Christianity and Human Rights Reconsidered

This is the first global examination of the historical relationship between Christianity and human rights in the twentieth century. Leading historians, anthropologists, political theorists, legal scholars, and scholars of religion develop fresh approaches to issues such as human dignity, personalism, religious freedom, the role of ecumenical and transatlantic networks, and the relationship between Christian and liberal rights theories. In doing so they move well beyond the temporal and geographical limits of the existing scholarship, exploring the connection between Christianity and human rights, not only in Europe and the United States, but also in Africa, Latin America, and China. They offer alternative chronologies and bring to light overlooked aspects of this history, including the role of race, gender, decolonization, and interreligious dialogue. Above all, these chapters foreground the complicated relationship between global rights discourses – whether Christian, liberal, or otherwise – and the local contexts in which they are developed and implemented.

Sarah Shortall is Assistant Professor of History at the University of Notre Dame. Her work has appeared in *Past and Present*, *Modern Intellectual History*, the *Journal of the History of Ideas*, and *Boston Review*. She is the author of *Soldiers of God in a Secular World: The Politics of Theology in Twentieth-Century France* (forthcoming).

Daniel Steinmetz-Jenkins is Postdoctoral Fellow in the History Department at Dartmouth College. He is currently the managing editor of *Modern Intellectual History* and is the former editor of *The Immanent Frame*. He is the author of *Raymond Aron and Cold War Liberalism* (forthcoming) and the co-editor, with Stephen Sawyer, of *Foucault, Neoliberalism and Beyond* (2019).

Human Rights in History

Edited by

Stefan-Ludwig Hoffmann, University of California, Berkeley
Samuel Moyn, Yale University

This series showcases new scholarship exploring the backgrounds of human rights today. With an open-ended chronology and international perspective, the series seeks works attentive to the surprises and contingencies in the historical origins and legacies of human rights ideals and interventions. Books in the series will focus not only on the intellectual antecedents and foundations of human rights, but also on the incorporation of the concept by movements, nation-states, international governance, and transnational law.

A full list of titles in the series can be found at:
www.cambridge.org/human-rights-history

Christianity and Human Rights Reconsidered

Edited by

Sarah Shortall
University of Notre Dame

Daniel Steinmetz-Jenkins
Dartmouth College

Shaftesbury Road, Cambridge CB2 8EA, United Kingdom

One Liberty Plaza, 20th Floor, New York, NY 10006, USA

477 Williamstown Road, Port Melbourne, VIC 3207, Australia

314–321, 3rd Floor, Plot 3, Splendor Forum, Jasola District Centre, New Delhi – 110025, India

103 Penang Road, #05–06/07, Visioncrest Commercial, Singapore 238467

Cambridge University Press is part of Cambridge University Press & Assessment, a department of the University of Cambridge.

We share the University's mission to contribute to society through the pursuit of education, learning and research at the highest international levels of excellence.

www.cambridge.org
Information on this title: www.cambridge.org/9781108440851

DOI: 10.1017/9781108341356

© Cambridge University Press & Assessment 2020

First published 2020
First paperback edition 2022

A catalogue record for this publication is available from the British Library

Library of Congress Cataloging-in-Publication data
Names: Shortall, Sarah, 1985– editor. | Steinmetz-Jenkins, Daniel, 1979– editor.
Title: Christianity and human rights reconsidered / edited by Sarah Shortall, University of Notre Dame, Indiana, Daniel Steinmetz-Jenkins, Dartmouth College.
Description: Cambridge, United Kingdom ; New York, NY, USA : Cambridge University Press, 2020. | Series: Human rights in history | Includes index.
Identifiers: LCCN 2020012021 | ISBN 9781108424707 (hardback) | ISBN 9781108341356 (epub)
Subjects: LCSH: Human rights – Religious aspects – Christianity. – History – 20th century.
Classication: LCC BT738.15 .C476 2020 | DDC 261.709/04–dc23
LC record available at https://lccn.loc.gov/2020012021

ISBN   978-1-108-42470-7   Hardback
ISBN   978-1-108-44085-1   Paperback

Contents

Figures

Contributors

CARLO INVERNIZZI ACCETTI is Associate Professor of Political Theory at the City University of New York, City College, and Associate Researcher at the Center for European Studies of the Paris Institute of Political Studies (Sciences Po). He is the author of *Relativism and Religion: Why Democratic Societies Do Not Need Moral Absolutes* (Columbia University Press, 2015) and *What Is Christian Democracy? Politics, Religion and Ideology* (Cambridge University Press, 2019).

P. MACKENZIE BOK is Lecturer in Social Studies at Harvard University, Faculty of Arts and Sciences. She is an intellectual historian who specializes in the young John Rawls and his path to writing *A Theory of Justice*. A Marshall Scholar, she earned her PhD at St John's College, Cambridge, winning the Quentin Skinner, Sara Norton, and Prince Consort and Thirlwall Prizes. Her published work also received the Society for US Intellectual History's Dorothy Ross Prize. In 2019, Kenzie was elected to the Boston City Council.

JULIAN BOURG is Associate Professor in the History Department at Boston College. His first book, *From Revolution to Ethics: May 1968 and Contemporary French Thought* (McGill-Queen's University Press, 2007; 2nd ed. 2017), won the 2008 Morris D. Forkosch book prize from the *Journal of the History of Ideas*. He is currently writing a conceptual history of terrorism since the eighteenth century.

JAMES CHAPPEL is the Hunt Family Assistant Professor of History at Duke University. He is the author of *Catholic Modern: The Challenge of Totalitarianism and the Remaking of the Church* (Harvard University Press, 2018). He comments on Catholic affairs for *Commonweal* and other public-facing venues.

ELIZABETH FOSTER is Associate Professor of History at Tufts University. She is the author of *Faith in Empire: Religion, Politics, and Colonial Rule in French Senegal, 1880–1940* (Stanford University Press, 2013), which won the 2014 Alf Andrew Heggoy Prize of the French Colonial

Historical Society. In 2019, she published *African Catholic: Decolonization and the Transformation of the Church* with Harvard University Press. Her work has been supported by fellowships from Fulbright, the American Council of Learned Societies, and the National Endowment for the Humanities.

UDI GREENBERG is Associate Professor of History at Dartmouth College. He is the author of the prize-winning *The Weimar Century: German Émigrés and the Ideological Foundations of the Cold War* (Princeton University Press, 2015), as well as multiple articles on modern European thought and politics.

DAVID M. LANTIGUA is Assistant Professor of Moral Theology/Christian Ethics at the University of Notre Dame. He is the co-author of *Comparative Religious Ethics: A Narrative Approach to Global Ethics* (Wiley-Blackwell, 2011) and *Bartolomé de las Casas and the Defense of Amerindian Rights: A Brief History with Documents* (University of Alabama Press, 2020), and the author of *Infidels and Empires in a New World Order: Early Modern Spanish Contributions to International Legal Thought* (Cambridge University Press, 2020).

VINCENT LLOYD is Associate Professor of Theology and Religious Studies at Villanova University. He is the author or editor of eleven books, including *Black Natural Law* (Oxford University Press, 2016), *Religion of the Field Negro* (Fordham University Press, 2018), and, with Jonathon Kahn, *Race and Secularism in America* (Columbia University Press, 2016). He co-edits the journal *Political Theology* and directs the Villanova Political Theology Project.

JOHN MILBANK is Research Professor of Religion, Politics and Ethics at the University of Nottingham. He is the author of *Theology Social Theory*, *Being Reconciled: Ontology and Pardon*, *Beyond Secular Order*, and numerous other books. Milbank delivered the Stanton Lectures at Cambridge in 2011.

SAMUEL MOYN is the Henry R. Luce Professor of Jurisprudence and Professor of History at Yale University. Moyn is a specialist in the history of human rights, the law of war, international law, and modern intellectual history. His books on human rights include *The Last Utopia*, *Christian Human Rights*, and *Not Enough: Human Rights in an Unequal World*.

CAMILLE ROBCIS is Associate Professor of French and History at Columbia University. Her first book, *The Law of Kinship: Anthropology, Psychoanalysis, and the Family in France* (Cornell

University Press, 2013), won the 2013 Berkshire Conference of Women Historians Book Prize. Her second book, *Disalienation: Politics, Philosophy, and Radical Psychiatry in France*, is forthcoming with the University of Chicago Press. Her essays have appeared in *Modern Intellectual History*, *Yale French Studies*, *Social Text*, *French Historical Studies*, *Discourse*, *South Atlantic Quarterly*, and the *Journal of Modern History*, among others.

SARAH SHORTALL is Assistant Professor of History at the University of Notre Dame. Her book *Soldiers of God in a Secular World: The Politics of Theology in Twentieth-Century France* is under contract with Harvard University Press. In addition, her work has appeared in *Past & Present*, *Modern Intellectual History*, the *Journal of the History of Ideas*, and *Boston Review*.

DANIEL STEINMETZ-JENKINS is a postdoctoral fellow in the History Department at Dartmouth College. He is currently the managing editor of *Modern Intellectual History* and is the former editor of *The Immanent Frame*. He is the author of *Raymond Aron and Cold War Liberalism* (Columbia University Press, forthcoming). He is the co-editor, with Stephen Sawyer, of *Foucault, Neoliberalism and Beyond* (Rowman & Littlefield). His work has appeared in *Modern Intellectual History*, the *Journal of the History of Ideas*, the *Journal of the American Academy of Religion*, and elsewhere.

CHRISTOPHER TOUNSEL is Assistant Professor of History and African Studies at Pennsylvania State University. He is a 2019 recipient of the Woodrow Wilson Career Enhancement Fellowship, and his book *Chosen Peoples: Christianity and Political Imagination in South Sudan* is forthcoming from Duke University Press.

ALBERT WU is Assistant Professor and Chair of the Department of History at the American University of Paris. His first book, *From Christ to Confucius: German Missionaries, Chinese Christians, and the Globalization of Christianity, 1860–1950*, appeared with Yale University Press in 2016.

GENE ZUBOVICH is Assistant Professor in the Department of History at the University at Buffalo, SUNY. He is the author of *The Global Gospel: Christian Human Rights and the Fracturing of the Twentieth-Century United States* (forthcoming) from the University of Pennsylvania Press.

Preface

Samuel Moyn

In a short time, the study of the relation of Christianity to human rights has passed a critical threshold. Not long ago, except for a dispute among Roman Catholic scholars about origins reflecting a twentieth-century dilemma about whether to treat rights as appalling or indispensable, it was still common to claim that Christianity must have "contributed" somehow to the making of human rights. And the chief reason for this tradition was a larger historiography of human rights that understood its task to be the acknowledgment of influences and the accumulation of precedents.

Nowadays the intellectual situation looks entirely different. From one perspective the intra-Catholic dispute about human rights has been generalized. A default liberalism has been newly challenged from perspectives outside the mainstream, many of which can allow for nagging doubts about the beneficence of rights, or radical interpretations that profoundly transform their ethical and political bearing. To be sure, Karl Marx himself offered an excoriating treatment of rights and the critical legal studies movement revived it a few decades ago. But then, over the same period, liberalism itself clove to rights frameworks like never before in its own contested history, especially after the publication of John Rawls's *Theory of Justice* in 1971. So it is hard to doubt that the past few years have opened up an intensity of challenge to "human rights" such as would have been surprising shortly before.

From another perspective, the historiographical terrain for stories about where rights came from has undergone a seismic shift of massive proportions. A more or less uncritical historiography of rights that grew over several decades around the turn of the millennium was challenged soon after, starting with Lynn Hunt's *Inventing Human Rights* (2007). The effect was augmented because, whatever the prior efforts to reconstruct the history of rights generally (and the relation of Christianity to them), an altogether new push to discern the origins of human rights appeared thanks to the great new age of the internationalization of the principles in global politics in the era straddling the Cold War's end. At

xi

first this push shared something of the ratification of human rights as the morality at the end of history of some complacent liberal histories. But in short order a more fully critical spirit prevailed and "the dark sides of virtue" became fashionable to highlight, whether because of entanglements of human rights with the hierarchies of geopolitics or neoliberalism.

In short, disputes around both rights themselves and stories of their origins transformed out of all recognition the setting for making claims about how Christianity fit in. This volume marks another stage in that transformation, as scholars clear the wreckage of prior contests for new engagements, or even begin in earnest in taking up new stances on the relationship between Christianity and human rights. A number of the chapters take up my lectures on *Christian Human Rights* (2015), but this volume is far more than merely a referendum on it from diverse perspectives. An essential purpose of this book, indeed, is to leave the debates sparked by any one position behind, in order to move fully into an age of scholarship with the hallmarks of every mature field: it is always critical but also always pluralistic. For that reason, even when they do directly engage my own book, various chapters are best read as establishing a range of interpretive options for continuing disagreement. Fortunately, when it comes to Christianity and human rights now, there is a conversation in which no one gets the last word.

This is especially true insofar as some of the chapters shift the timeline far toward the present from the middle of the twentieth century where others linger, while another set of authors explores far beyond the transatlantic geography of initial discussions. For that matter, historians of the United States have insisted that their evidence suggests a very different landscape than historians of Europe have depicted even when they have striven to include American Christianity – and other authors push the geography of inquiry into Africa and Asia too.

At the end of the exercise, if anything stands out, it is the question of what risks loss – including loss when Christianity receives too much attention as a source of human rights ideals and practices. After all, in the long history of Christianity, affirmations of and resistance to human rights may never have been much more than marginal and other concerns prevailed – and the same could occur again in the future. It is possible that the greatest risk is that Christianity, whether it invented human rights or not, and whether its agenda is advanced through appeal to them or not, is reduced when its relation to human rights is at the forefront.

Acknowledgments

The editors would like to thank Michael Watson, Emily Sharp, and the series editors at Cambridge University Press for supporting this project and shepherding it through to its completion, as well as the anonymous readers who provided invaluable comments on earlier drafts of the essays in this volume. Thanks as well to Stephanie Taylor, Richards Paul, and Ami Naramor for seeing the manuscript through the production phase. We would like to thank the Institute for Scholarship in the Liberal Arts at the University of Notre Dame for providing funding for the index and Pam Scholefield for creating the index. Finally, we would like to thank *Humanity* and *South Atlantic Quarterly* for permission to reprint material from chapters 4 and 6, respectively.

Introduction

Sarah Shortall and Daniel Steinmetz-Jenkins

In 2008, Pope Benedict XVI marked the sixtieth anniversary of the Universal Declaration of Human Rights in a statement before the General Assembly of the United Nations. The pope celebrated the legacy of this all-important document, which had made human rights the "common language and the ethical substratum of international relations." While acknowledging that the Declaration was the product of a convergence between various religious and cultural traditions that shared a commitment to the dignity of the human person, Benedict nevertheless singled out the specific contribution that the Christian tradition had made to the genesis of the international human rights movement.

In his speech, the pope praised the United Nations' (UN) efforts to promote human rights around the world. But he also raised grave concerns about the dangers lurking in a mistaken interpretation of the nature and foundations of these rights. Human rights are rooted in the objective and universal dictates of natural law, the pope argued, but some had forgotten this and risked "yielding to a relativistic conception, according to which the meaning and interpretation of rights could vary." The problem lay in the "thin" understanding of rights advanced by mainstream liberalism, which stripped these rights of their religious and ethical foundations and defined them in purely abstract, formal terms. "When presented purely in terms of legality," Benedict warned, "rights risk becoming weak propositions divorced from the ethical and rational dimension which is their foundation and their goal."[1] He therefore called on the assembly to recapture the original meaning of the Declaration by anchoring human rights in the unchanging dictates of natural law, by reminding people of the duties that necessarily go along with these rights, and by redoubling their efforts to protect religious freedom in particular.

---

[1] Benedict XVI, "Address to the General Assembly of the United Nations" (April 18, 2008): https://w2.vatican.va/content/benedict-xvi/en/speeches/2008/april/documents/hf_ben-xvi_spe_20080418_un-visit.html.

Benedict's comments at the UN reveal the complicated relationship between Christianity and human rights. On the one hand, the pope presented the Catholic Church as a staunch advocate for human rights, and even attributed the emergence of a modern idiom of rights and international justice to the influence of a much older theological tradition associated with early modern Scholasticism. On the other hand, the pope signaled the distance that continues to separate the Catholic account of human rights from the mainstream liberal discourse that informs much constitutional and international law, which accounts for the Church's long-standing suspicion of the rights tradition that emerged from the French Revolution. Benedict's remarks are thus a testament to the important contributions that Christianity has made to the development of modern human rights, as well as to the continuing tensions that exist between religious and secular accounts of their foundation, scope, and legitimacy.

The nature and history of the relationship between Christianity and human rights has long been a source of vigorous debate among historians, theologians, and philosophers. A standard line of interpretation, often put forward by Christian scholars, suggests that contemporary rights talk grew out of the "Judeo-Christian" tradition and locates the origins of this discourse in the Bible, Scholasticism, or the Protestant Reformation. This perspective has a long history and has most recently been defended by legal scholar John Witte, philosophical theologian Nicholas Wolterstoff, and canon law historian Brian Tierney.[2] In contrast, the standard secular interpretation of the origins of human rights, reaffirmed most recently by Jonathan Israel, maintains that human rights are the product of the Enlightenment revolt against religion.[3] *Pace* Israel, a secular Enlightenment perspective on human rights, is not necessarily incompatible with a longue durée perspective on their pre-Enlightenment

---

[2] John Witte, *The Reformation of Rights: Law, Religion and Human Rights in Early Modern Calvinism* (Cambridge: Cambridge University Press, 2009); John Witte and Frank Alexander, *Christianity and Human Rights: An Introduction* (Cambridge: Cambridge University Press, 2011); Nicholas Wolterstoff, *Justice: Rights and Wrongs* (Princeton, NJ: Princeton University Press, 2008); Brian Tierney, *The Idea of Natural Rights: Studies on Natural Rights, Natural Law and Church Law, 1150–1625* (Grand Rapids, MI: Eerdmans Press, 1997); Annabel Brett, *Liberty, Right and Nature: Individual Rights in Later Scholastic Thought* (Cambridge: Cambridge University Press, 1997) and "Human Rights and the Thomist Tradition," in *Revisiting the Origins of Human Rights*, ed. Pamela Slotte and Miia Halme-Tuomisaari (Cambridge: Cambridge University Press, 2015), 82–102.

[3] Jonathan Israel, *Democratic Enlightenment: Philosophy, Revolution, and Human Rights, 1750–1790* (New York: Oxford University Press, 2011). On the eighteenth-century origins of human rights, see also Lynn Hunt, *Inventing Human Rights: A History* (New York: Norton, 2007).

Christian origins. The attempt to bring both traditions together, something now associated with the notion of "post-secularism," has been articulated by German philosopher Jürgen Habermas, who argues that secular human rights emerged out of the "Judeo-Christian tradition."[4] What unites these conflicting approaches, whether secular or theological in outlook, is their emphasis on the long historical roots of contemporary human rights discourse. Taken together, they constitute what can be described as the "traditional" or "classical" historiography of human rights.

In the past ten years, a "new" historiography of human rights has emerged that has challenged these sorts of narratives. Far from seeking the origins of human rights in the distant Judeo-Christian past, or the somewhat less distant past of the age of Enlightenment and democratic revolution, scholars have begun to show that international human rights are in fact a remarkably recent invention.[5] This has led to a reconsideration of the more recent religious past and the role that Christian ideas and actors in particular played in the rise of international rights projects during the twentieth century. For instance, Samuel Moyn – the scholar who pioneered the new historiography of human rights – has argued that human rights first emerged in Europe during the 1930s and 1940s, as "a project of the Christian right not the secular left."[6] Marco Duranti has echoed this claim, revealing the instrumental role that Christians played in the "conservative human rights revolution" that led to the creation of the European Court of Human Rights.[7] This Christian conception of human rights, Moyn and Duranti contend, was taken up by Christian Democratic parties and enshrined in documents like the Universal Declaration of Human Rights or the European Convention on Human Rights, and thus played a key role in the construction of a conservative Cold War order. Other scholars, meanwhile, have focused on the way Christian concepts were translated into secular laws governing religious freedom and thus continue to shape how

---

[4] Jürgen Habermas, *Time of Transitions* (New York: Polity Press, 2006), 150–151. See also Habermas' conversation with Benedict XVI in *The Dialectics of Secularization* (San Francisco: Ignatius, 2006).

[5] See esp. Samuel Moyn, *The Last Utopia: Human Rights in History* (Cambridge, MA: Belknap/Harvard University Press, 2010); *Human Rights in the Twentieth Century*, ed. Stefan-Ludwig Hoffmann (Cambridge: Cambridge University Press, 2010); Hoffmann, "Human Rights and History," *Past & Present* 232 (2016): 279–310.

[6] Samuel Moyn, *Christian Human Rights* (Philadelphia: University of Pennsylvania Press, 2015), 8.

[7] Marco Duranti, *The Conservative Human Rights Revolution: European Identity, Transnational Politics, and the Origins of the European Convention* (Oxford: Oxford University Press, 2017).

national and international law manages, among other things, the status of religious minorities.[8]

The focus of this scholarship, by and large, has been on what Christianity can tell us about human rights and not the reverse. In some cases, the goal of recovering the Christian roots of such projects seems above all to cast doubt on the legitimacy or universality of human rights. And yet the past five years have also witnessed the emergence of a vibrant new scholarship on the twentieth-century history of Christianity, which takes seriously the ideas and aims of Christians themselves. A new generation of scholars has offered fresh insights into how Christians encountered the modern world and negotiated the challenges of twentieth-century politics, from the rise of fascism and communism, to the postwar development of Christian Democracy, to the end of empire.[9] Many of these authors have expanded upon, but also complicated, Moyn's account of the relationship between Christianity and human rights.[10] Some have delved more deeply into the twentieth-century Christian sources of human rights theory – most notably, ideas about dignity, religious freedom, and the human person.[11]

---

[8] For the new global politics of religious freedom, see Elizabeth Shakman Hurd, *Beyond Religious Freedom: The New Global Politics of Religion* (Princeton, NJ: Princeton University Press, 2015); Saba Mahmood, *Religious Freedom in a Secular Age: A Minority Report* (Princeton, NJ: Princeton University Press, 2015); *Politics of Religious Freedom*, ed. Winnifred Sullivan, Elizabeth Shakman Hurd, Saba Mahmood, and Peter Danchin (Chicago: University of Chicago Press, 2015); Linde Lindkvist, *Religious Freedom and the Universal Declaration of Human Rights* (Cambridge: Cambridge University Press, 2017); Anna Su, *Exporting Freedom: Religious Freedom and American Power* (Cambridge, MA: Harvard University Press, 2016).

[9] A small sampling of some of the most recent works includes: James Chappel, *Catholic Modern: The Challenge of Totalitarianism and the Remaking of the Church* (Cambridge, MA: Harvard University Press, 2018); Giuliana Chamedes, *A Twentieth-Century Crusade: The Vatican's Battle to Remake Christian Europe* (Cambridge, MA: Harvard University Press, 2019); Sarah Shortall, *Soldiers of God in a Secular World: The Politics of Catholic Theology in Twentieth-Century France* (Cambridge, MA: Harvard University Press, forthcoming); Piotr Kosicki, *Catholics on the Barricades: Poland, France, and "Revolution," 1891–1956* (New Haven, CT: Yale University Press, 2018); Darcie Fontaine, *Decolonizing Christianity: Religion and the End of Empire in France and Algeria* (Cambridge: Cambridge University Press, 2016); Elizabeth Foster, *African Catholic: Decolonization and the Transformation of the Church* (Cambridge, MA: Harvard University Press, 2019); Udi Greenberg, "Protestants, Decolonization, and European Integration, 1885–1961," *Journal of Modern History* 89, no. 2 (2017), 318–354.

[10] See, for instance, the roundtable devoted to Moyn's *Christian Human Rights*: "Christianity and Human Rights," *The Immanent Frame* (May 29, 2015–July 28, 2015): https://tif.ssrc.org/category/exchanges/book-blog/book-forums/christian-human-rights/. See also the special issue of the *Journal of the History of Ideas* devoted to Christianity and the new historiography of human rights, which includes articles by Sarah Shortall, Gene Zubovich, Paul Hanebrink, and Dan Edelstein: "Special Forum on Christianity and Human Rights," *Journal of the History of Ideas* 79, no. 3 (July 2018), 407–495.

[11] Piotr Kosicki, "Masters in Their Own Home or Defenders of the Human Person? Wojciech Korfanty, Anti-Semitism, and Polish Christian Democracy's Illiberal Rights-Talk," *Modern Intellectual History* 14, no. 1 (2017), 99–130; Udi Greenberg, "Catholics,

Others have disputed the identification between Christian human rights and conservative politics, pointing to the progressive and anti-racist Christian voices that helped to push human rights to the forefront of international law in the interwar and Cold War eras.[12] Finally, scholars working on Latin America, Africa, and Asia have questioned the extent to which historical arguments about the relationship between Christianity and human rights in Europe and North America can be applied to other parts of the world.

This volume brings together, for the first time, this rich new historiography on human rights and Christianity by leading scholars in the fields of history, law, theology, and political theory. The chapters offer fresh readings of some of the key themes and concepts explored in Moyn's recent work, such as dignity, personalism, religious freedom, the role of ecumenical and transatlantic networks, and the relationship between Christian and liberal rights theories. But they also move well beyond the temporal and geographical limits of the existing scholarship, exploring the connection between Christianity and human rights, not only in Europe and the United States, but also in China, Sudan, Latin America, and West Africa. In the process, they offer alternative chronologies and bring to light overlooked aspects of this history, including the role of race, gender, decolonization, and interreligious dialogue. Above all, these chapters foreground the complicated relationship between global rights discourses – whether Christian, liberal, or otherwise – and local variations.

By bringing together these essays, this volume showcases the new historiography on Christianity and rights, which moves beyond the traditional and predominantly confessional literature on this subject. Part I offers a set of general reflections on the relationship between Christian and liberal rights theory since the French Revolution, in conversation with Moyn's recent work. The chapters in Part II focus on the European Catholic encounter with human rights from the 1930s to the present. Part III turns to American Protestant voices, while Part IV examines the relationship between Christianity and human rights beyond Europe and North America. *Christianity and Human Rights Reconsidered* thus provides the first global account of the historical relationship between Christianity and human rights. In the process, it

---

Protestants, and the Tortured Path to Religious Liberty," *Journal of the History of Ideas* 79, no. 2 (July 2018), 461–479.

[12] Sarah Shortall, "Theology and the Politics of Christian Human Rights," *Journal of the History of Ideas* 79, no. 2 (July 2018), 445–460; Gene Zubovich, "American Protestants and the Era of Anti-Racist Human Rights," in the same volume, 427–443; P. MacKenzie Bok, "Did the Christians Ruin Rights?" *New Rambler Review* (February 15, 2016): https://newramblerreview.com/book-reviews/history/did-the-christians-ruin-rights.

promises to reshape our understanding of both human rights theory and the history of Christianity in the twentieth century.

Human Rights Reconsidered

As historians have shown, Christians made crucial contributions to the development of the human rights model that found expression in documents like the Universal Declaration of Human Rights, the European Convention on Human Rights, and the postwar constitutions of European states. In making this case, they have privileged figures like Catholic philosopher Jacques Maritain, who believed that it was possible for believers and nonbelievers to reach a practical agreement on a common charter of human rights. Such rights, he reasoned, ultimately come from God, but because they are inscribed on the human heart in the form of natural law, it is possible to apprehend them without having access to Christian revelation. This is why Maritain believed that human rights could function as a *"civic or secular* faith" ultimately rooted in Christianity but also intelligible to non-Christians.[13] Several of the following chapters build upon this historiography. Gene Zubovich (Chapter 7), for instance, recovers the contributions of liberal Protestants such as William Ernest Hocking to the mid-century debates at the UN. P. MacKenzie Bok (Chapter 8) reveals the little known influence of Maritain on John Rawls, while Camille Robcis (Chapter 6) shows how a Catholic concept of dignity made its way into secular French law.

But what emerges even more forcefully from the chapters in this volume, and where they break new ground, is the extent to which Christian accounts of human rights and dignity frequently *do not* fit the prevailing rights model enshrined in democratic constitutions and international law. Catholics and Protestants may have embraced the language of human rights and dignity in the course of the twentieth century, but this does not mean that they embraced a *liberal* conception of human rights. Instead, they were often profoundly critical of the grounds, implications, and limits of mainstream liberal rights discourse. The contributions to this volume thus reveal the extent to which human rights were and remain a highly contested terrain.

Many of the chapters highlight the divergence between Christian and liberal accounts of human rights. As Carlo Invernizzi Accetti (Chapter 4),

---

[13] Jacques Maritain, *Man and the State* (Washington, DC: Catholic University of America Press, 1998), 110 (emphasis in original). Maritain's most robust theorization of human rights is *The Rights of Man and Natural Law* (New York: Charles Scribner's Sons, 1943).

Julian Bourg (Chapter 2), Udi Greenberg (Chapter 5), and John Milbank (Chapter 1) show us, Catholics in particular have long taken issue with the individualist premises of the subjective rights claims so central to the liberal tradition. Christians see several problems with this model. In the first place, it threatens to dissolve the social bond by prioritizing the rights of the individual at the expense of the equally important duties we possess as members of a community. In addition, many Catholics have complained that a purely formal and subjective account of human rights serves to decouple them from any substantive notion of the good, to which such rights and human life itself are necessarily oriented. To do this, as Pope Benedict has argued, is to build one's house on the sand of relativism. Instead, like the pope, many Catholics have sought to anchor human rights in the ostensibly objective foundations of natural law. Finally, many Christians have taken issue with the way documents like the 1789 Declaration of the Rights of Man and Citizen empower the state by allowing it to define and enforce rights claims. These sorts of philosophical differences are far from insignificant. They have made many Christians wary of the prevailing rights tradition that emerged with the eighteenth-century revolutions and that continues to inform the work of international organizations. If many Christians came to embrace human rights in the course of the twentieth century, then, it is by no means clear that they meant the same thing by these rights as their non-Christian counterparts. And this suggests that we need to attend not only to the way Christians have contributed to the rise and spread of human rights as a global movement, but also to the way they have contested or transformed these rights. In other words, it is crucial to consider *which* rights we are talking about when we talk about human rights.

This question has important implications for the politics of Christian rights discourse. For historians like Samuel Moyn and Marco Duranti, the fact that Christian human rights emerged in the 1930s and 1940s out of a rejection of the liberal tradition of the rights of man is evidence that this was a fundamentally conservative project.[14] They point to Christians' efforts to limit individual rights claims by anchoring them in a higher moral order – one that imposes duties as well as conferring rights – as proof that this "was a reactionary program masked in revolutionary garb."[15] And yet to reject liberalism is not necessarily to embrace conservatism. As many of the chapters in this volume demonstrate, the

---

[14] Moyn, *Christian Human Rights*; Duranti, *Conservative Human Rights Revolution*.

[15] Marco Duranti, "The Holocaust, the Legacy of 1789 and the Birth of International Human Rights Law: Revisiting the Foundation Myth," *Journal of Genocide Research* 14, no. 2 (2012), 159–186, at 179.

Christian critique of individual rights could just as easily emerge from the left. David Lantigua (Chapter 12) shows us how liberation theologians in Latin America rejected the prevailing rights discourse emanating from America and Europe on the grounds that it was complicit in the spread of neoliberalism, and instead forged their own account of human rights rooted in the "preferential option for the poor." Vincent Lloyd (Chapter 9) uncovers a vernacular black Christian tradition of human dignity exemplified in the life and work of Paul Robeson – a vision Robeson believed the Soviet Union had come closer to realizing than his own country had. Meanwhile, James Chappel (Chapter 3) draws our attention to the way European Catholics like Jacques Maritain and Emmanuel Mounier rallied to the defense of workers' rights and the rights of colonized peoples as early as the 1930s.

This is not to say that Christian human rights should be viewed as a left-wing rather than a right-wing project. Instead, what emerges from the following chapters is a powerful sense of the political plasticity of Christian rights discourse. As Julian Bourg and James Chappel remind us, Christian human rights claims could take a variety of different forms. They could be taken up by far-right Catholics like Robert Linhardt and Henri Massis or by those on the left like Emmanuel Mounier; they could be deployed as a weapon against fascism or as part of a Christian crusade against communism; they could be emancipatory or exclusionary. The common denominator uniting these opposing positions was a critique or at least a suspicion of secular, liberal rights discourse. For John Milbank, this critique suggests that Christianity might still have something valuable to teach us about the limitations of the dominant account of human rights that prevails today. And indeed, the Christian critiques traced in this volume anticipated many of the charges that contemporary scholars have leveled against the human rights project. Whether they see it as complicit in the rise of neoliberalism and the expansion of state power, or simply as "not enough" to redress the economic and environmental crises facing our world, secular scholars continue to reiterate many of the same critiques Christians have long raised.[16]

But as Udi Greenberg and Julian Bourg remind us, the Christian critique of liberal rights theory also comes with its own political baggage. In our effort to recuperate the insights of this tradition, it is therefore

---

[16] See, for example, Wendy Brown, "'The Most We Can Hope For...': Human Rights and the Politics of Fatalism," *South Atlantic Quarterly* 103 (Spring/Summer 2004), 451–463; Giorgio Agamben, *Homo Sacer: Sovereign Power and Bare Life*, trans. Daniel Heller-Roazen (Stanford, CA: Stanford University Press, 1998). The phrase "not enough" comes from Moyn's latest work, *Not Enough: Human Rights in an Unequal World* (Cambridge, MA: Belknap/Harvard University Press, 2018).

equally important to attend to its potential pitfalls. When Christians reject a purely formal account of human rights in favor of a "thick" understanding of the ends to which these rights must be directed, or when they seek to limit the rights of the individual through the imposition of corollary duties, the risk of coercion and exclusion looms large. As Bourg points out, Christianity may well offer a richer and more substantive foundation for human rights than the liberal model can afford, but it does so at the risk of excluding or discriminating against non-Christians. Where, in other words, do non-Christians fit into a robustly Christian rights framework? The chapters by Robcis, Greenberg, and Bourg raise this problem specifically as it pertains to the status of Muslims in contemporary Europe and America. It is worth remembering that a regular ploy of certain right-wing populists today is to say that human rights cannot be disconnected from the Judeo-Christian tradition, when making their Islamophobic cases for why immigration stands to undermine "Western civilization."[17] And while it seems excessive to blame contemporary Islamophobia on the Christian critique of liberal rights, these chapters draw our attention to the limits of this critique and the things that are worth saving in the liberal tradition. In reconsidering the relationship between Christianity and human rights, the chapters in this volume thus draw our attention to both the value and the limits of human rights as they have found expression in constitutional and international law. Indeed, it is precisely the tension and contestation between Christian and liberal rights theory that opens up the possibility for thinking these rights anew.

Christianity Reconsidered

If the chapters in this volume push us to rethink the foundations, value, and politics of human rights, they also go beyond the existing historiography by shedding new light on the history of Christianity in the twentieth century. In his preface to this volume, Samuel Moyn suggests that focusing on human rights, which remained a relatively marginal concern for many Christians, may limit our understanding of the richness and complexity of twentieth-century Christianity. It is therefore crucial to cast a wider net. Given that so many Christians were wary of the prevailing secular and liberal rights tradition, they often avoided adopting the language of rights themselves. Indeed, the reader may well be struck by how

[17] For this position, see the interesting essay by Rogers Brubaker, "The New Language of European Populism: Why 'Civilization' Is Replacing the Nation," *Foreign Affairs* (December 10, 2017): www.foreignaffairs.com/articles/europe/2017-12-06/new-language-european-populism.

many of the chapters that follow engage with human rights only indirectly. Instead, Christians often addressed the question of rights through a variety of cognate concepts with deeper roots in their own theological traditions – especially ideas of personhood and dignity. To grasp the full range of Christian engagement with human rights, it is crucial to explore these cognate concepts, and one of the major goals of this volume is therefore to examine the relationship between theories of rights and related ideas such as humanism, personalism, and dignity.

A number of the chapters take up the theme of dignity in particular and explore whether this concept should be conceived as an extension or limitation of human rights discourse. In her chapter, Camille Robcis explores the Catholic genealogy of the idea of dignity that has found its way into French law since the 1990s. While acknowledging that alternative accounts of dignity can yield different political outcomes, she argues that the Catholic model that has emerged from debates over the reproductive rights of women and same-sex couples, as well as the famous controversy over the Muslim headscarf, was specifically designed to restrict individual rights. Here, dignity functioned as a corporate concept – an appeal to the rights of *humanity* over and against the rights of specific human beings – in order to shore up public order and police national belonging. Vincent Lloyd likewise highlights the distance between the vernacular black Christian concept of dignity and the vision of human rights enshrined at the UN. If Paul Robeson chose this language of dignity, however, it was precisely because he believed it offered greater possibilities for the emancipation of oppressed and marginalized groups than the abstract language of human rights could. For Robeson, dignity was not something possessed inherently by all human beings but something *performed* in and through the struggle against oppression. While Lloyd and Robcis offer very different accounts of the politics of dignity, both present it as a limit or alternative to human rights. On the other hand, as P. MacKenzie Bok and Gene Zubovich show us, many Christians, such as William Ernest Hocking and the young John Rawls, seem to have viewed human rights and dignity as more or less interchangeable.

Another concept Christians frequently preferred to the language of human rights was that of the person. Samuel Moyn has shown the outsized role that the cryptic interwar movement known as "personalism" played in the genesis of international human rights discourse in the 1940s, and most of the chapters in this volume also draw attention to the significance of personalism for the history of Christian human rights.[18]

---

[18] See esp. chapter 2 in Moyn, *Christian Human Rights*.

The movement itself remains elusive and difficult to define, largely because there were so many different kinds of personalism and because personalists tended to define themselves above all by what they were not. As Jacques Maritain put it, "there are at least a dozen personalist doctrines, which at times have nothing more in common than the term person."[19] The chapters in this volume certainly bear this out. They reveal that there were both Catholic and Protestant forms of personalism, as well as multiple theological strands within each of these traditions, not to mention regional and national variations. Perhaps the most famous of these was articulated in the 1930s by French Catholics who looked to the person as the basis for a "third way" between liberal individualism and totalitarian collectivism.[20] In contrast to the "individual" so central to liberal theory, the person was conceived first and foremost as a spiritual and a social being. It is therefore not surprising that Christians used this concept to distinguish their account of rights from the secular, liberal tradition of the "rights of man," preferring instead to champion the dignity and rights of the person.

But because personalism was explicitly conceived as a spiritual alternative to the dominant political ideologies of the day, its politics are notoriously difficult to classify. Historians have long wrangled over whether interwar personalists like Emmanuel Mounier should be seen as closet fascists or crypto-communists, but the chapters in this volume show that personalism could and did have a variety of political implications.[21] And this helps to explain the political plasticity of the Christian rights theories that emerged from it, as noted earlier. The reason for this is what Milbank refers to in his chapter as the "orthogonality" of Christian thought in relation to secular politics. If concepts like dignity and the person contain multiple political possibilities, it is precisely because they were not conceived as political terms, but rather as ethical or theological ones. And this "orthogonality" may also help to

---

[19] Jacques Maritain, *The Person and the Common Good*, trans. John J. Fitzgerald (Notre Dame, IN: University of Notre Dame Press, 1966 [1947]), 2.

[20] The standard reference work on this subject remains Jean-Louis Loubet del Bayle, *Les Non-conformistes des années trente: une tentative de renouvellement de la pensée politique française* (Paris: Seuil, 1969).

[21] John Hellman stresses Mounier's links to fascist circles and his involvement in the Vichy regime's National Revolution in *The Knight-Monks of Vichy France: Uriage, 1940–1945* (Montreal: McGill-Queen's University Press, 1993) and *Emmanuel Mounier and the New Catholic Left, 1930–1950* (Toronto: University of Toronto Press, 1981). Others instead stress his Resistance credentials and his relationship to Communism: Michael Kelly, *Pioneer of the Catholic Revival: The Ideas and Influence of Emmanuel Mounier* (London: Sheed and Ward, 1979); Kosicki, *Catholics on the Barricades*; Michel Winock, *Histoire politique de la revue 'Esprit', 1930–1950* (Paris: Seuil, 1975).

explain the political ambivalence of human rights more broadly. Both secular and religious accounts of human rights tend to frame them as an ethical or legal check on the realm of power politics – one that transcends the logic of right and left. Like personalism, then, human rights can mean different things to different people, and this is precisely what ensures both their popularity and their political indeterminacy.

The other reason why Christian human rights can yield such a range of political outcomes is of course the internal diversity of the Christian tradition. In the first place, Catholics, Protestants, and Orthodox Christians have not always approached the question of human rights in the same way. As the chapters by P. MacKenzie Bok, Gene Zubovich, and Vincent Lloyd indicate, American Protestants in particular fit somewhat awkwardly into existing accounts of mid-century Christian human rights that tend to privilege the role of European Catholics. This is partly because mainline American Protestants have had a much less vexed relationship to liberal democracy and the legacy of the Enlightenment than the Catholic Church has. Indeed, Udi Greenberg argues in his chapter that the long-standing Catholic suspicion of human rights was fueled at least in part by the notion that religious freedom was a specifically "Protestant" idea. He shows how this rather old idea that the Protestant Reformation had given birth to a subjective conception of rights, which in turn paved the way for the rise of modern individualism and secular liberalism, continued well into the twentieth century and even informs contemporary Catholic critiques of human rights and religious freedom.[22] On the other hand, Bok's chapter suggests that there was perhaps more continuity than we might expect between the Protestant and Catholic approaches to human rights, by revealing the little-known connection between Jacques Maritain and John Rawls.

What these chapters suggest is that it is just as important to attend to the theological differences *within* the Catholic and Protestant traditions as between them. If liberal Protestants like Hocking helped to frame the debate on human rights at the UN, many Protestants took a very different view on the subject. In fact, Nicholas Wolterstorff's recent work reveals

---

[22] For an overview of this argument and its contemporary representatives, see Udi Greenberg and Daniel Steinmetz-Jenkins, "The Cross and the Gavel," *Dissent Magazine* (Spring 2008): www.dissentmagazine.org/article/cross-gavel-secularism-religious-liberty-asad-milbank. Prominent examples include Brad Gregory, *The Unintended Reformation: How a Religious Revolution Secularized Society* (Cambridge, MA: Belknap/Harvard University Press, 2012); John Milbank, "The Reformation at 500: Is there any Reason for Celebration?" *ABC Religion and Ethics* (October 30, 2017): www.abc.net.au/religion/the-reformation-at-500-is-there-any-cause-for-celebration/10095254; William T. Cavanaugh, *The Myth of Religious Violence: Secular Ideology and the Roots of Modern Conflict* (New York: Oxford University Press, 2009).

that many of the most influential Protestant theologians of the twentieth century – Karl Barth, Emil Brunner, Paul Ramsey, John Howard Yoder, Anders Nygren, Stanley Hauerwas – embraced a theology of "agapism" that was distinctly at odds with the rhetoric of rights. From this perspective, as Wolterstorff puts it, "anybody who talked about natural rights to a group of Protestants in the latter half of the twentieth century and the first decade of the twenty-first was likely to receive the rejoinder, 'We should not be talking about rights; we should be talking about love.'"[23] Similar divisions existed within the Catholic Church, where Jacques Maritain's vision of human rights as a "secular faith" capable of speaking to both Christians and nonbelievers ran up against competing theological accounts of the nature, value, and political implications of human rights.[24] This is why it is so crucial to attend, as so many of the chapters in this volume do, to the theological traditions that inform Christian rights theory. But other factors also account for the internal diversity within a particular tradition. We cannot assume, for instance, that the position of the Vatican exhausts the Catholic Church's relationship to human rights, and the chapters in this volume therefore focus not just on the pronouncements of the Church hierarchy, but on the attitudes of theologians and lay people as well. Racial difference has also mediated the history of Christian human rights in critical ways, as the chapters by Lloyd and Elizabeth Foster (Chapter 11) attest. In sum, there were not one, but many forms of Christian human rights in the twentieth century, and the chapters in this volume testify to the remarkable internal diversity within the Christian tradition.

Perhaps the most significant contribution that this volume makes to restoring this internal diversity is to expand the geographical focus beyond Europe and North America, which have tended to dominate the existing scholarship. This allows us to explore whether Christian human rights were a distinctively North Atlantic project and to what extent Christians in Africa, Latin America, and Asia identified with it. Indeed, what is most striking about the chapters in Part IV is how marginal human rights often seem in relation to the dominant challenges Christians faced in these regions: poverty, decolonization, and the need to build an indigenous church. In regions where Christians are a minority, human

---

[23] Nicholas Wolterstorff, "Christianity and Human Rights," in *Religion and Human Rights: An Introduction*, ed. John Witte and Christian Green (Oxford: Oxford University Press, 2011), 42–55, at 46. Note that Wolterstorff himself eschews this line of thinking.

[24] See Shortall, "Theology and the Politics of Christian Human Rights." On the debate on human rights within the Catholic tradition, see David Hollenbach, *Claims in Conflict: Retrieving and Renewing the Catholic Human Rights Tradition* (New York: Paulist Press, 1979); Ethna Regan, *Theology and the Boundary Discourse of Human Rights* (Washington, DC: Georgetown University Press, 2010).

rights have furnished a useful language with which to make political claims, as Christopher Tounsel (Chapter 13) shows us. But the long-standing entanglement between Christianity and colonialism, as well as ongoing global inequalities of wealth and power, have significantly complicated the history of Christian human rights in the Global South. For many Christians in these regions, human rights seemed like a European or American export that was foreign to their own needs and traditions. Latin American liberation theologians, for instance, viewed the Carter administration's rights talk as complicit in the rise of neoliberalism, or worse, as an ideological cover for American military intervention in Latin America. But rather than rejecting human rights out of hand, David Lantigua shows us, these theologians elaborated their own competing rights theory rooted in the preferential option for the poor and the concrete challenges facing Latin Americans. Elizabeth Foster recounts a similar struggle to "decolonize" the Church on the part of West African Catholics such as Alioune Diop. While he condemned the institution's Eurocentrism and its colonial legacy, Diop nevertheless believed that Catholicism alone could promise a truly universal humanism and guarantee the dignity of the Third World. Finally, Albert Wu (Chapter 10) shows how the debate over the rights of Christians in China was bound up with the question of whether they could participate in traditional Chinese rites. Looking beyond the borders of Europe and North America thus gives us a very different perspective on the history of Christian human rights. Above all, it highlights the tension between the universalist language of both Christianity and human rights, and their historical ties to European culture and power.

The relationship between Christianity and human rights is of course far from static because, like human rights, Christianity too has a history. In addition to offering a richer account of the geographical and confessional diversity within the Christian tradition, the chapters in this volume help us to see how Christian approaches to human rights and dignity have changed over time. Much of the scholarship on this subject has privileged the mid-century moment, from the rise of personalism in the 1930s to the drafting of the Universal Declaration of Human Rights and the European Convention on Human Rights in the late 1940s and early 1950s. The following chapters push this chronology backward to explore earlier developments in the 1910s and 1920s, as well as forward to account for how Christian rights discourse has changed since the 1940s and has set the terms for contemporary debates on religious freedom, secular law, and minority rights. This longer chronology allows us to move beyond simplistic accounts of the relationship between religion and modernity, which tell a progressive story of how the churches gradually "made their peace" with the modern language of individual rights. Taking a longer view allows us to grasp the ways in which Christian rights discourse has changed over time, how it has emphasized different questions or conveyed different political priorities, and how it continues to differentiate itself from other typically modern rights models. There are not one but many forms of Christian human rights. By recovering this diversity, the chapters in this volume offer a richer account of both human rights and the history of Christianity.

Part I

General Reflections

1 The Last Christian Settlement
A Defense and Critique, in Debate with Samuel Moyn

John Milbank

I

Samuel Moyn's *Christian Human Rights* stands at the intersection of two debates: one concerning the history of rights-talk, the other concerning the political character of what historians increasingly recognize as the last European Christian revival during the 1930s, culminating in the last political-cultural Christian settlement right across the West, and even the globe, after 1945.[1]

At the further margin of both these concerns, only hinted at in the current book and yet considerably orienting its perspectives, lies the question as to why this settlement so suddenly collapsed, eventually ushering in an era of undiluted secular liberalism that includes, as Moyn suggests, a new and more purely secular, yet also unprecedentedly apolitical dominance of human rights.

Essentially out of sight, or invoked only in the last chapter of Moyn's book in a too-complacent manner, remains the contemporary fact that the reiteration of liberalism in our own day, as after World War I and with Weimar, has started to come unstuck, to be once more challenged by populist, quasi-fascistic and to a degree renewed state socialist advocacy.[2] It was just such a situation, one could argue, that the Christian revival of the 1930s tried to address in a "nonconformist," creative and coherent way that today looks once more highly relevant.[3]

Therefore one could also read Moyn's book as a clever attempt to suppress this relevancy and instead treat nonconformist communitarianism as but a reactionary hangover from the deep European past, and even as too close to fascism for comfort. In what follows, I try to make this case by addressing simultaneously both of Moyn's main concerns: the modern

---

[1] Samuel Moyn, *Christian Human Rights* (Philadelphia: Pennsylvania University Press, 2015).
[2] Moyn, *Christian Human Rights*, 137–167.
[3] See Philippe Chenaux, *De la chrétienté à l'Europe* (Tours: CLD, 2007).

history of human rights and the exact character of modern Christian political advocacy.

II

In either case, one must unreservedly welcome Moyn's commitment to historical rigor and desire to deny false continuities and lazy anachronisms. The 1960s were indeed such a watershed that we find it very difficult to believe that the existential stances, religiosity and mores of the twentieth century prior to that point were so very different. Thus most of the TV dramas set before that decade manage to get the clothes (if not always the makeup) more or less right, but scarcely the conversation, accents and behavior, bar the occasional negative registration that these decades fell well short of current standards of political correctness and were supposedly complacent as to the needs for state protection of adults and minors from all sorts of menaces.

Above all, as Moyn stresses, in the wake of other fine historians, we find it hard to imagine that up till so very recently religious assumptions remained normative and were even boosted in the face of rival totalitarianisms, both during peace and later at war, despite much deliberate (and by no means inevitable) organized secular opposition.[4] This includes, as Moyn so well details in this book, a myopia as to the nature of the human rights first advocated after 1945 and a false assumption as to the smooth gradient of rights-recognition from then until now.

For as Moyn argues here and elsewhere, two further phases of rights-talk have intervened since this initial one.[5] A second one tended to yoke rights to movements for national liberation and thereby revived the French revolutionary notion of rights, which saw them as protecting the smaller person and smaller property from the greater equivalents, and as only valid and enforceable if regarded as the rights of the "citizen" as well as of the human being as such.

The third and current phase alone articulates fully a discourse of exclusively "human" rights, focused on all sorts of emancipations of individual types and choices, as well as on the limitations of torture and other forms of legal abuse, cruelty and withholding of defensive succor. This discourse is more individualized and internationalized and so

---

[4] Moyn, *Christian Human Rights*, 1–24; and see Maurice Cowling, *Religion and Public Doctrine in Modern England*. Vols. 1–3 (Cambridge: Cambridge University Press, 1980–2001).

[5] Moyn, *Christian Human Rights*, 101–136; Samuel Moyn, *The Last Utopia: Human Rights in History* (Cambridge, MA: Harvard University Press, 2010); Samuel Moyn, *Human Rights and the Uses of History* (London: Verso, 2014).

depoliticized. Without any serious linking to international governance, but only to international tribunals that on their own lack the teeth of enforcement, the "rights of man," or now of the human being as such, have become unyoked from the "rights of the citizen." This latter right had been closely linked to the aggregated rights of the majority of citizens to rule, even if these two perspectives – of liberalism and democracy, respectively – are obviously in an aporetic tension with each other.

The consequence of this unyoking, as Moyn indicates, is that rights can now mean anything and everything and are not necessarily linked with democracy at all – indeed they may tend to inhibit any collective action and to encourage a purely formal mediation between rival claims by the law and the market, constitutionally embedded and immune to any serious popular challenge. He tends further to imply that this unyoking leaves rights once more prey to theological capture, as may be instanced by the return of "dignity" talk in our own day, even if this now takes predominantly Kantian forms, which it did not in the early twentieth century, as Moyn rightly says.[6]

On the other hand, if his remedy for either axiological anarchy or a new embrace of religion is a repoliticization of rights discourse, then it is perhaps not clear just how this can be possible in a globalized era without a difficult move to international governance, whose liberal character, as presumably desired by Moyn, might risk further popular democratic disaffection that is allied to a concern for place and ineffable local identity.[7] The nonvalidity of such concerns appears to be rather implied than discussed by him.

Neither does Moyn consider the way in which the stronger linking of the rights of the human being to the rights of the citizen always risks the cancelling of those rights outside the sway of polity, or their suspension in an emergency – exactly the reason why the Christian thinkers he discusses tended to diagnose dialectically a totalitarian drift of Rousseauian liberalism itself, and considered that all rights required an extra-human foundation that was transcendent rather than political. At times Moyn seems to assume that these diagnoses were just grounded in religious bias rather than emergent from a serious and still relevant analysis. But is it not the case that the contemporary tendency to try to reinforce "right" with "dignity" is related to our valid reactions of shock and horror to the easy suspension of supposedly universal rights in conditions of claimed emergency and with respect to persons who have become or are deemed to be stateless?

---

[6] Moyn, *Christian Human Rights*, 25–64; John Milbank, "Dignity rather than Right," *Open Insight* 5, no. 7 (2014), 77–124.

[7] See Dani Rodrik, *The Globalisation Paradox* (Oxford: Oxford University Press, 2011).

All the same, these philosophical lacunae in no way detract from the importance of Moyn's insistence that right and dignity are unnatural bedfellows, in both philosophical and historical terms. As he contends, a discourse of foundational subjective right – assuming freedom as naturally given "self-possession" (Hobbes and Locke), or else as a spiritual "dignity" of free choice lying prior even to any kind of ownership (Rousseau and Kant) – was historically developed as an *alternative* to the discourse of "natural law," even though there is a story to tell about how the latter, through the work of Francisco Suarez and others, gradually drifted in a natural rights direction.[8] Classically, natural law was not founded upon given freedom, or upon even any uninterpreted natural "facts" whatsoever, but upon the assumption of a divine government of the cosmos, which guided also human beings explicitly through their free conscience in terms of an intuited sense of equity.[9] This discourse therefore assumed the inherent justice of certain modes of action, goals and ways of relating. It embodied a philosophy of the common good, taken to include objective standards of individual flourishing, variegated according to proper social roles, besides holistic goods that can only be shared and striven for collectively, since they amount to more than the sum of their parts.

Despair of the reality of such an order, or of human participation within it (a despair that, to begin with, was itself perversely theological) led to novel and rival proposals for the grounding of human politics upon natural rights. Although Samuel Moyn is correct to say that seventeenth-century notions of self-grounding subjective right were intended to protect an existing order of property and contract, one must still see continuity as well as inversion (as he tends exclusively to stress) between this legacy and that of the late eighteenth-century revolutionary epoch. The emancipatory irruption of more dispersed freedoms linked to smaller properties still assumed the new subjective foundation, displacing older natural law. For this reason, a more conservative understanding of this foundation remained latent and liable to re-erupt (as so often in the United States) as well as less national-political construals, both individualist and internationalist, with roots going back to Grotius. And one can note here the still continuing debates as to whether after all Hobbes really favored king or Parliament and whether Locke was really a defender of the estate owner or of the smallholder.[10]

---

[8] See Jean-François Courtine, *Nature et empire de la loi: études suaréziennes* (Paris: Vrin, 1999).

[9] See Russell Hittinger, *The First Grace: Rediscovering the Natural Law in a Post-Christian World* (Wilmington, DE: ISI Books, 2003).

[10] Jeffrey R. Collins, *The Allegiance of Thomas Hobbes* (Oxford: Oxford University Press, 2005); James Tully, *A Discourse on Property: John Locke and His Adversaries* (Cambridge: Cambridge University Press, 2008).

For these reasons Moyn is somewhat in danger of suppressing genea-logical continuities with respect to modern right, even if one can alto-gether agree with him that these had no real precedents before the late medieval (and largely Franciscan) proto-construction of something like the Hobbesian outlook.[11] This is not to deny his insistence on the rup-tures that result in different archaeological levels (The Seventeenth Century/ The Revolutionary Epoch/ Christian/ Liberationist/ Globalized Rights), but it is to suggest an inherited and uncertain epige-netic potential within rights that belies his implicit attempt to see the revolutionary model as both normative and normatively radical. In doing so, he ignores above all the fact that this normativity has often been subject to critique from the socialist left as well as from what he wants to deem the "reactionary" right.[12]

None of this, however, in any way qualifies the truth of his insight that the Catholic assertion of "dignity" in the nineteenth century arose in opposition to revolutionary rights and was made in the name of natural law and communitarian values.[13] Nevertheless, Moyn's too easy and historically vague usage of labels like "conservative" and "reactionary" causes him at times to underplay the degree to which, already in the nineteenth century, Catholics were trying to unharness their tradition from association with ancien régime absolutism and dynasticism, whose assumptions and practices were after all not primordial for the Catholic inheritance, but rather themselves a specific mode of *modern* polity, often making just the same pessimistic anthropological assumptions as to nat-ural human anarchy, or putting forward equivalent "enlightened" tech-nocratic remedies, as their liberal opponents.

In this context, for Catholics to refuse the "modern" in either mode was not necessarily to be "conservative." To view things in this way, as Moyn does, is itself to take contemporary frames of reference of modernity for granted and to fail to see that "liberal" or "reactionary" may be equally and specifically *modern* options. By begging the most vital questions at issue in this fashion, Moyn seems to just assume that the orthogonality of Catholic thinkers is a species of self-deluded vaunting, rather than a perhaps genuinely prescient perception of our modern political condition.

Moyn's view that Catholic "dignity" at first referred only to groups, and only later to individuals, is not wholly accurate.[14] From the outset the "dignity of labor" necessarily meant that the individual worker is fully

[11] See John Milbank, "Against Human Rights: Liberty in the Western Tradition," *Oxford Journal of Law and Theology* 1, no. 1 (2012), 1–32.
[12] See Costas Douzinas, *The End of Human Rights* (London: Hart, 2000).
[13] Moyn, *Christian Human Rights*, 25–64.   [14] Moyn, *Christian Human Rights*, 31–34.

a human being and must be accorded the full respect due to all humans as humans. It is easy to find quotations that confirm this.[15] In this respect the nineteenth-century Thomistic revival did not have to wait upon twentieth-century personalism, because Aquinas's texts themselves strongly link dignity with personhood. The complexity of his usage of "person" (grounded in Trinitarian and Christological dogma as well as Latin etymology for which *persona* means "mask") allows for a highly complex interplay between player and performance, the inherent and the assumed, human nature and human social role, necessary to a creature understood to be an *animal sociale*.[16] This inherent theological fluidity of the notion of person already forbids the outright contrast of "group" and "person" that Moyn wishes to impose upon it.

A shift in the application of "dignity" from group to individual is crucial to Moyn's argument as to what happened with Christian thought in the later 1930s and 1940s.[17] He is surely not completely incorrect about this alteration, or wrong as to its main cause: a growing worry about the totalitarian import of any political collectivism. All the same, it would be more accurate to speak of a shift of emphasis and not a change from one perspective to another with which it is incompatible, precisely because the dignity of role already assumed the dignity of the individual "performer" of that role in the way that I have just described – just as the dignity of the human essence assumes the dignity of the individual, personal "performer" of that essence (the Roman, Trinitarian and Christological echoes here being crucial).

Indeed, Moyn effectively concedes that this is after all merely a shift in emphasis – though maybe that concession strengthens his argument as to "conservative" continuity – by allowing that the group-focused "corpora-tist" Catholics of Vichy often fully embraced Jacques Maritain and Emmanuel Mounier's personalist language, while inversely the new Irish Republic, though refusing Iberian-style fascism (or its near-equivalent), still encouraged a mode of corporatism under the name of "vocationalism."[18]

---

[15] See, for example, Mika LaVeque-Manty, "Universalising Dignity in the Nineteenth Century," in *Dignity: A History*, ed. Remy Debes (Oxford: Oxford University Press, 2017), 301–322, citing Leo XIII in *Rerum Novarum* at 318–319.

[16] See Milbank, "Dignity versus Right."   [17] Moyn, *Christian Human Rights*, 25–100.

[18] Note also that corporatism was also espoused on the left – by Emile Durkheim and Marcel Mauss, for example, in France, and by elements of the Labour Party in Britain. See Paul Hirst, *Associative Democracy* (Cambridge: Polity, 1993), Jonathan Boswell, *Community and Economy: The Theory of Public Cooperation* (London: Routledge, 1994) and Maurice Glasman, *Unnecessary Suffering: Management, Markets and the Liquidation of Solidarity* (London: Verso, 1996). For the combination of personalism and corporatism in François Perroux, the main economist of the nonconformist organ, *Esprit*, see *François Perroux: Les Dossiers*, ed. François Denoël (Paris: L'Age de L'Homme, 1990).

If personalism remained to a degree corporatist, then inversely corporatism was quite naturally blended with personalism, in the case of François Perroux and others, as Moyn does not sufficiently allow. But once one does so allow, then it becomes questionable as to whether the switch to "civil society" Catholicism and away from state corporatism was merely opportunistic and negatively fearful.

And in fact, insofar as Moyn rightly says that personalism did not originally embrace subjectively grounded "human rights," he tends to agree with this verdict. Nevertheless, he seems to imply that the main ground for the switch to "civil society" Catholicism was dread of an emergent totalitarianism that was markedly secular and so outside the Church's control and spiritual influence.

However, the official papal condemnation of Action Française in 1926, and Maritain's break with Charles Maurras, was mainly inspired by a belated realization of the heretical character of this movement, led by an atheist, whose sham mode of integralist "theocracy" was to instrumentalize religion toward the achievement of entirely secular and nationalistic ends.[19] Against this, Maritain's proclamation of the "priority of the spiritual" was no novelty, but a recovery of primordial Catholic truth. Even his project of a "new Christendom" tended to renew (if somewhat imperfectly) a Patristic and earlier medieval distinction between the higher suasive *auctoritas* exerted by the Catholic Church and the mere coercive *potestas* exerted by the state.[20] As the title of *Humanisme Intégrale*,

---

[19] This point also fails to figure in John Hellman's *The Communitarian Third Way: Alexandre Marc and Ordre Nouveau, 1930–2000* (Montreal and Kingston: McGill-Queen's University Press, 2002). There is no doubt about the importance of this book on several counts: the balancing of Mounier's importance against that of Marc, the founder of the Ordre Nouveau, which ran somewhat in parallel to Mounier's circle around the journal *Esprit*; the revelation of just how far a postwar obscuring of older Pétainist links has concealed from us the earlier tremendous fluidity between left and right and between third-way personalism and the softer, more left-wing and socialist versions of fascism and Nazism; the way in which so many famous French religious and secular thinkers and actors "repackaged" essentially the same nonconformist thinking (Marc's term) after the war as left rather than right. However, it far too often argues by chains of innuendo: so and so knew so and so who knew so and so who was a Nazi, etc. The interactions at times of nonconformists with Nazis and fascists are read as proof of their right-wing extremism, where they could more plausibly and less anachronistically be read as the relative moderation of some fascists and Nazis. Origins in Maurrasianism or flirtations with Vichy are viewed as far more significant than later repentances from both these things – altogether without warrant.

[20] See John Milbank, *Beyond Secular Order* (Oxford: Blackwell, 2013), 203–205. At times Maritain and his associate, theologian Charles Journet, still too much thought of the Church's authority, after Robert Bellarmine's seventeenth-century model of "indirect power," in terms of a jurisdictional power to intervene when supernatural concerns are involved. This was at once too greatly to restrict the scope of spiritual authority and at the same time to conceive it too much on a this-worldly model. This is indicated both by

which set forth this vision, proclaims, a more freely theocratic "integral-ism" is not here abandoned, but rather more properly asserted as the idea of a culture formed and guided by the Church through the adoption of proper natural social and political structures and educative procedures that can be oriented toward the human supernatural end. It is now politics, not religion, that is the mere means.[21] In politico-social terms the shift implies that intermediary corporate bodies are not to be sub-verted by state control and that their "social" independence of the poli-tical is guaranteed by the spiritual protection of the Church.

This mode of rupture with the French mode of "fascism" is all-important. It shows that the issue of the primacy of the spiritual, which includes the irreducibility of *esprit* to the corporeal, mechanical and manipulable, is both central to and sufficient for understanding the cleavage between personalism and fascism. Yet Moyn seems to half go along with the thesis that would see all or most "third-way" thinking as incipiently fascistic.[22] Thus he notes that perhaps the majority of French personalists were indeed ex-Maurrassians and implies that what was

---

Henry de Lubac and much later by Emmanuel Mounier in his *Feu le Chrétienté* (Paris: Desclée de Brouwer, 2013), 94–95.

[21] Jacques Maritain, *Integral Humanism: Temporal and Spiritual Problems of a New Christendom*, trans. Joseph W. Evans (Notre Dame, IN: Notre Dame University Press, 1973). In this respect it has to be recognized – though almost no one does – that *intégrisme* was reworked not only by Maritain but yet more by the *nouvelle théologie*, who, unlike Maritain's still Baroque Thomism, rejected (like the real Aquinas) any "purely natural end" with no orienting outlook toward the supernaturally donated beatific vision. Thus, as Hellman points out, its later exponents – Chenu, Congar, Daniélou, de Lubac – were all, to begin with, just like Maritain and Gilson, and indeed Simone Weil (so politically similar to the English "Tory Anarchist" George Orwell) closely associated with the Ordre Nouveau and *Esprit* (and indirectly linked to the emerging Protestant "ecologists" around Jacques Ellul and Bernard Charbonneaux in the Toulouse region, besides the Barthian Protestant personalist Denis de Rougemont in Switzerland) and so also, in albeit various different ways to "integral" projects for a New Christendom and a Christian philosophy. Many of these people's original relationship to Vichy was ambivalent and even de Lubac at first lectured at Marchal Pétain's academy at Uriage, before migrating to resistance in Lyon. For me, however, this recognition is unproblematic – here integralism has been purged of an instrumentalizing of the spiritual and a free play of the secular is fully allowed (as also by Gilson and Maritain), even though the ultimate test of political legitimacy must (as for official Catholic doctrine) be its promotion of Christian spiritual ends and so of human salvation, which is primarily the life of charity. And all these ambiguities with regard to Maurrassianism and Vichy apply *also* to the (eventually secular) intellectual figures of Merleau-Ponty, Lyotard, Paul de Man, Bataille, Nancy and Blanchot, as well as to the greatest modernist architect who was as close to the Dominicans and to Thomism in France as Eric Gill and David Jones were in Britain, Le Corbusier. Among politicians, the same goes for Charles de Gaulle and still more of course for François Mitterrand, who may privately never have really abandoned his earlier nonconformist royalism.

[22] Zeev Sternhell, *Neither Right nor Left: Fascist Ideology in France*, trans. David Maisel (Berkeley: California University Press, 1986).

involved in their exit was mainly expediency, Catholic obedience and a switch in tactics and vocabulary.

But this ignores, for one thing, the eventual strong influence upon all these people of certain thinkers, Catholic or religious, especially Charles Péguy, who (for all their anti-liberal romanticism) had not succumbed to Maurrassian rhetoric and blandishments.[23] For another, it tends to yield to the allure of a false syllogism. The false syllogism goes: fascism is defined as a blend of left-wing socialism and right-wing traditionalism; personalism is also such a blend, therefore personalism is fascistic. Yet this is to select what is historically the wrong major premise. A more accurate one would be that, ever since the French Revolution, various modes of "orthogonal" politics have existed, refusing at first both the ancien régime and individualist liberalism, and later both state socialism and the untrammeled free capitalist market. These modes include the originally *main line* of socialism and one could add that they include to a degree even most nineteenth-century liberalism, which sought to qualify individualism with organicism, or sometimes to define itself mainly in terms of a more ancient constitutionalism and generous sense of forbearance, forgiveness and generosity ("liberality" in the older meaning).[24] Moyn rightly notes (with some disapproval) that even in the case of the American Constitution the Bill of Rights is only a liberal supplement, and not its whole foundation, as in the French instance.

Viewed in this alternative perspective, orthogonality looks less like a Christian eccentricity concealing always authoritarian and perhaps fascistic dispositions, and more like the voice of suppressed common sense (as both Chesterton and Orwell regarded it), refusing dangerous extremes and looking to achieve a certain just and sustainable balance in human affairs.

Surely one could argue that Catholics in the 1930s (along with several Protestants and Russian orthodox exiles like Nikolai Berdyaev, as Moyn stresses) were in part trying to rearticulate such a voice? They could see that undiluted liberal individualism was already tending to cultural anarchy (incipient in the 1920s, especially in Weimar), financial instability and a disguisedly imperial American capitalist domination. They were not rejecting moderation, but several extreme ideologies, including Wilsonianism. Their suspicions of undiluted parliamentary democracy were a logical response to the rise of Mussolini and Hitler to power via popular vote. In consequence they sought to balance it both by a greater

---

[23] See John Milbank, "Foreword: Charles Péguy and the Betrayal of Time," in Charles Péguy, *Notes on Bergson and Descartes*, trans. Bruce K. Ward (Eugene OR: Wipf and Stock, 2019), ix–xxxiv.
[24] See Duncan Forbes, "What Is Liberalism?" *Political Theory* 42, no. 6 (2014), 1–22.

influence of informing, educative wisdom, and by a democracy more rooted in the practical good sense of craft and trade. They also thought that a greater allowance for direct participatory democracy in vocation and locality would tend to satisfy natural human political energies that otherwise get diverted into the hysteria of mass causes of "identity" of all kinds. In wishing to refuse the inherent injustice of capitalist appropriation, based on a treatment of men as machines, they wished, as Moyn himself records, to avoid the equal mechanization of people achieved by state welfarism and bureaucratic control of industry.

To counter all this, they spoke of "personalism." Moyn's presentation of this current is scarcely adequate or fair.[25] He glosses over the fact that it had some modern, neo-Kantian roots (e.g., C. B. Renouvier) as well as older, medieval ones, and plays down the Jewish contribution of Buber et al. to make it appear both more exclusively traditionalist and exclusively Christian.

Then he speaks of it as if it were inherently obscure and evasive.[26] Yet, with perfect cogency, in the face of the modern individual versus collective and action versus structure problematics, it suggested instead that we live in webs of relationship, formed through imitative action, yet such that the relational bond permitting imitation is always already there. The good sense of this implicitly informs much social theory to this day.

A paradoxical but coherent connection was also made between relationality and individual uniqueness. Whereas the isolated liberal individual, taken as an absolute starting point, is thereby uninvested and so uncharacterizable, and therefore becomes a bare atom ironically replaceable by any other atom, the connected and situated individual enjoys both a unique perspective and unique attributes. For this reason such a real, rounded "person" possesses a value equivalent to the whole of humanity. This human whole is more than its parts because its parts are not simply

---

[25] Moyn, *Christian Human Rights*, 66–100.

[26] The same is true of John Hellman. Indeed, he contemptuously brushes off this accusation made against him by a reviewer (*Communitarian Third Way*, 204, n. 7) as if it were just obvious that personalism was a farrago of nonsense. Thus no attempt is made over 200 pages to explain this philosophy, nor indeed communitarianism, nor the existentialist "Christian Nietzscheanism" of Alexandre Marc that was influential on Mounier. One is instead left with the implication that the latter must have been nasty or semi-Nazi. In reality it concerned a non-denial of the basic goodness of vital forces and a thoroughly Pauline attempt to see Christian virtue as always creatively singular and nonreactive – in other words as not just endeavoring, like the moral law in St. Paul's interpretation, to restrict the impact of a prior evil. Also it concerned a refusal of either a liberal or a Marxist politics of *ressentiment* that distorts the Christian defense of the weak and abused into an assault on the strong and virtuous, whereas a virtuous strength is really crucial to the exercise of charity. It is quite possible that the later Nietzschean turn of the secular French left in the 1960s is fundamentally indebted to Marc's legacy, if one examines various individual biographies.

parts, but monadic integrities that fully echo the entire essence of the whole and are all of them equally essential to its entirety.

In addition, personalism insisted on the irreducibility of soul to body, with spirit comprising both, as for all Christian and biblical tradition. This was to defend the human free will and powers of discernment and judgment, without which any sort of democracy in the best sense would lose all ground of possibility.

Finally, in the case of Mounier, there is a certain reckoning with the Marxist legacy that gives the lie to any notion that he had merely conservative antecedents.[27] In a manner that avoids any "merely" personal and ahistorical discourse, Mounier, also thinking in the traditions of "French spiritualism" stretching back to Maine de Biran, locates the very heart of the personalist problematic in the circumstance that the human animal has a unique power to transform his environment, yet is forever faced with the problems with which this presents him – the problems of "alienation" for Hegelian-Marxist tradition and of the formation of relatively good or bad habits for the Biranian one.[28]

Mounier argues that negotiating these problems involves always a focus on three sites of mediation: the body (and here he shares something in common with that eventually renegade Christian personalist and former writer for *Esprit*, Maurice Merleau-Ponty), property and the family. In excess of either Marxism or liberalism these are all to be regarded as non-owned "openings" to all the various alterities of nature and culture and neither to be over- or under-stressed in consequence. They necessarily mediate what nonetheless lies beyond their reach: the intra-psychic space of souls where, as Augustine stressed, we can all enjoy noncompetitively something at once and without rivalry, like sunlight.

If this was the ultimate ground of Mounier's personalism, then it also consciously bore the stamp of a psychic ground for socialism. In this respect his postwar leftward drift was no aberration and Moyn ignores the fact that the "nonconformist" groups were deeply influenced, just like

---

[27] Emmanuel Mounier, *Revolution personnaliste et communitaire* (Paris: Broché, 1935); *A Personalist Manifesto* (London: Longmans, Green & Company, 1938); *Be Not Afraid: Studies in Personalist Sociology*, trans. Cynthia Rowland (London: Rockliff, 1951); *Personalism* (Notre Dame, IN: Notre Dame University Press, 1970).

[28] Hellman tends to overstress by comparison the influence on Mounier et al. of Max Scheler and other German thinkers. Scheler was more transcendentalist and acosmically dualist than the French tradition of "spiritual realism" upon which they also drew, although his realist phenomenology indeed allowed him to see sympathetic feeling as truly registering the feelings of other in an intentionally interpersonal and not merely egoistically projective way. For the Biranian influence, see Gérard Lurol, *Emmanuel Mounier: Génèse de la personne* (Paris: Harmattan, 2000). See also Max Scheler, *The Nature of Sympathy* (London: Routledge, 2008).

the more obviously left-leaning Lyon Jesuits, by the traditions of French socialism, about which they both wrote, in collaboration.[29]

For this reason one must qualify Moyn's statement that the Catholic left was always a minority compared to the Catholic right. The observation is perfectly true and yet it can suppress the degree to which socialism itself is not historically "of the left" in any straightforward sense, and the strong influence of socialism also on Catholics of the right and center. Even "Christian Democracy" did not begin as a simply conservative party, although it rapidly became such; instead, its name was supposed to echo as much as to rival the name "Social Democracy," and to qualify it with a more spiritualist and federalist (less statist and nationalist) emphasis, not really a "right-wing" one.[30] After all, even today the average European Christian Democrat would surely be seen as a dangerous commie in many of the "dry" counties of the United States.

Given his dubious propensity to mis-describe the personalists as simply "conservatives" or even "reactionaries," Moyn fails to state what clearly distinguished them from the fascists and Nazis – and we need to remember that even in the latter case there was a more left-wing, more distinctly

---

[29] See again their collective production with contributions by Alexandre Marc and Henri de Lubac amongst others, *Traditions Socialistes Françaises.* The fact that these authors no doubt were seeking a specifically "French" and in this sense "national" socialism (in the tradition of Charles Péguy) does not automatically render them Hitlerian or fascistic. Marc here argues that the French working class would return to a measured patriotism if the political state were not so alienated from the body of the country. The main ally of the nonconformists (and of Maritain) in Italy, Dom Luigi Sturzo, was in fact one of Mussolini's main opponents – even if one cannot ignore some nonconformist flirtation with the Italian fascist fringes. Étienne Gilson, for example, supported Mussolini's invasion of Ethiopia – though he was rebuked in the pages of *Esprit* for this (Hellmann, *Communitarian Third Way,* 260, n. 194). Hellman rather plays down the fact that Marc himself migrated from Vichy to resistance during the course of World War II. For the records of Catholic resistance, mostly emergent from the same nonconformist root, see François Bédarida and Renée Bédarida, *La Résistance Spirituelle, 1941–1944: Les cahiers clandestins du Témoignage chrétien* (Paris: Albin Michel, 2001). For a defense of Mounier in relation to Vichy, see Bernard Comte, "Emmanuel Mounier devant Vichy et la revolution national en 1940–41: L'histoire réinterpretée," *Revue de L'Histoire de L'Eglise en France* 71, no. 187 (June–December 1985), 253–279. Comte convincingly argues that initially Mounier thought that Nazism and fascism were going to triumph and was trying to work out how to live with this while opposing it – an opposition the Vichy authorities quickly detected and so imprisoned him until he was freed in Lyon in 1942, after which he passed into work for the resistance. In the short term, of course, Mounier proved wrong. Yet one must remember that earlier he was almost alone even within *Esprit* in denouncing Munich. And in the very long term his fears of an eventual fascist rather than communist victory look prescient at the time of writing in the year 2019. All the same, beyond the case of Mounier it is impossible to escape the stronger Vichy affiliations of other aficionados of *Esprit* like Perroux, Loustou, Chevalier, Galey and Bergery. Some of these took cabinet or administrative positions.

[30] After World War II, Alexandre Marc threw much of his energy into the cause of European federalism, often with the support of Jacques Delors.

socialist faction. This was not a semi-dishonest veering toward the individual more than the group, as he suggests, but much more specifically the refusal of a state-centralized totalitarian *mode* of corporatism, subverting the true character of corporate bodies as intermediate institutions, along with a false mystical cult of race and nation in place of the true priority of the supernatural.[31] Just by reason of this refusal of a bastardized "spirit," where fascism was too fixated on the centralized sovereign state, personalism spelled itself out constitutionally as "federalism," meaning both political subsidiarity within states and the sharing and pluralizing of sovereignty across their borders, in line with one current of political Romanticism stretching back to Novalis.[32]

This refusal places them far nearer to moderate socialism and qualified liberalism than it does to the secular radical right. The latter's mode of orthogonality was indeed perverse, but that does not tarnish all third ways (of which fascism and Nazism are undeniably examples) with the same creosoting brush. Indeed, the very statism of the radical right, with its associated nationalism and racism, renders it *insufficiently* orthogonal and all too modern by comparison.

Moyn seems dismissive of those who have argued that fascism stands in a dialectical relation to liberalism. However, all the evidence, then as again now, would seem to suggest that indeed in the face of extreme individualism and loss of reciprocal participation people flee to the other modern pole of a kind of drugged collective identity and state worship. It is equally the case that liberalism, then as now, prepares the way for fascism by requiring an excessively strong central state apparatus in

---

[31] This is clearly true, for example, of François Perroux, even when he was arguing that some elements of Hitler's German new order were authentically corporatist and personalist. See Hellman, *Communitarian Third Way*, 105. One also needs sometimes to distinguish the enthusiasm for a revived Holy Roman Empire amongst the Benedictine monks of Maria-Laach in Germany, who included the great liturgist Odo Casel (so crucial for new Catholic liturgical thought in the twentieth century), from their admitted degree of seduction by the Third Reich, whose political basis was in reality racist and nationalist in a Prussian lineage, and so not akin to a much older mode of "south-looking" imperialism (in the tradition of Ferdinand II and the Sicilian connection) at all. Thus it is significant that for all this seduction they still sheltered the fugitive Konrad Adenauer. Carl Schmitt was close to Maria-Laach in his more Catholic phase, when his work could be saluted, for example by Christopher Dawson. Ernst Kantorowicz is one representative of a much more "south" and Roman-leaning, rather than "east" oriented German imperialism. See Chenaux, *De la chrétienté à l'Europe*, 46–52. For Schmitt's most Catholic political work, in which he seems to eschew his usual Hobbesian sovereignty doctrine (explicitly disavowing *Leviathan*) in favor of a fine exposition of "representation" as inherently Christian, see *The Necessity of Politics: An Essay on the Representative Idea in the Church and Modern Europe* (London: Sheed and Ward, 1931).

[32] Chenaux, *De la chrétienté à l'Europe*, 37–102.

order to enact a merely formal order without interpersonal connection and to police the ensuant anarchy that the latter constantly engenders.

III

However, the main thrust of *Christian Human Rights* concerns the postwar mutation in the Catholic articulation of human dignity that permitted it also to include human rights.[33] Again Moyn is astute in calling attention to this shift. And again, undoubtedly, as he is not altogether able to deny, it was triggered by a concern with the gross indifference to and abuse of human life but recently witnessed. Beyond Moyn one might venture that if, recently, dignity has been re-added to right, then earlier right was added to dignity under similar impulses. Quite simply, at a certain rhetorical level, a verbal doubling indicates a redoubled wish to protect and to guard individual human existence.

Of course Moyn is right to say that, in terms of this postwar concern, the full dimensions and meaning of the Holocaust were not immediately registered, yet one could argue that he also underplays the degree to which it was.[34] Conversely, the tendency of the recent "Holocaust industry" to let this horror, albeit central, overshadow all the other horrors and totalitarian dimensions of Nazism is somewhat dubious. Nazism, after all, did not arise because of an unprecedented extremity of anti-Semitism; the latter arose because of Nazism. There is a danger here in so far particularizing that one loses sight of the universal damage and danger.

Most of all that applies to Moyn's complaint that the Nazis were accused of "crimes against humanity," rather than crimes against the Jews in particular, and presumably also the Roma, disabled people, mental health patients, terminally ill people and homosexuals. Yet in every case the wider accusation against the Nazis is the more radical one, because it wishes to insist that all these categories of people are fully human, such that only the Nazis' denial of this could have caused them to discard them like animals or worse. Equally, the phrase implies that crimes against any subgroup of human people is a crime against all of us, thus properly eliciting our expanded solidarity.

Moyn's short-sightedness at this point is of a piece with his earlier inability to see that the "dignity of work" is also the dignity of the worker as an individual human, especially because humans never exist in the abstract, but only as having a particular identity and a particular set of commitments. It is precisely a merely formal respect for human beings, and ultimately just for the human will in the abstract, that constitutes the

[33] Moyn, *Christian Human Rights*, 65–136.   [34] Moyn, *Christian Human Rights*, 90.

inadequacy of liberalism. For this sort of respect tends to be compatible with any and every abuse in reality; one can always claim, like Albert Eichmann, that a formal essence has been left untouched – even the free will, if it is taken in a Fichtean fashion as the irreducible possibility of an inner ironic reserve.

Thus Moyn's entire implied philosophical perspective seems to veer between an empty universal formalism on one hand and a desire to segregate the claim rights and claimed damages of various different identities on the other. Such particularism, unmediated by the universally human, both disallows the overall context and primacy of mediating, distributional justice, and also risks an infinitesimal deconstruction into various subhuman or transhuman species. For to refuse some sort of transcendently grounded universalism inevitably leaves a merely posited universal empty and so provokes a disaggregation into types. This bears negative witness to the truth that lay at the heart of the personalist case, that only the holistic individual person, irreducible to type identity, genuinely manifests the universal and the transcendent.[35]

Moyn's more general and primary point is that Christians dishonestly appropriated the language of rights after World War II.[36] His case is that, in reality, right is almost entirely assimilated to dignity in perpetuation of a specifically Christian political project. And up to a point he is correct. The "rights" now spoken of in the postwar epoch are often correlated with duties and are regarded as claim rights only in relation to claims that one may legitimately make on the basis of natural law.

For example, if it is just and right to teach or to heal people, then students and patients have consequent rights, both human and civil, to make claims for education and treatment upon teachers and doctors. Yet this implies no post-Hobbesian *derivation* of right from the fact of human freedom or its assumed legitimacy. In consequence, it does not imply a natural or civic right to be educated or healed as *primary*. Instead this arises as a secondary consequence of the duty of humans in general to educate and to heal each other. And the legitimate mounting of a civil claim right in these directions assumes the prior existence of a collective duty-based system upon which one can exert such a claim. But to *commence* with a right to be educated or to be healed as a ground for educative or medical policy tends to ignore the unavoidable truth that education and medicine depend entirely upon a system of *mutual* support in which teachers and doctors are socially enabled, paid and

[35] See John Milbank, "The All: A Philosophico-political Polemic," *The Immanent Frame* (February 16, 2018); https://tif.ssrc.org/2018/02/16/the-all-a-philosophico-political-polemic/.
[36] Moyn, *Christian Human Rights*, 89–100.

rewarded, however that be organized. Here a greater realism and a nobler, more transcendent foundation for rights are actually in strong accord.

Moyn rightly indicates that most Christian Democrats were hostile to notions of "welfare rights" construed along the lines of subjective foundations, precisely because they wished to locate subjective rights in the context of distributional and equitable natural law. It may be correct to say that already at this time existed a mounting (but, as we have just seen, incoherent) social democratic discourse of foundational rights to welfare. Yet in the case of the establishment of the British "welfare state," it was initially regarded as the logical extension of a system of mutual support, grounded in duty and charity rather than foundational rights, in the wake of such figures as R. H. Tawney. Natural and civil rights to treatment were only seen as arising in relation to this naturally equitable objective foundation.

But the problem here is that if a merely objective natural law grounding of subjective claims were all that were involved in the new adding of rights to dignity, as Moyn seems to suggest, then there would, after all, be *no historical contradiction* about this blend. For as the best historians have shown, medieval canon law and Thomas Aquinas himself expanded the classical jurisprudential legacy to include subjective claim rights in this non-foundational sense.[37]

There could only then be a contradiction if in fact Catholics and other Christians of this period tried indeed to combine natural law dignity with modern subjectively grounded subjective claim rights. But at least in the instance of the very influential postwar Maritain, that is precisely the case. And it is therein and therein only that a historical and philosophical incoherence lies, as the Catholic jurisprudential philosopher Michel Villey later identified.[38] Maritain indeed speaks of the "self-mastering individual" who is a Kantian "end in himself" as the ultimate source of natural right, and in a now totally un-Thomistic manner traces natural law back primarily to the divine electing will.[39]

Therefore my complaint about the postwar Catholics would be just the opposite to that of Moyn – not that they diluted right with dignity, but that they diluted dignity with liberal right.

---

[37] See Milbank, "Against Human Rights."

[38] Michel Villey, *La formation de la pensée juridique moderne* (Paris: Presses Universitaires de France, 2013).

[39] Jacques Maritain, *The Rights of Man and the Natural Law*, published together with *Christianity and Democracy*, trans. Doris C. Anson (San Francisco: Ignatius, 2011), esp. 206–207.

To a considerable degree Mounier and other members of the *Esprit* group saw this, but the insight notably took them in a more socialist rather than modern conservative direction, inspired both by a desire for Europe to follow a third way between the USA and the USSR, and at times by some naiveté about the latter for which they have received retrospective excoriation from Bernard Henri-Lévy and others. But for all that Moyn is correct in seeing this faction as a minority, its alienation from the start of the European project tended, as Philippe Chenaux suggests, to dilute personalism and weaken the radically federalist ambitions of the European pioneers.[40] These ambitions became instead eventually divided between the Gaullist idea of a mere unity of nations and a highly technocratic and apolitical notion of federal unity, as inspired by Jean Monnet, who lay outside the personalist current of thinking.

Yet even allowing for its inadequacy and compromised character, the genuine Christian Democratic tempering of liberalism seems both admirable and moderate. The implication that it was, on the contrary, deplorable and merely "conservative" (a word that at times for Moyn seems to be equivalent to "Christian") would seem tacitly to go along with the liberal dismantling of that settlement, first culturally in the 1960s and 1970s and then economically in the 1980s. Yet this would have to include also, for reasons we have seen, the fatal dismantling of the British Socialist–High Tory compromise of the 1950s and of the American New Deal, whose partially Christian inspiration Moyn also indicates.[41]

But for many people, perhaps for most of us, there must rather be massive cause for regret here. The last Christian settlement, of which Moyn like other historians speaks, delivered unparalleled prosperity in the West, unprecedented peace in Western Europe and less insecurity for most people. It nurtured strong families and greatly extended education; despite a feminist deficit it also hugely advanced the political and civic participation of women, as Moyn's own secondary sources explicitly underline.[42]

It would seem that one can come to Moyn's assumed or hinted negative verdict only if one defines progress entirely in terms of much later exclusive obsessions with as yet unemancipated human identities: obsessions that tend to require us to cast what was experienced at the time as a period of renewal as after all belonging to the dark gothic past – a requisite now duly provided by endless TV drama series.

---

[40] Chenaux, *De la chrétienté à l'Europe*, 103–143.
[41] Moyn, *Christian Human Rights*, 68, 93.
[42] Martin Conway, "The Rise and Fall of Western Europe's Democratic Age, 1945–1973," *Contemporary European History* 13, no. 1 (2004), 67–88.

However valid some of these new emancipatory concerns may be, it seems one-sided to let this measure of success discount other ones of economic justice and the greater contentment of majorities.

IV

All that can probably be conceded to Moyn here is that the treatment of women truly remained for long in the twentieth century a blind spot amongst Christian thinkers, for all the great women among their number like Simone Weil, Madeleine Delbrel, Edith Stein, Dorothy Day and Dorothy L. Sayers.

This matter warrants more explanation, because the pre-rigorist bishops in France of the period 1820–1850 already showed much concern for female well-being, extending notably to the view that birth control must be left to the conscience of couples.[43] Just why rigorism survived so strongly and was often even intensified with respect almost exclusively to matters of sex, gender and birth (the background to *Humane Vitae* being truly a quirky and minority one), besides at times restricted views on women's roles in society, has perhaps not yet been fully accounted for.

All the same, the personalists (including Mounier and Maritain, besides Edith Stein and Dietrich von Hildebrand in Germany) engaged in a sophisticated critique of liberal feminism that insisted on a corporeally and spiritually based sexual difference, but newly embraced gender equality, both in theory and to a considerable degree in social practice. It likewise asserted the interpersonal complementarity of the sexes, while also insisting on the unified personhood of each male and female taken alone, which must include a certain psychological integration of the sexual other.[44] In the case of Karol Wojtyła, much of this was finely developed and yet at times implausibly distorted through its linkage with the unnecessary rigorism as to certain specific policies and too limited a vision of women's public role. The consequences of the latter have undoubtedly been dire: already in the 1920s some Churchmen noted the disaffection of intelligent women and in the 1960s this became a mass exodus.[45]

Yet the exodus by no means concerned women alone, and most commentators wrongly assume the 1960s revolt to have been inevitable and

---

[43] See Claude Langlois, "Sexe, modernité et catholicisme. Les origines oubliées," *Esprit* (February 2010), 110–121.

[44] See Prudence Allen, "Man-Woman Complementarity: The Catholic Inspiration," *Logos* 9, no. 3 (2006), 87–108; Emmanuel Mounier, "La femme aussi est une personne," *Esprit* (June 1936), 292–297. Hellman's accusations of a blanket sexism and anti-feminism are simply inaccurate.

[45] See Callum Brown, *The Death of Christian Britain* (London: Routledge, 2009).

natural, when in reality the protest of an unprecedentedly privileged generation, often the children of heroes and heroines, warrants far more attempt at historical explanation.[46]

V

The furthest reach of Samuel Moyn's concerns in *Christian Human Rights* relates, however, not to the post-1968 moment, but to the post-9/11 moment and to the twenty-first century so far. Here he suggests that our current responses to Islam show that rights to religious freedom have been too much construed in Christian terms.[47] In this instance, despite the ruptures of phases two and three of postwar human rights, a certain legacy of phase one, of specifically "Christian human rights" still perniciously endures.

Here again I would invert the verdict. Rather, a notion of toleration rooted in Christian belief that assent to God must be uncoerced was already in the first phase too much contaminated by an expression in terms of "rights." For, as Moyn indicates, if rights are grounded in freedom of individual choice, there is no need to privilege religion at all, even though this seems so immediately counterintuitive (and rightly so) for any lover of liberty. One does so only by positive analogy with one's own religious legacy, extending a measure of toleration to that which is sufficiently akin to it and therefore acceptable – for Christianity acknowledgment of such affinity readily extends to all the major world religions, rooted in the common axial legacy.[48] All real historical religious toleration (as opposed to sheer indifference) has proceeded on this basis and otherwise – as Moyn indicates with half-approval – any sheerly objective and secular espousal of absolutely free rights of belief and opinion is really a part of a secular campaign to extirpate the public influence, and so the deep social and psychological reality, of religious practice.

In this context, no sheerly secular approach could possibly favor Islam, which still less than Christianity accepts any hard-and-fast sacred/secular distinctions. Moyn simply glosses over the crucial point that the surely unreasonable total public ban on the veil has been advocated by the

---

[46] With respect mainly to French Catholicism, Guillaume Cuchet suggests as primary causes rather the bureaucratization of the Church and the loss of its sense of mystical distance, already under way in the 1950s, but shockingly sealed for many by the impact of Vatican II. See *Comment Notre Monde a Cessé D'être Chrétien* (Paris: Seuil, 2018), 267–276.

[47] Moyn, *Christian Human Rights*, 137–167.

[48] See John Milbank, "The End of Tolerance: On the Decline of Religious Freedom and the Return of Religious Influence," *ABC Religion and Ethics* (August 24, 2017): www .abc.net.au/religion/the-end-of-tolerance-on-the-decline-of-religious-freedom-and-the /10095472.

French secular regime and far less so by Christians. Indeed, those like Pierre Manent and now Emmanuel Macron himself in France looking for a more generous policy toward Muslims are advocating both a qualification of *laïcité* and a nurturing of a stronger sense of some analogy between the Islamic *ummah* and the Catholic Church.[49] Moyn's tergiversations concerning laws used against both communism and claimed Islamic excesses make in the end no significant point other than that in *either case* both the spiritual and the political identity of Europe are obviously considered to be involved and in neither case is it considered that this can lightly be put at risk.

In reality it is clear that one should have just the opposite anxiety to Moyn – a fear that Christian witness, practice and symbolism is less and less tolerated in Europe, while the Islamic equivalents are much more so, and that crimes committed by Muslims under alien and often barbaric cultural assumptions (though often not genuinely grounded in the best Islamic traditions) go under-detected out of fear of racist accusations.[50] Secular liberals collude in this situation in the name of pluralism and in the hope that this will yet further undermine Christian hegemony, even though it also compromises their own liberal values. Of course the dangers of this strategy backfiring are overwhelming.

In the same spirit of his approach to Europe and Islam, Moyn clearly wishes to tarnish the Christian nonconformists with the brush of ethnocentrism. But their failure to condemn colonialism, which he points up, was once more shared with overwhelming numbers of socialists of this epoch. Neither is this failure obviously or entirely culpable: to the contrary, a reaction against the pseudo-radicalism of simplistic anti-imperialism is today emergent. Increasingly it is apparent that dogmatic anticolonialism has tended to endorse the still worse imperialism of anarchic corporate power colluding with tribally exclusive nationalisms linked to dubious ideologies, whether communistic, fascistic or neoliberal.[51]

VI

One can base a political civilization upon *something*, a deep, complex and profound tradition like Christianity, or upon a void bridged by formality and eventually by terror, as we are now seeing in the case of identity

---

[49] Pierre Manent, *Beyond Radical Secularism: How France and the Christian West Should Respond to the Islamic Challenge* (New York: St. Augustine's Press, 2016).

[50] Douglas Murray, *The Strange Death of Europe: Immigration, Identity, Islam* (London: Bloomsbury, 2017).

[51] See Bruce Gilley, "The Case for Colonialism," *Third World Quarterly* (December 24, 2017), 1–17; Helen Andrews, "Where Zimbabwe Went Wrong," *National Review* (December 18, 2017).

politics turned poisonous, through its impossible attempt to supply us with a new anti-universal. When the founding upon a void has been attempted, stutteringly or suddenly as in 1789, 1917, 1968 or 1989, sooner or later one engenders either an atavistic populist reaction or a "progressivist" demand for a purely scientific and technocratic future, as with current "accelerationism" and the espoused policies of China. The dialectical reversal has only been slower since 1968 than since 1919, because of the great durability and therefore slower erosion of the 1945 settlement that was established under largely Christian auspices.

But we are now back in that moment of reversal. And so we are once more in a moment when a Christian personalist and postliberal vision is trying to respond, in a manner inevitably linked with a newly attempted cultural and ecclesial Christian revival.[52] The hidden reality of the recent past, which Moyn has so rightly disinterred, figures now less as a specter, as he supposes or desires, than as a resurrected possibility.

---

[52] See John Milbank and Adrian Pabst, *The Politics of Virtue: Postliberalism and the Human Future* (London and New York: Rowman and Littlefield, 2016).

2　The Alpine Climb between Paris and Rome

Julian Bourg

The eminent philosopher of law John Finnis has penned a particularly stern critique of Samuel Moyn's *Christian Human Rights*.[1] Finnis is a notable voice in revived reflection on natural law and natural rights as well as a tireless commentator on the Catholic intellectual heritage.[2] Given Moyn's argument that the Catholic Church led the way in the mid-twentieth-century promotion of human rights as a newly salient paradigm, one might have thought Finnis to be largely sympathetic to his account. The reverse is true. The two are in deep, seemingly irreconcilable opposition. Beyond serious political and methodological disagreement, their substantive differences ultimately culminate in the standoff between two long-established positions – implied, though never explicitly articulated – on one hand, Finnis's view that modernity is basically hostile to Catholicism, and on the other, Moyn's excavation of a dominant strain of Catholicism that is hostile to modernity. Extremes obviously meet in the shared assessment that Catholicism and modernity are inimical. To be sure, the category of modernity has in recent decades been subjected to thoroughgoing critiques. In spite of obvious limitations, however, the concept remains a useful shorthand. For behind such generalities are very concrete stakes regarding questions of tradition, religion, secularity, history, plurality, the individual/person, sociality, rights, and so forth. That contemporary rights talk is secular or at least nondenominational, potentially compatible with religion without being reducible to particular faith communities, is a modern proposition. At the same time, the essential insight of the recent post-secular moment has been that religion has never gone away.

Rather than the contrast of Jerusalem and Athens, posed long ago by Tertullian and renewed in the past century by Leo Strauss, with Finnis

---

[1] Samuel Moyn, *Christian Human Rights* (Philadelphia: University of Pennsylvania Press, 2015); John Finnis, "On Moyn's *Christian Human Rights* (2015)," *King's Law Journal*, 28, no. 1 (2017), 12–20; Moyn, "Tradition and Beyond: Christian Human Rights in Debate," *King's Law Journal*, 28, no. 1 (2017), 27–34.

[2] John Finnis, *Natural Law and Natural Rights*, 2nd ed. (Oxford: Clarendon Press, [1979] 2011); Finnis, *Collected Essays*, 5 vols. (Oxford: Oxford University Press, 2011).

and Moyn we confront a mountainous conceptual divide, itself distinctly modern, between Rome and Paris, the Vatican's perdurance and the French Revolution's legacy.[3] Although not entirely wrong to find themselves on opposite slopes of a shared judgment – they are arguing about real matters – both Finnis and Moyn end up assuming familiar stances. One of the great merits of the theme of Christian human rights is that its contradictions expose fundamental impasses: here, Catholic rejection of the secular foundations on which much rights talk rests and anti-Catholicism as a long-standing cornerstone of secular modernity. Today such oppositions may all at once seem incomplete, ironically proximate, outdated, and more relevant than ever. The theme of Christian human rights highlights tensions between Catholic eternalism and modern historicism, foregrounds possible Catholic rapprochement with key aspects of modernity, and exposes the inadequacies of individualist human rights regimes. It thus also points toward new vistas. For in spite of real, persisting differences between religious and nonreligious worldviews, the notion of Christian human rights suggests possible forms of mediation and dialogue that are attractive today.

Finnis vs. Moyn

Finnis thinks Moyn is wrong that Christians recently embraced human rights. Such rights, he believes, are rooted in natural law and religious commitments.[4] Nominalist attention to terminology and contextualist attention to contingency are ultimately superficial because the conceptual possibility of human rights is based in truths that are metaphysically real and supra-historical. Thus, Thomas Aquinas was "talking about human rights even though he did not use that phrase." To be sure, Finnis acknowledges that rights claims occur within "circumstances."[5] Yet the admission shapes his argument no more than Moyn's inverse concession that traditions and chronologies surpassing his punctualist histories of human rights during the 1940s and 1970s matter. In other words, Finnis's eternalist suspicion of historicism is mirrored in reverse by Moyn's historicist suspicion of the longue durée. A good deal of Moyn's

---

[3] Tertullian, *Prescription against Hereticks and the Apologeticks of St. Theophilus, Bishop of Antioch to Autolycus, against the Malicious Calumniators of the Christian Religion*, trans. Joseph Betty (Oxford: Printed at the Theatre, 1722), 12–87, at 24; Leo Strauss, "Jerusalem and Athens: Some Introductory Reflections," *Commentary*, 43 (1967), 45–57.

[4] For the possibility of decoupling natural law and religion, see Dan Edelstein, "Not Church History?" *The Immanent Frame* (June 3, 2015): https://tif.ssrc.org/2015/06/03/not-church-history, and Edelstein, *On the Spirit of Rights* (Chicago: University of Chicago Press, 2018).

[5] Finnis, "On Moyn's *Christian Human Rights*," 15.

response to Finnis focuses on the methodological contrast between his own "secular and external" critical-explanatory approach and Finnis's "internalist," "apologetic," and hermeneutical one.[6]

Finnis's prioritization of nature and revelation over historical contingency, and thus of *order* over *right*, is on display in his reading of Article 9 of the European Convention for the Protection of Human Rights and Fundamental Freedoms (November 4, 1950). Article 9(1) states that "everyone has a right to freedom of thought, conscience and religion," including the right to change religion. Article 9(2) details limits on such rights that "are necessary in a democratic society in the interests of public safety, for the protection of public order, health or morals, or for the protection of the rights and freedoms of others."[7] In *Christian Human Rights*, Moyn argues that claims for such a "democratic minimum" had reflected Cold War, anticommunist anxieties and the promotion of Christian Western civilization. The mid-twentieth-century assertion of religious freedom as a human right thus expressed desires to "marginalize" or "ensure the postponement of" a secularism embodied by the Soviet Union. Moyn points out that the first contemporaneous invocation of Article 9(2) had been in favor of West Germany's 1957 effort to ban the Communist Party. In a considerable irony, recent efforts to limit the religious freedom of Muslims in Europe in the guise of a secularist democratic minimum have forgotten the anti-secularist motives that first inspired the 1950 European Convention. In between that moment and our own, the thoroughgoing de-Christianization of Europe had created the conditions for this new, secularist interpretation.[8]

In Finnis's view, the "content" of rights cannot "be specified" without the kind of considerations found in Article 9(2).[9] Since there can be no rights without order, priority should have been given to Article 9(2) limitations over Article 9(1) rights. The possibility that Article 9(1) rights are themselves foundational – the right to change itself providing a stable, orderly ground – is not acceptable. Indeed, the permanence of change would have seemed strange to Aristotle. For Finnis, the fact that there are neighbors precedes my claim to a right to play my music as loudly as I want, and furthermore, primary social norms (don't be loud) underlie secondary legal articulation. Such norms derive at least in part from tradition, and Finnis has a particular tradition in mind – Catholic Christianity – whose holistic metaphysical realism he emphasizes. He

---

[6] Moyn, "Tradition and Beyond," 27.
[7] European Convention for the Protection of Human Rights and Fundamental Freedoms (November 4, 1950): www.echr.coe.int/Documents/Convention_ENG.pdf, 11.
[8] Moyn, *Christian Human Rights*, 140–141, 144, 161.
[9] Finnis, "On Moyn's *Christian Human Rights*," 15.

refers to the "worthy and sustainable patterns of life" expressed by Christianity as they relate to character, conduct, and community interaction. Rights and duties are mutually conditioning through the telos of human flourishing and fulfillment. Compared to such a substantive or thick understanding of persons embedded in social frameworks, the formalist language of rights seems thin, vacuous, or pernicious. Individuals cannot flourish alone, and rights talk is merely "a way of expressing moral-political judgments" that have priority (both anteriority and precedence).[10] The specific point can be extended more generally to the communitarian position that that, if socially embedded traditions did not satisfy human needs, they would not endure.

In a sense, Moyn and Finnis are both committed to forms of realism. Finnis's realism is metaphysical, and he possesses a card the eternalist can always play: the contingent world is forever out of sync with divine or natural perfection. The apparent is subordinate to the real, and this world cannot be the site of ultimate normative or explanatory meaning since it is incidental whether one is trying to follow natural law in the fourteenth century or the twenty-first. To be sure, the anti-historicist has a very hard time explaining how and why social facts and norms change, why new ones evolve, and how we might substantially and meaningfully separate the past from the present, for example, with respect to slavery in Athens or Article 1, section 2 (the "three-fifths clause") of the US Constitution. In his reply to Moyn, Finnis cites his 1992 Étienne Gilson lecture on historical consciousness and theological foundations in which he responded to Catholic thinkers inspired by Bernard Lonergan's contrast of historical and classical worldviews. There, he wondered if the historical worldview, whose "plausibility" he somewhat oddly related to "the massive growth of historical information" as opposed to, say, any fundamental reorientation in the human experience of time, could handle the possibility of "universal principles." Implicitly criticizing by way of Lonergan the distinctive historical turn of certain strains of twentieth-century Catholic thought from Étienne Gilson to Pierre Teilhard de Chardin and Henri de Lubac, Finnis sought to show how thinkers such as Aristotle and Aquinas had already arrived at similar perspectives with greater consistency. Whatever its merits, however, the strategy replayed the problem it claimed to address since all claims that appeal to God and nature are themselves historically situated.[11] For Moyn, in contrast, contingent

---

[10] Finnis, "On Moyn's *Christian Human Rights*," 17.
[11] Finnis, "Historical Consciousness and Theological Foundations," in *Collected Essays*, vol. 5, *Religion and Public Reasons*, 140–141.

circumstances are real; the historical world is intelligible through rational, evidence-based analysis; understanding norms requires explanation and not merely justification; and history is our common, nondenominational lot. A punctualist historiography is at home here, but Moyn has an understandably harder time with middle- or long-term historicization, and historicism always faces the risk of self-dissolution. Where one stands depends on where one sits: Finnis's and Moyn's divergent views on eternalism and historicity determine which kind of context each emphasizes in making sense of human rights. In other words, different basic commitments lead to different methodological positions, which in turn yield divergent substantive conclusions.

Moyn finds Finnis's foundationalism potentially noxious for two converging reasons. First, specifying limitations on rights ahead of time risks capricious or imperious abridgment. Majorities can easily impose noxious social norms on minorities; the principle of public safety, for instance, can obviously be invoked to curtail rights in abusive ways. For Moyn, abuse would involve the violation of an underlying democratic ethos that gives life to rights – his own version of a democratic minimum. That "minority rights" may become a majoritarian social norm implies a contingent historical evolution from nonrecognition to recognition. Second, with respect to Christian "patterns of life," Moyn is concerned that substantive notions of "human good" and "communal life" can themselves be restrictive and oppressive since they may preemptively decide which social acts are permissible and thus foreclose other possible goods.[12] In other words, while substantive rationality possesses the advantage of meaningful social content, it also has the disadvantage of potentially chauvinist exclusions that degrade the democratic ethos. Natural law may provide arguments against crimes against humanity, but as a matter of historical record, the category of natural law has also been used, for instance, to justify slavery and genocide. Again, the metaphysical realist can always play the card that says that excess or abuse were ipso facto never a true manifestation of natural law at all but rather reflected an incorrect apprehension of it. In any case, Finnis's references to "chattel slavery; abortions of convenience; [and] non-voluntary euthanasia" gesture toward the ethico-political stakes of the debate between contingent democratic norms and suprahistorical natural law.[13]

If Moyn and Finnis cannot see eye to eye on ontological and epistemological matters, or on limiting rights and foregrounding substantive goods, in other ways they may nonetheless approach one another, their

---

[12] Finnis, "On Moyn's *Christian Human Rights*," 16.
[13] Finnis, "On Moyn's *Christian Human Rights*," 17n18.

movements echoing across the snowy peaks. For starters, they are both suspicious of individualist human rights regimes. The cumulative effect of Moyn's critical history of human rights, from *The Last Utopia: Human Rights in History* (2010) to *Not Enough: Human Rights in an Unequal World* (2018), has been to expose the shortcomings of present-day pieties.[14] He has insisted on the recent, contingent origins of paradigms popularly understood as based on eternal verities, and he has exposed the political failings, notably with respect to global inequality, of ethical human rights regimes. In *Not Enough*, he has embedded his earlier insights about the 1940s and 1970s within the story of now-hobbled welfare projects that previously pursued sufficiency and equality together. Building on the suggestion presented earlier in this chapter that substantive rationality faces the tension between meaningful social content and potentially chauvinist exclusion, as a corollary one might say that formal rationality possesses the advantage of protective shielding but the disadvantage of empty proceduralism. With different motives and relying on different criteria, Finnis too is obviously dissatisfied with contemporary human rights. "I actually think Finnis is profoundly correct," Moyn writes, "about the need to achieve a richer approach to social morality than contemporary human rights law and movements frequently allow."[15] In short, they share a common concern – the weaknesses of an individualistic notion of human rights – while pursuing very different solutions. Moyn believes that social rights are made a posteriori through historical effort; Finnis holds that they are ultimately found a priori in a metaphysically real cosmology. Might they agree, however, that the social context of rights precedes their individualization – both the enumeration of distinct rights and the identification of "the individual" as bearer of them? The obvious problem is that social-historical contexts include both inherited traditions and undetermined possibilities. *That* is the mountain.

Moyn's suggestion to "reclaim the history of duties" signals a route for possible encounter (to borrow a term dear to the Catholic intellectual tradition). Contemporary liberalism and human rights, he says, have lost sight of a long-standing project – namely, thinking rights in relation to duties. The contemporary tendency to underestimate "obligations" is "unbalanced," whereas some nineteenth-century liberals had relied on duties as counterweights to rights. Moyn highlights Giuseppe Mazzini's broad vision of cosmopolitan "social interdependence" that "sought

---

[14] Samuel Moyn, *The Last Utopia: Human Rights in History* (Cambridge, MA: Harvard University Press, 2010); Moyn, *Human Rights and the Uses of History*, 2nd ed. (London: Verso, 2017); Moyn, *Not Enough: Human Rights in an Unequal World* (Cambridge, MA: Harvard University Press, 2018).

[15] Moyn, "Tradition and Beyond," 32.

a balance between individual emancipation and collective obligations" and that was rooted in human "perfectibility." Notwithstanding Mazzini's own mobilization against the Church as an impediment to Italian nationalization, in retrospect, such a vision actually sounds awfully Catholic. Or perhaps Catholics in the twentieth century came to sound Mazzinian. One wonders if the concepts of interdependence, of the "eventual unification of humanity," and of the "collective foundations of the good life" might at some level be compatible with the kind of perspective and commitments Finnis expresses.[16] Might *emancipation* and *holism* be consonant idioms? Grasping such potential affinity would require Finnis to ease off on the requirement that interdependence be founded in Christian natural law, and it would require Moyn to ease off his suspicion that tradition is essentially coercive. Neither "pining for lost medieval syntheses" nor Enlightenment anti-religiosity may be adequate for generating non-noxious, non-imperious forms of individuality, equality, social justice, and common good.[17]

Moyn seeks to preserve the gains of post-Enlightenment autonomy while drawing attention to its limits. He explicitly opposes the view that "rights ought to *depend* on the assumption of duties," a view that he ascribes to those today "whose true purpose" in invoking duties "is a return to tradition won by limiting the rights of others."[18] It is a sentiment he repeats in his reply to Finnis when he writes that both medieval and modern Christianity have often provided "a rationale for the unjustifiable rule of some over others, as all historical religions have chiefly been."[19] I would like to make three comments. First, Moyn is simply right to insist on the "repressive 'patterns of life'" that Christians have "imposed" on others, not least the long tradition of Christian anti-Semitism.[20] Anti-Semitism is the permanent temptation of Christianity as a supersessionist religion, and contrition, atonement, and penance are resources internal to Christian traditions with which in future centuries to continue to confront that theological racism. The cosmopolitan democratic voice also rightly raises questions about Catholic views on women and sexual minorities. Second and related, Moyn tracks a distinctively "conservative" version of Christianity. Such are the reasonable contours of his study of the surprising genesis of Christian human rights by actors and dynamics principally on the political right. Religious traditions certainly can be coercive, but they also possess resources for social solidarity.

---

[16] Moyn, "Reclaiming the History of Duties," in Moyn, *Human Rights in History*, 153, 155–158, 160.
[17] Moyn, "Tradition and Beyond," 32.
[18] Moyn, "Reclaiming the History of Duties," 165.
[19] Moyn, "Tradition and Beyond," 32.   [20] Moyn, "Tradition and Beyond," 30.

Beyond the looseness with which the label conservative is employed –
presumably anyone who gets married, has children, or follows the religion
of one's parents can be considered conservative – the more serious issue is
the degree to which any "restriction" on "personal entitlements" involves
"submission."[21] Even if Moyn is right that many of the particular mid-
twentieth-century Catholics he examines did view restriction as submission, the more general question about how to balance rights with restrictions (e.g., duties) may still stand. Moyn clearly wants to avoid claiming
that we are bound only by the duties we individually choose, which would
lead back to Kantian atomism. Yet in many places around the world
today, notions of social autonomy and duty seem invariably to engage
religious traditions. It therefore may be worth parsing a little more the
differences between tradition as coercion and tradition as elective affinity.
Perhaps Moyn's apparent worry that religion in general and Catholicism
in particular are structurally coercive actually points to a mundane political problem: protecting the lifeworlds of minorities against the tyranny
of majorities. This requirement certainly applies to the experience of non-
Christians in predominately Christian countries but also seems germane
to minorities in all societies where majority faiths exist, notably
Buddhism, Hinduism, Islam, and Judaism.

This leads to the third point: Moyn may not take his own commitments
to contingency far enough. While he asserts that the "peregrinations" of
the Church are "far more a matter of adaptation to climate than inevitable
working out of original truth," and although his final word to Finnis is the
simple truth that "traditions do change," he tends to take religiously
committed voices at face value, as if accepting the eternalism of
Christianity is the entry price for understanding its internal logics, discourses, and practices.[22] A commitment to historical contingency might
entail the strong view that even if historical actors believe and say that they
answer to the eternal, they themselves may not fully grasp the fortuity of
their own claims. Historicism admits no exceptions. Even a weaker, more
charitable view might hold that religious discourse can be, as Hans
Blumenberg said of rhetoric, "a form of rationality itself – a rational way
of coming to terms with the provisionality of reason."[23] Reference to
eternity may be one way to come to terms with contingency. Amos
Funkenstein, for instance, went even further in exploring and excavating
the coherent rationalities of the theological imagination; even from his

---

[21] Moyn, "Tradition and Beyond," 31–32.
[22] Moyn, "Tradition and Beyond," 28–29, 34.
[23] Hans Blumenberg, "An Anthropological Approach to the Contemporary Significance of
Reason," in *After Philosophy: End or Transformation?*, ed. Kenneth Baynes,
James Bohman, and Thomas McCarthy (Cambridge, MA: MIT Press, 1987), 452.

perspective of ontological agnosticism, Christianity quite literally *made sense*.[24] Again, this is not to underestimate the "repressive 'patterns of life'" that have indeed stemmed from eternalist positions, neither is it to exclude the possibility that religion ought to be subject to democratic means testing (here, the notion of democratic minimum returns as the prerequisite for participation in a noncoercive, non-exclusionary ethos). Rather, following the commitment to historical contingency all the way through may involve engaging another paradox: not taking Catholic worldviews so seriously in order to take them more seriously. For if both Finnis and Moyn agree that Catholicism is essentially eternal, static, conservative, and only more superficially subject to "circumstances" and "peregrinations," then both may underestimate the mechanisms, rhythms, and dynamics of change for an institution that "thinks in centuries." Here, more unselfconsciously than deliberately, they both scale the heights of a well-mapped terrain where one faces the question: can Catholics ever be modern?

The Never-Ending Story

Moyn and Finnis act out enduring tensions between anti-Catholic modernity and modern anti-Catholicism. A thumbnail sketch of this long-term conceptual relationship is useful in order to historicize their discord. This detour will lead back to the issue of stasis and the prospects for moving beyond it. Again, personification is shorthand, since to speak of "moderns" or "Catholics" is to refer to ideal types. The concept of the modern itself can be seen to have deep roots within Christian culture, from the Incarnation as epochal consciousness to debates between *moderni* and *antiqui* in Christendom to the notion of secularization as "a disguised version of what went before."[25] More familiar is the fact – both trite and freighted with significance – that a radical rupture between modernity and Catholicism occurred between the sixteenth and eighteenth centuries. Magisterial accounts such as those by Blumenberg and

---

[24] Amos Funkenstein, *Theology and the Scientific Imagination from the Middle Ages to the Seventeenth Century*, preface by Jonathan Sheehan (Princeton, NJ: Princeton University Press, [1986] 2018).

[25] Robert B. Pippin, *Modernism As a Philosophical Problem* (Cambridge, MA: Blackwell, 1991), 17; Matei Calinescu, *Five Faces of Modernity: Modernism, Avant-Garde, Decadence, Kitsch, and Postmodernism* (Durham, NC: Duke University Press, 1987), 14–16; Martin Jay, "Blumenberg and Modernism: A Reflection on *The Legitimacy of the Modern Age*," in *Fin-de-siècle Socialism and Other Essays* (New York: Routledge, 1988), 150. The classic statement of translational continuity between Christian and secular notions of temporality is Karl Löwith, *Meaning in History: The Theological Presuppositions of the Philosophy of History* (Chicago: University of Chicago Press, 1949).

Funkenstein locate resources for this rupture within the complex terrain of Christian theology itself.[26] Nevertheless, "the standard account of modernity" recounts how Christian "typological" time of *non nova, sed nove* (not the new, but anew) was replaced by "the epoch of Being conceived under the sign of the *novum*" (the new) and by "homogeneous, empty time."[27] Since the 1790s, the French Revolution has been a metonym for this centuries-long conflict. Moderns have celebrated it as the victory of reason and rights over superstition and medieval hierarchy, while Catholics have viewed it as an assault (the 1789–1790 nationalization of Church property, dissolution of religious orders, and clergy loyalty oaths). It is actually difficult to determine whether Paris or Rome "declared war" first.[28]

Catholicism has long served as a foil against which the modern defines itself – that is, modernity has understood itself in part as anti-Catholicism. This is noticeably the case in the myriad accounts of modernity that appeared in the 1960s–1990s (such as those just cited). Crises of confidence in modernity fed investigations of its origins. Of course, sunset reflections often highlighted enduring tropes available since the 1500s: modern approaches to nature and social emancipation rejecting guarantees of divine transcendence, *tradition* and *superstition* serving as code words for Catholicism among Protestants and non-Christians. Robert Pippin, for example, points to the modern critique of "the claims of tradition, the ancestors, and especially the Church (the public status of reason, it was hoped, could provide the social integration and cultural stability long a function of tradition and religion)."[29] Galileo Galilei was a victim, Voltaire a hero, and so on.

Yet the image of Catholicism in modern eyes is somewhat blurry. For a worldview committed to the possibility of meaningful change over time, its judgment of the Church is remarkably static. There is no mistaking the way that the Catholic Church has and continues to serve moderns as the case par excellence of what they are not: a premodern or antimodern, archaic, and dogmatic contrariety. Indeed, modernity needs the concept

---

[26] Hans Blumenberg, *The Legitimacy of the Modern Age* (Cambridge, MA: MIT Press, 1983); Funkenstein, *Theology and the Scientific Imagination*.

[27] Stephen Toulmin, *Cosmopolis: The Hidden Agenda of Modernity* (Chicago: University of Chicago Press, 1992), 13; Antoine Compagnon, *The Five Paradoxes of Modernity* (New York: Columbia University Press, 1994), 8–9; Gianni Vattimo, *The End of Modernity: Nihilism and Hermeneutics in Postmodern Culture* (Baltimore, MD: Johns Hopkins University Press, 1988), 168; Walter Benjamin, "Theses on the Philosophy of History," in *Illuminations*, ed. Walter Benjamin (New York: Schocken Books, 2007), 261.

[28] Moyn, "Tradition and Beyond," 30.

[29] Pippin, *Modernism As a Philosophical Problem*, 4.

of the premodern or antimodern Church as an essential part of its own foundational self-understanding, its identity requiring this other against which to define itself. The analogy to non-Western and colonized peoples, whose differentiation function is well established in critical scholarship, can only ever partially apply since colonial subjects never occupied positions of domination akin to the Church's. From natural science and technology to democracy to capitalism to progressivism, and beyond, in spite of all its variety, the standard account of modernity has echoed a basic refrain: *at least we're not Catholic.*

Modern anti-Catholicism is not merely phantasmic. Catholics have decidedly helped reinforce the judgments of their modern critics. Catholic antimodernity hardened in the 150 years after the French Revolution, defensiveness drawing on and reinforcing narratives of persecution familiar to the Christian tradition. Traditionalism, reaction, and conservativism, as well as more difficult-to-classify adaptive engagements such as Catholic social thought, expressed both resistance and alternatives to ascendant secular modernity. From Pius IX's *Syllabus errorum* (1864), which rejected the notion that reason could be the "sole arbiter of truth" and "ultimate standard," to Pius X's *Pascendi dominici gregis* (1907), which targeted the growing influence of secular philosophy and historical criticism among "modernist" Catholic thinkers, to the interwar era on which Moyn focuses, Catholic integralism has had a range of manifestations, from critiques of capitalism to accommodation to fascism.[30] In its dialectical relationship with the modern from the eighteenth through the twentieth centuries, Catholicism often fulfilled its assigned oppositional role. Nevertheless, anti-Catholic modernity and Catholic antimodernity are not exactly reciprocal. The former exists as part of the foundational imaginary and mythos of an era and worldview. The latter has included a range of reactive and proactive responses to changing historical conditions. Narratives of persecution and victimization are limited by the fact that Catholics in the modern era have been perpetrators as well as casualties.

The Catholic Church did not display very much patience with the language of modernity as an era and worldview until the Second Vatican Council (1962–1965). Yet, in another tremendous irony, at the very moment when the Church began explicitly to embrace that paradigm, many people were starting to have serious doubts about it. The

---

[30] Pius IX, *Syllabus errorum* (December 8, 1864): www.papalencyclicals.net/pius09/p9syll .htm. See also *Quanta cura* (December 8, 1864): www.papalencyclicals.net/pius09/p9q uanta.htm; Pius X, *Pascendi dominici gregis* (September 8, 1907): www .papalencyclicals.net/pius10/p10pasce.htm. See also *Lamentabili sane exitu* (July 3, 1907): www.papalencyclicals.net/pius10/p10lamen.htm.

Pastoral Constitution on the Church in the Modern World, *Gaudium et Spes*, with which Vatican II closed and which was communicated by Paul VI on December 7, 1965, engaged with postwar modernization theory under the shadow of possible atomic catastrophe. Offering a critical diagnosis of modern reality while prescribing a global role for the Church, the constitution explicitly acknowledged that "the human race is involved in a new stage of history" characterized by "[p]rofound and rapid changes" and the shift from "a rather static concept of reality to a more dynamic, evolutionary one."[31] "Modern man is on the road," the document asserted, "to a growing discovery and vindication of his own rights."[32] The moment presented both opportunities (global interdependence and unity) and dangers (disaggregation, atheism, destructive war technologies). Highlighting the themes of marriage and family, culture, socioeconomic life, politics, and peace, *Gaudium et Spes* concluded by calling for "sincere and prudent dialogue" with all people; for dignity, human rights, and religious toleration to be causes of global concern; for the duty to reduce suffering; and for the Church to go "forward together with humanity and experience the same earthly lot which the world does. She serves as a leaven and as a kind of soul for human society as it is to be renewed in Christ and transformed into God's family."[33]

Leaven, soul, renewed in Christ, transformed – what could these terms possibly mean to non-Catholics and non-Christians? Such language is prima facie unacceptable to the Christopher Hitchenses and Richard Dawkinses of the world, even if notions of human society and human family might compute. All religions in the late modern era have faced the challenge of negotiating fidelity to traditions and engagement with non-denominational pluralism. It falls to Catholics and Christians to translate their own vocabulary – poetry not prose – into terms comprehensible to those outside their particular communities (extending the spirit of the 1963 Constitution *Sacrosanctum Concilium* that shifted from Latin to vernacular). This task has been especially pressing for many Catholics since the 1960s when, belatedly to be sure, the battles of the nineteenth century no longer seemed worth fighting in the face of more urgent needs. Although Catholics still debate whether Vatican II went too far or not far enough, sustained reflection on Catholic modernity and modern

---

[31] Paul VI, *Gaudium et Spes* (December 7, 1965), §3–5: www.vatican.va/archive/hist_coun cils/ii_vatican_council/documents/vat-ii_const_19651207_gaudium-et-spes_en.html.
[32] Paul VI, *Gaudium et Spes*, §41.
[33] Paul VI, *Gaudium et Spes*, §21, 40. More generally, in 1966 Blumenberg could note the contemporary "theological justification of secularization." Blumenberg, *The Legitimacy of the Modern Age*, 6. The position was reinforced at the time in the United States by the emergent sociology of religion of Harvey Cox, Peter Berger, David Martin, and others.

Catholicism decidedly emerged in the mid-1970s and persisted into the late 1990s.[34]

However, just as Catholic thinkers were considering the possibility of reconciling what had long been split asunder, others outside the Church were placing the entire modern paradigm in question. I referred earlier to this field of sunset reflection during the 1980s and 1990s. Toulmin expressed a common mood in 1992:

> Today, the program of Modernity – even the very *concept* – no longer carries anything like the same conviction [it once did]. If a historical era is ending, it is the era of Modernity itself. . . . What looked in the nineteenth century like an irresistible river has disappeared in the sand, and we seem to have run aground. . . . [W]e are now stranded and uncertain of our location. The very project of Modernity thus seems to have lost momentum, and we need to fashion a successor program.[35]

Bruno Latour had anticipated the sentiment the previous year: "[Y]ou can feel that the heart is gone. The will to be modern seems hesitant, sometimes even outmoded."[36] One successor program involved the historiographical retrieval of past exclusions, exceptions, and hybrids that did not fit the standard account of the modern, such revisionism setting into relief modernity's past and present distortions and contradictions. Toulmin himself appreciated the relationship between theoretical reorientation and the historical record, writing that "the dividing line between Medieval and Modern times rests more on our philosophical assumptions than we had supposed. Now that rationality too is open to challenge, the traditional picture of a medieval world dominated by theology yielding to a modern world committed to rationality must be reconsidered."[37] If all was not well with the modern, then long-excluded religious perspectives might have occasion to return. Some found themselves having to confront

---

[34] Langdon Gilkey, *Catholicism Confronts Modernity: A Protestant View* (New York: Seabury, 1975); Joseph Fichter, "Restructuring Catholicism," *Sociological Analysis*, 38, no. 2 (Summer 1977), 154–166; James Hitchcock, *Catholicism and Modernity: Confrontation or Capitulation?* (Ann Arbor, MI: Servant Books, 1979); Jay P. Dolan, "A Catholic Romance with Modernity," *Wilson Quarterly*, 5, no. 4 (Autumn 1981), 120–133; Gabriel Daly, "Catholicism and Modernity," *Journal of the American Academy of Religion*, 53, no. 4 (December 1985), 773–796; *The Debate on Modernity*, ed. Claude Geffré and Jean-Pierre Jossua (London: SCM Press, 1992); Philip Gleason, *Contending with Modernity: Catholic Higher Education in the Twentieth Century* (New York: Oxford University Press, 1995); Charles Taylor, "A Catholic Modernity?" in *A Catholic Modernity? Charles Taylor's Marianist Award Lecture, with Responses by William M. Shea, Rosemary Luling Haughton, George Marsden, and Jean Bethke Elshtain*, ed. James L. Heft (New York: Oxford University Press, 1999).

[35] Toulmin, *Cosmopolis*, 3.

[36] Bruno Latour, *We Have Never Been Modern* (Cambridge, MA: Harvard University Press, [1991] 1993), 9.

[37] Toulmin, *Cosmopolis*, 12.

what Max Weber would have called an inconvenient fact: Catholicism had ceased to be a potent or vital cultural force in the modern era – except for all those people for whom it was. Others with religious commitments could appreciate the incongruity: the fact that religion had never gone away was an obvious point that seemed to have dawned on moderns rather late in the day. When in 1985 Augustinian priest Gabriel Daly wrote that "modernity is not what it used to be," he meant it in a different sense and took it in a different direction than, say, Jean-François Lyotard's diagnosis of the "postmodern condition" six years earlier.[38] Still, they were on the same page.

The late twentieth- and early twenty-first-century return of religion included both broad social contexts – the Iranian Revolution, the 1980s Moral Majority alliance of American evangelicals and Catholics (and subsequent culture wars), the decline of secular Zionism, the pivot date of September 11, 2001, and so forth – as well as attendant, rarefied academic discourses – radical orthodoxy, the post-secular, political theology, and inevitably secularism once again. Yet the return of religion in the so-called postmodern moment also helps illuminate the pontificates of John Paul II and Benedict XVI, who clearly decided that Vatican II had gone "too far" and joined the broader critique of modernity's limitations, exclusions, and blind spots. Why accommodate the Church to a worldview in clear crisis and to an era that might be ending? For if modernity itself was unraveling, then it was too late to seek rapprochement between it and Catholicism, and the post- could breathe new life into anti-modern Catholicism. In 1998, John Paul II wrote that "the currents of thought which claim to be postmodern merit appropriate attention," while reaffirming an older ecclesiastical critique of modern philosophy: reason's "one-sided concern to investigate human subjectivity" led to anthropocentrism, skepticism, agnosticism, and relativism.[39] Where Paul VI had engaged postwar modernization theory, Benedict XVI seemed to recall an earlier era when he attacked Francis Bacon and denounced the "dictatorship of relativism."[40]

---

[38] Daly, "Catholicism and Modernity," 781. Jean-François Lyotard, *The Postmodern Condition: A Report on Knowledge*, trans. Geoff Bennington and Brian Massumi (Minneapolis: University of Minnesota Press, 1984).

[39] John Paul II, *Fides et ratio* (September 14, 1998), §§ 5 and 91: http://w2.vatican.va/content/john-paul-ii/en/encyclicals/documents/hf_jp-ii_enc_14091998_fides-et-ratio.html.

[40] Benedict XVI, *Spe Salvi* (November 30, 2007), §16–17: http://w2.vatican.va/content/benedict-xvi/en/encyclicals/documents/hf_ben-xvi_enc_20071130_spe_salvi.html; Cardinal Joseph Ratzinger, "'Pro Eligendo Romano Pontifice': Homily of His Eminence Cardinal Joseph Ratzinger, Dean of the College of Cardinals" (April 18, 2005): www.vatican.va/gpII/documents/homily-pro-eligendo-pontifice_20050418_en.html.

Thus, at the turn of the twenty-first century it was possible for the Catholic mind to cheer the return of religion while decrying secularism, as well as to opt for global pluralism, reinvestment in the Catholic intellectual heritage, or both. The entire story is filled with stark contrasts and gray ambiguities. Neither John Paul II nor Benedict XVI rehearsed authoritarian affinities normal only a few decades before, and the contemporary Church has been a global voice on religious freedom, human rights, economic disparity and poverty, peace, and the environment. Yet the limits of Vatican II "bringing up to date" (*aggiornamento*) are no less clear, for instance, with respect to gender and sexuality. This context also helps explain why Pope Francis seems so refreshing to some and so terrifying to others (Finnis refers to "the present syncretistic, secularizing and shambolic pontificate").[41] Francis concluded the 2015 Synod on the Family by cautioning against "burying our heads in the sand" and by calling for the Church "to open up broader horizons, rising above conspiracy theories and blinkered viewpoints."[42] The previous year, in a talk to a group of university students, he had said that "research" can help "reach an ambitious goal": "to heal the rift between the Gospel and modernity through the approach of cultural mediation, an itinerant mediation which, without denying cultural differences, indeed by valuing them, becomes the horizon of positive planning."[43] Even as a metaphor, the notion of research does important work: it suggests open-ended activity and assumes that one has things to learn, since one does not have all the answers. Such mediation might involve what Jürgen Habermas has described as possible translations and mutual historical learning processes between religious and secular idioms.[44] Would this be to go too far or not far enough? Such a question itself expresses the dialectic between Catholicism and modernity that provides essential conditions of possibility for Finnis and Moyn's confrontation, which, though ephemeral, in other ways seems eternally recurrent.

---

[41] Finnis, "On Moyn's *Christian Human Rights*," 18.

[42] Edward Pentin, "Pope Francis' Closing Speech of Synod on the Family," *National Catholic Register* (October 24, 2015): www.ncregister.com/blog/edward-pentin/pope-francis-closing-speech-of-synod-on-the-family.

[43] *Message of Pope Francis to the Italian Catholic Federation of University Students (FUCI)* (October 14, 2014), §2: http://w2.vatican.va/content/francesco/en/messages/pont-messages/2014/documents/papa-francesco_20141014_messaggio-fuci.html.

[44] A spate of publications has appeared between Jürgen Habermas, *Religion and Rationality: Essays on God, Reason, and Modernity* (Cambridge, MA: MIT Press, 2002), and Habermas, *Auch eine Geschichte der Philosophie*, 2 vols. (Berlin: Suhrkamp Verlag, 2019).

Summiting

In spite of the advantages their generality affords, we have rightly grown dissatisfied with the kind of large-scale narratives traced in the previous section. Framing Moyn and Finnis's exchange this way folds them into a sequence, a before-and-after whereby past and future, tradition and modernization, vie for noncontradictory preeminence. Obviously, the sufficient reasons of history are a good deal messier. The very notion of Christian human rights complicates simple story lines, and Moyn's work joins an emerging historiography of twentieth-century Catholicism actively melting glacial oppositions between inward-looking Church histories and critical "secular" ones that sideline Catholicism as a historical force.[45] James Chappel, for instance, takes issue with the preceding account of the never-ending story, especially insofar as it tracks what he calls a "consensus narrative" of Catholic rapprochement with modernity: the search for a Catholic Third Way since the late nineteenth century, the defanging of reactionary options after 1945, and the qualified victory of modernizing forces at Vatican II.[46] He emphasizes instead the multiple "tactics" and "strategies" during the 1930s and 1940s through which Catholic attempts to "overturn modernity" were replaced by the advocacy of "Catholic forms *of* modernity."[47] Such forms were divided into two tendencies: mainstream "paternal" anticommunism and marginal "fraternal" antifascism. Although open to authoritarian politics during the interwar period, by the 1950s paternal Catholicism morphed into Cold War Christian democracy, forming an accord with the minoritarian fraternal orientation that lasted through Vatican II. Ultimately, the sexual

---

[45] John Connelly, *From Enemy to Brother: The Revolution in Catholic Teaching on the Jews, 1933–1965* (Cambridge, MA: Harvard University Press, 2012); Gerd-Rainer Horn, *The Spirit of Vatican II: Western European Progressive Catholicism in the Long Sixties* (Oxford: Oxford University Press, 2015); Piotr Kosicki, *Catholics on the Barricades: Poland, France, and "Revolution," 1939–1956* (New Haven, CT: Yale University Press, 2018); Giuliana Chamedes, *A Twentieth-Century Crusade: The Vatican's Battle to Remake Christian Europe* (Cambridge, MA: Harvard University Press, 2019); Sarah Shortall, "Theology and the Politics of Christian Human Rights," *Journal of the History of Ideas*, 79, no. 3 (July 2018), 445–460; Shortall, *Soldiers of God in a Secular World: The Politics of Catholic Theology in Twentieth-Century France* (Cambridge, MA: Harvard University Press, forthcoming). An analogous development has occurred in revisions of the role of religion in one of modernity's primal scenes, the Enlightenment. See Michael Printy, *Enlightenment and the Creation of German Catholicism* (Cambridge: Cambridge University Press, 2009); David Sorkin, *The Religious Enlightenment: Protestants, Jews, and Catholics from London to Vienna* (Princeton, NJ: Princeton University Press, 2011); Ulrich Lehner, *The Catholic Enlightenment: The Forgotten History of a Global Movement* (New York: Oxford University Press 2016).

[46] James Chappel, *Catholic Modern: The Challenge of Totalitarianism and the Remaking of the Church* (Cambridge, MA: Harvard University Press, 2018), 9. Moyn cites his former student's dissertation favorably in *Christian Human Rights*, 35–39.

[47] Chappel, *Catholic Modern*, 5, 7–8.

politics of the 1960s revived the conflicts of the interwar era, and Catholics have been oscillating between the two tendencies ever since. John Paul II and Benedict XVI can be read as paternal Catholic moderns and Francis as a fraternal one. The point is that the longitudinal, sequential choice of either Catholic or modern now seems less compelling than side-by-side lateral tensions: the multiple ways of being Catholic and modern and how tensions embody compatibilities irreducible to propositional rationality. In other words, disjunctive either-or reasoning is often too narrow to grasp the conjunctive logics of actual historical experience.

To be sure, complexity cannot obviate stark contrasts, especially those that point toward diverging normative conclusions. While Chappel's notion of paternal Catholicism confirms Moyn's view that the religious notion of dignity has been fully compatible with antidemocratic politics, as with the example of gender and the Irish constitution,[48] the fraternal tendency challenges Moyn's emphasis on religion's coercive dimensions. He and Chappel have different readings of Jacques Maritain in particular. Chappel calls Maritain's *Integral Humanism* (1936) an antifascist, anti-racist, and anti-capitalist tract. Its emphasis on "civic fraternities," he claims, broke with the paternalists by embracing Popular Front–era coordination with communists, a "horizontal" notion of the family based on the "relationship" of marriage (whereas paternalists stressed procreation), and a pluralist civil society in which associations such as trade unions and different religious communities could flourish.[49] By the mid-1940s, Maritain's fraternalist anti-statism meant human rights. Still, Moyn's suspicions about Maritain, whose "communitarian framework" he generally portrays as paternalistic, are not baseless.[50] The "ambiguity" of personalism enabled it to be taken in a variety of directions at the time, and they continue to feed varying interpretations today.[51] Altogether, the debate on Christian human rights productively reveals a specific

---

[48] Moyn, *Christian Human Rights*, 43–44. In Chapter 3 of this volume, "Explaining the Catholic Turn to Rights in the 1930s," Chappel highlights paternalists Robert Linhardt and Henri Massis, whose attraction to mixed constitutions and corporatism pointed personalism toward rights talk while remaining forthrightly disposed toward authoritarianism.

[49] Chappel, *Catholic Modern*, 111–112; Chappel, "All Churches Have Heretics: On Catholicism, Human Rights, and the Advantages of History for Life," *The Immanent Frame* (June 5, 2015): https://tif.ssrc.org/2015/06/05/all-churches-have-heretics-on-catholicism-human-rights-and-the-advantages-of-history-for-life; Moyn, "Christianity, Contemporary Legacies, and the Critique of Secularism," *The Immanent Frame* (July 30, 2015): https://tif.ssrc.org/2015/07/30/christianity-contemporary-legacies-and-the-critique-of-secularism.

[50] Moyn, *Christian Human Rights*, 83.

[51] Moyn, *Christian Human Rights*, 69. David Brooks, "Personalism: The Philosophy We Need," *New York Times* (June 14, 2018): www.nytimes.com/2018/06/14/opinion/personalism-philosophy-collectivism-fragmentation.html; John Milbank, "Dignity, Not Rights:

contradiction: simplistic oppositions are inadequate to historical complexity, and at the same time, strong contrasts meaningfully persist. It has mattered and still matters if Christianity is a singularly dispositive frame for rights and democracy or if Christianity is a particular cultural position within a nondenominational democratic rights frame. The requirement that Christian "patterns of life" provide a substantive foundation for political life is obviously much more stringent and potentially anti-pluralist than the more solicitous notion that Christianity is compatible with rights and democracy – maintaining fidelity to its mission while accepting that it is one voice among many.

Sharp divisions make for impasses, but blocked paths also inspire the search for alternate routes. Rights talk obviously draws on and seeks to address basic structural problematics of modern politics, between individual and society, person and community, freedom and solidarity, and so forth. The interwar era saw a variety of Third Way projects; some were creative and unrealized, others were problematic and destructive. In his own way, Moyn too seeks to transcend static antinomies, from his invocation of a corrective history of duties to his call to revive the neglected politics of equality. Reasserting the "moral significance of modernity" means affirming and defending the value of autonomy against externally imposed constraint, and at the same time, redressing through social solidarity an atomism of rights entirely compatible with inequality.[52] The problem may not necessarily be secularity per se but secularism poorly understood and inadequately applied, perhaps including unconsciously repeated anti-religious prejudice.[53] To return to an earlier discussion, the suspicion that religious tradition is tantamount to coercion might contend with the fact that political life in general, including egalitarian solidarity, also involves limitation. Positive freedom requires restriction: staying in school to become educated, the discipline of going to the gym to improve one's health, fidelity in order to experience the joys of partnership. Since the Enlightenment we can, of course, imagine following rules that we ourselves make, and under the circumstances of such freedom, identification with tradition can be elective and not merely compulsory. Still, the post-secular moment has made us aware that alternative and multiple modernities include the religious.[54] The task of

---

Against Liberal Autonomy," *ABC Religion and Ethics* (January 8, 2016): www.abc.net.au/religion/dignity-not-rights-against-liberal-autonomy/10097418.

[52] Moyn, "Tradition and Beyond," 32n6.

[53] Compare Moyn, *Christian Human Rights*, 166–167, and Joan Scott, *Sex and Secularism* (Princeton, NJ: Princeton University Press, 2017).

[54] *Alternative Modernities*, ed. Dilip Parameshwar Gaonkar (Durham, NC: Duke University Press, 2001); *Multiple Modernities*, ed. Shmuel N. Eisenstadt (New Brunswick, NJ: Transaction Publishers, 2002).

creating nonsectarian, emancipatory forms of life adequate to our global space, it seems, requires all hands on deck. It may be that the Catholic Church has things to contribute to the conversation, from the preferential option for the poor to the notion of a historical, pilgrim people that "waits in joyful hope" for lions and lambs to lay down together. Moyn's critical history of Christian human rights augurs the possibility of distinguishing between pernicious and salubrious interpretations of Christian concepts of the common good, personhood, holism, integration, flourishing, and fulfillment. Critical democratic means testing is indeed a crucial supplement to self-corrective hermeneutics. By the same token, living traditions do not merely repeat or act out past conjunctures; if they are alive, they are not just ghostly presences. In short, there is a difference between, on one hand, imposing a prefigured holism on others and, on the other, working with others to repair the broken world.

Still, there is no getting around the fact that divides remain, high mountains with slick slopes and thin air. The era of intense antagonism may be gone, but vestiges of Catholic antimodernity and modern anti-Catholicism persist as deeply embedded habits of mind, ready-at-hand repertoires. Some non-Catholics see Church teachings and structures as based on pre- or non-modern premises in conflict with certain widely accepted norms. Some Catholics see themselves as victims of "the last acceptable prejudice," their identities excluded from dialogues structured by anti-Catholic presuppositions and codes.[55] The "promise and predicament [of] Catholic intellectual life," to borrow a phrase, may continue to reside in the Church's perpendicular, bisecting relationships to non-Catholic forms of life: different, unwelcome, familiar, challenging, promising, frustrating.[56] Catholics do not always make it easy, especially when they sometimes make it difficult for others. Finnis finds the principle of democratic necessity too constrictive, believing that it culminates in judicial activism run amuck, even though he seems to find acceptable the notion that Christianity uniquely provides necessary foundational guidance.[57] Echoes of authority structures that derive from the medieval and Renaissance eras continue to haunt this perspective. Yet we live in history, there are no time machines, and there have always been many Catholicisms; the Alpine metaphor itself recalls the distinction between the Gallican Church and ultramontanism. All faith communities are

---

[55] Philip Jenkins, *The New Anti-Catholicism: The Last Acceptable Prejudice* (New York: Oxford, 2003); Mark S. Massa, SJ, "The New and Old Anti-Catholicism and the Analogical Imagination," *Theological Studies* 62 (2001), 549–570.

[56] *In the Lógos of Love: Promise and Predicament in Catholic Intellectual Life*, ed. Father James L. Heft, SM, and Una M. Cadegan (New York: Oxford University Press, 2016).

[57] Finnis, "On Moyn's *Christian Human Rights*," 16.

divided between their particular idioms and, as *Gaudium et Spes* put it, the "earthly lot" of multiplicity to which "dialogue" is one rather useful response. It is even plausible to imagine theological arguments for pluralism as fecund creation, a type of objective realism adequate to our own day.[58] If it is true that "not recognizing itself in its adversary, the Enlightenment both grasps and misunderstands faith," it is also the case that Catholics are sometimes like the Greeks, speaking the language of universality while often failing to acknowledge their own parochialisms.[59]

---

[58] John Courtney Murray, *We Hold These Truths: Catholic Reflections on the American Proposition*, intro. Peter Augustine Lawler (Lanham, MD: Rowman and Littlefield, [1960] 2015).

[59] Charles Taylor, *Hegel* (Cambridge: Cambridge University Press, 1975), 172, 183.

Part II

European Catholicism and Human Rights

3   Explaining the Catholic Turn to Rights in the 1930s

James Chappel

The history of human rights has taken a welcome pluralist turn in recent years. In place of singular origin stories, looking to the 1780s or the 1940s or the 1970s, scholars have recognized that the discourse of human rights has multiple inflection points and multiple origins.[1] Indeed, how could it be otherwise, given that it combines two of the most protean concepts of the past two millennia: "rights" (or *ius*) and "the human," each with complex intellectual histories stretching into the classical past? Who is the agent of human rights, what sorts of claims can be made in its name, and what body or institution is tasked with granting those rights? The answers to these questions have varied tremendously, creating differences in kind and not simply of degree.

The pluralist turn allows us to move past singular accounts, either heroic or tragic ones, in the name of more granular questions, and questions capable of answer with the uncertain light of the historian. The pious celebration of human rights discourse as an unqualified good does not stand up to the historical record. As Samuel Moyn, Marco Duranti, and others have shown, human rights have a checkered and sometimes uncomfortable history. Sometimes celebrated as the universalist endpoint of political-moral thinking, these histories have shown that human rights discourse has often been employed as a cudgel against other, possibly more emancipatory, forms of universalism. And yet, at the same time, the equally pious critique that sees human rights as the eager midwife of neoliberalism does not match the evidence, either. As scholars from multiple fields have shown, human rights have provided a globally legible discourse for justice movements, often involving women's issues, and have done much more than distract historical agents from class politics.[2]

---

[1] Stefan-Ludwig Hoffmann, "Human Rights and History," *Past and Present* 232 (2016), 279–310; Samuel Moyn, "The End of Human Rights History," *Past and Present* 233 (2016), 307–322.

[2] Sally Engle Merry, *Human Rights and Gender Violence: Translating International Law into Local Justice* (Chicago: University of Chicago Press, 2006); Lori Allen, *The Rise and Fall of Human Rights: Cynicism and Politics in Occupied Palestine* (Stanford, CA: Stanford

Human rights, it appears, have been employed in multiple registers and for incommensurate purposes. It is misguided, therefore, to search for a "unit idea" in this chaos of discourse, as though an aid worker in contemporary Palestine and an eighteenth-century intellectual were giving voice to recognizably similar ideas when they invoked human rights. This might seem like a dispiriting turn for the field, and a dismaying transition from exciting scholarship to familiar pointillism. In fact, though, it allows a new and historically crucial set of questions to emerge. Why did certain groups turn toward a discourse of human rights at a certain time? What problems did it solve for them, and what blind spots did it create in specific times and places? Answering these questions might not cast any light on contemporary invocations of human rights, although if asked and answered enough it might lead to a hypothesis as to why, and in what circumstances, human rights emerge as a plausible vessel for moral and political claims.

The search for plural origins of rights talk has led, among other places, to the Catholic Church. Human rights have never been the province of international lawyers or bureaucrats alone; inside the Church, human rights became in the mid-twentieth-century a lingua franca for an organization with more than one billion adherents. How did this happen, and when, and why? This is one of the central questions for the history of human rights, but the answer is still opaque. It has been broached by a number of scholars, notably Marco Duranti, J. Bryan Hehir, Piotr Kosicki, Samuel Moyn, and Rudolf Uertz.[3] However much light they have shed, they share a surprising omission. Each of them points to the period from 1933 to 1945 as a major point of inflection (in this chapter, I simply refer to this period as the 1930s, considering texts written between Hitler's rise to power and the end of the war). The 1930s themselves, however, are not the main topic of investigation for these

---

University Press, 2013); Elora Haim Chowdhury, *Transnationalism Reversed: Women Organizing against Gendered Violence in Bangladesh* (Albany: State University of New York Press, 2011).

[3] Marco Duranti, *The Conservative Human Rights Revolution: European Identity, Transnational Politics, and the Origins of the European Convention* (New York: Oxford University Press, 2016), chap. 6; J. Bryan Hehir, "The Modern Catholic Church and Human Rights: The Impact of the Second Vatican Council," in *Christianity and Human Rights: An Introduction*, ed. John Witte Jr. and Frank S. Alexander (New York: Cambridge University Press, 2010), 113–134; Piotr Kosicki, "Masters in Their Own Home or Defenders of the Human Person? Wojciech Korfanty, Anti-Semitism, and Polish Christian Democracy's Illiberal Rights-Talk," *Modern Intellectual History* 13 (2015), 1–32; Samuel Moyn, *Christian Human Rights* (Philadelphia: University of Pennsylvania Press, 2015); Rudolf Uertz, *Vom Gottesrecht zum Menschenrecht. Das katholische Staatsdenken im Deutschland von der französischen Revolution bis zum II. Vatikanische Konzil* (Paderborn: Schöningh, 2004). See also the forum in *Journal of History of Ideas* 79, no. 3 (July 2018).

historians. They argue, in different ways, that the turn toward rights in the 1930s was a minority phenomenon, although the particular group in question differs. In any case, that story is meant as a harbinger, perhaps ironic, of the postwar moment in which it is presumed that the shift toward rights attained its full flower.

If we bracket the human rights revolution that took place after the phrase made its way into the Atlantic Charter, a new set of questions emerges that sidesteps the ironic emplotment of these histories. First, to what extent did Catholics come to adopt a discourse of human rights in the 1930s – was it a minor phenomenon that exploded in significance after the war, or was it already a mainstream discourse? Second, *why* did they do so, and what problems did it solve for them? And third, what varieties of Catholics rights talk existed – was it a firm dogma, or a fluid discourse through which various social theories could find voice? Through an analysis of the Catholic public sphere, the encyclical literature, and especially a close reading of four Catholic defenses of rights, this chapter attempts to answer these questions, thereby providing a more rigorous and capacious understanding of Catholic rights talk in the 1930s.

I conclude that "human rights" emerged as a discursive Catholic strategy in the 1930s: the moment when Catholic thinkers came to accept the legitimacy of the secular nation-state, and at which point rights talk served to explain the duties and limits of that state project.[4] They attained dominance in the Church, therefore, at a different moment than they did so in secular institutions like political parties or international organizations. Catholics did so in different ways, however, because they had such different political projects. Rights talk may have altered the form in which Catholics made political arguments, but they did not revolutionize their content. The rights turn, that is, marked a shift in Catholic attitudes toward the state more than it did a shift in attitudes toward capitalism, racism, universalism, or even individualism.

The first question concerns the scope of Catholic rights discourse in the 1930s. Previous scholars, even when operating with rather small source bases, have presumed that the Catholic rights turn was a minority phenomenon. An analysis of the enormous print archive of the 1930s Church shows that the transition to rights talk was more profound than previously recognized, involving official and lay sources alike. One obvious place to look is the encyclical literature, where the discourse of individual rights took on an unparalleled significance. Considerations of the encyclical

---

[4] This analysis is corollary to the one I pursued in James Chappel, *Catholic Modern: The Challenge of Totalitarianism and the Remaking of the Church* (Cambridge, MA: Harvard University Press, 2018).

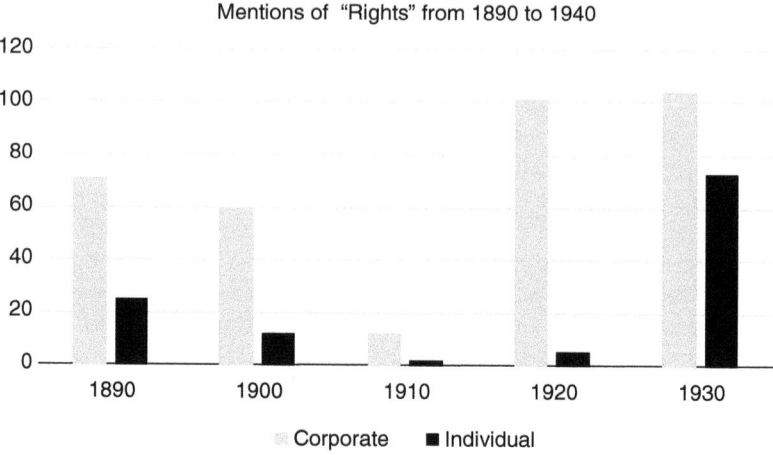

Figure 3.1 Mentions of "rights" in encyclical literature from 1890 to 1940

literature are often impressionistic, but their manageable scope renders them amenable to quantitative analysis. This graph collates every mention of "rights" in encyclical literature between 1890 and 1940.[5] Between 1890 and 1930, whenever "rights" were mentioned, the bearer of those rights was normally a corporate body: the Church, most commonly, but also the family, the school, or the working class ("God," another corporate entity in Catholic thought, was another common rights bearer). In the 1930s, this changed, and Catholic dogma became increasingly concerned with the individual as a bearer of rights. Between the 1920s and 1930s, mentions of corporate rights in the encyclical literature remained essentially constant. The number of references to individual rights, however, exploded from five to more than seventy (note that the number of encyclicals per year remained roughly the same). Or, put another way: between 1890 and 1930, individual rights were invoked, on average, once per year. Between 1930 and 1940, individual rights were mentioned seven times as frequently.

---

[5] I am not including the data here because it is challenging to be precise. There are two main reasons for this. The first is the issue of language. Encyclicals were normally released in Latin, but sometimes in other languages (Italian, Spanish, and German encyclicals were also released in the 1930s). That is often a translation already, as the drafting process was often multilingual. For simplicity's sake, I used (official) English translations in my own accounting, but it is possible that an accounting in a different language would yield slightly different results. The second is that, given the ponderous nature of the encyclical genre, it can sometimes be challenging to locate a precise invocation of rights into one of these two categories.

Encyclicals are a useful index of what is happening on the ground, but are insufficient in themselves. They are, perhaps, overused by scholars of the Church because they are so easily available online. Catholics in the past did not have such easy access to the pope's words, which had to be mediated first by bishops and clergymen who might choose to selectively report their contents or to ignore them altogether. The encyclicals, therefore, should always be considered alongside an analysis of the Catholic public sphere itself, which Catholics on the ground could regularly access. The Church did not understand itself through encyclicals alone, but also through a dense web of newspapers, youth and women's movement newsletters, trade union bulletins, and the like.

At least in France, Germany, and Austria, rights discourse became ubiquitous in this Catholic print culture in the mid-1930s. It is of course challenging to be quantitative when dealing with so many millions of pages, so examples will have to suffice. In France, to take one, a Catholic politician wrote an "Essay on the Notion of the State" (1935) in which he condemned "totalitarian states" for their "great contempt for the rights of the person." In *Latin Culture and Social Order*, a book released the same year, the master of the Dominican order in France discussed "the enduring rights of the human person." As with Catholic political discourse more generally, most but not all of this was located on the political right. The first draft of the Vichy constitution, prepared in 1941 by the National Council, declared that "the state recognizes and guarantees the rights of the human person."[6] In Austria, arch-conservatives like Georg Moenius argued that the spirit of the "West" presumed respect for "the right of the individual and the personality." Defenders of Engelbert Dollfuß at the regime-sponsored journal *The Christian Corporate State* celebrated the "rights of the person" and described the state as a "defender of rights." Even supporters of National Socialism like Bishop Alois Hudal praised ancient Rome as "the cradle of human rights and the personality."[7]

---

[6] Jacques de Broze [i.e., Alibert], "Essai sur la notion d'Etat," *Revue du XXème Siècle* 3 (January 1935), 15–23, here 19; Martin-Stanislaus Gillet, *Culture latine et ordre social* (Paris: Flammarion, 1935), 234. For the constitution, see Michèle Cointet, *Le Conseil national de Vichy: vie politique et réforme de l'Etat en régime autoritaire, 1940–1944* (Paris: Aux amateurs de livres, 1989), 413.

[7] Moenius cited in Elke Seefried, *Reich und Stände: Ideen und Wirken des deutschen politischen Exils in Österreich, 1933–1938* (Düsseldorf: Droste, 2006), 190; Walter Münster, "Das Wesen des Föderalismus," *Christliche Ständestaat* 4, no. 33 (August 22, 1937), 784–786, here 785; Dietrich von Hildebrand, "Staat und Ehe," *Christliche Ständestaat* 2, no. 42 (October 20, 1935), 1002–1004, here 1003; Alois Hudal, *Deutsches Volk und Christliches Abendland* (Vienna: Tyrolia, 1935), 28.

Hudal was not alone: a number of German-speaking Catholics mobilized human rights in the 1930s in the name of Catholic-Nazi rapprochement. One Bavarian theologian wrote in 1934, the year after Hitler's rise to power, of the "ineffable dignity" and "primeval rights" of the individual.[8] Otto Schilling, a convinced Nazi and one of the leading theologians in Germany, argued along similar lines in his *Defense of Catholic Morality* (1936). "The command of the hour," he insisted, "is the integration of all Christian thinkers and friends of Christian culture in the struggle against the enemies of Christianity." As did other Catholics across Europe, Schilling claimed that the Church respected the "dignity [and] personality of men," as explained by natural law. "Nobody," he argued, "protects natural human rights more faithfully and loyally than the Church."[9]

While this evidence is impressionistic, it is at least enough to demonstrate that Catholic rights talk was widespread, and it was not confined to the progressive or "Christian Democratic" minority of Catholic intellectuals. We can turn, then, to our second question: *why* did so many Catholics, including both supporters and opponents of political reaction, come to adopt rights talk in the 1930s? What work did "human rights" do for them, faced as they were with the rise of fascism and communism, fearful for the future of their Church and their values? To properly answer this question requires a close reading of texts. Both human rights and the Catholic Church are slippery subjects. Human rights are normally presented as self-evident, and are not frequently defended in strict philosophical or even theological terms (even the normal Christian understanding of God as the granter of rights is not always germane, given that God is often presented as an entity bearing rights that we are bound to respect). The narration of their history requires, therefore, less a history of a philosophy than an attention to how, when, and why rights talk emerged as common sense in a particular ecology of contexts. In this section and the next, we see that the political crisis of the early 1930s led rights talk to emerge as a plausible political discourse for Catholics because it allowed them to make claims on modern states using a superficially "modern" language, albeit one with deep roots in Catholic theology. It did not involve a new attitude toward "individualism," which remained anathema as ever, but it did mobilize a newly conciliatory attitude toward the modern state – a state that, in the 1930s, was often a fascist one.

---

[8] Wilhelm Moock, "Der Einzelne und die Gemeinschaft," *Hochland* 32, no. 1 (1934–1935), 193–203, here 194, 198.

[9] Otto Schilling, *Apologie der katholischen Moral* (Paderborn: Schöningh, 1936), 5, 240, 238.

To understand the emergence of rights in context, I focus on two rights-defending texts by two engaged Catholic intellectuals, one German and one French. Both were mainstream in the sense that they, like most of their fellow Catholics, were interested in finding ways to cohere Catholicism with political authoritarianism in the name of anticommunism and Western civilization. By looking carefully at the work that rights did in the texts, and the contexts in which they appeared, this analysis will help us to understand the Catholic turn to rights (the next section focuses on the more "leftist" turn to rights, which was not dominant but nonetheless deserves our attention).

The first figure, a German Jesuit named Robert Linhardt, is particularly interesting because Rudolf Uertz, one of the most distinguished intellectual historians of the twentieth-century Church, has singled him out as a central player in the Church's turn to rights. He was, indeed, the author of the first text that scholars like Uertz and myself have found to place individual rights talk at the center of a reasonably coherent and extensive social-theoretical text. But a text of what sort? Here Uertz fell prey to the tendency to believe that rights talk has one history and one *telos*. He described Linhardt as a forerunner of Christian Democracy and expressed uncertainty as to why he was banned from preaching after the war. The answer, it turns out, is that Linhardt was a convinced and public National Socialist.[10]

Linhardt's turn to rights actually began in 1932, with his *Social Principles of Saint Thomas of Aquinas*. Following Uertz, though, I focus on his book *Constitutional Reform and the Catholic Conscience* (1933), which more transparently embodies Linhardt's previously expressed belief that the Church should "go with the times" and "adapt to them."[11] Unlike Linhardt's earlier work, it was a short and sparsely footnoted pamphlet, clearly designed more as a temporal intervention than a work of lasting scholarship. *Constitutional Reform* came out in early 1933, just as Hitler was dismantling the Weimar Republic. The text clearly conveyed Linhardt's despair at the failure, both intellectual and political, of political Catholicism. The Center Party had for decades represented the Catholic voice in the Reichstag, but in the early 1930s the party was in crisis. Under the

---

[10] Uertz, *Vom Gottesrecht zum Menschenrecht*, 347–359. On his Nazism, see Thomas Forstner, *Priester in Zeiten des Umbruchs. Identität und Lebenswelt des katholischen Pfarrklerus in Oberbayern 1918 bis 1945* (Göttingen: Vandenhoeck & Ruprecht, 2014), 214–216.

[11] Robert Linhardt, *Die Sozialprinzipien des heiligen Thomas von Aquin. Versuch einer Grundlegung der speziellen Soziallehren des Aquinaten* (Freiburg i.B.: Herder, 1932), 134 et al. for rights, 224 for this quotation.

controversial leadership of Heinrich Brüning, the Center was taking Germany toward dictatorship and austerity. A few weeks after Linhardt finished his book, the party would agree to support Hitler's takeover and dissolve itself.

The book was an attempt to think through the political role of Catholicism given the abject failure of political Catholicism as a parliamentary phenomenon. Linhardt began by declaring that the Weimar Constitution is dead and that all Germans, Catholics included, must look for "rational" and not "utopian" means to arrive at a better one. Catholics, he contended with some justification, had primarily argued in the negative, about what they did not want, instead of providing a positive vision of their own. The notion of the "political middle," which had long guided Center politics, was rejected out of hand.[12] Theologically, Linhardt insisted, Catholics had been confusing the "secondary, practical regulative principle" of mediation with the first principles that were the proper concern of the Church. Catholics, he urged, must stop compromising, recognizing that Catholic constitutionalism is not "at some arithmetical middle" between democracy and dictatorship, but represents a complete and robust tradition of its own.[13]

Insofar as Catholics had a positive political vision at all, it tended to be organized around the noble scholastic principle of the "common good" (*Gemeinwohl, summum bonum*). Linhardt found much to appreciate in this tradition, especially in that it allowed for significant flexibility to suit different national characters and historical situations. And yet, in the end, he did not find it much more regulative than the formula of the "political middle." It was not wrong, he thought, but "paltry and insufficient." Specifically, a focus on the common good kept Catholics from making any constitutional recommendations whatsoever, because any regime, including the formal democracies and total dictatorships barred by Catholic doctrine, could plausibly claim to defend the common good.[14]

And yet, as Rüdiger Graf has suggested of the Weimar discourse of crisis more broadly, Linhardt saw the collapse of Weimar as an opportunity for new thinking and for a political order that would be more congenial to the Catholic tradition.[15] As Linhardt was a good Thomist, his

[12] On the tradition that Linhardt rejected, see Stefan Gerber, *Pragmatismus und Kulturkritik. Politikbegruungung und politische Kommunkationn im Katholizismus der Weimarer Republic (1918–1925)* (Paderborn: Schöningh, 2016); Peter Tischleder, *Der Staat* (Mönchengladbach: Volksvereins-Verlag, 1926).

[13] Robert Linhardt, *Verfassungsreform und katholisches Gewissen* (München: J. Pfeiffer, 1933), 4–7.

[14] Ibid., 9, 10–11, 13–14.

[15] Rüdiger Graf, "Either-Or: The Narrative of 'Crisis' in Weimar Germany and in Historiography," *Central European History* 43 (2010), 592–615.

positive program involved a defense of the "mixed constitution," which Aristotle, Aquinas, Bellarmin, Suarez, and many others had defended. The idea was that there were virtues of democratic, aristocratic, and monarchist rule, and that the best constitution would take advantage of them all.[16] For some readers, this may have seemed a letdown, given that the basic principle was so familiar. The angel, however, was in the details. Innovations in Catholic theory tend to proceed through the supposed return to older sources and traditions, as the Dominicans around Le Saulchoir were doing in France.[17] And yet a pure return is never possible and the translation of older ideas into modern contexts necessarily involves reinvention. To see how, consider how Linhardt defined the nature of each governing principle – in ways more reminiscent of twentieth-century political science than thirteenth-century scholasticism.

Linhardt's version of the "monarchist" principle, for instance, clearly derived from the contemporary work of Carl Schmitt rather than from Aquinas. Aquinas's own view of kingship was put forth centuries before a modern state apparatus or conception of sovereignty existed. His own pre-Westphalian account of sovereignty was most concerned with the category of the *summum bonum* – a stipulation Linhardt had already rejected as insufficient. For Linhardt, the virtue of the monarch was that he represented the sovereign power of the decision and the "political unity" of authority that could rise above the endless squabbling of civil society. All constitutions, he insisted, must give the state the "highest authority," extending beyond the "political detail work of lawgiving and administration" (this distinction between authority and governance was central to Schmitt's legal theory but foreign to Aquinas). This authority would emerge only in emergency situations, but was, Linhardt argued, central to the nature of the state.[18]

Linhardt's book was no apologia for dictatorship, however, and he was quick to emphasize Aquinas's concern for the mixed constitution. He updated the aristocratic and democratic principles for the context of Germany in early 1933, distinguishing them from their feudalist and parliamentary versions, respectively. The aristocratic principle mandated that the best and brightest, in the cultural and ethical sense, should somehow be identified and given a central role in governing. They

---

[16] Linhardt, *Verfassungsreform*, 18–19.

[17] For a recent introduction to this dialectic, see Jon Kirwan, *An Avant-garde Theological Generation: The* Nouvelle Théologie *and the French Crisis of Modernity* (New York: Oxford University Press, 2018).

[18] Linhardt, *Verfassungsreform*, 27. For Aquinas on sovereignty, see James Turner Johnson, *Sovereignty: Moral and Historical Perspectives* (Washington DC: Georgetown University Press, 2014), chap. 2.

provided a check on the Führer. However well-intentioned such a leader might be, Linhardt argued, he would still be hamstrung by original sin, and granting dictatorial power to any one man was an affront to human dignity, which required a "right of participation" [*Mitbestimmungsrecht*] to those who were capable of it. Specifically, he suggested the introduction of a chamber of elites drawn from professional organizations, churches, and universities. The democratic principle, therefore, did not require one man, one vote, and in fact militated against it. Instead, it meant that those groups of citizens who were up to the task should have a say in governance. Specifically, Linhardt wanted to grant voting rights to the elderly, soldiers, and parents over rebellious workers and youth.[19]

Thus far, Linhardt's analysis was not especially novel. The important twist came with his belief that Catholic constitutionalism was built on concern for "human dignity" and the "human person." If collectivists denied the person altogether, and liberal individualists presumed the lonely egoist, Catholic thinkers argued, following Aristotle, the individual person has a certain "natural essence" that can find expression only in communities, including marriage, the family, the profession, and the state. The state, while legitimate, was a derivation of the "inalienable human right" possessed by the person to fulfill his or her essential being, as God intended. Moreover, the very purpose of the state was "to protect the inalienable rights of the person," "facilitating the most dignified possible existence for its members."[20]

This might not seem like a particularly fascist or even authoritarian form of Catholic political thought. But delivered in the year 1933, it was clearly a brief for the form that a Catholic philo-Nazism might take. Indeed, what else could it have been? Linhardt was clear that Weimar was finished, that the Center Party had been a disaster, and that communism was inherently anti-Catholic. It is possible that he was hoping for a Catholic authoritarianism along the lines of Franz von Papen, but evidence from other sources indicates that Linhardt was a convinced National Socialist, as von Papen would become too.[21] The zeal for corporatist representation and mixed government was the *form* that Catholic philo-Nazism was taking in the early months of 1933. Wilhelm Schwer, the only contemporary authority that Linhardt cited positively, made similar arguments, as did Theodor Brauer. The Catholic zeal for

---

[19] Linhardt, *Verfassungsreform*, 30–31, 33, 37–39, 18.   [20] Ibid., 24–29.
[21] On these figures, see Larry Eugene Jones, "Catholic Conservatives in the Weimar Republic: The Politics of the Rhenish-Westphalian Aristocracy, 1919–1933," *German History* 18 (2000), 61–85; Christoph Hübner, *Die Rechtskatholiken, die Zentrumspartei und die katholische Kirche in Deutschland bis zum Reichskonkordat von 1933* (Berlin: Lit Verlag, 2014).

Nazism, that is, had little to do with the Führer principle and much to do with a (misguided) sense that Hitler was going to pursue a form of corporatist, anti-liberal, and anticommunist politics. This was, in fact, the logic Linhardt pursued explicitly in a long front-page article for a Bavarian newspaper at the end of the year.[22]

Before stepping back and thinking analytically about this text and its significance, it is useful to examine one more Catholic defense of rights to ensure that we are exploring the Catholic turn to rights and not only the vicissitudes of Robert Linhardt. A few years later, another Catholic political thinker, who would also lend his talents to the Nazi takeover of Europe, penned another defense of rights.

Since the Dreyfus Affair, Henri Massis had been a well-known Catholic reactionary, aligned with both Charles Maurras and the younger *Jeune droite* (more than anyone else, he was a transition figure between these two generations of French reaction).[23] Massis's intellectual formation was rather different from Linhardt's. Like Maurras, he venerated Aquinas and the natural law tradition more as symbols of order and reason than as a specific, textual tradition: for his actual intellectual apparatus, he relied more on the tradition of French conservative thought that included figures like Maurras, Joseph de Maistre, Fustel de Coulanges, and Augustin Cochin. Like Linhardt, he published throughout the 1920s without being interested in rights.

Over the course of the 1930s, though, Massis changed his mind about rights and began to give them pride of place – a process that reached its peak with his 1939 book *Leaders: The Dictators and Us*. In some ways it is a parallel text to Linhardt's, given that it was one of the last books of French Catholic political thought to be published before Hitler took over the country. It represents, like Linhardt's pamphlet, an attempt to think through the role of the Church in a Europe threatened by Nazism – but not published directly under Nazi rule. And like Linhardt, Massis was a celebrant of the new authoritarianism, entering the service of Marshal Pétain's Vichy government in 1940 (he was, incidentally, on the committee to draft the rights-defending, but never enacted, Vichy constitution quoted earlier in this chapter).

The book was a collection of interviews with and reflections on the new crop of Catholic dictators taking power across Europe: Mussolini,

---

[22] Schwer and Brauer, both convinced corporatists, collaborated on a short-lived Catholic-Nazi journal called *Deutsches Volk*. Robert Linhardt, "Von dem Sinn der neuen Zeit," *Bayerischer Kurier* 77, no. 364/5 (December 31, 1933), 1–2. On this theme more generally, see Chappel, *Catholic Modern*, chap. 2.

[23] Paul Mazgaj, *Imagining Fascism: The Cultural Politics of the French Young Right, 1930–1945* (Newark: University of Delaware Press, 2007).

Franco, and Salazar (some had been published before, but they were updated with a new preface for the 1939 volume). Like Linhardt, Massis began by discussing a political crisis and the vacuity of old solutions. "We are manifestly witnessing," Massis claimed, "the general crisis of political systems."[24] In the wake of liberalism, the options were totalitarianism, either communist or Nazi, or some kind of authoritarianism, and only the latter was acceptable to the Catholic conscience.[25] Mussolini, he argued, pointed the way. Even more than the Russian Revolution of 1917, the Italian coup of 1922 was a "global revolution": "the first revolution of order." He insisted, as Linhardt was doing with Hitler, that Mussolini was not a pure dictator, but that he oversaw a corporatist reconstruction cognizant of legitimate authorities throughout the social body. The genius of Mussolini was that he represented the spirit of the West: "an ensemble of cultures united by a certain conception of man, penetrated by Christianity."[26]

Like Linhardt, Massis believed that a democratic regime, without the introduction of monarchist and aristocratic principles, would descend into tyranny. He too rejected the "pretended affinities between the rights of the human person and democratic regimes." Massis did so in a different key, however. Uninterested in the niceties of Thomist theology, he drew instead on the French sociological tradition to claim that unfiltered democracy (or republicanism, in the French debate) was disastrous. From its origins in the thought of Auguste Comte, that tradition had been concerned with the relationship between the individual and the social whole, seeking to understand how those two poles might exist without one swallowing the other. This often involved the novel formulation of "the human person," as in Massis's quote cited earlier (Émile Durkheim used that phrase too, to distinguish the sociologically sanctioned cult of the individual from the bankrupt and atomizing sort).[27] One of the great debates in that tradition concerned the possibility of protecting the human person in a republican or democratic regime. Durkheim famously believed that it could, while Massis's own master, Charles Maurras, disagreed. Maurras believed, like Massis after him, that the location of sovereignty in the people led corrupt parliamentarians to

---

[24] Henri Massis, *Chefs. Les dictatures et nous* (Paris: Plon, 1939), 4.
[25] The Catholic turn to rights should be read alongside the kindred turn toward antitotalitarianism, for which see James Chappel, "The Catholic Origins of Totalitarianism Theory in Interwar Europe," *Modern Intellectual History* 9 (2011), 261–290.
[26] Massis, *Chefs*, 5, 10.
[27] The Dreyfusard invocations of the "human person" have not been much remarked. For an example, see Paul Deschanel, Jean Jaurès, and André Ribot, *Le budget et la politique étrangère de la France: Discours prononcés à la Chambre des Députés du 19 au 29 janvier 1903* (Paris: Édouard Cornély, 1903), 169.

massively expand social programs to garner popularity, which would lead in the end to *étatisme* and the end of liberty (this was essentially Tocquevillean, as filtered through a conservative historian named Augustin Cochin[28]). This debate set the parameters for Massis's invocation of human rights, with the caveat that he had access to the new concept of "totalitarianism" to designate individual domination by the state.[29]

This is the context in which Massis turned to human rights, presuming with Linhardt that political legitimacy rested on their proper articulation and defense. "Rights," for Massis, designated those proper claims of the human individual on society that would be overwhelmed by the "totalitarian" state. That totalitarian regime, he believed, was a natural successor of its democratic predecessor. The problem with totalitarianism, Massis argued, was that it violated "personal dignity" and "the primacy of the human person." What was necessary, instead, was a regime that rightly understood the role of elites, authority, and history. A regime of that sort could build support on the appeal of emotion, faith, and sentiment rather than parliamentary horse-trading. Massis believed that examples existed across Europe already. In his interviews with Mussolini, Salazar, and Franco, he claimed to find a model for what an authoritarian France might look like – one that would, as Mussolini did, defend "the rights of the human person."[30]

Abstracting from the specific national contexts of these two texts, we can identify the commonalities to understand how the turn to rights emerged from the more general situation facing European Catholics in the 1930s. The first striking commonality is that neither text was interested in the Church *qua* institution, representing a striking departure from the main line of Catholic political thought since the French Revolution. A great deal of difference separated the legitimists of the nineteenth century (Bonald, de Maistre), the papal tradition (Leo XIII, Pius XI), and the more republican Catholic thinkers of the early twentieth century (Sangnier, Mausbach). And yet they had all presumed that the relevant political question was whether or not Catholic *institutions*, notably the Church itself, religious orders, and Catholic schools, could survive in a given political framework. Linhardt and Massis simply ignored that question. Linhardt explicitly rejected the politics of the Catholic Center Party. Moreover, his Catholic constitutionalism had precisely nothing to

---

[28] On Maurras and Cochin, see Pierre Lafarge, "Les Sociétés de Pensée et la Démocratie Moderne," in *Le Trésor de l'Action française*, ed. Pierre Pujo (Lausanne: L'Age d'Homme, 2006), 31–33; Charles Maurras, "La Politique," *L'Action Française* 13, no. 33 (February 13, 1926), 1.

[29] Massis, *Chefs*, 17–18.   [30] Ibid., 16, 67.

say about the role that the Church as a concrete institution was to play in the new order. Massis did something similar. *Leaders* was clearly a Catholic book, full of praise for Roman principles of order. And yet he said nothing at all about Catholic institutions, or about the need for the state to recognize Catholicism as an official state religion. Indeed, he praised Salazar's realism in his decision to keep Church and state separated, and even to keep Portugal's rather lax divorce legislation in place.[31]

The second notable similarity between the two is that, while not committed to Church-state fusion, they *also* were critical of liberal democracy. They both believed that democracy was in crisis and, at least in its liberal form, was en route to the historical dustbin. In its place, they proposed some kind of anti-liberal politics that would marry monarchist principles with "Western" culture, respect for the family, and anticommunism. They were both, therefore, somewhere on that broad spectrum of Catholic authoritarianism. Liberalism led not to a healthy pluralism, they thought, but to domination – a criticism they leveled also at Catholic politicians who sought common ground with others to defend the liberal state.

Linhardt and Massis, therefore, turned to human rights as a conceptual resource to confront a particular and shared problem. The ages of the Catholic state and of Catholic parliamentarianism were over, they believed, so Catholics had to pursue new strategies for a post-liberal, authoritarian age in which the modern nation-state seemed to be an unsurpassable horizon. They welcomed that age as the final overcoming of liberalism, but they recognized too that Catholic teaching had to be mobilized to place limits around the newly empowered state. Both saw that the commitment to a dense Catholic institutional life was a nonstarter, so they pivoted toward a new kind of rights discourse that focused on claims that human persons could make as individuals. Even in an age of authoritarian and non-Catholic rule, the believer could live a recognizably Catholic life if she was entitled to own property, found a family, and worship freely (the corporate life of the family and Church were still implicated, of course, but the crucial distinction is that those corporate entities are not designated as the bearer of rights as such).

Linhardt and Massis forged a variety of social Catholic ethics that could be at home in and provide guidance to an age of furious state-building. Human rights, for them, were the handmaiden to Catholic authoritarianism. While this helps us to understand a great deal about the Church's transition to rights as a whole in the 1930s, it should not lead us to the familiar, ironic story of "reactionary human rights." Antifascist Catholics,

---

[31] Ibid., 121.

faced with the same set of historical circumstances, made a rights turn, as well – but in a very different way.

This becomes apparent through an investigation of the rights talk of Jacques Maritain and Emmanuel Mounier. They shared many assumptions with Massis and Linhardt (Maritain and Massis had once been close friends). All four of them were disgusted by secular liberalism; all four sought to move beyond the stale debates of fin de siècle Catholicism; all four were comparatively uninterested in defenses of the Church *qua* dense network of clergy-led institutions. Here, though, the similarities end. Maritain and Mounier were more inspired by antifascism than by anticommunism and derived a different variety of rights talk from the social Catholic tradition (it is no accident that they were both French, given that Paris was the "capital of anti-fascism," but similar forms of rights talk could be found amongst anti-Nazi Germans like Dietrich von Hildebrand and Eberhard Welty[32]). Theirs was not the mainstream rights discourse of the Church, either during or after the 1930s.[33] It is worthwhile to recover it, however, to show that human rights, in this time and place at least, was politically protean, and was not inherently "conservative" in the interwar years.[34]

For Mounier, the central text was the *Manifesto in the Service of Personalism* (1936). It was written during the Popular Front of Léon Blum – an antifascist movement that Mounier supported.[35] He rejected both the fascist and communist versions of modernization, but his support for antifascist forces in France and Spain makes clear that he saw the former as the greater evil (this would lead him, after World War II, to his notorious defenses of Stalinism). Mounier's invocations of rights, while equally rooted in Catholic social teaching, were substantially different from Massis's and Linhardt's, which focused more on civil and religious rights

---

[32] Anson Rabinbach, "Paris, Capital of Anti-Fascism," in *The Modernist Imagination: Intellectual History and Critical Theory*, ed. Warren Breckman, Peter E. Gordon, A. Dirk Moses, Samuel Moyn, and Elliot Neaman (New York: Berghahn, 2009), 183–209; Hildebrand, "Staat und Ehe"; Eberhard Welty, OP, *Gemeinschaft und Einzelmensch* (Leipzig: Pustet, 1935).

[33] It might seem obvious that Maritain had more of an impact on the Church's trajectory than Massis or Linhardt. That might be true as a matter of individual fame and influence, but as a matter of ecclesiastical history more generally it seems to me that the Massis/Linhardt track remained dominant, if not overwhelmingly so. For more on this, see Chappel, *Catholic Modern*, chaps. 4–6.

[34] The "dissident" and minority turn to human rights in the Catholic 1930s has been discussed before by Samuel Moyn. Unlike him, however, I do not see a straight line between that turn and the more conservative appropriations, then or later. Samuel Moyn, "Personalism, Community, and the Origins of Human Rights," in *Human Rights in the Twentieth Century*, ed. Stefan-Ludwig Hoffmann (Cambridge: Cambridge University Press, 2010), 85–106.

[35] He was not alone, as explored in Paul Christophe, *1936: Les Catholiques et le Front populaire* (Paris: Editions Ouvrières, 1986).

than on social or economic ones. "The first right of the economic person," Mounier declared, is "the right to a basic income [*minimum vitale*, what we might now call a UBI]." In line with the very first declarations of rights from the eighteenth century, as well as the more recent Soviet constitution, Mounier affirmed that "the right to work" is "an inalienable right of the person." The manifesto presents a cacophony of surprisingly progressive rights claims: women should have not only the right to equal pay for equal work but also the "right to a household salary" for housewives to be deducted from their husbands' paychecks. He derived a robust anticolonialism, and even a politics of indigeneity, from his illiberal theory of rights: the person's "natural right to fulfill himself in the community of his choice overflows the bounds of both nations and races," leading to a recognition of "the rights of the first occupants" against "capitalism imperialism" and its "rational exploitation of the globe."[36]

Mounier, therefore, turned to rights for a similar contextual reason but mobilized them in the name of a distinct political-theological project. Jacques Maritain's turn to rights can be explained similarly. Maritain had once been close friends with Massis, pursuing the same kind of monarchist project. After the papal condemnation of the Action française, however, he had struck a different course, becoming personally and spiritually closer to Mounier. Ironically, though, he actually turned to rights rather later than his peers. They are more or less ignored, for instance, in *Integral Humanism* (1936, based on lectures given in 1934). He built his analysis around the human person, to be sure, and he presumed the same eclipse of liberal modernity, but he did not see a rights-defending state as the answer. He was not explicitly opposed to rights, as he might have been earlier, but his search for a morally pure, almost saintly, and quasi-anarchist politics in the 1930s had little call for them.[37]

Maritain's turn to rights, temporally, confirms the general trend: it took place once he determined that his own brand of celestial politics would have to make peace with the secular nation-state. This did not happen for Maritain until the war: in the 1930s, as I have discussed elsewhere, Maritain was searching for some kind of nebulous "third way" between theocracy and the secular nation-state. Not until the war did he begin to publicly argue that secular nation-states, as currently constituted, were worthy of Catholic support. *Les droits de l'homme et la loi naturelle*, published in America in 1942, proceeds from the same premises as the other three texts discussed in this chapter. The age of clericalism and liberalism

---

[36] Emmanuel Mounier, *Oeuvres, vol. 1 (1931–1939)* (Paris: Seuil, 1961), 593, 597, 567–588, 632.

[37] For more on Maritain's 1930s itinerary in context, see Chappel, *Catholic Modern*, chap. 3.

were both over, Maritain presumed, and Catholics needed to adopt new strategies for a world of religious pluralism. But his version of rights talk had more in common with Mounier's than with Linhardt's. Despite later historians' linkage of Maritain with Christian Democracy, the rights talk Maritain espoused in the 1940s bore almost no resemblance to the conservative anticommunism of the Christian Democratic era.[38]

Maritain, that is, called for an antifascist form of human rights linked with dramatic political and social transformation, rather than an anticommunist form that was so easily enlisted into authoritarianism. Drawing on Teilhard de Chardin, Maritain argued that rights are a component of social progress and of increasing "political and social emancipation." Rights, that is, are not a rearguard defense, but part of the "progressive movement of humanity" toward "justice," "civic amity," and "equality."[39] While human rights would come to refer primarily to civil and political rights in order to embarrass communists, this was not all that Maritain had in mind. He did defend such rights, including the right to equality before the law, public employment without racial discrimination, freedom of expression, and freedom of association. He also defended, as equally significant, a rather robust set of social rights, including the right to free trade unionism, the right to work, the right to public assistance, and the right to a just wage, defined as one that would allow the worker and his family to have a "sufficiently human standard of living." These social rights in particular, Maritain claimed, would evolve over time, given that the war was leading to enormous economic dislocations and the potential for a new and more personalist reorganization of the economy.[40]

One interesting point of comparison is that Maritain, like Linhardt, aimed to proceed directly from scholastic political philosophy, and particularly the long-venerated notion of a mixed government. Maritain, however, interpreted that mixed government in quite a different way. Linhardt had argued for a straightforward application of the principles, hoping that the National Socialist movement to come might protect some vestige of aristocratic and democratic rule. For Maritain, this was too literal. His interest in historical progress and analogical reasoning led him to argue that, in the new world of pluralism and liberty, the goal was to

---

[38] As Marco Duranti has shown in *Conservative Human Rights Revolution*, that was more likely to come from opponents of Maritain and recovering monarchists like Louis Salleron. For my attempt to rupture the assumed linkages between Maritain and Christian Democracy, see my *Catholic Modern*, chap. 4.

[39] Jacques Maritain, *Oeuvres complètes*, ed. Cercle d'études Jacques et Raïssa Maritain, vol. 8 (Fribourg:Éditions Universitaires, 1988), 633–634, 641, 643.

[40] Ibid., 675–676, 678–679, 691, 682–685.

preserve the *principles* of monarchy and aristocracy – namely, unity and vigor – without any affection whatsoever for previous institutional manifestations. This, he believed, could be done in a personalist and pluralist democracy through an enlightenment and enfranchisement of the masses themselves (it was no accident that Maritain's other writings during the war concerned pedagogical theory).[41]

These four stories show us the shape of the Catholic turn to rights in the 1930s. In all four cases, Catholics turned toward rights when previous forms of Catholic politics failed – whether that form was Catholic monarchism, parliamentarianism, or something else. At some point in the 1930s, Catholic thinkers came to grudgingly accept that the secular nation-state, in some form or another, was the horizon of political expectations in a modern age. Rights talk emerged as a discursive toolbox to help them explain what shape that state should take and how Catholic principles might be incarnated in it. Beyond this, though, rights talk was surprisingly malleable, capable of coherent employment by reactionaries and philo-socialists alike.

This story inflects the broader narrative of human rights history in two major ways. First, it suggests that the crisis of the 1930s played a larger role in that history than is normally believed. That interwar decade should be viewed as a crucible in its own right, rather than as an antechamber to the more consequential explosion of rights talk during and especially after the war. In line with recent works by Philip Nord, Quinn Slobodian, and many others, this suggests that the tectonic shifts in political-moral thinking did not result from the war alone, but rather from a longer and slower phenomenon in which empires fell, economies cratered, and secular nation-states sought to forge new forms of modernization, political economy, and citizenship. This model makes the most sense of the Catholic turn to rights.[42]

Second and related, it reminds us of just how malleable "rights talk" can be. Sometimes its advent is viewed as a welcome transition to universalism, and sometimes as an exhausted turn away from emancipation. The truth is that rights talk is as amorphous as its competitors and can be turned in a great variety of directions. The human rights of the Catholic 1930s were not "liberal" or "conservative" or "humanist." They were, simply, Catholic – expressing all of the contradictions of a Church in transition, explicable more through the local political projects of Catholic agents than through the long sweep of human rights history.

---

[41] Ibid., 652.

[42] Philip Nord, *France's New Deal: From the Thirties to the Postwar Era* (Princeton, NJ: Princeton University Press, 2010); Quinn Slobodian, *Globalists: The End of Empire and the Birth of Neoliberalism* (Cambridge, MA: Belknap, 2018).

4 Catholic Social Doctrine and Human Rights
From Rejection to Endorsement?

Carlo Invernizzi Accetti

The Catholic Church is today widely regarded as one of the staunchest advocates of human rights: a perception that Vatican authorities have done much to uphold over the course of the past few decades.[1] Since at least the second half of the 1960s, references to the notion of human rights have been pervasive in the official discourse produced by the Catholic Church, and this institution is also deeply implicated in the material support of a vast array of "humanitarian" organizations across the world.[2]

Nevertheless, when the notion of human rights appeared on the stage of world history during the so-called democratic revolutions of the end of the eighteenth century, the position Vatican authorities adopted with respect to it was one of radical rejection. In a message he addressed to French bishops on March 10, 1791, for example, Pope Pius VI declared that human rights are "contrary to religion and society."[3] This remained the Vatican's official position throughout the nineteenth century and well into the twentieth. Indeed, even at the time of the United Nations' 1948 Universal Declaration of Human Rights, the Vatican's reaction remained cold, if not openly hostile. In light of the importance the notion was later to assume within the framework of Catholic doctrine, it is, for instance, surprising to note that this declaration was not mentioned once in the whole body of texts produced by Pope Pius XII, the pontiff in office at the time.

The first explicit mention of the 1948 declaration in an official Vatican document is found in the encyclical *Pacem in Terris* promulgated by Pope John XXIII in 1963. And it was only after this that the Catholic Church

---

[1] This chapter is a reprint of Carlo Invernizzi Accetti, "Catholic Social Doctrine and Human Rights: From Rejection to Endorsement?" *Humanity* 9, no. 2 (2018), 271–295.
[2] For an interesting collection of statistics relating to this, see the volume on "The Geopolitics of the Vatican" of the journal *Diplomatie* 4 (August–September 2011). See also the annual report published by Catholic Relief Services, available at: http://annual report.crs.org/.
[3] Cf. Pius VI, *Quod Aliquantum* (March 10, 1791): www.papalencyclicals.net/Pius06/index .htm.

progressively restyled itself as an advocate of human rights. From the point of view of intellectual history, this poses the question of what doctrinal developments informed this ostensible change in the Vatican's position. More specifically: does this point to a substantive transformation in the Church's attitude with respect to modernity, or is it rather the case that in order to rally behind human rights, the Vatican transformed their original meaning more than its own traditional doctrine?

The argument advanced in this chapter is that, over the course of the past half-century, the Vatican has developed a distinctive doctrine of human rights at odds with the liberal conceptions implicit in the first declarations of the end of the eighteenth century, as well as with the dominant theories of human rights prevalent in today's secular academia. Thus, in answer to the question posed earlier: the Catholic Church effectively *co-opted* human rights by transforming their original meaning. As a consequence, almost all the grounds for the Church's previous opposition to human rights remain latent in the Church's current doctrine, although this is now presented in terms of a *specific conception* of human rights, rather than a critique of the notion itself.[4]

This thesis challenges existing narratives on the relationship between Catholicism and human rights in several significant ways. First, it nuances the relatively widespread idea that human rights are in some important sense "inherently Christian."[5] As Samuel Moyn has pointed out, the

---

[4] I should emphasize here that what I refer to as "the Catholic Church's" position on human rights only strictly refers to *the Vatican's* official doctrine as codified in the set of papal encyclicals and conciliar documents promulgated over the course of the past century and a half. By this, I do not mean to deny the internal heterogeneity and complexity of Catholicism as an intellectual and religious phenomenon. As Charles Curran notes in the introduction to his *Catholic Social Teaching*, Catholicism is "a world unto itself"; however, a well-established tradition exists of scholarly commentary focusing exclusively on the corpus of Catholic social teaching "as found in papal and hierarchical documents." See Charles Curran, *Catholic Social Teaching: A Historical, Theological and Ethical Analysis* (Washington, DC: Georgetown University Press, 2002), 1–2. This restriction of focus – and the attendant habit of referring to "the Church's" position when one actually means to refer only to its established hierarchy's official doctrine – can be justified with reference to the magisterial role the hierarchy is assumed to play within the framework of the Catholic faith itself, which implies that the Vatican is entitled to speak with authority about what Catholicism as a whole stands for. Of course, a comprehensive study of the relationship between Catholicism and human rights would require taking into account a much broader set of sources than can form the basis for a single chapter. However, at a minimum, we can say that such a broader study could not afford to ignore the body of sources examined here. For, while it is true that Catholicism as a whole can't be reduced to the Vatican's official doctrine, it is also the case that the latter remains Catholicism's intellectual bedrock, as well as its authoritative guide.

[5] For a clear statement of this thesis, see, for instance, Nicholas Wolterstorff, *Justice: Rights and Wrongs* (Princeton, NJ: Princeton University Press, 2008). See also John Finnis, *Human Rights and Common Good: Collected Essays* (Oxford: Oxford University Press, 2011).

trouble with this thesis "is not so much that Christianity accounts for nothing, as that it accounts for everything."[6] "Without Christianity," Moyn writes, "our commitment to the moral equality of human beings is unlikely to have come about, but by itself this has no bearing on most forms of political equality," since it obscures the fact that for a large part of its history organized Christianity "has stood for values inimical to those we now associate with human rights."[7] The challenge for the intellectual historian is therefore to uncover some of the more "proximate" and "concrete" processes that led mainstream Christianity (and in particular the Catholic Church) to explicitly endorse human rights over the course of the past few decades, beyond abstract generalities concerning the influence of "Christian values" on the development of Western culture.

While accepting Moyn's starting point, this chapter seeks to both extend and revise some aspects of his narrative. First of all, whereas Moyn focuses almost exclusively on what he calls the "trans-war" period between the beginning of the 1930s and the end of the 1940s, I want to show that a lot of important intellectual work in the development of a distinctively Christian doctrine of human rights also took place since the 1960s, in the body of texts generally assumed to constitute the corpus of Catholic social doctrine. This leads me to focus on a different period and a more specific set of sources compared to Moyn's book: encyclical letters, conciliar documents, and papal pronouncements promulgated over the course of the past half-century.

Second, and perhaps more important, I want to challenge an idea that seems to run implicitly through Moyn's text – namely, that the development of a Christian conception of human rights in the middle part of the twentieth century laid the conditions for the later reappropriation of this notion by left-leaning secular liberals beginning in the 1970s. This gives the impression that a direct line of *continuity* can be traced between the Christian conception of human rights elaborated in the middle part of the twentieth century and the one that dominates today.[8] In contrast, what I want to bring out is that the Catholic conception of human rights developed over the course of the past half-century was explicitly construed in *opposition* to a rival secular or liberal conception. Thus, rather

---

[6] Samuel Moyn, *Christian Human Rights* (Philadelphia: University of Pennsylvania Press, 2015), 6.

[7] Ibid., 6–7.

[8] In this respect, for instance, Moyn writes that: "It is Christians who did much and perhaps most to welcome and define the idea of human rights in the 1940s, as well as some of its core notions such as the importance of human dignity which nobody else was yet making central in 1942. . . . And so, when liberal democracy later came in Western Europe it was in a conservative and religious form graced by a commitment to human dignity that signaled enormous *continuity* with the past" (ibid., 7–8) (emphasis added).

than feeding into the contemporary liberal consensus on human rights, the development of a Catholic doctrine of human rights points to the parallel existence of at least two distinct and irreconcilable conceptions of human rights, which have continued to coexist with – or rather *against* – one another over the course of the past decades.

Finally, this argument also lays the ground for a broader contribution to the existing literature on the intellectual foundations of human rights, which will only be sketched out here, but which challenges the very widespread idea that such rights are currently the object of an "over-lapping consensus" between a variety of different philosophical and poli-tical standpoints.[9] If the key thesis I am seeking to advance is true – namely, that the Catholic Church's conception of human rights remains at odds with the liberal one implicit in the first declarations as well as most contemporary secular literature on this topic – it follows that a more accurate description of the current philosophical status of human rights may be to view them as the *sites of an intellectual and political struggle*. What this alternative formulation brings out more clearly is that significant disagreement continues not just on the ultimate justification of human rights but also on their substantive meaning.

To flesh out and justify these claims, this chapter is divided into two parts. In the first, I reconstruct the reasons for the Catholic Church's initial opposition to human rights, in order to call into question the facile associations sometimes made between the traditional Christian doctrine of natural law and the notion of human rights. In this part I show that, within the framework of Catholic social doctrine, the notion of human rights was initially associated with an "individualist" and "contractualist" conception of the social order, ultimately founded on human autonomy. This was considered inconsistent with the traditional Christian doctrine of natural law, which asserts that human beings are part of a divinely ordained "order," which inscribes them in certain predetermined rela-tionships of authority and obligation, construed as independent of their will.

In the second part I examine the doctrinal developments that allowed the Catholic Church to endorse the notion of human rights, considering the grounds for its previous opposition to them. This analysis is intended to show that the substantive core of Catholic social doctrine has not

---

[9] For a clear statement and discussion of this idea, see, for instance, Charles Taylor, "Conditions of an Unforced Consensus on Human Rights," in *The Politics of Human Rights*, ed. Obrad Savic (London: Verso, 1999), 101–119. See also Joshua Cohen, "Minimalism About Human Rights: The Most We Can Hope For?" *Journal of Political Philosophy* 12, no. 2 (2004), 190–213; and Jack Donnelly, "The Relative Universality of Human Rights," *Human Rights Quarterly* 22, no. 2 (2007), 281–306.

changed very much, despite its ostensible realignment. Instead, the Catholic Church has progressively developed its own doctrine of human rights, which effectively recasts them as logical corollaries of the traditional Christian doctrine of natural law, while maintaining all the grounds for its previous opposition to liberalism, secularism, and individualism. Thus, instead of operating as a "synthesis" between Christianity and liberalism, contemporary Catholic doctrine on human rights merely restates the traditional grounds for its opposition to them, at a higher level of abstraction – that is, in terms of what human rights *mean* rather than whether they should be endorsed.

Elements for a Catholic Critique of Human Rights

The doctrinal reasons for the Catholic Church's initial opposition to human rights can be summed up in terms of three core objections by Vatican authorities against the way in which such rights were understood when they emerged on the stage of world history in the context of the so-called democratic revolutions of the end of the eighteenth century.

The first and most basic objection stems from a categorical distinction between two rival conceptions of the nature of man and the grounds for social order. On one hand, Catholic social doctrine has traditionally posited a conception of man as a "creation of God," from which it has derived the idea that submission to His authority is man's primary duty, and consequently the only possible foundation for a legitimate social order. This vision has been set against an alternative conception of man as a purely "natural" creature subject only to his (or her) will – which has in turn been assumed to be logically correlated to a conception of the social order as founded on the principle of freedom rather than authority.

Pius IX articulated this categorical distinction very clearly in the encyclical letter *Quanta Cura*, which was written to accompany and introduce the famous "Syllabus of Errors" the Vatican promulgated in 1864. The text begins by asserting that "our Lord, the Creator" has entrusted the Catholic Church with the task of "nourishing the whole Lord's flock with words and faith of salutary doctrine" in order to "guide them" toward salvation.[10] The underlying assumption is therefore that man is inherently subject to God's authority, whose commandments are in turn mediated by the Catholic Church. Hence the pope later states that "all true felicity flows abundantly upon man from our august religion and its

---

[10] Pius IX, *Quanta Cura* (December 8, 1864), §1: www.papalencyclicals.net/Pius09/p9quanta.htm.

doctrine and practice; and happy is the people whose God is their Lord."[11]

In contrast to this, Pius IX then delineates an alternative conception of man, stemming from what he describes as "forgetting our Creator" and "abjuring his power."[12] The claim is that a purely "naturalistic" conception of man necessarily leads to the view that the social order is founded on "human will" rather than divine authority. Thus, the idea that a social order can be founded exclusively on the principle of autonomy is seen as resulting from a denial of the sovereign authority of God over man: "Where religion has been removed from civil society," the pope writes, "and the doctrine and authority of revelation repudiated, the genuine notion of justice is darkened and lost ... Thence it appears why it is that some, utterly neglecting and disregarding the surest principles of sound reason, dare to proclaim that the people's will, manifested by what is called public opinion or in some other way, constitutes a supreme law, free from all divine and human control."[13]

Within the terms of this basic opposition between authority and autonomy as grounds for social order, Pope Pius IX clearly situates the notion of human rights in the latter camp. In commenting on some of the implications of the "dangerous doctrine" of popular sovereignty, for instance, he writes that:

From this totally false idea of social government, they [i.e., its advocates] do not fear to foster the erroneous opinion, most fatal in its effects on the Catholic Church and the salvation of souls ... that liberty of conscience and worship is each man's personal right, which ought to be legally proclaimed and asserted in every rightly constituted society; and that a right resides in every human being to an absolute liberty, which should be restrained by no authority, whether ecclesiastical or civil.[14]

The first and most basic objection the Catholic Church has historically developed against human rights is therefore that such rights are predicated on an "irreligious" conception of man and the grounds for the social order, which ultimately refers to an idea of individual *autonomy* rather than divine *authority*.

In the decades following Pius IX's formulation of this objection, the Church progressively reformulated its basic concern for a reassertion of divine authority against individual autonomy by fusing it into a broader recovery of Thomist theology as the intellectual foundation for its social doctrine. In the thought and writings of Leo XIII, for instance, we find the idea that God created the universe as a purposive "order" oriented toward

---

[11] Ibid., §8.   [12] Ibid., §9.   [13] Ibid., §4.   [14] Ibid., §3.

the ultimate goal of human salvation.[15] Within the framework of this overall conception of the universe first emerged the scope for recognizing the legitimacy of certain personal "rights," understood as the logical corollaries of the duties individuals must conform to in order to respect and foster the overall purposive equilibrium of the universe. In the encyclical *Immortale Dei* of 1885, for instance, Leo XIII writes that "in the constitution of the natural order We have just described, divine and human things are equitably shared; the rights of citizens assured to them, and fenced round by divine, by natural, and by human law; the duties incumbent on each one being wisely marked out, and their fulfillment fittingly insured."[16]

It is important to point out here that these personal "rights" are not understood as subjective *entitlements*, in the sense of individual claims against others to have certain basic liberties respected. Rather, they are understood as objective correlates of the *duties* all individuals have to respect the natural order of authority willed by God. The notion of duty is therefore assumed to be logically prior to that of right, rather than vice versa. This becomes explicit when, later in the same text, Leo XIII goes on to deplore "all those tenets of unbridled license which, in the midst of the terrible upheavals of the last century, were wildly conceived and boldly proclaimed as the principles and foundation of a new conception of law that is at variance on many points not only with the Christian but even the natural law."[17] The second key objection against human rights traditionally articulated by Catholic social doctrine is therefore that such rights invert the specific order of priority between rights and duties implicit in the classical notion of natural law.

Finally, the third line of Catholic social doctrine's objection against human rights concerns the presumed *consequences* of founding the social order on subjective freedom as opposed to divinely ordained authority. Throughout almost all the official documents the Catholic Church promulgated in the period between the end of the eighteenth century and the

---

[15] In the encyclical *Immortale Dei*, for instance, Leo XIII articulates this form of neo-Thomism as follows:

The Almighty has so combined the forces and springs of nature with tempered action and wondrous harmony, that all of them most fitly and aptly work together for the great purpose of the universe. ... Indeed, when more fully pondered, this mutual coordination has a perfection in which all other forms of government are lacking, and from which excellent results would flow, were the several component parts to keep their place and duly discharge the office and work appointed respectively for each. (Cf. Leo XIII, Immortale Dei (November 1, 1885), §§14–17: www.papalencyclicals.net/Leo13/l13sta.htm)

[16] Ibid., §17.   [17] Ibid., §24.

first half of the twentieth, we find a recurring pattern according to which the "modern" doctrines of liberalism and popular sovereignty are assumed to lay the condition for a degeneration of the moral standards of society, thereby leading to a collapse of the social order into anarchy and conflict, and finally to a violent reassertion of order through sheer tyrannical force. Commenting in 1832 on some of the consequences of the "recent political turmoil," for instance, Pope Gregory XVI wrote in his encyclical *Mirari Vos* that "now is truly the time in which the powers of darkness winnow the elect like wheat. ... Depravity exults; science is impudent; liberty dissolute. ... So the restraints of religion are thrown off, by which alone kingdoms stand. We see the destruction of public order, the fall of principalities, and the overturning of all legitimate power."[18]

In sharp contrast with the dominant understanding of human rights throughout the first century and a half of their existence, therefore, the Catholic Church initially refused to understand them as potential bulwarks against the threat of tyranny or political abuse. On the contrary, it portrayed them as part and parcel of a "modern mentality" that was inviting a breakdown of the social order and thereby laying the conditions for the emergence of some new kind of tyranny, or even – as it later came to be known – totalitarianism. The Catholic Church had posited a sort of *immanent dialectic* in the kind of individual freedom that human rights claim to protect, which ultimately makes it result in an even worse kind of oppression.

Toward a Catholic Doctrine of Human Rights?

Given the premises so far established here, it is perhaps not so surprising that the path that led the Catholic Church to its eventual endorsement of human rights was both long and arduous. In the remaining parts of this chapter, I attempt to reconstruct the twists and turns of this path in order to assess the extent to which it involved a substantive departure from the Church's original position on human rights, by comparing the elements of novelty and continuity within it.

The Prehistory of a Catholic Doctrine of Human Rights

In *Christian Human Rights*, Samuel Moyn traces the intellectual roots of the contemporary understanding of human rights to the development of a distinctively Christian doctrine of the rights of the "human person"

---

[18] Gregory XVI, *Mirari Vos*, §5.

during the so-called trans-war years between the 1930s and 1940s.[19] To be sure, the concept of human "personality" already had deep roots within the history of Christian moral and political theology. It can, for instance, be found in the work of Thomas Aquinas, where it is occasionally used to refer to the specific position human beings occupy within the overarching "order" of creation that for him constitutes the core of *ius naturale*. It was however only during the first few decades of the twentieth century that the idea of a human "person" began to be referred to as the bearer of a set of subjective rights, understood as logical correlates of the objective duties individuals owe one another – and especially God – in virtue of this overarching order.

In his Christmas radio address of 1942, for instance, Pope Pius XII began by asserting that "the origin and primary scope of social life is the conservation, development and perfection of the human *person*, helping him to realize accurately the demands and values of religion and culture set by the Creator for every man and for all mankind."[20] On this basis he then went on to articulate a doctrine of the inherent rights of the human person:

> He who would have the Star of Peace shine out and stand over society should cooperate, for his part, in giving back to the human person the dignity given to it by God from the very beginning. ... He should uphold respect for and the practical realization of the following fundamental personal rights; the right to maintain and develop one's corporal, intellectual and moral life and especially the right to religious formation and education; the right to worship God in private and public and to carry on religious works of charity; the right to marry and to achieve the aim of married life; the right to conjugal and domestic society; the right to work, as the indispensable means towards the maintenance of family life; the right to free choice of state of life, and hence, too, of the priesthood or religious life; the right to the use of material goods; in keeping with his duties and social limitations.[21]

Moyn's argument is that this doctrine laid the foundations for the Catholic Church's later endorsement of human rights because it effectively carved out the space for a conception of subjective rights that is not inconsistent with the traditional Christian doctrine of natural law, but rather ends up reasserting it in a backhanded way, since the rights enumerated here are merely the logical corollaries of duties that the Church has long held to be implicit in the "natural order" willed by God. This is what Moyn is suggesting when he asserts that the doctrine of the inherent rights

[19] Moyn, *Christian Human Rights*, 65 100.
[20] Pius XII, "Christmas Radio Message 1942": https://w2.vatican.va/content/pius-xii/en/s peeches/1942.index.html.
[21] Ibid.

of the human person was "part and parcel of a reformulation of conservatism in the name of a vision of moral constraint, not human emancipation or individual autonomy."[22]

While there is no denying that the Vatican's appropriation of a doctrine of personalism in the "trans-war" years of the twentieth century represented a crucial step in the path that led it to its later endorsement of human rights, my contention is that it would be a mistake to read it as an endorsement of human rights as previously understood. For, in almost all the writings Moyn focuses on, the notion of a human "person" is kept carefully distinct – and indeed opposed – to the abstract idea of the human "individual" taken to be the subject of the liberal conception of human rights implicit in the first declarations of such rights.

My contention is therefore that the development of a doctrine of the inherent rights of the human "person" during the trans-war years ought perhaps more properly to be considered as forming part of the *pre*history of a Christian doctrine of human rights, rather than its beginning or foundation. That history only really began once the Catholic Church reversed its previous position of opposition and explicitly endorsed the notion of "human rights" (as opposed to the inherent rights of the human "person") itself. This happened only several decades later, in close connection with the events that led to the Second Vatican Council and its aftermath. It is therefore to an analysis of the relevant parts of Catholic social doctrine in *that* period that I now turn.

The Encyclical Pacem in Terris

A conventional starting point to begin reconstructing the Catholic Church's current position on human rights is the encyclical *Pacem in Terris* promulgated by Pope John XXIII in 1963, the first official Vatican document to mention the 1948 declaration explicitly and to formally endorse it.[23] This document ought, however, to be situated within the context of the broader pontifical mission John XXIII pursued under the aegis of the concept of "renewal" (*aggiornamento*). The latter was intended as a counterpoint to the Church's previous policy of "intransigent" refusal of the entire intellectual framework of modernity, which John XXIII felt was marginalizing the Catholic Church within the

---

[22] Moyn, *Christian Human Rights*, 10.

[23] On this point, see David Hollenbach, *Claims in Conflict: Retrieving and Renewing the Catholic Human Rights Tradition* (New York: Paulist Press, 1979); Robert Traer, *Faith in Human Rights: Support in Religious Traditions for a Global Struggle* (Washington, DC: Georgetown University Press, 1991); Daniele Menozzi, *Chiesa e Diritti Umani* (Bologna: il Mulino, 2012).

context of modernity and therefore impairing its capacity to fulfill its evangelical and pastoral mission.[24]

In this respect it is important to point out that the new approach did not (and was never meant to) imply a repudiation of the substantive critiques the Church had previously leveled against what it perceived as the "errors" of modernity. Like all the most important transformations in Catholic doctrine, this methodological shift was both understood and presented as a way of placing greater emphasis on a previously ignored aspect of the issue, without thereby denying the validity of anything stated before.[25] Within the framework of this overall doctrine, the specific intellectual operation John XXIII carried out in the encyclical *Pacem in Terris* consists in affirming that some aspects of the modern notion of human rights overlap with the traditional Christian doctrine of natural law and the Catholic Church can therefore accept them.

The encyclical accordingly begins with a restatement of the already very well-established idea that a "divinely established order" is inscribed in the structure of the universe itself, which prescribes a set of reciprocal rights and duties amongst all human beings and God.[26] However, instead of making the inference that the Vatican had traditionally drawn from this premise – that is, that the modern notion of human rights must therefore be "contrary to religion and society" – John XXIII suggests that *some* aspects of the modern notion of human rights are compatible with it:

Any well-regulated and productive association of men in society demands the acceptance of one fundamental principle: that each individual man is truly a person. His is a nature, that is, endowed with intelligence and free will. As such he has rights and duties, which together flow as a direct consequence from his nature. . . . Once this is admitted, it follows that every basic human right draws its authoritative force from the natural law, which confers it and attaches to it its respective duty. Hence, to claim one's rights and ignore one's duties, or only half fulfill them, is like building a house with one hand and tearing it down with the other.[27]

---

[24] On the pontifical doctrine of Pope John XXIII and more specifically on his use of the notion of *aggiornamento*, see Christian Feldman, *Pope John XXIII: A Spiritual Biography* (London: Crossroad, 2000); *Aggiornamento? Catholicism from Gregory XVI to Benedict XVI*, ed. Karim Schelkens, John A. Dick, and Jürgen Mettepenningen (Boston: Brill, 2013).

[25] On the complex interplay between change and continuity with the history of official Catholic doctrine, see Charles Curran, *Change in Official Catholic Moral Teachings* (New York: Paulist Press, 2003).

[26] Cf. John XXIII, *Pacem in Terris* (April 11, 1963), §§1–3: www.vatican.va/holy_father/jo hn_xxiii/encyclicals/documents/hf_j-xxiii_enc_11041963_pacem_en.html.

[27] Ibid., §§9–30.

Although this passage is often seen as containing the first explicit endorsement of a notion of human rights by the Catholic Church, in light of the previous section of this chapter, at least three key elements should stand out: first of all, the normative foundation for the legitimacy of human rights is here assumed to lie in a Thomist conception of "natural law." Second, these rights are considered valid only to the extent that they are conceived of as inextricably tied to a correlative set of "duties." Finally, the principal point of imputation of such rights is not taken to be the human being as such, but rather the human "person."

Each of these three features points to an important element of continuity between the reasoning behind John XXIII's ostensible endorsement of human rights and the Church's previous critiques of this notion. For, as I pointed out earlier, the normative foundation for these critiques lies precisely in the Thomist conception of *ius naturale* as a "divinely ordained natural order" that prescribes a set of reciprocal rights and duties amongst the elements of creation. On this basis, the Catholic Church had already for a long time been arguing that human beings could be considered bearers of certain personal rights, as long as such rights were deduced from objective duties ultimately owed to God and not vice versa.

The real originality in John XXIII's statement lies in his concession that certain aspects of the modern doctrine of human rights are compatible with the traditional Catholic doctrine of natural law. This amounts only to a very qualified endorsement of such rights, which does not really change the substance of Church's previous position, because it still implies that wherever there may be a divergence between human rights and the traditional doctrine of natural law, the latter stands.

The Second Vatican Council

The elements of reservation implicit in John XXIII's endorsement of human rights were developed further by the Second Vatican Council of 1962–1965. While reiterating many of the same arguments contained in John XXIII's seminal encyclical, for instance, the pastoral constitution *Gaudium et Spes* also contains a detailed analysis of the dangers attendant upon an incorrect interpretation of the meaning and grounds for such rights. Consider, for instance, the following passage from the document in question:

By no human law can the personal dignity and liberty of man be so aptly safeguarded as by the Gospel of Christ which has been entrusted to the Church. ... The Church, therefore, by virtue of the Gospel committed to her, proclaims the rights of man; she acknowledges and greatly esteems the dynamic movements of today by which these rights are everywhere fostered. Yet these movements must be penetrated by the spirit of the Gospel and protected against any kind of false autonomy. For we are tempted to think that our personal rights are fully ensured only when we are exempt from every requirement of divine law. But this way lies not the maintenance of the dignity of the human person, but its annihilation.[28]

What we see reemerging here is a theme already at the heart of the Church's previous criticisms of human rights – namely, that if human communities diverge from the guidance offered by the "spirit of the Gospel," as legitimately interpreted by the Catholic Church, they run the risk of falling back into a "false" conception of liberty, which in turn underwrites a specific kind of political rule that ends up "annihilating" the very idea of freedom on which it was initially based. This is precisely the point I raised earlier when I spoke of the Church positing an "immanent dialectic" in the conception of subjective rights as individual liberties or entitlements, whereby its concrete application necessarily ends up producing forms of political rule that contradict the principles and values on which it is based in the first place.

The only real difference between that idea and what is being asserted in the passage just quoted lies in the way it spells out the implications of this reasoning: whereas previous Catholic social doctrine had taken this dialectic as grounds for a rejection of the notion of human rights as such, the Second Vatican Council prefers to state that human rights can be considered legitimate *to the extent* that they are "penetrated by the spirit of the Gospel" – that is, to the extent to which human rights "overlap" with the traditional Christian doctrine of *ius naturale*, as legitimately interpreted by the Catholic Church.

To be sure, it would be a mistake to underestimate the historical significance of such passages. As I have already pointed out, many of the most important transformations within official Catholic doctrine happened through gradual changes in emphasis and subtle terminological shifts. From this perspective, the fact that the Church came to explicitly endorse a notion – that of "human rights" – that it had previously vehemently rejected is certainly of enormous historical importance, since it opened the way for a whole new mode of engagement between the Catholic Church and the political discourse of modernity. So there is no denying here that the Church's endorsement of the notion of human rights *cut both ways*, in the sense that it involved a measure of transformation in the substance of traditional Catholic social doctrine at the same time as it put forward a new and distinctive doctrine of human rights.[29]

---

[28] Ibid., §41.   [29] See Curran, *Change in Official Catholic Moral Teachings.*

The question I am addressing here, however, is whether this transformation is more adequately understood as a substantive change in the core of traditional Catholic social doctrine, or rather, as a conceptual co-optation that ended up transforming the meaning of human rights more than the substance of traditional Catholic social doctrine itself. To answer this question, it is necessary to compare the relative degrees of change and continuity in the set of doctrinal statements being evaluated. And it is from this perspective that I wish to emphasize the elements of continuity at work here. For, whereas most of the existing literature on the relationship between Catholic social doctrine and human rights has tended to portray the encyclical *Pacem in Terris* and the Second Vatican Council as moments of radical break, my contention is that the elements of continuity are actually preponderant. This suggests that the Church's ostensible endorsement of human rights at this juncture of its recent history is more adequately interpreted as a case of conceptual co-optation.

The Pontificate of Paul VI

The pontificate of Paul VI is generally considered the high point of the Church's rapprochement with human rights, since at several junctures during this time Paul VI came close to suggesting that the reservations still expressed in the encyclical *Pacem in Terris* and then further elaborated by the Second Vatican Council could in principle be overcome. In a message addressed to the president of the General Assembly of the United Nations on the twentieth anniversary of the 1948 declaration of human rights, for instance, Paul VI refers to this document as a "precious testament to the ideal of a human community proposed to the whole of humanity," adding that "the Church seeks not to impose structures or establish legal norms for the City of Man, but does insist that these norms be inspired by the principle of respect for human rights, and by the promotion and preservation of the same rights."[30]

Here too, however, it may be legitimate to introduce a note of caution. Statements such as this need to be read within the context of the broader doctrinal framework that informed Paul VI's pontificate and, as several commentators have pointed out, in light of the influence Jacques Maritain exercised on Paul VI's doctrinal outlook.[31] In particular, one key thesis

---

[30] Paul VI, Message delivered at the Teheran conference for the celebration of the twentieth anniversary of the United Nations Universal Declaration of Human Rights (April 15, 1968): www.vatican.va/holy_father/paul_vi/messages/pont-messages/documents/hf_p-v i_mess_19680415_confer-teheran_sp.html.

[31] On this point, see, for instance, Philippe Chenaux, *Paul VI et Maritain. Les rapports du "montinianisme" et du "maritainisme"* (Rome: Istituto Paolo VI, 1994). See also Peter Hebblethwaite, *Paul VI: The First Modern Pope* (New York: Paulist Press, 1993).

Paul VI took over from Maritain's theology is the idea that human rights ought to be viewed as a manifestation of the "evangelical spirit" assumed to be at work in human history – that is, as a "profane" manifestation of the "Christian ferment" assumed to guide humanity throughout its "pilgrimage in time" toward the ultimate goal of final redemption.[32]

On this basis, Paul VI's main contribution to the Church's doctrine on human rights can be described as a "historicization" of the key idea John XXIII introduced in the encyclical *Pacem in Terris*, which recast the overlap between traditional Christian doctrine and the modern notion of human rights as a distinctive feature of the contemporary historical epoch. Thus, Paul VI proposed to interpret human rights as the "historical expression" of the requirements imposed at the present time by the traditional Christian conception of natural law.

This "historicization" of the relationship between the traditional Catholic doctrine of natural law and human rights certainly laid the grounds for a greater openness toward the latter, since it introduced a dynamic element in the Church's attitude with respect to human rights, which potentially cleared the way for an even fuller rapprochement in the future. At the same time, however, it is also important to note that the corollary of this reasoning is the introduction of a certain element of *contingency* in the relationship between human rights and traditional Christian doctrine. For, if human rights are only the expression of the requirements imposed by the immutable principles of justice at this stage of human history, it follows that in the future such rights might cease to fulfill this function, and therefore that the Catholic Church might be required to withdraw its support for them.

Indeed, strictly speaking, if one accepts the Maritainian doctrine that human history corresponds to a gradual process of fulfillment of God's providential plan,[33] it follows that since human history is manifestly not completed yet, there must necessarily remain some "errors" or at least "imperfections" in our current understanding of this plan. Through this reasoning, Paul VI was able to carve out the conceptual space for a re-actualization of the criticisms the Catholic Church had traditionally advanced against the notion of human rights, directing them against the persistent elements of "imperfection" in the current interpretation of the immutable principles of justice implied by the Christian faith. In a speech he delivered before the foreign diplomatic corps accredited to the Vatican in 1978, for example, the pope recalled almost all the standard grounds

---

[32] Cf. Jacques Maritain, *Christianity and Democracy, Followed by the Rights of Man and Natural Law* (San Francisco: Ignatius Press, 2012).

[33] Cf. Jacques Maritain, *Du régime temporel et de la liberté* (Paris: Desclée De Brouwer, 1933).

for the Church's traditional opposition to the notion of human rights
when he asserted that:

Human rights are today the object of much attention and discussion. This is
almost always done with the realization of a higher conception of justice, either
real or presumed, in mind. However, not all the claims that are advanced in this
guise are equally reasonable or feasible. For, some remain encrusted by individualist pretensions, or tainted by a form of utopian anarchism, while others are even
morally inadmissible. ... Nonetheless, on the whole, and to the extent that it
stems from an aspiration or a tension towards a higher conception of justice, this
increased interest in a space of freedom and responsibility is favorable to the full
development of the human person and therefore a positive fact which needs to be
encouraged. The Church follows it and will continue to follow it with sympathy,
all the while providing the light and guidance it requires.[34]

This passage clearly shows that, even at the high point of its rapprochement with human rights, the Catholic Church never repudiated its condemnation of the aspects of this notion it had always considered
incompatible with the traditional Catholic doctrine of natural law. On
the contrary, the Church's endorsement of human rights has always been
understood as a specification, and therefore a reaffirmation, of this doctrine, and of the political consequences that follow from it. This implies
that there are *some* elements within the notion of human rights that the
Catholic Church has at certain moments of its history thought it could
come to terms with, and others that it couldn't. But the decisive criterion
has always remained an elaboration of the traditional doctrine of natural
law, not a concern for human rights as such. The difference between these
two respective ideas was to come even more to the fore during John Paul
II's pontificate.

The "Neo-intransigentist" Turn

Under John Paul II's guidance, the elements of ambivalence still present
in the Church's position on human rights during Paul VI's pontificate
were radicalized. Although the notion of human rights remained pervasive in almost all of John Paul II's pronouncements, he much more starkly
subordinated the Church's endorsement of human rights to their substantive conformity with traditional Catholic doctrine, and thereby also
the Church's magisterial role in discriminating between the "acceptable"
and "unacceptable" aspects of the notion.

---

[34] Paul VI, Speech delivered before the diplomatic corps accredited to the Vatican
(January 14, 1978): www.vatican.va/holy_father/paul_vi/speeches/1978/january/docu
ment/hf_p-vi_spe_19780114_corpo-diplomatico_fr.html.

This can be observed, for instance, in the encyclical *Evangelium Vitae*, which contains the most sustained exposition of John Paul II's views on human rights, and is accordingly worth examining in some detail here. The thrust of the argument developed in this document lies in the opposition between two rival conceptions of "the basic rights of the human person": one according to which such rights are founded on the "recognition of" and "participation in" a "divinely ordained natural order," and the other according to which such rights are founded on the "self-assertion" of a "monadic individual" independent of any concern for a higher authority.[35] By applying this distinction to the issue of the correct interpretation of the "right to life" – which for John Paul II constitutes the "ground" and "stepping-stone" for all other rights – the encyclical reaches the conclusion that the conception of human rights as grounded on the "self-assertion" of monadic subjects is ultimately *self-defeating*, because it implies that the subjects most in need of having their right to life protected (i.e., the "young," the "sick," and, in general, the "dependent") actually have the weakest claim to such protection, precisely because they are likely to be incapable of claiming and defending this right for themselves.[36]

This argument harks directly back to the idea of an "immanent dialectic" in the secular conception of human rights as individual entitlements, which we have found to be at the heart of all the Catholic Church's critiques of modernity since the end of the eighteenth century. It is, however, not the only commonality between the argument deployed by John Paul II in this encyclical and previous Catholic social doctrine. Another interesting element of overlap can be found in John Paul II's recovery of another recurrent theme from the Church's nineteenth-century "intransigentist" critique of modernity: the association of the specific kind of "individualism" taken to underpin the modern notion of human rights, with a form of "moral relativism" supposed to undermine the moral foundations of society and therefore to lay the grounds for a relapse into anarchy, disorder, and, ultimately, tyranny. Consider for instance the following passage from the same encyclical:

The eclipse of the sense of God and man [manifested in some of the contemporary interpretations of the notion of human rights] inevitably leads to a practical materialism, which breeds individualism, utilitarianism and hedonism. ... The values of being are replaced by those of having and the only goal which counts is the pursuit of one's own material well-being. The so-called "quality of life" is

---

[35] Cf. John Paul II, *Evangelium Vitae* (March 25, 1995), §§21–24: www.vatican.va/holy_fa ther/john_paul_ii/encyclicals/documents/hf_jp-ii_enc_25031995_evangelium-vitae_en .html.
[36] Ibid., §23.

interpreted primarily or exclusively as economic efficiency, inordinate consumerism, physical beauty and pleasure, to the neglect of the more profound dimensions – interpersonal, spiritual and religious – of existence.[37]

Almost all the themes touched upon in this passage can be retraced, virtually in the same terms, to the Church's previous denunciations of "moral relativism" since the end of the nineteenth century.[38] To be sure, this specific strand of the Catholic critique of modernity had been more or less suppressed throughout the official Church documents we have been considering up to this point – most probably because it did not fit very well with the Church's resolute alignment with the "Western" front in the context of the Cold War. However, it is interesting to note that as soon as this exogenous constraint was removed, the themes reemerged as part of John Paul II's critique of the conception of human rights he considers antithetical to Catholic doctrine, thereby marking a further element of convergence between his thought and the critiques of human rights developed by traditional Catholic doctrine prior to the onset of the Cold War.

Benedict XVI on Human Rights

Benedict XVI's pontificate developed along a line of overall continuity with the second part of John Paul II's. If anything, we can observe a stiffening of the "neo-intransigentist" stance adopted by the latter, for example in the condemnation of "moral relativism," which Benedict XVI made into the backbone of his pontifical message by linking it to the presumed threat of a "relapse" into a new and more subtle form of "totalitarianism."[39]

This can be observed, for example, in the text of a speech he delivered on the occasion of the sixtieth anniversary of the Universal Declarations of Human Rights, in which he asserted that:

> It is evident that the rights recognized and expounded in the declaration apply to everyone by virtue of their common origin in the divinely ordained natural law. . . . Removing human rights from this context would mean restricting their range and yielding to a relativistic conception. . . . Thus, today, efforts need to be redoubled in the face of pressure to reinterpret the foundation of human rights and to

---

[37] Ibid., §23.

[38] For a detailed reconstruction of the history of the discourse of anti-relativism in the tradition of Catholic social thought, see Carlo Invernizzi Accetti, *Relativism and Religion: Why Democratic Societies Do Not Need Moral Absolutes* (New York: Columbia University Press, 2015).

[39] Benedict XVI, *Caritas in Veritate* (June 29, 2009): www.vatican.va/holy_father/benedict_xvi/encyclicals/documents/hf_ben-xvi_enc_20090629_caritas-in-veritate_en.html.

compromise their inner unity, so as to move away from the protection of human dignity towards the satisfaction of material interests and egoistic needs. The declaration was adopted as a common standard of achievement and cannot be applied according to selective choices that merely run the risk of contradicting the unity of the human person and thus the indivisibility of human rights.[40]

In this passage it is possible to discern, *in nuce*, almost all the elements of the doctrine of human rights developed by John Paul II, complemented by a clarification of the link with the issue of "moral relativism." The conception of human rights Benedict XVI proves willing to endorse is founded on a recognition of the "divinely ordained natural law" that stems from the supreme authority of God. This is contrasted to an alternative interpretation that stems from a "relativistic conception" of human rights, in turn connected to both "materialism" and "individualism." In this way, Benedict XVI recovered the link between the Church's previous critique human rights and the individualism and materialism of contemporary societies.

Finally, it is also worth noting that in the last sentence of the passage, Benedict XVI also alludes to the idea of an "immanent dialectic" whereby the latter interpretation of the conceptual foundation for human rights runs the risk of contradicting the very principles and values on which such rights are founded in the first place. What we see reemerging here is therefore another recurrent theme from the Church's nineteenth-century "intransigentist" doctrine – namely, the idea that civil coexistence amongst human beings is possible only through a recognition of the inherent truth of the Christian faith, and therefore a subordination to the magisterial authority of the Catholic Church.[41]

Contemporary Developments

Compared to the analysis conducted earlier, a much more difficult challenge is raised for the intellectual historian by the task of situating the available pronouncements of the newly elected Pope Francis I on human rights. This is the case not only because this pope's election remains relatively recent but also because a distinctive feature of this pope's discourse appears to be precisely its elusiveness. In his effort to find

---

[40] Benedict XVI, Speech delivered before the General Assembly of the United Nations on the occasion of the sixtieth anniversary of the Universal Declaration of Human Rights (April 18, 2008): www.vatican.va/holy_father/benedict_xvi/ speeches/2008/april/docu ments/hf_ben-xvi_spe_20080418_un-visit_en.html.

[41] For a general appraisal of Benedict XVI's doctrine on human rights making this point, see Thomas Rourke, *The Social and Political Thought of Benedict XVI* (Lanham, MD: Lexington, 2010).

consensus, patching over the tensions and misunderstandings generated by the "neo-intransigentist" stance of his two predecessors, this pope has been led to *dilute* the doctrinal import of his statements on human rights, adopting positions that can be interpreted as agreeable from a variety of different points of view, but also adapting his message to the specific audience at hand.

The result has been an oscillation between statements that seem to hark back to a position more similar to the one developed by Pope Paul VI, and others that instead continue along the lines delineated by John Paul II and Benedict XVI. In a speech he delivered on the occasion of World Peace Day on January 1, 2014, Francis I appeared to provide an almost unqualified endorsement of human rights when he asserted that "the Church speaks out loudly in order to make world leaders hear the cry of pain of the suffering and put an end to every form of hostility, abuse and the violation of fundamental human rights."[42] However, in an apostolic exhortation he delivered at the Vatican on November 24, 2013, concerning the issue of the right to life of unborn fetuses, Francis I outlined a position that appears much more ambivalent and, indeed, reticent on human rights:

Frequently, as a way of ridiculing the Church's effort to defend the right to life, attempts are made to present her position as ideological, obscurantist and conservative. Yet her defense of unborn life is closely linked to the defense of each and every other human right. It involves the conviction that a human being is always sacred and inviolable, in any situation and at every stage of development. . . . Once this conviction disappears, so do solid and lasting foundations for the defense of human rights, which would always be subject to the passing whims of the powers that be.[43]

Such oscillations make it difficult to provide even a preliminary assessment of Francis I's overall position on human rights. However, what I have sought to demonstrate throughout this chapter is that, whichever inclination ultimately prevails – whether the more open-minded posture reminiscent of Paul VI's statements on human rights, or the more reticent positions taken by John Paul II and Benedict XVI – the substance of the Church's position on human rights is bound to still have many elements in common with the doctrinal framework that underwrote its previous opposition to it. The basic reason is that, throughout its most recent twists and turns, Catholic social doctrine has remained grounded in a Thomist

---

[42] Francis I, Message for the celebration of the World Day of Peace (January 1, 2014): http://w2.vatican.va/content/francesco/en/messages/peace/documents/papa-frances co_20131208_messaggio-xlvii-giornata-mondiale-pace-2014.html.

[43] Francis I, *Evangeli Gaudium* (November 24, 2013): http://w2.vatican.va/content/francesco/en/apost_exhortations/documents/papa-francesco_esortazione-ap_20131124_evangelii-gaudium.html.

conception of *ius naturale* as a "divinely ordained natural order," which is profoundly at odds with the individualistic metaphysics that informs the liberal conception of human rights.[44] Thus, the only way for the Catholic Church to endorse human rights has been to ascribe this notion a different meaning, which turns out to overlap with the Church's own doctrine in many significant ways without removing any of the grounds for the previous opposition between them.

Conclusion

The conclusion I reach is that the Catholic Church can only be said to have come to endorse human rights on the condition of introducing a distinctive and original conception of such rights, which is irreducibly *at odds* with the liberal one implicit in the first declarations of such rights from the end of the eighteenth century and most contemporary secular theorizations.[45] Far from feeding into one another, these two rival conceptions of human rights have always been kept distinct – and indeed opposed to one another – within the framework of Catholic social doctrine. Thus, even today, many of the most important grounds for the Church's initial opposition to a liberal conception of human rights remain latent in its doctrine, even though the Church has now restyled itself as an advocate for a specific conception of human rights, rather than a critic of the notion itself.

To be sure, this conclusion is not meant to deny that the Church's ostensible realignment on the question of human rights has been of major historical importance. On the contrary, the Catholic Church's explicit endorsement of a notion of human rights has been a central component in a new and distinctive mode of engagement with the political discourse of modernity. However, the key question I have sought to answer is whether this mode of engagement is best understood as involving a substantive transformation of traditional Catholic social doctrine or rather as a form of conceptual co-optation that has transformed the inherited meaning of

---

[44] For other discussions of the relationship between "modern" conceptions of human rights and "classical" doctrines of natural law that substantiate this point from a variety of different perspectives, see also Leo Strauss, *Natural Right and History* (Chicago: University of Chicago Press, 1953); Richard Tuck, *Natural Right Theories: Their Origin and Development* (Cambridge: Cambridge University Press, 1979); Michel Villey, *Le Droit et Les Droits de l'Homme* (Paris: Presses Universitaires de France, 1983).

[45] For an analysis of the continuities between the "original" conception of human rights implicit in the first declarations of the end of the eighteenth century and more contemporary theorizations of human rights within the framework of secular academia see Justine Lacroix and Jean-Yves Pranchère, *Human Rights on Trial* (Cambridge: Cambridge University Press, 2018).

this notion more than the core of Catholic social doctrine itself. It is from this perspective that I have maintained that the elements of continuity have trumped the conceptual innovations, and therefore that the Church's current doctrine on human rights is best understood as a form of conceptual co-optation.

This conclusion casts some doubt on the relatively widespread idea that human rights have emerged as the object of an "overlapping consensus" between a plurality of different religious (notably Christian) and philosophical (notably liberal) standpoints.[46] For, if it is to be taken seriously, this thesis would seem to imply that, despite some lingering disagreements over the intellectual grounds for the justification of human rights, Christianity and liberalism should in principle agree on a specific list of such rights, which they both in principle stand for. My analysis shows that is *not* the case, inasmuch as the specific conception of human rights the Catholic Church currently endorses proves to be based on a neo-Thomist conception of natural law irreducibly at odds with the liberal conception of individual autonomy that underpins most secular theories of human rights. Thus, human rights ought perhaps more appropriately be described as the site of an ongoing intellectual and political *struggle*, rather than the object of an "overlapping consensus."

Indeed, this ongoing struggle over the meaning of human rights may perhaps be one of the reasons for their contemporary prominence in both intellectual and political discourse. In commenting on the essential indeterminacy of the notion of the human "person" prior to its appropriation by Catholic thinkers during the first half of the twentieth century, for instance, Samuel Moyn has written that "its ambiguity was, in a sense, its genius; since it signaled the identity of the opposition clearly, while leaving flexibility about what the alternative program was."[47] Although Moyn himself does not extend this logic to the notion of human rights itself, something similar may be said of it too. The "genius" of human rights – and one of the reasons for their contemporary success as a unifying language of politics – may be precisely their indeterminacy – which allows them to function as the terrain of an ongoing political struggle, rather than the weapon of any one side within it. This conclusion should not, however, be allowed to obscure the fact that what is at stake in the contemporary struggle over the meaning of human rights is a concrete political difference that ultimately has to do with whether *freedom* or *authority* is considered the foundation of social order.

[46] See note 8.   [47] Moyn, *Christian Human Rights*, 69.

5 Radical Orthodoxy and the Rebirth of Christian Opposition to Human Rights

Udi Greenberg

Few Christian intellectual movements have drawn as much attention over the past two decades among nonpracticing readers as the Anglo-American school of "radical orthodoxy." Comprised of Catholic and Catholic-inspired writers, it has especially sparked interest among left-leaning scholars, who have found in them a rare Christian ally in the quest to create a more equal and egalitarian world. Indeed, while the group's writings defy simple political labeling, the causes its leaders advocate have often aligned with the left. British theologian John Milbank, for example, radical orthodoxy's most prominent writer, has called for major economical redistribution, international solidarity against atavistic nationalism, and opposition to the West's military interventions in the Middle East. William Cavanaugh, his American counterpart, has mobilized in support of immigration, anti-capitalism, and anti-racism, and has decried American churches' increasing alignment with conservative partisanship. Such positions have helped radical orthodoxy enjoy considerable attention not only among Christian readers but also among several left-leaning audiences. From philosopher and Marxist icon Slavoj Zizek to the British socialist "Blue Labour" think tank, its ideas have been embraced like those of few other theological schools.[1]

The cause that in particular has drawn left-leaning scholars' attention to radical orthodoxy has been its opposition to the concept of human rights, especially the right to religious freedom. According to Milbank and Cavanaugh, the liberal conception of religious rights – the idea that the

---

[1] For the cooperation between Milbank and Zizek, see, for example, their *The Monstrosity of Christ* (Cambridge, MA: MIT Press, 2011); *Theology and the Political: The New Debate* (Durham, NC: Duke University Press, 2005); *Paul's New Moment* (Grand Rapids, MI: Brazos Press, 2010). For Blue Labour's utilization of radical orthodoxy's concepts, see Ian Geary and Adrian Pabst, *Blue Labour: Forging a New Politics* (London: I. B. Tauris, 2015), 256 onward. For the utilization of radical orthodoxy's ideas for the critique of Western foreign policy, especially the War on Terror, see Johannes Grow, "The Perpetual State of Emergency," *Telos* (June 2014): www.telospress.com/the-perpetual-state-of-emergency/.

secular state should guarantee religious equality to all its subjects – was not as liberating as its advocates like to claim. By empowering states to regulate religion, and thus to determine what counts as "healthy" or "appropriate" religious behavior, religious liberty laws in fact deepen state control and inevitably breed discrimination. This line of thinking resonated with a growing group of scholars, such as philosopher Talal Asad, who have criticized religious freedom from the left as a tool of Western oppression and violence, especially against Muslims. It is no accident, these scholars contend, that European courts increasingly invoke religious freedom as justification to ban Muslim clothes (especially the veil) and that American leaders use it as justification to bomb Muslim-majority countries. These deplorable actions, so the argument goes, reveal religious liberty's inherently imperialist and intolerant nature. Asad and others who share his convictions therefore often cite and utilize radical orthodoxy's ideas. The works of Milbank and Cavanaugh seem like a useful ally in the left's quest to establish a truly pluralist and religiously tolerant society in which all groups live as equals.[2]

What has often gone less noted in this intellectual borrowing, however, is the old source on which radical orthodoxy's new critique drew. Alongside its innovations, it also resurrected an old and conservative Catholic intellectual tradition that opposed human rights and religious freedom and denounced them as the product of the Church's worst historical enemy: the Protestant Reformation. Throughout the eighteenth and nineteenth centuries, conservative Catholics sought to discredit liberalism, democracy, and religious liberty (which they saw as intertwined) by tracing them to the Protestants' disastrous assault on the Catholic Church. These modern principles, so the logic went, all emerged from Luther's understanding of faith as a personal matter, which bred animosity toward institutions and communities and ultimately led to moral relativism and nihilism. While this line of thinking, which sometimes assumed a clear moral hierarchy between Catholic teachings and all other religions, was pushed to the margins of Catholic thought in the second half of the twentieth century, radical orthodoxy brought it back to life. Especially Milbank and Cavanaugh attributed the modern era's ills, from neoliberalism to nationalism, to Protestantism and its celebration of religious freedom. This logic enticed Milbank to go as far as suggesting that Europeans abandon the quest for religious equality, especially toward the Muslim minority. The model for healthy spiritual

---

[2] See, for example, Talal Asad, *Formations of the Secular* (Stanford, CA: Stanford University Press, 2003), 178 onward; Elizabeth Shakman-Hurd, *Beyond Religious Freedom* (Princeton, NJ: Princeton University Press, 2015), 59.

life, he claimed, was European medieval Christendom, in which the Catholic majority and religious minorities lived under separate and unequal legal systems. This claim, to be sure, was never embraced by all writers in the orbit of radical orthodoxy. But it put the critique of religious freedom at the service of religious discrimination.

Recognizing the links between earlier Catholic polemics and radical orthodoxy's new critique of religious freedom is valuable for two reasons. First, it contributes to the ongoing debate about the origins and nature of religious liberty. Over the past few years, scholars have claimed to uncover religious freedom's roots in the Reformation, Enlightenment thought, European colonialism, or post–World War II reconstruction. Was it a stable concept, they wondered, whose consequences continued to unfold over decades and centuries, or did its meaning change dramatically over time?[3] What has often been absent from these discussions is the history of opposition to religious freedom. Perhaps the ways in which critiques of rights evolved can help shed light on how thinkers debated and understood these rights. Second, this genealogy can also raise important questions about radical orthodoxy's value for the effort to create a more religious egalitarian society. If Milbank and Cavanaugh's critique of religious freedom sometimes echoes conservative arguments, and in Milbank's case, even comes close to Islamophobia, what does this mean for its emancipatory potential? What would the world look like if religious freedom was indeed removed? Would it open the door for new and more tolerant arrangements, or would it risk the return of older and harsher hierarchies?

Religious Liberty and Protestantism in Catholic Thought

In the years and decades that followed the French Revolution, few concepts sparked as much anxiety among Catholic thinkers as the right to religious liberty. The Church, theologians and popes proclaimed, may tolerate some of the "rights of man and citizen" announced by the revolutionaries, but it could certainly not accept the notion that the state should remain neutral in religious matters.[4] According to Catholic

---

[3] For a few prominent examples from this vast scholarship, see, for example, John Witte, *The Reformation of Rights: Law, Religion, and Human Rights in Early Modern Calvinism* (New York: Cambridge University Press, 2007); Joan Scott, *The Politics of the Veil* (Princeton, NJ: Princeton University Press, 2007); Samuel Moyn, *Christian Human Rights* (Philadelphia: University of Pennsylvania Press, 2015); Linde Lindkvist, *Religious Freedom and the Universal Declaration of Human Rights* (New York: Cambridge University Press, 2017).

[4] On the early Catholic debates regarding human rights, see Dan Edelstein, "Christian Human Rights in the French Revolution," *Journal of the History of Ideas* 79, no. 3 (2018), 411–426.

dogma, the Church and its hierarchies represented God's truth on earth; it was therefore its duty to repress "heresies" and impose its teachings through state institutions, to use them as the Vatican's "secular arm." The price of succumbing to religious freedom appeared especially clear after the abolition of Catholicism's special status as state religion was quickly followed with horrifying anticlerical violence. For many, it seemed self-evident that religious liberty was the Revolution's worst and most lasting legacy, one bound to breed indifferentism, nihilism, and anarchy. For the rest of the nineteenth century, opposing religious freedom thus remained central to the Church's teaching. From Pope Gregory XVI's *Mirari vos* (1832) to Pius IX's *Syllabus of Errors* (1864), pontiffs routinely wondered if there was "any sane man who would say poison ought to be distributed [and] sold publicly ... because some antidote is available and those who use it may be snatched from death again and again?"[5] If the Church was occasionally willing to suspend this norm and endorse state neutrality in religious matters, it was only in countries where Catholics formed a minority, like Britain. Formally, tolerance was a strategic concession, a temporary arrangement until Catholic dominance could be established.[6]

This opposition to religious liberty, however, was animated not only by the rejection of new liberal and secular principles. If many conservative Catholics recoiled at the Revolution and its ideas, it was in part because they saw it as a cover for Protestantism, the church's historic enemy, and its centuries-old quest to destroy Catholicism. As early as 1791, the Catholic pamphlet *The Causes and Agents of the Revolution in France* lamented that a secret "league" or "cabal" of Protestants plotted the Revolution in order to bring the Church's downfall. Another pamphlet decried the Revolution's hostility to the monarchy, the Church's political ally, and claimed it "reeked" of "Luther and Calvin."[7] The conflation of modern republicanism with the Reformation quickly spread and became the mainstream in the circles of the right's "counter-Enlightenment." Philosopher Joseph de Maistre, one of conservative Catholicism's leading lights, explained in 1798 that the Protestants' assault on the Church devastated their belief in any order and hierarchy and was responsible

---

[5] The quote is from Gregory XVI, *Mirari vos* (August 15, 1832): www.papalencyclicals.net/Greg16/g16mirar.htm.

[6] For helpful background, see, for example, Joseph A. Komonchak, "Religious Freedom and the Confessional State: A Twentieth Century Discussion," *Revue d'Histoire Ecclésiastique* 95 (2000), 634–650.

[7] Cited in Bryan Banks, "The Protestant Origins of the French Revolution," *Journal of the Western Society for French History* 42 (2014), 65–74, here 68.

for the Revolution's ultimate turn to terror.[8] Throughout the nineteenth century, freedom of religion in particular stood at the center of this narrative, evidence of Luther's devastating legacy in the modern world. The Reformation, several polemicists claimed, with its belief in every believer's access to divine teachings through the Bible, conceived of religion as a private matter. Rather than tradition or institutions, it was individual belief that mattered and determined the truth; no authority could claim superior access to God's will. For traditionalists like Catalan theologian Jaume Balmes, this was why Protestants' ultimate goal, which continued to animate secular revolutionaries, was to force religion out of the public sphere, strip it of its communal elements, and empty it of any claim to objective truth. As he explained in his hugely popular *Protestantism and Catholicity Compared* (1842), Protestantism's conception of religious freedom was an extension of its "nihilism" and part of its diabolical plan to destroy religion altogether.[9]

The persistence of such beliefs meant that the proliferation of liberal constitutions after World War I in Europe, and their enshrining of religious liberty, only further sustained Catholic anxieties about a Protestant infiltration. Widely read works of Catholic thought, such as Jacques Maritain's *Three Reformers* (1925) or Henri Massis's *Defense of the West* (1927), went so far to claim that the Luther-inspired notion of religious neutrality continued to breed new anti-Christian forces, especially "Godless" Communism.[10] Such conflation of religious freedom, Protestantism, and Communism proved so popular that it survived World War II and reemerged in the early Cold War, even as Catholics strategically deployed religious freedom against Communist persecutions. In 1953, in a spectacular and highly publicized address in Rome, Secretary of the Holy Office Cardinal Alfredo Ottaviani explained why the Church should continue to oppose universal freedom of religion and could use it only as a temporary tool where it was in the minority. Such resistance, he claimed, was necessary so Catholic countries such as Spain and Italy would legally expel Protestant missionaries (which they

---

[8] See, for example, Joseph de Maistre, "Reflections on Protestantism in its Relations to Sovereignty," in *Critics of the Enlightenment*, ed. Christopher Olaf Blum (Wilmington, DE: ISI Books, 2004), 133–156; J. M. Roberts, "The Origins of a Mythology: Freemasons, Protestants, and the French Revolution," *Bulletin of the Institute of Historical Research* 44 (1971), 80–93; and Darrin M. McMahon, *Enemies of the Enlightenment: The French Counter-Enlightenment and the Making of Modernity* (New York: Oxford University Press, 2001), esp. 77–80.

[9] Jaume [Jaime] Balmes, *European Civilization: Protestantism and Catholicity Compared in Their Effects on the Civilization of Europe* (Baltimore, MD: Murphy, 1851 [1842]).

[10] Jacques Maritain, *Three Reformers* (London: Sheed & Ward, 1926); Henri Massis, *Defense of the West* (New York: Harcourt, 1928).

routinely did in the 1950s). According to Ottaviani, Protestant missions sought to inject their notions of neutrality into the body of Christian states and were thus analogous to Communist spies, which Western countries also expelled. In fact, Ottaviani claimed anti-Protestantism and anti-Communism were not merely analogous, but virtually the same. "The majority of 'converts'" to Protestantism in Italy and Spain, he scoffed, were "authentic Communists."[11]

Such harsh rhetoric, however, could not hide the sea change that by that point was undermining Catholic opposition to both Protestantism and religious freedom. As James Chappel and others have recently shown, the 1930s and 1940s, and the experience of facing Europe's brutal dictatorships, produced new thinking among Catholics, especially toward other Christians. For many, Nazism's violent efforts at biological engineering and especially Communism's frightening expansion in the early Cold War made previous enemies such as Protestants and liberals look less threatening than before. Perhaps, some Catholic thinkers now wondered, they should be regarded as allies. In this new environment, Catholics began to shed their opposition to both Protestantism and religious liberty. Catholic politicians such as West German chancellor Konrad Adenuaer founded joint Catholic-Protestant and anti-Communist parties; theologians such as Yves Congar and John Courtney Murray led a crusade to change Catholic thought on state-Church relations. In the 1960s, these campaigns reached a successful conclusion when the Catholic Church embraced their causes as its formal dogma. Gathering for the Second Vatican Council in Rome, the bishops declared Protestants "brethren in faith" (in 1964) and then accepted religious liberty as compatible with the Church's teachings (in 1965).[12]

By the beginning of the twenty-first century, peace with Protestants and religious liberty were so widely accepted that even conservative hard-liners celebrated them. In fact, religious freedom became a mutual battle cry of both conservative Catholics and Protestant evangelicals, who became allies in the evolving culture wars and invoked freedom of religion for a variety of joint causes, from opposition to same-sex marriage to

---

[11] Alfredo Ottaviani, *Duties of the Catholic State in Regard to Religion* (Kansas City, MO: Angelus Press, 1954), 23.

[12] On the 1930s and 1940s, see James Chappel, *Catholic Modern: The Challenge of Totalitarianism and the Remaking of the Church* (Cambridge, MA: Harvard University Press, 2018), and Moyn, *Christian Human Rights*. On Vatican II, see, for example, John W. O'Malley, *What Happened in Vatican II* (Cambridge, MA: Belknap/Harvard University Press, 2008); Giuseppe Alberigo and Joseph A. Komonchak, *History of Vatican II* (Maryknoll, NY: Peeters, 2003). I discuss the links between Catholic thinking about religious freedom and Protestantism in "Catholics, Protestants, and the Tortured Path to Religious Liberty," *Journal of the History of Ideas* 79, no. 3 (July 2018), 461–479.

public funding of church playgrounds. In 2012, this new consensus received an especially forceful articulation, when a group called "Evangelicals and Catholics Together" published an impassioned statement against US employers' legal duty to provide contraception as part of their workers' healthcare coverage. Signed by hundreds of church leaders and prominent theologians, it claimed religious freedom had *always* been a cherished Christian principle that both Catholics and Protestants should forever defend.[13] For a moment, it seemed that accommodating Protestants and religious liberty became a Catholic consensus. The long intellectual campaign against both seemed to be fading from memory.

Radical Orthodoxy and the Critique of Rights

Yet it was exactly at that moment, when the Catholic commitment to religious freedom seemed secure, that the newly created movement of radical orthodoxy began to question it. According to the writers of this group, the Catholic Church's postwar compromise with liberalism and religious freedom had come at an enormous cost. By accepting liberalism's relegation of religion to the private sphere and its insistence that public policy be shaped without reliance on religious logic, Catholics had diminished their ability to advocate for important causes from immigration to climate change. Even worse, by making peace with religious liberty, Catholics had accepted the discrimination that liberalism inadvertently breeds. They granted state institutions the authority to regulate religion, which sooner or later it was bound to use against them. While this line of thinking both echoed and resonated with a left-leaning critique of human rights, it drew from the tradition of conservative Catholic thinkers. Without mentioning de Maistre or Balmes, radical orthodoxy resurrected elements of their logic. As was the case for those earlier critics, writers associated with radical orthodoxy described religious liberty as part of Protestantism's heretical and tragic legacy. And at least for one prominent member of this school, the conclusion of this narrative pointed to anti-egalitarian notions of religious hierarchies.

The first and most prominent writer to point in this direction was British Anglican theologian John Milbank, who strongly identified with the Catholic tradition. First in his tome *Theology and Social Theory* (1991), and in multiple essays since, he outlined what would become the main critique of religious freedom from the left: the claim that the liberal conception of rights imposed an individualist concept on what were

---

[13] Evangelicals and Catholics Together, "In Defense of Religious Freedom," *First Things* (March 2012): www.firstthings.com/article/2012/03/in-defense-of-religious-freedom.

communitarian ideals. According to Milbank, liberalism and Catholic Christianity held profoundly dissimilar views of human relations, politics, and legitimacy, and indeed of human nature itself. While liberalism celebrated individual autonomy and independence as the basis for all collective order, the Catholic Church believed humans can live meaningfully only as members of larger collectives, such as family, profession, or communities (whether local, national, or regional). This difference is best reflected in the concepts that undergird their respective political theories. While liberals maintain that society should protect individuals' "rights," Catholics are interested in defending "dignity," a term that for Milbank signifies a person's membership in a community. In Milbank's telling, if the Catholic Church has claimed since the Second Vatican Council that individual rights and Catholic dogma are compatible, this was an unfortunate mistake. The Catholic reforms "concede[d] too much to liberal democracy," he explained, because "Catholicism remains at bottom incompatible with liberal notions of rights and democracy." In fact, any effort at reconciling the two was bound to fail. "Right and dignity stand for two radically opposed political philosophies and indeed for the two *most* opposed political philosophies."[14]

Nowhere is this tension between liberalism and Christianity more apparent for Milbank than in the principle of religious liberty. In their obsession with individual autonomy, Milbank maintained, liberals conceive religious freedom as a protection from any pressure to conform to religious norms. Instead of accepting religious communities' rights to promote their vision of collective life – for example, restricting marriage to heterosexual couples or banning assisted suicide – they have come to view any form of collective religious advocacy as an "inevitable infringement on the non-negotiable rights of others, whether as human beings or as citizens." This approach predictably diminished religious authorities' legitimate demand that individuals follow their group's religious teachings. Secular liberals may "allow group rights up to a point, but in the end, individual rights are foundational and must prevail." In their thinking, "why should the rules of a religious body ever be allowed to override the political and natural rights of a member of that body?" For Milbank, this attitude meant that liberalism, by its very logic, was bound to encroach on religious communities until it eradicated their ability to make any meaningful demands from their members. "A pure secularism of voided

---

[14] See, for example, John Milbank, *Theology and Social Theory: Beyond Secular Reason* (Oxford: Blackwell, 2006), and "Against Human Rights: Liberty in the Western Tradition," *Oxford Journal of Law and Religion* 1, no. 1 (2012), 203–234. The quotes are from "Dignity Rather than Right," *Revista de filosofia Open Insight*, 4, no. 7 (January 2014), 77–124.

content," he warned, "where only the language of rights counts as to value, would seem to require a tolerance so open as to disallow the authenticity of any traditional religion committed to a primarily communal identity." Religious liberty, then, was far from a tool of tolerance. If anything, it was an engine for anti-religious, and in particular anti-Christian discrimination. Indeed, Milbank decried liberals for their alleged hypocrisy in enforcing secular principles, which he claimed were always directed against Christians but rarely against Muslims. That they were scandalized by bans on the Muslim veil but would advocate for preventing Christmas celebrations from taking place in public spaces showed how much their animosity was ultimately anti-Christian.[15]

An equally blistering attack was soon launched by American Catholic theologian William Cavanaugh, who helped popularize radical orthodoxy's message among anthropologists, political scientists, and legal scholars. In several books and essays, Cavanaugh has traced liberal writers' conception of religion as a primitive, irrational, and violent force. It was this vision, he lamented, that led them to support the regulation of religious practice – for example, prohibiting churches' partisan advocacy in the United States – and to view such regulation as necessary for peace and progress. Cavanaugh, however, employed Michel Foucault's critique of liberalism to maintain that the result was ironically increased oppression. The more state authorities intervened in religious matters, the deeper they infiltrated their subjects' intimate and spiritual lives, rewarding loyalty to state institutions and punishing dissent. Modern and liberal regulation belief and rites, then, was not substantially different than its increasing control over labor, health, or sexuality. It was part and parcel of states' alarming quest to produce a complement, productive, and obedient subject.[16]

To drive the point home, Cavanaugh also radically challenged the key historical narrative that liberals have often utilized to justify their call for religious control, about the birth of religious liberty from the bloody religious conflicts of the sixteenth and seventeenth centuries. Rather than clashes between fanatical Christians that were followed by peaceful religious state neutrality, he wrote in his much-discussed *The Myth of Religious Violence* (2009), those wars *resulted* from declining religious authority and increasing secular state power. In this revisionist telling,

---

[15] John Milbank, "The End of Tolerance: The Decline of Religious Freedom and the Return of Religious Influence," *ABC Religion & Ethics* (August 24, 2017): www .abc.net.au/religion/articles/2017/08/24/4723769.htm (unpaginated). For similar claims, see also his "Against Human Rights."

[16] William T. Cavanaugh, *Torture and the Eucharist: Theology, Politics, and the Body of Christ* (Oxford: Blackwell, 1998), esp. 77–79, 101–102.

early modern states sought to take over churches' wealth and authority, especially the loyalty of their subjects. In the process, they "exacerbated and enforced ecclesial differences, ultimately breeding religious warfare." In fact, these massacres and military clashes were a symptom, and not a cause, of the emerging liberal division between the "secular" and "religious" spheres, which did not exist beforehand. Their violence was meant to guarantee the states' control over politics and economics while limiting the churches' authorities to the private sphere, where they could regulate beliefs, rites, and family relations, but nothing more. "The so-called wars of religion," he bluntly wrote, "appear as wars fought by state-building elites for the purpose of consolidating their power over the church and other rivals." The states that ultimately emerged from these wars were therefore not religiously neutral, but more powerful than ever, and with increased aspirations to dominate their subjects' lives. As he put it, "the state did not rein in and tame religion but became itself sacralized." For Cavanaugh, this genealogy showed that current-day liberals were not promoting freedom. Unknowingly, they helped further the long project of expanding state power.[17]

As was the case for Milbank, religious liberty encapsulated in Cavanaugh's eyes liberalism's most damaging consequences for believers. According to Cavanaugh, in their campaign to acquire total control over their citizens, states have increasingly narrowed their definition of "legitimate" religious practice entitled to legal protection. Churches and communities, which were sources of competing authority, lost their ability to claim legal rights; only individuals could invoke religious freedom as a tool against oppression. As a result, religion risked becoming a strictly private matter. Instead of a set of collective rules, norms, and rituals, states and believers mistakenly viewed religion as an individual preference with no bearing on collective political or economic issues. For Cavanaugh, this meant that Christians had to oppose the logic and language of religious freedom. If they accepted it, he warned, they were implicitly accepting the individualist conception of religion, abandoning claims for collective or corporal rights, and thus forfeiting their ability to use the Church's teaching to mold state laws in fields such as economics, healthcare, or immigration. To be sure, utilizing religious liberty may have tactical value. It may, for example, allow Catholic employers to claim exemptions from state requirements that they provide contraception to women (a demand Cavanaugh supported). Yet, according to

[17] William T. Cavanaugh, *Myth of Religious Violence: Secular Ideology and the Roots of Modern Conflict* (New York: Oxford University Press, 2008), 162, 177. The claim also appears in his *Theopolitical Imagination: Christian Practice of Space and Time* (New York: Bloomsbury, 2002), esp. 9–52.

Cavanaugh, the price of such small victories was far too high. Accepting the logic of individual rights denied the Church the ability to promote its broader vision of collective human good; for example, it could not justify comprehensive immigration reform or radical economic redistribution (both causes Cavanaugh also supported). For Cavanaugh, all of this meant that freedom of religion, rather than protecting and empowering Christians, in fact crippled their action. As he put it in his *Field Hospital* (2016), "we need more than an appeal to freedom of belief ... we need a robust defense of the idea that our God is the God of all creation," and whose laws should shape every citizen's life.[18]

While these claims gained Milbank and Cavanaugh considerable enthusiasm from scholars on the left, what has gone less noticed is the homology of their historical narratives and earlier Catholic critique of religious liberty. Like de Maistre or Balmes before them, writers associated with radical orthodoxy routinely drew on anti-Lutheran polemics to show that state neutrality in religious matters is never neutral; it is the product of and a cover for Protestantism's perversity. Milbank's *Theology and Social Theory*, for example, was laced with denunciation of Luther's responsibility for secularism. "The Protestant Reformation," he decried, "completely privatized ... the sacred and concurrently reimagined human action and society as a sphere of autonomous, sheerly formal power," leading to today's spiritual wasteland.[19] For Milbank, who associated his own Anglican Church more with traditional Catholicism than with the Protestant schism, the reformers drew from earlier Christian developments (especially the school of nominalism) to remove ethics and politics from divine authority, and thus led to secularization. As he put it, Luther's "religious reform ironically ran the danger of encouraging secularization, since it unintentionally suggested the possibility of an ethical and political order without God." In fact, like the counterrevolutionaries of the eighteenth and nineteenth centuries before him, Milbank attributed all the malaise of the modern world to Protestant teachings. "The Reformation and its legacy," he thundered, were the "disaster that broke Europe apart, as it today incipiently remains, and blinded us to nature's real enchantment, at the same time and from the outset."[20]

---

[18] William T. Cavanaugh, *Field Hospital* (Grand Rapids, MI: Eerdmans, 2016), esp. 234–248, here 244, 246, 247.

[19] Milbank, *Theology and Social Theory*, 9.

[20] The quote is from Milbank, "The End of Tolerance." See also his "Alternative Protestantism: Radical Orthodoxy and the Reformed Tradition," in *Radical Orthodoxy and the Reformed Tradition: Creation, Covenant, and Participation* (Grand Rapids, MI: Baker Academic, 2005), 25–41.

Cavanaugh similarly traced the menace of religious liberty to Luther. The reformers, he mourned in *Field Hospital*, devastated spiritual and institutional authority. By celebrating the individual's ability to access God through scripture, they undermined the right of churches, hierarchies, and institutions to have privileged access to truth, and thus to enjoy religious, legal, or political privileges. For Cavanaugh, this was the ideology that produced "the modern conception of rights as inhering in individuals and the modern conception of religion as a matter of individual personal preference." Like Milbank, Cavanagh proclaimed that this development had ominous consequences even beyond the specific threat it posed to Catholicism. If individuals could decide for themselves how to understand the Gospel, he claimed, there was no basis on which any notion of collective good could be based, which was bound to lead to moral relativism. Cavanaugh thus warned that the consequence of this process was the weakening of social solidarities and groups of any kind, and their replacement by all-controlling states. The Reformation's worst legacy was "the debilitation of any intermediate associations that stood between the state and the individual, because they were the only bearers of shared notions of the good … the real conflict in modern political history has not been, as is so often stated, between State and individual, but between State and social group."[21]

Indeed, radical orthodoxy both reflected and helped fuel the rebirth of Catholic polemics against Protestantism and its legacies. Reversing half a century of inter-confessional peace, several Catholic writers resurrected in the early twenty-first century the stark dichotomies of earlier eras: the notion that Catholics defend communitarian models, while Protestants (and everyone who subscribes to modern ideas) are deeply individualists, which directly feeds into confusion and nihilism. No one articulated this new intellectual agenda more than historian Brad Gregory, whose *The Unintended Reformation* (2012) and *Rebel in the Ranks* (2017) marked the apogee of the revival of Catholic polemics (and enjoyed lengthy appreciations from Milbank and Cavanaugh). Luther, Gregory maintained, with his principle of *sola scriptura*, unleashed centuries of doubt regarding institutions and traditions' ability to teach the truth. This directly led to the French Revolution, to modern bureaucratic state power, and to our own "Kingdom of Whatever," an atomized and consumption-obsessed society in which no one cares about values. For Gregory, the Protestant principle of religious liberty was at the very heart of this unfolding catastrophe. "Because *individuals* disagreed about the meaning of God's

---

[21] Cavanaugh, *Field Hospital*, 244.

word," he lamented, "*individuals* ... had to be the bearers of rights, beginning with the right to religious liberty."[22]

This reliance on anti-Protestant tropes reflected more than superficial similarities between earlier and current writings. Milbank utilized the logic of earlier anti-Protestant polemicists and their opposition to religious hierarchies to reflect on contemporary tensions, most importantly between Christianity and Islam. In his most recent writings, Milbank claimed that Christians' most urgent dilemma was their relationship to Europe's Muslim communities. This was not due to European states' panicked efforts to criminalize Muslim clothes (like the veil) and rituals, as many left-leaning writers complained. On the contrary, the problem was the threat that Islam, "this nomadic and imperial religion," posed to Christians. In Milbank's telling, because secular liberals found no value in Christianity and its heritage, they allowed Islam to establish a "sub-polity under Shari'a law within European cities." European courts and governments, despite some faint efforts at taming extremism, granted Muslim clerics religious liberty and allowed the imposition of Islam's "strict requirements for fasting, food preparation, segregation of men and women, [and] tendencies of dress" on entire populations. For Milbank, this dystopian reality proved the inability to establish true equality between religions, even under the liberal principle of religious liberty. It was natural for religious communities to express their teachings in the public sphere, and if one (Christianity) were denied this right, others (Islam) would soon replace it.[23]

For Milbank, therefore, Christianity's survival depended not only on dislodging the liberal notions of equal rights, but on their replacement with a different legal model, which would draw on Europe's Middle Ages. According to Milbank, the time had come to discard what he called liberalism's "simple space," where one universal law applies equally to all citizens. In its place, he suggested a "complex" or "gothic space," which would replicate medieval Christendom's system in which individual rights and privileges were tied to certain groups and communities. While in Milbank's earlier writings, "complex space" was meant to encourage economic distribution and solidarity,

---

[22] Brad Gregory, *The Unintended Reformation: How a Religious Revolution Secularized Society* (Cambridge, MA: Belknap/Harvard University Press, 2012), 215. See also his *Rebel in the Ranks: Martin Luther, the Reformation, and the Conflicts That Continue to Shape Our World* (New York: Harper, 2017).

[23] John Milbank, "Shari'a and the True Basis of Group Rights: Islam, the West, and Liberalism," in *Shari'a in the West*, ed. Rex Ahdar and Nicholas Aroney (Oxford: Oxford University Press, 2013), 43–58. See also Milbank, "The End of Tolerance."

more recently its purpose has been to establish religious differences.[24] In a post-secular Europe, he explained, Christianity would regain its privileged position in organizing collective lives: it would dictate religious holidays, marriage laws, and education policies. In turn, non-Christian communities would be granted some autonomy – say to manage their own marriage laws – but would accept a secondary status. They would be allowed to run their own businesses according to their traditions, but would not be able to shape the majority's lives or demand equal footing in public affairs. For Milbank, such an attitude was not a vision for a utopic or distant future, but "should govern our treatment *today* of Islam in the West . . . It is not deplorable that our Western sense of what valid religion consists in is an inherently Christian one."[25]

To be sure, not all writers associated with radical orthodoxy share these sentiments. And Cavanaugh, even though he has not written in detail on Christian-Muslim relations, has harshly criticized those who attribute inherently violent impulses to Muslim communities.[26] Yet in Milbank's writings, radical orthodoxy has been put to the service of very old traditions. It has joined the more conservative wing of the Catholic Church, which once again has been calling for the enshrinement of Catholic doctrine into legal documents. No one represented this way of thinking more forcefully than Joseph Ratzinger (later Pope Benedict XVI), who explained in 2004 why Christianity must become the heart and center of a then-planned European constitution, even at the expense of equality to its Muslim minority. Secular Europeans' failure to "embrace our own heritage of the sacred," he bemoaned, is not only a denial of "the identity of Europe," but the product of "a peculiar Western self-hatred that is nothing short of pathological." Milbank and Ratzinger may depart on other issues, but on that point, they were in agreement. Once again, state laws and the notion of collective rights have been conceived as the faith's "secular arm."[27]

Conclusion

The ways in which writers associated with radical orthodoxy have revived Catholic polemics against Protestantism, and then, in Milbank's case, used it in order to justify clear hierarchies between Christians and

---

[24] John Milbank, "On Complex Space," in *The Word Made Strange: Theology, Language, and Culture* (Oxford: Blackwell, 1997), 268–292.

[25] Milbank, "The End of Tolerance."

[26] See, for example, his *The Myth of Religious Violence*, esp. 211–230.

[27] Joseph Ratzinger, "The Spiritual Roots of Europe: Yesterday, Today, and Tomorrow," in *Without Roots: The West, Relativism, Christianity, Islam*, ed. Joseph Ratzinger and Marcello Pera (New York: Basic Books, 2006), 51–80, here 78–79.

Muslims, has implications beyond contemporary Christian thought. For Milbank and Cavanaugh's ideas have enjoyed special resonance among left-leaning critics of religious freedom, who seek to establish a more religiously egalitarian world. Progressive writers like Saba Mahmood and Elizabeth Shakman-Hurd, for example, despite the considerable differences between them, have echoed the claim that religious liberty emerged from Protestantism's uniquely individualist conception of religion. It was in part for this reason, they lament, that its export beyond Protestant-majority countries often fosters discrimination and violence. Talal Asad, perhaps secularism's most prominent critic, went so far as to adopt Milbank's concepts in an effort to imagine a legal order more hospitable to Muslims in Europe. Milbank's "complex space," he wrote in his pathbreaking *Formations of the Secular* (2003), in which religious groups would be granted special rights, provides the key to a more equal future.[28]

Given Milbank's own prescription for Christian-Muslim relations, there is considerable irony in this intellectual borrowing. Indeed, while the progressive critique of religious freedom has powerfully highlighted its potentially discriminatory consequences, it has not always recognized the tradition it may end up serving. Conservative Catholics, after all, were the first to decry religious liberty – and secularism as a whole – as Protestantism's dark legacy. And, according to this tradition, the alternative has to be a harshly hierarchical model. Of course, sharing the diagnosis for secularism's limits does not mean sharing the proposed solution. The horizons of religious freedom's progressive critics, after all, is the formation of a truly egalitarian future. Still, it is worth wondering if the persistent presence of hierarchical tradition in some contemporary writing does not shows the dangers that potentially await in a world beyond religious freedom. If states were to recognize its imperfections and abolish religious legal protections, can we be sure that a more inclusive and tolerant world awaits?

It may be, then, that for the critique of religious freedom to advance its cause, it would have to depart from its condemnation of religious freedom as a rigid concept that cannot be freed of its strict Protestant origins. If the Catholic dogma on religion and law can be reformed in the mid-twentieth century, why can secular religious laws not be transformed and expanded to respond to a new era? There is no obvious reason why progressive lawyers and thinkers cannot redefine it to include more religious

---

[28] Saba Mahmood, *Religious Freedom in a Secular Age: A Minority Report* (Princeton, NJ: Princeton University Press, 2015); Hurd, *Beyond Religious Freedom*; Talal Asad, *Formations of the Secular*, 187 onward.

practices. And there is no reason that social activism cannot pressure courts to embrace such measures and defend previously marginalized minorities (just as they have successfully done in expanding the once-narrowly heterosexual definition of marriage). Like their critiques, the right of religious freedom and secularism as a whole can be both reactionary and progressive, geared toward both inclusion and exclusion. Perhaps what is needed is not their discarding but their extension, without the polemical narratives that for two centuries have uncovered their liberating potential.

6 The Biopolitics of Dignity

Camille Robcis

> Let us not allow, within a free nation, monuments of slavery, even voluntary.
> – Pierre Anastase Torné, French deputy, April 6, 1792

A few days after the shocking attacks on the offices of *Charlie Hebdo* in January 2015, several French political leaders called for the revival of the "crime of national indignity" as a possible sanction against terrorists of French citizenship.[1] As Prime Minister Manuel Valls put it, such a measure – backed up, according to surveys, by 76 percent of the French population – would "mark with symbolic force the consequences of the absolute transgression that a terrorist act constitutes."[2] Under French law, national indignity did indeed have a particular history and signification, one that was not simply "symbolic" but in fact quite concrete. As historian Anne Simonin shows, "national indignity" was invented in 1944 by the legal experts of the Resistance as an exceptional measure to punish, retroactively, the supporters of the Vichy regime who had collaborated with the Nazi occupiers and promoted anti-Semitic legislation. Between 1945 and 1951, around 100,000 citizens were accused of indignity and punished by "national degradation." In practical terms, this meant that they were stripped of their civic rights and their possessions, banned from exercising certain public positions and professions (lawyers, bankers, teachers), and forbidden to live in particular regions of France. National indignity was an alternative to prison and to

---

[1] This piece appeared in a slightly modified version as "The Biopolitics of Dignity," *South Atlantic Quarterly* 115, no. 2 (April 2016), 313–330. I am grateful to the editors, Richard Keller and Sara Guyer, for encouraging me to write this piece and also to Carolyn Dean, Charlotte Duc-Bragues, Stéphanie Hennette-Vauchez, Mitchel Lasser, Samuel Moyn, Bruno Perreau, Aziz Rana, Todd Shepard, Miranda Spieler, Judith Surkis, and Caterina Toscano for all their advice, comments, and suggestions. All translations from the French are mine unless otherwise indicated.

[2] Geoffroy Clavel, "Terrorisme: 76% des Français pour l'indignité nationale, les mesures du gouvernement jugées 'appropriées.'" *Huffington Post* (February 5, 2015): www.huffing tonpost.fr/2015/02/05/terrorisme-indignite-nationale-mesures-gouvernement-appro priees_n_6612898.html?utm_hp_ref=france.

the death penalty that nonetheless imposed a form of "social or civic death," to use Simonin's terms. Although political indignity was originally formulated during the Terror as the antithesis of fraternity (primarily to convict émigrés and to justify the guillotine for those who conspired against the Republic), it was reimagined during the Liberation as a moral politics, as a way to "purge" the Vichy heritage and to purify the Republic. As Simonin writes, national indignity served to codify the crime of *lèse-République* and to single out the new figure of the internal enemy: the *vichyiste*.[3]

Given this history, it is easy to understand why so many French politicians invoked national indignity in the aftermath of the national trauma that *Charlie Hebdo* represented. Indignity appeared as a perfect tool, in a state of exception, to punish the new internal enemy who had attacked the Republic: the terrorist. But if indignity was linked in both cases to the revival of the Republic, by 2015 the notion was also deeply entangled with the question of national belonging. Indeed, none of the perpetrators of the *Charlie Hebdo* attacks was a foreign citizen. Saïd Kouachi, his brother Chérif Kouachi, and Amedy Coulibaly were all born and raised in France. Yet, in the weeks after the murders, much of the conversation focused on the social origins of these three young men: where they were born, where they grew up, where they traveled, where they converted to Islam, why they had failed to integrate or why France had failed to integrate them. This was the context in which the right demanded that the government strip away French citizenship from any terrorist who might hold a second nationality, and in which several political leaders proposed to resuscitate national indignity for French citizens convicted of terrorism.[4] In effect, national indignity could bring about a form of "civic death" targeted at French jihadists – Coulibaly and the Kouachi brothers, for example. More specifically, national indignity offered the government a legal way to expel French citizens from the national community without violating the Universal Declaration of Human Rights, which affirms the "right to a nationality" and explicitly forbids any nation from "arbitrarily depriving" someone of his or her nationality – a concern particularly salient for the writers of this 1948 document given the fate of European Jews during World War II.[5]

---

[3] Anne Simonin, *Le déshonneur dans la République: une histoire de l'indignité, 1791–1958* (Paris: Bernard Grasset, 2008), 20.

[4] "L'"indignité nationale', une piste envisagée par l'Élysée," *Le Figaro* (January 20, 2015): www.lefigaro.fr/politique/2015/01/20/01002-20150120ARTFIG00087-l-indignite-natio nale-une-piste-envisagee-par-l-elysee.php.

[5] www.un.org/en/documents/udhr/. Hannah Arendt famously addressed the relationship between statelessness, rights of man, and dignity in her 1951 *The Origins of Totalitarianism*.

My interest in these recent discussions of national indignity is that they bring to light the historical, legal, and political ties between dignity, security, public order, and citizenship. Although this longer history of the Liberation is crucial to explain the current return to indignity, the history of dignity in French law is also extremely revealing. Indeed, throughout the 1990s, the notion of "human dignity" flourished in French legal, political, and intellectual circles. Even though a handful of scholars cautioned against this sudden enthusiasm, academic journals, experts, politicians, and lawyers referred to human dignity as the self-evident, transcendental, and inalienable foundation of the individual and of society.[6] To be sure, French judges and legal scholars were not alone in their celebration of human dignity. In recent years, courts in Canada, South Africa, India, Mexico, and many other countries have grounded their rulings in the unquestionable principle of human dignity, and various constitutions written recently have chosen to foreground the notion. The European Court of Human Rights has been referring to dignity for years now, and the first article of the 2000 European Charter of Fundamental Rights, modeled on the 1949 German Basic Law, posits human dignity as "inviolable."[7] In the United States, the Supreme Court has appealed to dignity in many of its recent decisions, for example, in *Lawrence* v. *Texas*, which in 2003 struck down sodomy laws and reaffirmed the dignity of homosexuals in their "intimate and personal choices," and most recently, in *Obergefell* v. *Hodges*, which emphasized the "equal dignity" of same-sex couples in the eyes of the law as it legalized same-sex marriage throughout the United States.[8]

In its current formulation, dignity appears remarkably simple, since it posits that we should value the human person simply because he or she is human. Yet, as many scholars point out, the concept has been used on both sides of some of the most controversial debates – abortion, assisted

Simonin also warned against the reestablishing of national indignity to punish terrorists in the aftermath of *Charlie Hebdo* because it would create "non-subjects of law": "Indignité nationale: 'La France aurait beaucoup à perdre,'" *Le Monde* (January 22, 2015): www .lemonde.fr/politique/article/2015/01/22/indignite-nationale-la-france-aurait-beaucoup-a-perdre_4561226_823448.html.

[6] Among the first critiques of human dignity in France, we can list the following examples: Marcela Iacub, *Le crime était presque sexuel et autres essais de casuistique juridique* (Paris: EPEL, 2002); Denys de Béchillon, "Porter atteinte aux catégories anthropologiques fondamentales?" *Revue Trimestrielle de Droit Civil* (2002); Cayla Olivier and Thomas Yan, *Du droit de ne pas naître: à propos de l'affaire Perruche* (Paris: Gallimard, 2002); Charlotte Girard and Stéphanie Hennette-Vauchez, *La dignité de la personne humaine: recherche sur le processus de juridicisation* (Paris: Presses universitaires de France, 2005).

[7] www.europarl.europa.eu/charter/pdf/text_en.pdf.

[8] www.law.cornell.edu/supct/html/02-102.ZO.html.

suicide, bioethics, gay rights, freedom of expression – to argue exactly opposite cases.[9] As Reva Siegel highlights, lawyers have turned to dignity to defend a woman's right to an abortion but also to protect the fetus; to argue for gay rights such as marriage but also to forbid them as violations of the most basic social norms.[10] Sometimes dignity operates as a synonym or corollary of human rights, other times as a tool to limit them. Hence, much of the recent debate over dignity in the United States – at least in the fields of philosophy and of law – has focused on whether the notion is, can be, or should be normatively useful.[11]

My own interest in dignity is neither legal nor philosophical but historical. More specifically, my goal in this chapter is to trace the genealogy through which dignity in France has come to be associated with national belonging and public order, as evidenced in the example of *Charlie Hebdo*. My argument is thus twofold. First, I want to suggest that the notion of dignity circulating in French law since the 1990s is a corporatist one. Rather than promote abstract individual freedom, this notion of dignity insists on the obligations that the individual has toward the community, toward the social, and, in its most recent formulations, toward France. In this sense, the French version of dignity is theoretically much closer to that of political Catholicism and personalism than to the Kantian or liberal understanding of dignity (such as the one underpinning Anthony Kennedy's opinions in recent years).[12]

Although dignity in France has been used to gain a few specific rights (mostly in labor and housing law), the term has primarily been used to *oppose* individual rights, liberalism, and legal positivism. More

---

[9] For a good summary of the debates around human dignity, see Christopher McCrudden, "In Pursuit of Human Dignity: An Introduction to Current Debates," in *Understanding Human Dignity*, ed. Christopher McCrudden (Oxford: Oxford University Press, 2013), 1–58.

[10] Reva Siegel, "Dignity and Sexuality: Claims on Dignity in Transnational Debates Over Abortion and Same-Sex Marriage," *International Journal of Contemporary Law* 10, no. 2 (2012), 355–379.

[11] See, for example, in recent years, Michael Rosen, *Dignity: Its History and Meaning* (Cambridge, MA: Harvard University Press, 2012); Jeremy Waldron, *Dignity, Rank, and Rights* (New York: Oxford University Press, 2012); George Kateb, *Human Dignity* (Cambridge, MA: Belknap/Harvard University Press, 2011). For a strong critique of the turn to dignity in gay rights, see Katherine M. Franke, "Dignifying Rights: A Comment on Jeremy Waldron's Dignity, Rights, and Responsibilities," *Arizona State Law Journal* 43 (2012), 1177–1200. For a call to move beyond the paradigm of dignity more broadly, see among others, Ranjana Khanna, "Indignity," *Ethnic and Racial Studies* 30, no. 2 (2007), 257–280.

[12] Samuel Moyn's *Christian Human Rights* (Philadelphia: University of Pennsylvania Press, 2015) is especially helpful to understand how human rights and dignity, as they emerged in the 1940s, had no obvious correlation with liberal democracy. Rather, Christian conservatives promoted them so as to provide a moralized political and social model that could counter communism and liberalism.

specifically, dignity has emerged as one of the best instruments to curb the perceived excesses of democracy and human rights, what many critics since the 1980s have called *droits-de-l'hommisme* or *démocratisme*.[13] Throughout the 1990s, various French legal scholars turned to dignity but also to other transcendental concepts such as the symbolic, the human person, the anthropological function of the law, the nondisposability of the body, and human ecology to counter the rhetoric of equality and privacy that lawyers and activists were mobilizing around the same time in hopes of acquiring specific rights. The law's purpose, they insisted, was not to grant individuals various rights that they considered "private" and idiosyncratic but to guarantee the social and psychic integration of all citizens into the national community: in other words, to guarantee their dignity. Dignity thus served to condemn pornography and sadomasochism (against the dignity of women), to oppose same-sex domestic partnerships, to prevent single women and homosexuals from having access to reproductive technologies, to sterilize transsexuals, and to outlaw surrogacy (all against the dignity of their potential children). Most recently, politicians brought up dignity to justify the 2010 law that banned the niqab and other "face coverings" in public spaces, and to cancel the performances of controversial comedian Dieudonné M'bala M'bala in 2014.[14]

This leads me to my second point. In French contemporary legal and political culture, dignity has become a way to regulate the border between public and private and, more generally, to define the boundaries of the nation as an imagined community. This is why dignity is so often tied to national belonging, social cohesion, the "common good," or, to use a recurring term, life-in-common: *le vivre-ensemble*. This is also why references to dignity have proliferated in cases concerning the expression and organization of gender, sexuality, religion, and race. As I want to suggest, in the French context, human dignity is best understood not as a value intrinsic to a person but as a project of biopolitical rule. In this sense, French dignity is fundamentally different from the American deployment of the term as synonymous with human rights and democratic inclusion. I propose instead to think of dignity as closer to *laïcité* and republicanism, in the sense that these three concepts – often used

---

[13] I examine the intellectual critique of this phenomenon of "excessive human rights" in Camille Robcis, "Republicanism and the Critique of Human Rights," in *France Since the 1970s: History, Politics and Memory in an Age of Uncertainty*, ed. Emile Chabal (London: Bloomsbury Academic, 2014), 225–243.

[14] On Dieudonné, see Jean-Marie Pottier, "Le lancer de nains peut-il bloquer un spectacle de Dieudonné?" in *Slate.fr* (January 6, 2014): www.slate.fr/france/81939/dieudonne-lancer-nain.

interchangeably and self-evidently – have progressively lost their historical meaning in order to signify the constraints on individual autonomy,
the process of disciplining subjects into a particular division of public and
private believed to be necessary because specifically, immutably, and
transcendentally French.

The Discovery of Dignity

As Stéphanie Hennette-Vauchez argues, human dignity did not become
a constitutional principle in French law until 1994.[15] Dignity was never
mentioned in the 1789 Declaration of the Rights of Man and the Citizen
or in any other of France's foundational legal texts. Although there were
traces of this legal concept prior to the end of the twentieth century, these,
as James Whitman shows, were mostly derived from the ancient notion of
dignitas, related to social and professional statuses, to rank and etiquette,
rather than a universal human nature.[16] Dignity entered the French legal
discourse in the 1980s through the vector of social law and the "defense of
the workers' dignity."[17] It was also important in cases pertaining to freedom of expression, as certain publications were fined for printing pictures
of dead bodies and other intimate scenes that judges believed had violated
the basic parameters of human dignity, as with the photos of François
Mitterrand's deathbed featured in *Paris Match* in 1996.

In July 1994, sixty-eight deputies, mostly from the right, called on the
Conseil Constitutionnel – France's highest constitutional authority – to
challenge various clauses in the series of laws that came to be known as the
"bioethics laws." These laws, eventually adopted by the parliament on

---

[15] Girard and Hennette-Vauchez, *La dignité de la personne humaine*; Stéphanie Hennette-
Vauchez, "Human Dignity in French Law," in *The Cambridge Handbook of Human
Dignity*, ed. Roger Brownsword and Dietmar Mieth (Cambridge: Cambridge
University Press, 2014), 368–374.

[16] James Whitman traces the evolution of *dignitas* to dignity as French society became more
democratic in James Q. Whitman, "The Two Western Cultures of Privacy: Dignity
versus Liberty," *Yale Law Journal* 113, no. 6 (2004), 1151–1221. See also
Stéphanie Hennette-Vauchez, "When Ambivalent Principles Prevail: Leads for
Explaining Western Legal Orders' Infatuation with the Human Dignity Principle,"
Legal Ethics 10, no. 2 (2007), 193–208.

[17] According to Alain Supiot, social law was responsible for promoting the principle of
human dignity after the Second World War: Alain Supiot, *Grandeur et misère de l'État
social* (Paris: Collège de France Fayard, 2013), 34. Interestingly, Supiot, currently
a professor at the Collège de France, has been one of the most important supporters of
this "anthropological turn" in law. Very much indebted to the work of Pierre Legendre,
Supiot has argued for the importance of dignity to ground social solidarity and resist the
marketization of culture and the dominance of positive law. See Alain Supiot, *L'esprit de
Philadelphie: la justice sociale face au marché total* (Paris: Seuil, 2010) and Alain Supiot,
Homo juridicus: essai sur le fonction anthropologique du droit (Paris: Seuil, 2005).

July 29, 1994, were the result of ten years of controversial debates that had played out in the political arena, in lower courts, in expert committees, in academic journals, and in the media, on contentious topics of bioethics including embryo research, surrogacy, assisted reproductive technologies, and organ transplants.[18] For complicated reasons related to the particularities of French family law and the political and social context of the 1990s in which same-sex and single-parent households were becoming more visible and demanding state recognition, the final version of the 1994 bioethics laws was extremely conservative, especially for reproduction.[19] After many heated discussions, the French government chose to ban surrogacy and to restrict assisted reproductive technologies to heterosexual couples of procreative age, married or living together for at least two years, who had been diagnosed with infertility. As legal scholar Marcela Iacub puts it, these laws were designed as a "perfect crime": they carefully covered all traces of medical intervention so that children could believe that they were the product of their parents' sexual act, as if technology had never intervened.[20] Thus, one of the most obvious and most disputed consequences of the 1994 bioethics laws was to ensure that it would be legally impossible for single individuals and for same-sex couples to have children and form families in France.

Yet, despite the bioethics laws' legal (and symbolic) consecration of the heterosexual reproductive family, the deputies who appealed to the Conseil Constitutionnel nonetheless argued that even these laws presented a fundamental challenge to "the constitutional principles of the right to life, equality, the right to the respect of the integrity of the person and of the human body, family law, the right to the genetic protection of humanity, the right to the health of the child and to the free fulfillment of his personality, personal responsibility and the separation of powers."[21] Although the deputies did not use the term *dignity* in their report, they referred to the "sacred character of human life" from which derive the "inalienable and sacred rights proclaimed in the Declaration of the Rights of Man and reaffirmed in the preamble of the 1946 Constitution." In addition, they warned against the potential of "soft eugenics" and insisted on the fact that the embryo was a "subject of law" (as opposed to an

---

[18] The full legal texts are available at: www.ladocumentationfrancaise.fr/dossiers/d000030-lois-de-bioethique-la-revision-2010-2011/historique-des-lois-de-la-bioethique. See also Stéphanie Hennette-Vauchez, *Le droit de la bioéthique* (Paris: La Découverte, 2009); Daniel Borrillo, *Bioéthique* (Paris: Dalloz, 2011).

[19] I examine this at length in Camille Robcis, *The Law of Kinship: Anthropology, Psychoanalysis, and the Family in France* (Ithaca, NY: Cornell University Press, 2013).

[20] Iacub, *Le crime était presque sexuel et autres essais de casuistique juridique*, 147.

[21] www.conseil-constitutionnel.fr/conseil-constitutionnel/francais/les-decisions/acces-par-date/decisions-depuis-1959/1994/94-343/344-dc/saisine-par-60-deputes.103208.html.

object), with all the "attributes of a human person" (as opposed to an animal). Finally, the deputies returned to the 1946 preamble to caution against anonymous sperm donation, which, aside from causing irremediable psychic damage to the child, would inaugurate a "new conception of the family." This, they argued, represented a direct affront to the vision of the family promoted by the writers of the 1946 Constitution of the Fourth Republic, who conceived of the family as the "natural community whose sole purpose [*vocation*] was to welcome children" and to "guarantee their harmonious development." As the deputies pleaded, the bioethics laws offered a perfect occasion for the constitutional judge to "affirm with vigor that the protection of the genetic patrimony of each human being and of *humanity as a whole* is a principle of constitutional value particularly necessary in our time." This was exactly what the Conseil Constitutionnel did in its decision of July 27, 1994.

Although the Conseil ultimately found the bioethics laws constitutionally sound, it addressed the concerns of the deputies using their own terms and arguing that these laws, in fact, supported and affirmed the general principles that they were calling for: "the primacy of the human person, the respect of the human being from the inception of life, the inviolability, integrity, and non-marketability of the human body, the integrity of the human race," and, they added, "the constitutional principle safeguarding the dignity of the human person."[22] To make their case and to claim human dignity as a constitutional principle, the members of the Conseil Constitutionnel relied on three statutes. First, they acknowledged the importance of individual freedom as proclaimed by articles 1, 2, and 4 of the Declaration of the Rights of Man and of the Citizen. But individual freedom, they noted, "needed to be reconciled with the other principles of constitutional value," principles that the court drew from the preamble to the 1946 Constitution. The decision thus cited at length the preamble's opening paragraph: "In the morrow of the victory achieved by the free peoples over the regimes that had sought to enslave and degrade the human person, the people of France proclaim anew that each human being, without distinction of race, religion or creed, possesses sacred and inalienable rights." From this passage, the Conseil Constitutionnel argued: "It follows that the protection of the dignity of the human person

---

[22] www.conseil-constitutionnel.fr/conseil-constitutionnel/francais/les-decisions/acces-par-date/decisions-depuis-1959/1994/94-343/344-dc/decision-n-94-343-344-dc-du-27-juillet-1994.10566.html. I have slightly modified the English translation provided by the Conseil Constitutionnel to preserve the idea of the *personne humaine*, which has a particular meaning and history in Roman law and in Catholic social thought: www.conseil-constitutionnel.fr/conseil-constitutionnel/root/bank/download/94343_344DCa94343dc.pdf. On the human person, see chapter 2 of Moyn, *Christian Human Rights* and part II of Olivier and Yan, *Du droit de ne pas naître*.

against all forms of enslavement or degradation is a principle of constitutional status." Finally, the Conseil concluded by citing a third statute, also drawn from the 1946 preamble: "The Nation shall provide the individual and the family with the conditions necessary to their development," and "the Nation shall guarantee to all, notably children [and] mothers ... protection of their health."

That the Conseil Constitutionnel based its decision on the preamble of France's last constitution (as opposed to the current 1958 Constitution) was not surprising per se. Indeed, following a landmark decision in 1971, the Conseil had agreed to consider various legal texts, including the 1946 preamble, as integral to France's constitutional norms, as its "constitutional bloc" (bloc de constitutionnalité). What was more surprising, however, was that it chose to use the term dignity when neither the deputies nor the authors of the 1946 Constitution actually had. As Samuel Moyn argues, it was during the interwar years that dignity first thrived in European legal and political circles.[23] More precisely, Moyn contends, Ireland was the first country to inscribe the protection of human dignity in its constitution of 1937. For Irish leaders, appealing to dignity was part of a broader strategy of preserving certain key aspects of Catholic social thought (notably the emphasis on the family and on the natural inequality of women) while rejecting a more reactionary and authoritarian version of Catholicism. Dignity, along with the notion of the "human person," offered a model of individualism distinct from both socialism, judged to be psychically and socially too homogenizing, and market-driven liberalism, considered too atomizing. In other words, in its early twentieth-century juridico-political iteration, dignity was always linked to community, to society, and to the family – a connection encouraged by Pope Pius XI, who was also adamant in his condemnation of totalitarianism and extreme liberalism. It was this version of what Moyn calls "religious constitutionalism" with dignity at its center that was taken up in the postwar period, first in the UN Charter in 1945, in the new constitutions of Christian Democratic states such as Italy and Germany, and in the 1948 Universal Declaration of Human Rights.

Although France was never a Christian Democratic state as such, it did have a strong tradition of social Catholicism, one that was especially vibrant – politically and intellectually – during the interwar years and one that played a central role in the Resistance.[24] During the Liberation and the Fourth Republic, many Social Catholic activists joined the

---

[23] Moyn, Christian Human Rights.
[24] For a short introduction, see James F. McMillan, "France," in Political Catholicism in Europe, 1918–1965, ed. Tom Buchanan and Martin Conway (Oxford: Oxford University Press, 1996), 34–68. See also James Chappel, Catholic Modern: The Challenge of

Mouvement Républicain Populaire (MRP), which emerged as one of the three leading parties in France in the 1945 and 1946 elections, along with the socialists and communists.[25] In the years after the war, French political leaders were extremely conscious of the need to mark a clear break with Vichy, to promote different values, and to create new institutions to uphold the restoration of republican legality. For the MRP, however, this mission was somewhat more difficult than it was for the socialists or the communists. Indeed, in the eyes of many Catholics, the Vichy regime had implemented the kind of strong corporatist social policy anchored in the family that they had lobbied for since the late nineteenth century.[26] To be sure, many leftist Catholics rejected the overt racism of the État Français and the authoritarianism of Philippe Pétain – two of the many reasons why so many Catholics joined the Resistance. But how could the Republic be resolutely "social" and "humanistic" without hewing too closely to the Vichy experiment?[27]

The two constitutive assemblies elected in 1946 to draft a new constitution for the Fourth Republic were acutely aware of this dilemma, especially the representatives of the MRP, which after the June elections became the dominant party in France. Throughout the legislative debates on the constitution and especially its preamble, MRP deputies insisted on the importance of "curbing" liberalism with a strong social policy anchored in the concepts of dignity, the person, and a revised human rights. As MRP deputy Lionel de Tinguy du Pouët put it, "What we want is a mandatory and complete declaration of rights. ... We want the condemnation of the liberalism and the individualism of 1789. ... We want the affirmation of the pluralist community [*cité*] ... the freedom of

---

Totalitarianism and the Remaking of the Church (Cambridge, MA: Harvard University Press, 2018).

[25] Isser Woloch, "Left, Right and Center: The MRP and the Post-war Moment," *French History* 21, no. 1 (2007): 85–106.

[26] According to these Catholic family activists, the family was not simply important but actually constitutive of social bonds and solidarity. This was also the message of Pope Leo XIII in his 1891 encyclical *Rerum Novarum*. On Vichy family policy, see Francine Muel-Dreyfus, *Vichy et l'éternel féminin: contribution à une sociologie politique de l'ordre des corps* (Paris: Seuil, 1996); Kristen Stromberg Childers, *Fathers, Families, and the State in France, 1914–1945* (Ithaca, NY: Cornell University Press, 2003); Miranda Pollard, *Reign of Virtue: Mobilizing Gender in Vichy France* (Chicago: University of Chicago Press, 1998); Michèle Bordeaux, *La victoire de la famille dans la France défaite: Vichy 1940–1944* (Paris: Flammarion, 2002).

[27] This was a concern for the MRP but also for Charles de Gaulle, whose vision of social policy was very close to social Catholicism, especially in the field of family law: see chapter 1 of Robcis, *The Law of Kinship*. On De Gaulle and corporatism, see also Matthew H. Elbow, *French Corporative Theory, 1789–1948: A Chapter in the History of Ideas* (New York: Columbia University Press, 1953), 202–203. More generally, see Andrew Shennan, *Rethinking France: Plans for Renewal, 1940–1946* (Oxford: Clarendon Press, 1989).

groups [*groupement*], the freedom of the person and of the family, the freedom of the father in particular."[28] In the words of Maurice Guérin, also from the MRP, it was not enough to defend the essential rights of man proclaimed in 1789 because "the framers in 1789 ... could not foresee the social evolution and especially the economic evolution" that their revolution had brought about.[29] Dignity was one way to reframe human rights against liberalism but also against communism while insisting on the Republic's intrinsically social nature. As one MRP deputy, Jacques Bardoux, explained in reference to the preamble (of which he claimed to be the author):

Why ... did I write this text ... ? Because it seemed to me necessary to affirm, at the head of the declaration, the spirit, the objective, and the method of republican reconstruction after this war. ... What spirit? To affirm the supreme dignity of the human person. What method? To define the rights and guarantee the liberties of the human person. How? First, to return – by intensifying and then generalizing – to the foundations of French civilization in their origin and in human rights; to react, on all fronts, against the terrifying regression that totalitarian regimes represented, especially Hitler's regime.[30]

Bardoux's reference to totalitarianism is interesting and significant given his political trajectory. During the interwar years, Bardoux distinguished himself through aggressively anticommunist pamphlets. Elected to the Assembly in 1938, he supported Pétain in 1940 and eventually participated in Vichy's Conseil National, the administrative body created in 1941 to replace the parliamentary regime that had ended with the German occupation.[31] After the war, Bardoux was pardoned and reelected to the National Assembly.[32] Although Pétain and his associates were highly critical of the parliamentary regime of the Third Republic – which in their minds was responsible for the political instability, the social crisis, and the exacerbated individualism of the 1920s and 1930s – they believed it was important to set up some kind of legislative structure that

[28] *Journal Officiel*, Assemblée Nationale Constituante (August 23, 1946), 3303–3304. All the issues of the *Journal Officiel* of the Fourth Republic are available at: http://4e.republique.jo-an.fr/?f=a&y=&i=&s=&n=&d=&q=;.

[29] *Journal Officiel*, Assemblée Nationale Constituante (March 8, 1946), 640.

[30] *Journal Officiel*, Assemblée Nationale Constituante (April 9, 1946), 1632.

[31] Michèle Cointet, *Le Conseil National de Vichy: vie politique et réforme de l'état en régime autoritaire (1940–1944)* (Paris: Aux Amateurs de livres, 1989). See also Olivier Wieviorka, *Orphans of the Republic: The Nation's Legislators in Vichy France* (Cambridge, MA: Harvard University Press, 2009).

[32] Because so many Vichy supporters joined the MRP, the party was sometimes called by its opponents "Machine à Recycler les Pétainistes" ("machine to recycle Pétain supporters"). On these continuities, see Philip Nord, *France's New Deal: From the Thirties to the Postwar Era* (Princeton, NJ: Princeton University Press, 2010), Rémi Lenoir, *Généalogie de la morale familiale* (Paris: Seuil, 2003).

would function in the war's aftermath. Writing a constitution was part of this effort, and although the text was never made public (partly because of the refusal of the German authorities), the Conseil National did indeed finish a draft that Pétain signed on January 30, 1944. This new constitution, which was firmly communitarian (and which, for example, replaced universal suffrage with the family vote, as familialist activists had called for throughout the 1920s), proclaimed in its first article:

The liberty and dignity of the human person are supreme values and intangible goods. To guarantee them requires order and justice from the state, and discipline from the citizens. The constitution thus delimits the duties and rights of public power [*puissance publique*] and of citizens by instituting a state whose authority lies in the adherence to the Nation.[33]

If we consider these "transwar continuities," to use Philip Nord's helpful expression, then perhaps the absence of the term *dignity* in the final version of the 1946 Constitution is not merely accidental. Indeed, the MRP deputies who wrote the constitution were not all right-wing sympathizers like Bardoux. The party also included people like Maurice Schumann, who was a member of the Socialist Party (SFIO) prior to the war, or Francisque Gay, a close collaborator of Marc Sangnier at the Sillon, a movement that began in the 1890s to put an end to the long-standing battle between the Republic and the Church and to spread the ideas of social Catholicism within the left. For those who had fought Pétain, perhaps a direct reference to "dignity" would fail to provide the break from Vichy that seemed so necessary. From this perspective, the final version of the constitution promulgated in October 1946 could be read as a compromise: it kept many of the clauses, and certainly the "spirit," of Christian Democracy without using certain specific loaded terms.

Dignity and Public Order

The point of this detour through the 1940s is not to suggest that the Conseil Constitutionnel was thinking of Vichy's failed constitution or of the parliamentary debates around dignity during the Fourth Republic when it formulated its decision on the bioethics laws in July 1994. Rather, I want to argue that the version of dignity that legal scholars and politicians took up after this ruling was similar to the communitarian, anti-liberal, anti-totalitarian, and pro-family notion that persisted through Vichy and the Fourth Republic. The context of the 1990s was

---

[33] Projet de constitution du 30 janvier 1944: http://mjp.univ-perp.fr/france/co1944p.htm See also Etienne Le Floch, "Les projets de constitution de Vichy (1940–1944)" (Université Paris II Panthéon Assas, 2003).

significantly different from that of the 1940s, but, interestingly enough, the same animus against "savage liberalism" and totalitarianism pervaded many of the discussions. For critics of the bioethics laws, the deregulation of reproductive technologies was both the origin and the result of a particular liberal and capitalist (often termed "Anglo-Saxon") multiplication of rights *and* of a totalitarian erasure of sexual difference. Law, and family law especially, they argued, needed to preserve its normative and integrative capacity (believed to be transhistorical and universal) instead of simply reflecting social mores.

Thus, according to Muriel Fabre-Magnan, a professor of law at the Sorbonne and one of the main defenders of the notion of dignity in law, notably to condemn surrogacy, unlike the immediate postwar period when the "enemy was the state and the main threat was oppression and the loss of liberty," the real enemy was no longer the state but "barbarism and the risk of dehumanization [*déshumanisation*] brought about by the inordinate development of technology and of the market."[34] Dignity, Fabre-Magnan continues, served to restrain consent, the "modern juridical expression of individualism and liberalism," which had become "a keyword to lift all prohibitions and to legitimate all behaviors." Dignity did not aim to "protect a particular person, or even a category of persons, but humanity in general."[35] It accounted for "what exceeds man, what remains a transcendence despite what we have called the disenchantment of the world."[36] Or, as Fabre-Magnan puts it in "Sadomasochism Is Not a Human Right," nobody could renounce human dignity, neither for others nor for oneself, because "there is an aspect of the relationship of oneself with oneself which does not pertain to the sphere of the private but which has to do with the public sphere."[37]

This understanding of dignity as a safeguard against the "new totalitarianism" of capitalism and individualism, and as the last transcendent value to resist secularization and positivism, spread in legal journals, conferences, and publications throughout the 1990s and 2000s. It was defended in different ways by legal scholars such as Bernard Edelman, Alain Supiot, Catherine Labrusse-Riou, and Fabre-Magnan, as well as philosophers such as Sylviane Agacinski and Thibaud Collin, but also theologians like Olivier de Dinechin and France Quéré.[38] This vision of

---

[34] Muriel Fabre-Magnan, "La dignité en droit: un axiome," *Revue interdisciplinaire d'études juridiques* 58, no. 1 (2007), 1–30, here 5–6.

[35] Ibid., 21.   [36] Ibid., 25.

[37] Muriel Fabre-Magnan, "Le sadomasochisme n'est pas un droit de l'homme," *Conférence* 22 (Spring 2006), 291.

[38] See Bernard Edelman, *La personne en danger* (Paris: Presses universitaires de France, 1999); Catherine Labrusse-Riou, *Écrits de bioéthique* (Paris: Presses universitaires de France, 2007); Sylviane Agacinski, *Corps en miettes* (Paris: Flammarion, 2013); Supiot, *Homo juridicus*; Olivier de Dinechin, *L'homme de la bioéthique: entretiens avec Yves de*

dignity as the foundation of the social also circulated in the discussions and reports of the Comité Consultatif National d'Éthique (CCNE), a national ethics committee founded in 1983 to advise legislators on how best to regulate the new technologies that had developed in biology, medicine, and public health.[39] Much of the language adopted in the final version of the bioethics laws was taken directly from the CCNE reports and amended after the parliamentary deliberations in which dignity played, once again, a central role. Citing the works of Labrusse-Riou and of Edelman, Christine Boutin, for example, an elected representative with close ties to the Vatican and one of the few French politicians to publicly oppose abortion, opened her speech on the bioethics laws by asking the government to "give voice to moral principles, give voice to human dignity, give voice to the foundations of our humanist tradition."[40]

Boutin, who was also a key figure in the battle against same-sex partnerships and marriage, opposed the 1994 laws for failing to protect the embryo sufficiently. Legislators, according to Boutin, were still guided by science rather than by "the inalienable and sacred rights of man consecrated in the preamble of our 1946 Constitution."[41] It is also interesting to note that Boutin served as a consultant for the Pontifical Council for the Family founded by Pope John Paul II in 1981 to "promote the pastoral care of families" and "to protect their rights and dignities in the Church and in civil society."[42] As I argue elsewhere, dignity was especially important in the thought of John Paul II, who sought throughout his life to elaborate a new anthropology, a new conception of man and of society anchored in sexual complementarity, a new political model that could provide an alternative to liberalism and socialism at once.[43] Dignity, in other words, circulated in overlapping circles – legal, religious,

Gentil-Baichis (Paris: Desclée de Brouwer, 1999); *La dignité humaine en question: handicap, clonage* (Paris: Éditions de l'Emmanuel, 2004); France Quéré, *L'éthique et la vie* (Paris: Odile Jacob, 2006).

[39] The decisions of the CCNE are collected in *Travaux du comité consultatif national d'éthique*, ed. Didier Sicard (Paris: Presses universitaires de France, 2003). For a good presentation of the CCNE, see Dominique Memmi, *Les gardiens du corps: dix ans de magistère bioéthique* (Paris: Editions de l'Ecole des hautes études en sciences sociales, 1996).

[40] *Journal Officiel*, Assemblée Nationale (November 19, 1992), 5737: http://archives .assemblee-nationale.fr/9/cri/1992-1993-ordinaire1/081.pdf.

[41] Ibid., 5741.

[42] John Paul II, *Apostolic Constitutions* (1988): http://w2.vatican.va/content/john-paul-ii/en/ apost_constitutions/documents/hf_jp-ii_apc_19880628_pastor-bonus-roman-curia .html.

[43] See Camille Robcis, "Catholics, the 'Theory of Gender,' and the Turn to the Human in France: A 'New Dreyfus Affair'"? *Journal of Modern History* 87, no. 4 (2015), 892–923. See also Mary Anne Case, "After Gender the Destruction of Man? The Vatican's

political, and intellectual – and through a series of thinkers, lawyers, and politicians who navigated these different fields.

Even though the Conseil Constitutionnel played a crucial role in establishing dignity as a constitutional principle in French law in its 1994 bioethics decision, it was the Conseil d'État – France's highest court of appeals in administrative matters – that definitively inscribed dignity as a key component of public order in its famous "dwarf-throwing" decision of October 27, 1995. The case involved the owners of a nightclub in Morsang-sur-Orge, a Paris suburb, who, in October 1991, decided to organize dwarf-throwing competitions in which dwarves, dressed in protective suits, were thrown into the air before landing on a mattress. Alarmed by this form of "entertainment," the town's mayor shut down the event through a municipal order. Manuel Wackenheim, a twenty-four-year-old dwarf who claimed to have voluntarily participated in what he considered a form of work, challenged the decision in court demanding the right to exercise his profession. The case traveled through various administrative tribunals including that of Versailles, which in 1992 declared that dwarf throwing did not disturb any of the three pillars of public order (security, peacefulness, and public health) and that the mayor had violated Wackenheim's human rights.

Three years later, however, the Conseil d'État reversed the decisions of the lower courts, stating that, in fact, "the respect of the dignity of the human person was one of the components of public order." As such, the municipal police – whose role was to guarantee public good order and safety – was correct in suspending the show. Being projected into the air could not possibly be construed as a "right," the court continued, because throwing a person affected by a physical handicap was "in its very objective [*par son objet même*]" an infringement on the dignity of the human person.[44] The Morsang-sur-Orge decision, which became one of the most discussed legal cases in recent years, was remarkable on many fronts. As commentators noted, Morsang-sur-Orge inaugurated a new role for the judges of the Conseil d'État, who suddenly left their "splendid isolation" to enter the field of politics and actually *make* the law instead of simply applying it.[45] But for my purposes here, the decision confirmed that dignity could now redefine private entities (whether it be individual

Nightmare Vision of the 'Gender Agenda' for Law," *Pace Law Review* 31, no. 3 (2012), 802–817.

[44] Conseil d'État, Assemblée (October 27, 1995), #136727: www.legifrance.gouv.fr/affic hJuriAdmin.do?oldAction=rechJuriAdmin&idTexte=CETATEXT000007877723.

[45] This is, for example, the position of Cayla Olivier, "Le coup d'État de droit?" *Le Débat* 100, no. 3 (1998), 108–133. For more on the history of the Conseil d'État, see Bruno Latour, *La fabrique du droit: une ethnographie du Conseil d'État* (Paris: La Découverte, 2002).

consent or the privately owned nightclub) into public spaces subject to government regulation and intervention. Dignity, in other words, had become explicitly biopolitical.

Dignity, Catholicism, and Islam

Given the redefinition of dignity that proceeded from Morsang-sur-Orge, it is not surprising that the French government under President Nicolas Sarkozy turned to dignity once more when it sought a legal justification for its 2010 law banning "face coverings" in public spaces, a law specifically targeting the burqa and the niqab. Referring to "face covering" as a "communitarian manifestation of the rejection of the values of the Republic" and as a "symbolic and dehumanizing violence that hurts the social body," the government explained:

The voluntary and systematic covering of the face poses a problem because it is simply contrary to the fundamental requirements of life-in-common of French society [*le vive-ensemble*]. The defense of public order is not limited to the preservation of tranquility, public health, or security. It also allows the prohibition of certain behaviors that go directly against the rules essential to the republican social contract that founds our society. . . . This form of public reclusion, even when it is voluntary or accepted, evidently constitutes an infringement on the dignity of the person.[46]

Despite the fact that the Conseil d'État (this time serving as adviser to the state) expressed some reservations on the government's legal formulation – especially on the ambiguity that the category of dignity had acquired over the years – the Conseil Constitutionnel upheld the law, and the government signed it on October 11, 2010.[47]

Both this "face covering" law and the pleas to revive "national indignity" after the terrorist attacks on *Charlie Hebdo* reveal how dignity and national belonging have become intertwined in recent years. While the 1994 bioethics laws sought to control sexuality and to exclude homosexuality from reproduction (the reproduction of children but also of the nation), these other two cases point to the complex articulation of France, Islam, and secularism. As many scholars point out, the concept of *laïcité* has evolved significantly from its 1905 formulation as freedom of religion to its current "republican" mobilization, in which the state, in view of a "neutral public sphere," consciously regulates behaviors that were

---

[46] Assemblée Nationale, "Projet de loi interdisant la dissimulation du visage dans l'espace public" (May 19, 2010): www.assemblee-nationale.fr/13/projets/pl2520.asp.
[47] For a good analysis of the law in context, see Constantin Languille, "Logique juridique, logique politique. Le cas de la burqa," *Le Débat* 172, no. 5 (2012), 87–97.

recently considered intrinsically private – clothing or eating, for example.[48] It is in this sense that I suggested in the introduction that dignity, like *laïcité* and republicanism, has become a self-evident, trans-cendental, and de-historicized concept increasingly used to exclude certain bodies and certain communities from the limits of the nation. Just as the historicization of *laïcité* and republicanism is crucial to map the multiple forms and meanings that these concepts have taken since the eighteenth century, it seems equally important to bring to light this particular genealogy of dignity, which at the very least complicates the insistently secular self-understanding of French law.

---

[48] The 2008 "affaire Baby Loup" is a particularly good example of this *nouvelle laïcité*. See, for instance, Mayanthi L. Fernando, *The Republic Unsettled: Muslim French and the Contradictions of Secularism* (Durham, NC: Duke University Press, 2014); Stéphanie Hennette-Vauchez and Vincent Valentin, *L'Affaire Baby Loup ou la nouvelle laïcité* (Issy-les-Moulineaux: LGDJ, Lextenso éditions, 2014).

Part III

American Protestant Trajectories

7 William Ernest Hocking and the Liberal Protestant Origins of Human Rights

Gene Zubovich

In the summer of 1947, Charles Malik was busy at work revising the Universal Declaration of Human Rights (UDHR). As the rapporteur for the United Nations Commission on Human Rights, Malik had been inundated with rough drafts and suggested edits from dozens of countries and nongovernmental entities. But during this busy summer, he reached out for help from his former teacher at Harvard, philosopher William Ernest Hocking, who was enjoying his retirement in New Hampshire.[1] Hocking read the draft carefully and advised Malik that "every human being has one 'natural' right": to develop one's personality. The "liberal position in politics is weakened today, as it has long been weakened in law, by staking out elaborate and plural areas of individual right [*sic*] without showing their relation to each other and to their own central meaning."[2]

To get at this one central right, Hocking focused on the first article of the UDHR, which (in 1947) read: "All men are brothers. Being endowed with reason and conscience, they are members of one family. They are free, and possess equal dignity and rights." Hocking suggested tightening the connection: "To recognize the existence of 'reason and conscience' in another creature is to recognize 'freedom' and 'dignity'. ... Man has rights <u>because</u> he has freedom and conscience; why not say that, instead of making rights an addendum?"[3]

Hocking's attempt to explicitly root human rights in "freedom and conscience" did not find its way into the text of the UDHR. Nevertheless, Hocking's liberal defense of human rights in the 1940s merits our attention for two reasons. First, Hocking was an influential figure in the human rights debates of the 1940s, thanks to his close connections to Charles Malik and his longtime work with the Federal Council of

---

[1] The best biographical treatment of Hocking's retirement in Madison, New Hampshire, is John Kaag, *Philosophy: A Love Story* (New York: Farrar, Straus and Giroux, 2016).
[2] William Ernest Hocking to Charles Malik, August 3, 1947, folder 12, box 20, in Charles Habib Malik Papers, Manuscript Division, Library of Congress, Washington, DC.
[3] Ibid.

Churches, which historians now credit with playing an outsized role in the creation of the United Nations and the UDHR.[4] Second, Hocking is equally worthy of our attention because he was one of the earliest theorists and defenders of human rights. In the 1920s, he wrote the first formal philosophical defense of human rights in the United States.[5] By critically interrogating his work, this chapter looks at the origins and flowering of human rights discourse in the mid-twentieth-century United States.

Hocking's role in the human rights debates of the 1940s points to the important role of American liberal Protestantism in the conception and defense of human rights. Hocking was a devout liberal Protestant whose philosophical career revolved around religious questions. His body of work blended together elements of idealism, pragmatism, mysticism, and personalism – all of which circulated in the liberal Protestant milieu of the first half of the twentieth century. His contribution to the American human rights discourse should be understood in this religious context.

Human rights are often depicted as either a secular and liberal product of the Enlightenment or as originating in a religious and conservative milieu. The either/or distinction makes more sense for European history. In Europe, the Catholic Church reacted to the French Revolution and the ensuing secularization by moving in conservative and anti-republican directions until Vatican II in the 1960s. European Protestants had a more complicated relationship with liberalism in the nineteenth and twentieth centuries but during the mid-twentieth century – the key moment for the origins of human rights – Protestant neoorthodox theologians rejected a variety of liberal assumptions. The sharp divide between secular republicanism and religious conservatism was one of the governing divisions of modern European history.[6]

---

[4] Linde Lindkvist, *Religious Freedom and the Universal Declaration of Human Rights* (Cambridge: Cambridge University Press, 2017); Samuel Moyn, *The Last Utopia: Human Rights in History* (Cambridge, MA: Harvard University Press, 2010); John Nurser, *For All Peoples and All Nations: Christian Churches and Human Rights* (Washington, DC: Georgetown University Press, 2005), 112–117; Andrew Preston, *Sword of the Spirit, Shield of Faith: Religion in American War and Diplomacy* (New York: Knopf, 2012).

[5] William Ernest Hocking, *Present Status of the Philosophy of Law and of Rights* (New Haven, CT: Yale University Press, 1926).

[6] On the secular origins of human rights, see Lynn Hunt, *Inventing Human Rights: A History* (New York: W. W. Norton, 2008); Jonathan I. Israel, *Democratic Enlightenment: Philosophy, Revolution, and Human Rights, 1750–1790* (New York: Oxford University Press, 2013). Human rights histories of the United States are largely secular narratives by omission. See Elizabeth Borgwardt, *A New Deal for the World: America's Vision for Human Rights* (Cambridge, MA: Harvard University Press, 2007); Mark Philip Bradley, *The World Reimagined: Americans and Human Rights in the Twentieth Century* (Cambridge: Cambridge University Press, 2016). On the Christian roots of human rights, see Samuel Moyn, *Christian Human Rights* (Philadelphia: University of Pennsylvania Press, 2015).

In the history of the United States, however, drawing sharp distinctions between liberalism and religion makes little sense. Many Americans were both liberal and religious.[7] David Hollinger argues that American Protestants imported Enlightenment values into the United States and made them safe for an overwhelmingly religious nation. "In the United States," he contends, "the engagement of Protestant Christianity with the Enlightenment most often took the form of *accommodation*."[8] James Kloppenberg locates the origins of American liberalism and democracy largely in a "Judeo-Christian worldview."[9] William Ernest Hocking's pioneering work on human rights demonstrates that American human rights emerged out of the complex interaction between religious liberalism and secular Enlightenment values.

By arguing that the American understanding of human rights in the 1940s emerged partly out of the liberal Protestant milieu, which stood in stark contrast to the European religious scene, this chapter makes two arguments about the nature of human rights in this era. Hocking's defense of human rights was, first and foremost, a defense of religious liberty. Historians have shown that the history of religious liberty was interwoven with American and European imperialism.[10] But they have paid less attention to how intellectuals like Hocking came to associate religious liberty with decolonization. Hocking's intellectual trajectory shows that among liberal Protestants religious liberty, and human rights more generally, came to be understood in opposition to imperialism.

---

[7] Elesha J. Coffman, *The Christian Century and the Rise of the Protestant Mainline* (New York: Oxford University Press, 2013); Gary J. Dorrien, *The Making of American Liberal Theology: Imagining Progressive Religion, 1805–1900* (Louisville, KY: Westminster John Knox Press, 2001); Matthew Hedstrom, *The Rise of Liberal Religion: Book Culture and American Spirituality in the Twentieth Century* (New York: Oxford University Press, 2012); David A. Hollinger, *After Cloven Tongues of Fire: Protestant Liberalism in Modern American History* (Princeton, NJ: Princeton University Press, 2013); William R. Hutchison, *The Modernist Impulse in American Protestantism* (New York: Oxford University Press, 1982); Henry F. May, *The Enlightenment in America* (New York: Oxford University Press, 1976); *American Religious Liberalism*, ed. Leigh Eric Schmidt and Sally M. Promey (Bloomington: Indiana University Press, 2012).

[8] David A. Hollinger, "The Accommodation of Protestant Christianity with the Enlightenment: An Old Drama Still Being Enacted," *Daedalus* 141, no. 1 (Winter 2012), 76–88, here 77. Italics in original.

[9] James T. Kloppenberg, *Toward Democracy: The Struggle for Self-Rule in European and American Thought* (New York: Oxford University Press, 2016), 11. See also David D. Hall, *A Reforming People: Puritanism and the Transformation of Public Life in New England* (New York: Knopf, 2011); Amy Kittelstrom, *The Religion of Democracy: Seven Liberals and the American Moral Tradition* (New York: Penguin Press, 2015).

[10] Anna Su, *Exporting Freedom: Religious Liberty and American Power* (Cambridge, MA: Harvard University Press, 2016); Tisa Joy Wenger, *Religious Freedom: The Contested History of an American Ideal* (Chapel Hill: University of North Carolina Press, 2017).

Second, this chapter argues that human rights constituted a form of secularization of liberal Protestant thought at mid-century. For Hocking, and for many other liberal Protestants, human rights were a way of reconciling Protestant beliefs with a religiously diverse world by translating religious ideas into an ostensibly secular language. Although Hocking defended a theistic understanding of human rights, the theistic content of human rights made no reference to any specifically Christian beliefs. He defended a doctrine of human rights that was compatible with a wide variety of religious tradition – or no religion at all. Historians of the United States have noted that management of religious diversity has been the primary mechanism for the secularization of public life in the country.[11] By uprooting specifically Christian doctrines like original sin, natural law, and vicarious redemption from his defense of human rights, Hocking was also paving the way for a more secular cultural and intellectual life in the United States. As this chapter makes clear, Hocking's attempt to articulate and defend human rights was full of wrong turns and showed the limits of religious liberalism. For all of his faults, he demonstrates the important impact of religious liberalism on the broader course of the history of human rights.

* * *

William Ernest Hocking was born in Cleveland, Ohio, in 1873 into a middle-class family. His father was a struggling physician who moved from town to town before settling down in Joliet, Illinois, where young William grew up. Hocking was raised in a pious household and, in his teenage years, he became "twice-born" during a Methodist revival meeting. He intended to become an engineer during his years at Iowa State College at Ames, but an encounter with William James' *Principles of Psychology* shook his childhood faith and upended his career plans. Hocking decided to study with the pragmatist philosopher at Harvard.[12]

James was away on sabbatical when Hocking entered Harvard as a freshman, and Hocking studied during his first year with Josiah Royce. James and Royce were opposites in many ways. James pioneered

---

[11] On mid-twentieth-century American debates about religious pluralism as a vehicle for secularization, see K. Healan Gaston, *Imagining Judeo-Christian America: Religion, Secularism, and the Redefinition of Democracy* (Chicago: University of Chicago Press, 2019); Kevin Michael Schultz, *Tri-faith America: How Catholics and Jews Held Postwar America to Its Protestant Promise* (New York: Oxford University Press, 2011); Martin E. Marty, *Modern American Religion. Vol. 3* (Chicago: University of Chicago Press, 1999).

[12] Leroy S. Rouner, "Hocking, William Ernest," in *Biographical Dictionary of Christian Missions*, ed. Gerald H. Anderson (New York: Macmillan, 1998), 295. For a bibliography of Hocking's works, see Richard C. Gilman, *The Bibliography of William Ernest Hocking, from 1898–1951* (Waterville, ME: [self-published], 1951).

the field of pragmatism, a philosophical doctrine that rooted truth in experience and understood ideas to be transient, contingent, and social. Royce, who Hocking unexpectedly studied with, focused on metaphysics, by which he meant the study of things that do not change. James' absence moved Hocking into the orbit of the absolute idealist philosopher and shaped his interests. Hocking later returned to Harvard for graduate work, studying with Royce late in the philosopher's career, when Royce was moving toward accepting some pragmatic insights. From Royce, he learned that the goal of philosophy is to discover absolutes, especially the unifying principles that govern what Royce called the "Beloved Community" that encompassed the whole of humanity. Through classes with James, Hocking came to employ the notion of experience as a central component of his philosophical work.[13]

Upon graduating from Harvard with a PhD, Hocking worked at the University of California, Berkeley, and at Yale, and finally returned to Harvard in 1914, where he later received the only endowed chair in the Harvard philosophy department, the Alford Professorship in Natural Religion, Moral Philosophy, and Civil Polity, which he held until 1943.[14]

He received the most prestigious post in American philosophy because of his first and most important book, *The Meaning of God in Human Experience*. The book was published in 1912, in the context of an ongoing conversation among liberal Protestant philosophers and theologians that sought to vindicate their faith against its detractors while also making it compatible with modernity. The book was a study of the metaphysics of intersubjectivity, in which Hocking argued that knowledge of God is presupposed in knowledge of oneself and in social relationships.

What stood out in the book was his concept of "Negative Pragmatism." Hocking observed that certain kinds of over-rationalized religions strike people as false because their experience creates "a general disaffection from the religion of reason, and from its philosophical framework, absolute idealism."[15] He argued that experience can intuitively help us know if something is untrue. He turned James' pragmatist insight of "that which

---

[13] On James and Royce, see George Cotkin, *William James, Public Philosopher* (Baltimore, MD: Johns Hopkins University Press, 1990); Bruce Kuklick, *Josiah Royce: An Intellectual Biography* (Indianapolis, IN: Bobbs-Merrill, 1972); Gerald E. Myers, *William James, His Life and Thought* (New Haven, CT: Yale University Press, 1986); *William James and a Science of Religions: Reexperiencing the Varieties of Religious Experience*, ed. Wayne Proudfoot (New York: Columbia University Press, 2004).

[14] "Historical Note," Guide to the William Ernest Hocking Correspondence, 1860–1979, Harvard University, Cambridge, MA: http://oasis.lib.harvard.edu/oasis/deliver/~hou01777.

[15] Hocking, *The Meaning of God in Human Experience*, reprinted in *A William Ernest Hocking Reader: With Commentary*, ed. John Lachs and D. Micah Hester (Nashville: Vanderbilt University Press, 2004), 20.

works is true" into its inverse: "That which does not work cannot be true." Hocking explained what he meant:

> If a theory has no consequences, or bad ones; if it makes no difference to men, or else undesirable differences; if it lowers the capacity of men to meet the stress of existence, or diminishes the worth to them of what existence they have; such a theory is somehow false, and we have no peace until it is remedied.[16]

Experience can tell us what is false, but only metaphysics can tell us what is true.

The big question raised by *The Meaning of God in Human Experience* was whether individuals can know other individuals. Hocking argued that our knowledge of one another does not come from knowing each other's internal experience. "For where art thou? Not there, behind those eyes, within that head, in darkness, fraternizing with chemical processes."[17] It is in the common experience of nature – knowing that two individuals are experiencing the same thing and are both being shaped by it – that grounds our social reality. And it is in the natural world, which molds individuals into a community, that God can be found.

For Hocking, the idea of "personality" bridged the gap between James' pragmatism and Royce's idealism, and between experience and absolute truths. Personalism would be at the heart of the 1940s-era human rights. It would justify human rights as a defense of personality and would provide the distinctive language of "personality," "dignity," and the "human person" to the era's rights talk. According to Hocking in 1912, a personality is a psychological object that registers experience and shapes one's being. A personality is also a divine object that makes each individual connected to one another because each human personality is made in the image of God, and that shared identity as God's children binds each human person to one another.[18] This is a philosophical articulation of the theological postulate that "the fatherhood of God" creates "the brotherhood of man." In this way, he continued James' search for a viable, philosophically and scientifically defensible religious sensibility, and he remained committed to grounding philosophical speculation in

---

[16] Ibid., 24.

[17] William Ernest Hocking, *The Meaning of God in Human Experience: A Philosophic Study of Religion* (New Haven, CT: Yale University Press, 1912), 266.

[18] On American personalism, see Dorrien, *American Liberal Theology*, 286–355; Rufus Burrow Jr., *God and Human Dignity: The Personalism, Theology, and Ethics of Martin Luther King, Jr.* (Notre Dame, IN: University of Notre Dame Press, 1992); Gene Zubovich, "American Protestants and the Era of Anti-racist Human Rights," *Journal of the History of Ideas* 79, no. 3 (July 2018), 427–443. On European personalism, see John Hellman, *The Communitarian Third Way: Alexandre Marc's Ordre Nouveau 1930–2000* (Montreal: McGill-Queen's University Press, 2002); Moyn, *Christian Human Rights*.

experience. But he continued to insist, along with Royce, that metaphysics can clarify universal rules of conduct.[19] That commitment would lead him down the road to human rights.

* * *

The trouble for Hocking was that he articulated his blend of James and Royce at a moment when the two strands of philosophy they represented – idealism and pragmatism – became emblems of opposing sides during World War I. John Dewey had become a dominant figure in philosophy by the start of the Great War. Like Hocking, Dewey had early interests in religion and Hegelian idealism but had by this point abandoned his earlier faith and began articulating a pragmatic philosophy that discarded the quest to vindicate Protestant Christianity. Hocking, perhaps feeling some rivalry with this philosophical giant, had taken offense at Dewey's 1915 book *German Philosophy and Politics*. In it, Dewey argued that Kant was the progenitor of German militarism and he insinuated that idealism tends to lead to some form of despotism. He faulted Kant for telling "men that to do their duty is their supreme law of action, but [he] is silent as to what men's duties specifically are." In this way, Kant opened the way for the state to decide what men's duties are. In Kant's wake, Fichte and Hegel undid the separation of the "noumenal" and the "phenomenal," reading history as the revelation of the Absolute Spirit, with the state as the main agent of progress. As a result, the German people were conditioned to see the state as "God on earth" and to devote themselves religiously to their government. He concluded that "philosophical absolutism may be practically as dangerous as matter of fact political absolutism."[20]

For Hocking, these were fighting words. In a letter to *The New Republic*, which was Dewey's magazine of choice for his political essays, Hocking insisted that German idealism stood in contrast to the politics of the present. Germany's politics, in fact, resembled Dewey's pragmatism more closely than the worldviews of Kant or Hegel. Germany had abandoned any sense of absolute principles and was trampling on the rights of other nations. Worst of all, Hocking worried, Dewey "recommends to

---

[19] David A. Hollinger, "Damned for God's Glory: William James and the Scientific Vindication of Protestant Culture," in *William James and a Science of Religions: Reexperiencing Varieties of Religious Experience*, ed. Wayne Proudfoot (New York: Columbia University Press, 2004), 9–30.

[20] Dewey, "Reply to William Ernest Hocking's 'Political Philosophy in Germany,'" in *The Middle Works of John Dewey, 1899–1924, Volume 8: 1915, Essays, Germany Philosophy and Politics, Schools of To-morrow*, ed. Jo Ann Boydston (Carbondale: Southern Illinois University Press, 1991), 418–421. John Dewey, *German Philosophy and Politics* (New York: H. Holt, 1915).

American policy a more radical experimentalism; let us have done with absolute or fixed principles, such as 'nationality' or 'sacred rights'; let us regard everything as subject to test, discussion, measurement, compromise, adjustment, revision," he wrote sardonically.[21] To his mind, Dewey was attacking not only idealism but also the very purpose of philosophy, which (as Royce had argued) is to find absolute principles for the whole of humanity. After the war, Hocking would spend his time articulating a political defense of "sacred rights."

Despite these fights, the two philosophers remained collegial in other matters. After all, they both supported the war effort. Hocking came out early as a supporter of American preparedness for war.[22] Upon America's entry into the war, he took a multiyear leave of absence from Harvard, enlisting as a captain in the army and spending the war studying the morale of British and French troops.[23]

Like Dewey, Hocking had misunderstood the character of the war and was deeply disappointed with what seemed, in retrospect, his own undue exuberance. Neither man expressed his change of heart publicly. Like so many other liberal Protestants of the era, but unlike Dewey, Hocking wholeheartedly backed the League of Nations.[24] He valued the League so much that he cautioned readers of the *New York Times* in 1920 that "the habitual Republican voters who want a prompt and honest entry into the League (and I am one of them) can do no other than vote for the [Democratic presidential candidate] Cox."[25] Hocking became a devotee of Wilsonianism.[26]

The Great War saw the emergence of both Hocking and Dewey as public intellectuals. The war had sharpened the divide between idealism and pragmatism, and, thanks partly to Dewey's maneuvering, tied Hocking to a philosophical system that was losing its status in the American academy. The pragmatic elements of his thought became less

---

[21] Quoted in James Campbell, "Dewey and German Philosophy in Wartime," *Transactions of the Charles S. Peirce Society* 40, no. 1 (Winter 2004), 1–20. Quote on pp. 8–9.

[22] "Policing the World," William Ernest Hocking, Letter to the Editor, *Springfield Daily Republican* (December 15, 1915), 10.

[23] "Hocking, William Ernest," in *American National Biography Online*: www.anb.org/arti cles/20/20-00480.html. His observations were published as William Ernest Hocking, *Morale and Its Enemies* (New Haven, CT: Yale University Press, 1918). Robert B. Westbrook, *John Dewey and American Democracy* (Ithaca, NY: Cornell University Press, 1991), 231.

[24] Michael G. Thompson, *For God and Globe: Christian Internationalism in the United States between the Great War and the Cold War* (Ithaca, NY: Cornell University Press, 2015).

[25] William Ernest Hocking, "Professor Hocking Replies to Arguments of Pro-League Republicans," *New York Times* (October 25, 1920), 14.

[26] On the relationship between Wilsonianism and decolonization, which Hocking would come to support, see Erez Manela, *The Wilsonian Moment: Self-Determination and the International Origins of Anticolonial Nationalism* (Oxford: Oxford University Press, 2009).

appreciated and Hocking, whom the *New York Times* had once identified as "William James' successor," became known as a proponent of idealism.[27] Despite the complexity of his philosophy, he would thereafter be plagued by an association with German thought and politics.

* * *

Hocking's public fights with Dewey and his thoughts on the war and the League of Nations lacked the intellectual rigor of his early work. But they did create in him a desire to make his defense of "sacred rights" more systematic. His pioneering political writings in the 1920s, which included some of the earliest defenses of human rights, came out of this post–World War I context. He desired, in part, to rescue some of the wartime Wilsonianism and his own continued faith in the League of Nations. He waded into the philosophical grounding of the state and the law, producing "the first modern philosophical study of politics by an American," according to Bruce Kuklick.[28]

In his 1926 book, *Man and State*, Hocking voiced a defense of the state. He grounded his analysis in individual psychology. Each person has a will that demands to be enacted in history. But each person wants more than they can achieve, as individuals, and they need something beyond themselves to achieve their wills. That something is the state, which pools and rationalizes individual wills and allows them to endure beyond the life of the individual. The individual wills the state into being but the state is what allows the individual to become complete, he argued.[29] Hoping to differentiate his ideas from German idealists and their idolatry of the state, he insisted that individuals existed prior to the state and implied that God existed over and above the state. But the precise relationship between individuals, the state, and God remained unclear.

In 1926, the same year he published *Man and State*, Hocking also wrote a slim volume called *Present Status of the Philosophy of Law and of Rights*, which outlined his thoughts on human rights for the first time. The book came about because of a graduate course on legal theory that he co-taught with Roscoe Pound, then dean of the Harvard law school. In the book, Hocking continued his project of reforming absolute idealism as he

---

[27] Charles Armstrong Bennett, "Negative Pragmatism: William James's Successor's Philosophical Principle Is, That Which Will Not 'Work' Cannot Be True," *New York Times* (December 29, 1912), 55.

[28] Bruce Kuklick, *The Rise of American Philosophy, Cambridge, Massachusetts, 1860–1930* (New Haven, CT: Yale University Press, 1977), 491.

[29] On the complex relationship between religion, individuals, and the state, see William Ernest Hocking, *Man and the State* (New Haven, CT: Yale University Press, 1926), 375–379.

pushed back against the legal theory of two German neo-Hegelian philosophers. In particular, he criticized Josef Kohler, who argued that human rights are sometimes an impediment to progress.[30] Like Hegel, Kohler contended that humanity passes through stages of development and that each step is necessary, even if we judge it harshly from our own vantage point. Kohler used the example of slavery as a necessary stage that society must pass through that requires "the sacrifice of human life." "No one who looks at the matter entirely from the standpoint of ... human rights will be able to appreciate slavery in its historical development."[31]

Hocking drew on his earlier personalist writings to argue that slavery is wrong, not because it violates natural law or our own contemporary sensibilities, but rather because it violates the one human right that every individual possesses: the right to develop one's personality to its full capacity. For Hocking, this one human right to develop one's personality is always true in its outline – everyone has always had it and will always have it. It derived from religious life and is held to be true by all major world religions. But the content of that right would be filled out in historical time and revealed through experience. The development of one's personality occurs in history and is subject to the possibilities and limitations of the day. But the quest for developing human personality guides progress in every era. For that reason, the end of slavery showed that the expansion of individual rights and social progress were not only compatible, he argued, but inseparable.

Hocking believed that a "scale of values" derives from the right to develop one's personality. At the top of the scale are the rights that have the greatest "bearing on the development of the mental power in individuals."[32] Because developing one's personality is a process that requires self-possession, reflection, and a certain amount of trial and error, freedom of conscience is every person's first right. One must be free to think and believe in order to develop one's personality, which includes the ability to understand and follow the law. In virtue of the person's right to conscience, that person also has the right to control himself or herself, to persuade others, and to control nature. The person also has the "right to security" "of one's person," "of one's agreements or contracts," and "of one's property." In this way, he elaborated a plurality of classical liberal rights he believed should be recognized in virtue of every human being's possession of a personality. By making a religious conscience the source of all other rights, he rooted his defense of human rights in the classical Protestant idea of

---

[30] Hocking, *Present Status*.   [31] Quoted in ibid., 8.   [32] Ibid., 82.

the right to a personal conscience and the American idea of religious liberty.

By the 1930s, in the midst of the Great Depression and the New Deal, Hocking moved beyond these classically liberal conceptions of individual rights. He outlined his criticism of classical liberalism in 1937, when he published *The Lasting Elements of Individualism*. In the book, he identified three deficits of liberalism. First, it cannot maintain social unity in practice because the "I" usually comes before the "We." For example, liberalism has no theory of the social consequences of wealth accumulation. Second, liberalism promotes rights over duties. Third, liberalism cannot sustain itself. The very spirit that gives it force – an optimistic view of nature and progress – is undermined by the individualism it promotes. Like other liberal Protestants in the 1930s, Hocking defended the response of the US government to the Great Depression.[33]

Lasting Elements did not mention human rights, but the emphasis Hocking placed on the interconnection of rights and duties and on the state in playing a positive role in the achievement of rights differentiated his ideas from other conception of human rights. For example, Marco Duranti argues that the European Convention on Human Rights was shaped by a host of conservatives, from British libertarians to French communitarians, who had in common a fear of post–World War II left-wing majoritarian rule. Whereas the European Convention on Human Rights protected the power of corporations and the Catholic Church against the welfare state, Hocking defended a doctrine of human rights that left little room for natural law or church hierarchy. His conception of human rights was also not directed at placing limits on governmental power. And that fact left him open to criticism that he was moving in authoritarian directions.[34]

He argued that the rights derived from personality also endow people with duties toward one another and to God. Liberalism can save itself only by having the state more actively create unity and promote duty, he concluded in 1937. The state must be "commotive" – it must merge individual wills into one. It must establish duties commensurate to freedoms. The state should recognize that:

Freedom to express thought is for thinkers. ... Idea bearing should be as solemn a business as child bearing. ... To the hideous perils and absurdities of the Censorship, we must join the equally hideous perils, hypocrisies and humbugs

---

[33] William Ernest Hocking, *The Lasting Elements of Individualism* (New Haven, CT: Yale University Press, 1937).

[34] Marco Duranti, *The Conservative Human Rights Revolution: European Identity, Transnational Politics, and the Origins of the European Convention* (New York: Oxford University Press, 2017).

of No-censorship. .... The new state must do two things where the Liberal state attempted but one. It must restrict liberty for the sake of liberty.[35]

Reviewers condemned such recommendations. One scholar of fascism observed that Hocking's "theory of education seems closer to [fascist philosopher] Gentile's than to Dewey's, for he would postpone critical and reflective thought until adolescence, teaching the younger child only what is accepted. Thus he contends that a whole-hearted revolutionist is out of place in public schools but should have a hearing in colleges."[36] Another reviewer wondered, "There must be a 'sobering objective judgment' which checks the freedom of the irresponsible word-mouther. Can the state supply it, short of that fascism which the author also severely castigates?"[37]

Here were the criticisms Dewey had launched during World War I returning with a vengeance on the eve of World War II. Hocking's reliance on the state as a mechanism of social order led his ideas to be, once again, linked to authoritarianism. He paid little attention to institutions or social groups. "I am stupid about organizations and trust in God for the outcome," he once admitted.[38] His reliance on the state to do his philosophical work moved him toward a more authoritarian politics, even as he insisted that promoting individual human flourishing is the central function of the state. At the same time, the association of idealism with authoritarianism was a widely held truth in the philosophical profession and structured the reception of his work.

* * *

While Hocking's political ideas sometimes drifted toward authoritarian positions, his writings on international affairs put him squarely in the company of other Protestant liberals of the era. His Wilsonianism, which he expressed in several books and many articles on world affairs, came at a time when his star was waning in the philosophical profession. In his own department at Harvard, colleagues moved toward logical positivism and other outlooks that cared little about the broad, socially engaged questions that Hocking addressed in his culturally Protestant books.[39]

Although Hocking would eventually become a pariah in his own department, it is important not to overstate the point. First, his brand of

---

[35] Quoted in *Hocking Reader*, 331.
[36] Herbert W. Schneider, Review of *The Lasting Elements of Individualism*, in *American Historical Review* 44, no. 2 (January 1939), 316–317.
[37] H. A. L., Review of *The Lasting Elements of Individualism*, in *Journal of Philosophy* 34, no. 9 (April 1937), 250.
[38] Quoted in *Hocking Reader*, 332.
[39] On Harvard in the 1920s and 1930s, see Kuklick, *Rise of American Philosophy*.

philosophy thrived well into the 1940s and 1950s in some philosophy departments.[40] Second, his thought continued to inform work outside the academy, especially in philanthropic organizations, in government, and in religious institutions.[41] Third, he remained a major international figure long after his star was waning in American academia. His interest in Islam, Hinduism, and Buddhism – first expressed in *The Meaning of God* in 1912 – and his travel abroad meant that he was widely read in India, China, and other non-Western nations. Charles Malik, his former student, informed Hocking that "you will find now in many homes throughout the Arab world copies of your [textbook] *Types*, and because of this and of your well-known interest in this part of the world, a good many Arab intellectuals and politicians know much about you."[42] Well into the 1950s, Hocking's influence was affirmed by a social and political climate that celebrated America's Protestant heritage, and through non-governmental organizations and international scholarship that saw international affairs in religious terms. His ideas flourished in this milieu.

After World War I, Hocking began thinking about how states deal with one another in the international arena and, in 1928, he was offered the opportunity to travel to the Middle East. During his trip, he concluded that the world is full of tremendous diversity, and that diversity is largely structured by religious differences. "No one can enter the world of the Arab and of Islam and come out the same person in either outlook or affection," he wrote in an orientalist tone. Unlike other observers, he also affirmed the basic equality of Arabs. He sharply criticized British and French colonial administrators for their "malaise," driven by a sense of the "supposed inequality" of Arabs. He believed that nationalism was surging in the Middle East and argued in his 1932 book, *The Spirit of World Politics*, for the independence of Arab nations.[43]

In 1932, Hocking was invited to participate in a Rockefeller-funded study of the missionary project, which produced the controversial report *Re-thinking Missions*. He traveled with a group of Protestant leaders to

---

[40] For example, "Philosophy and theology were intertwined at Princeton in the early 1940s," argues P. MacKenzie Bok. See Bok, "To the Mountaintop Again: The Early Rawls and Post-Protestant Ethics in Postwar America," *Modern Intellectual History* 14, no. 1 (April 2017), 153–185, here 158.

[41] On Hocking's influence on religious institutions, see Gene Zubovich, "For Human Rights Abroad, against Jim Crow at Home: The Political Mobilization of American Ecumenical Protestants in the World War II Era," *Journal of American History* 105, no. 2 (September 2018), 267–290.

[42] Malik to Hocking, March 2, 1945, Folder 12, Box 20, Malik Papers.

[43] William Ernest Hocking, *The Spirit of World Politics, with Special Studies of the Near East* (New York, MacMillan, 1932). On orientalism, see Edward W. Said, *Orientalism* (New York: Vintage Books, 2003).

Japan, China, and other Asian nations to assess the Christian missionary endeavors under way there. On behalf of the commission, Hocking wrote a withering critique of missionary work, treating the Protestant venture as a failure. In *Re-thinking Missions*, Hocking sought to shift the focus of missionary work from proselytization to social work. Evangelization, rightly understood, would lead to more schools and hospitals and fewer attempts at conversion.[44] Like in his writings on the Middle East, he argued that missionaries should pay heed to the nationalist movements demanding colonial independence.[45]

Hocking had become a public critic of imperialism, and in 1932, he called on American Protestants to disassociate religious liberty from imperialism. The United States had long justified the colonization of the Philippines by arguing that it was promoting religious liberty in the colony. So too had European powers justified military interventions in China on the same grounds. This presented a problem for Hocking, who placed liberty of religion and conscience at the center of his defense of human rights. To reconcile his belief in human rights and his opposition to imperialism, he argued that human rights should never be imposed by force. He went so far as to speak out against proposals for "religious liberty" in treaties and international law. "If the liberty of religious propaganda is abetted by a Western government," he reasoned, "it becomes associated with the interest of that government."[46] Promoting religious liberty and human rights requires Asian countries to accept these ideas as their own and they will not do so as long as human rights are closely tied to American and European imperialism.

For Hocking, human rights were antithetical to imperialism. As he criticized the missionary movement, Hocking reiterated in *Re-thinking Missions* that "each individual soul matters in the sight of God" and is of "absolute worth." The "worth of the individual person" is the basis "of rights and also of duties."[47] In the same way that each individual must be free to discover what his or her duties are, so too must nations charter their own path free from the domination of others. And there is no guarantee that postcolonial countries will follow the right path in national development. Unlike Catholic theorists of human rights, Hocking could

---

[44] William R. Hutchison, *Errand to the World: American Protestant Thought and Foreign Missions* (Chicago: University of Chicago Press, 1987), 158–175.

[45] On the transformation in attitudes toward imperialism among American Protestant missionaries, see ibid.

[46] Quoted in Heather J. Sharkey, *American Evangelicals in Egypt: Missionary Encounters in an Age of Empire* (Princeton, NJ: Princeton University Press, 2007), 142. On Hocking and religious liberty, see Lindkvist, *Religious Freedom and the Universal Declaration of Human Rights*, 52–54. See also Su, *Exporting Freedom*.

[47] Hocking, *Re-thinking Missions*, 56.

not rely on natural law or religious hierarchy to constrain the freedom of each person and each nation to chart its own route in the development of personality.[48] He continued to believe that a certain amount of experimentation and experience is needed to work out the rights and duties that govern humanity.

Hocking believed in individual and national development without the guiding hierarchies of imperialism or religious establishments. But he assured his audience that "world culture" would help guide newly independent nations. The spread of modernity – including the proliferation of technology, science, and liberal religion – was creating a basis of commonality between diverse cultures. "World culture" was an early conception of globalization that served as a basis for universal norms like human rights. Without world culture, Hocking reasoned, there could be no universal human rights because the world would be radically pluralistic.

In Hocking's conception, world culture was identical to the liberal Protestant values he worked so hard to defend, while also being ostensibly respectful of global religious and cultural diversity. In his philosophical work, Hocking had defended the existence of a supreme being, supported scientific inquiry, and urged moral growth. What he understood as the essence of Christianity were not specific theological postulates that churchgoers heard on Sunday mornings but what he viewed as the best aspects of the West and of Christianity. He discarded the many particularities of Christianity for the sake of reaching common ground with other religious traditions. What was important for Hocking was that these essences of Christianity – industriousness, scientism, moral reflection, and self-possession – were being spread by world culture. And if traditional missionary work and Western imperialism now proved to be barriers to the spread of world culture, it was time for them to go.

Hocking's belief in "world culture" demonstrated the limits of Protestant universalism at mid-century in its attachment to the supremacy of Western culture and its resistance to cultural pluralism. Conceiving of a universal culture likewise allowed him to soften the impact of decolonization and nationalism on the American imagination. After all, he argued, rebellion against science, reason, and liberal religion in the Global South was relegated to the past. Nationalism today, he argued in 1932, would mimic the best aspects of Western thought. Even if the forms that world culture would take in India and China appeared in the guise of Hinduism and Buddhism, it would nonetheless resemble the Christian modernity of the West. For this reason, it was time to

---

[48] See Moyn, *Christian Human Rights.* On Jacques Maritain, see Lindkvist, *Religious Freedom and the Universal Declaration of Human Rights,* 34–37, 41–46.

disassociate the missionary project and the promotion of human rights from imperialism.[49]

His writings on missionaries were part of a growing criticism of imperialism and a broader counter-totalitarian mobilization by ecumenical Protestants across the North Atlantic West in the 1930s.[50] Earlier efforts to create unity among Protestants worldwide became politicized in that decade. The locus of the efforts of the Americans involved in these ventures was toward a new international organization to replace the failed League of Nations. They hoped to create a new world order that would ensure religious liberty, diminish the importance of national sovereignty in international affairs, and gradually end colonialism. As historians John Nurser, Andrew Preston, and Samuel Moyn have shown, religious figures turned to the language of human rights in the 1940s and became among their most ardent supporters, before a more secular version of human rights ascended in the 1970s.[51] Hocking joined this venture as a senior figure among these Christian statesmen. He worked closely with the Federal Council of Churches in shaping its massive advocacy program during World War II. This included Hocking's personal collaboration with John Foster Dulles in writing the "Six Pillars of Peace" in 1943 and in the critique of the Dumbarton Oaks proposal in 1945. The Federal Council of Churches also engaged in extensive lobbying of the State Department to support a human rights charter as part of the postwar settlement.[52]

Two years later, former student Charles Malik asked Hocking to critique an early draft of the UDHR. In this conversation Hocking once again emphasized the importance of reason and religion as the basis of rights, much as he had done in the 1910s and 1920s:

The possession of reason and conscience is the mark of the genus homo: Article 1 states that this quality transforms the genus into a "family" of "brothers." In other

---

[49] On the European Protestant embrace of decolonization, which was driven by anti-secular attitudes quite different from those of Hocking, see Udi Greenberg, "Protestants, Decolonization, and European Integration, 1885–1961," *Journal of Modern History* 89, no. 2 (June 2017), 314–354. Hocking clashed publicly with several of the European theologians Greenberg identifies, particularly Hendrick Kraemer. See J. Wesley Robb, "Hendrick Kraemer versus William Ernest Hocking," *Journal of the American Academy of Religion* 29, no. 2 (1961), 93–101.

[50] Mark Thomas Edwards, *The Right of the Protestant Left: God's Totalitarianism* (New York: Palgrave Macmillan, 2012); Justin Reynolds, "Against the World: International Protestantism and the Ecumenical Movement between Secularization and Politics, 1900–1952," PhD Diss., Columbia University, 2016; Thompson, *For God and Globe*.

[51] Moyn, *The Last Utopia*; Nurser, *For All Peoples and All Nations*; Preston, *Sword of the Spirit*.

[52] Gene Zubovich, "The Global Gospel: Protestant Internationalism and American Liberalism, 1940–1960," PhD Diss., University of California, Berkeley, 2015, 46–64.

words humanity cannot be a mere genus. Why not? Because men have to treat one another as being what they are! To recognize the existence of "reason and conscience" in another creature is to recognize "freedom" and "dignity." To accord "rights" to a being is not something else than recognizing his freedom and dignity; it is the same thing. Man has rights because he has freedom and conscience; why not say that, instead of making rights an addendum?[53]

Hocking's language was remarkably Kantian at a time when Kant was not a major figure in legal theory.

Hocking's view of human rights also made no sharp distinction between religious and secular conscience. As Linde Lindkvist argues, Hocking had a theistic understanding of human rights, which Malik shared.[54] But Hocking also took pains to root human rights in an expansive notion of world culture that had discarded a lot of theistic content. Unlike some other understandings of human rights, his defense was not a defense of the role of clergy, religious institutions, or religious law. Neither did it seek to adjudicate between the many warring belief systems of religious denominations in the United States or religions across the world. It was an explicit, if limited, attempt to find common grounds among the world's religions. He emphasized instead the role of nations and the role of individuals to chart their own course. In this way, Hocking defended a specific type of secularity, one that had certain historically Protestant assumptions at its core.[55]

Hocking's long-standing emphasis on "personality" helped constitute one of the discourses on human rights, whose language was reflected in the UDHR in phrases like "dignity and worth of the human person" – vocabulary otherwise alien to the American political tradition.[56] His thought on rights continued to prioritize conscience as the first right because of its centrality in the recognition between self and other, as it had been in his earliest work. His work on human rights also offered a solution to a problem posed for Protestant liberals: how to propagate

---

[53] Hocking to Malik, August 3, 1947, Folder 12, Box 20, Malik Papers.
[54] Lindkvist, *Religious Freedom and the Universal Declaration of Human Rights.*
[55] The literature on Protestants and secularism is vast. A good starting point is Talal Asad, *Formations of the Secular: Christianity, Islam, Modernity* (Stanford, CA: Stanford University Press, 2003).
[56] On discussions of the human family, see Bradley, *The World Reimagined.* See also Mary Ann Glendon, *A World Made New: Eleanor Roosevelt and the Universal Declaration of Human Rights* (New York: Random House, 2001); Carol Anderson, *Bourgeois Radicals: The NAACP and the Struggle for Colonial Liberation, 1941–1960* (Cambridge: Cambridge University Press, 2015); Zachary Steven Ramirez, "International Human Rights Activism in the United States during the Cold War," PhD Diss., University of California, Berkeley, 2013; Nurser, *For All Peoples and All Nations*; Paul Gordon Lauren, *The Evolution of International Human Rights: Visions Seen* (Philadelphia: University of Pennsylvania Press, 2003).

Christianity but also respect cultural differences. Human rights offered what he believed was a universal rendering of Protestant principles that were nonsectarian in character and part of the coming "world culture."

His long engagement with ideas of human rights serves as a helpful reminder that Hocking offered a popular and influential alternative to the political theology of mid-century Christian realists. From the 1930s to the 1950s, Reinhold Niebuhr, Walter M. Horton, Henry Pitney Van Dusen, and other realist theologians developed a critique of the Enlightenment and popularized an understanding of human nature centered on original sin.[57] Because their ideas emerged as a criticism of moral and international law, and because they viewed ambitious international projects with suspicion, realists never became interested in human rights. But the centrality of human rights to American Protestants in the face of realist indifference (and sometimes outright opposition) shows that even within their own religious community realists never achieved the authority historians have often ascribed to them.[58]

Hocking's career also reveals that it was a specific strain of Protestantism – Protestant liberalism – that undergirded mid-century human rights. Like Protestant realists, evangelicals rejected the human rights project of the 1940s. But the evangelical rejection came about for different reasons: human rights were too closely associated with theological liberalism, with an internationalism they found threatening, and because human rights cast off the particulars of the Christian faith that were central to the evangelical project.[59] While Hocking adhered to some historically Protestant positions, from the evangelical perspective he had discarded so many doctrines that his philosophical system was no longer plausibly Christian. Evangelical theologian Carl Henry condemned the entire post–World War II international order because it was "a global peace without any reference to the vicarious atonement and redemptive work of Christ."[60] And unlike Catholic theologians, who defended natural law and church hierarchy, virtually the only times Hocking spoke about church leaders was when he was chastising them. When he did

---

[57] Nicolas Guilhot, *After the Enlightenment: Political Realism and International Relations in the Mid-Twentieth Century* (Cambridge: Cambridge University Press, 2017), 69–114.

[58] Edwards, *The Right of the Protestant Left*; Terrance Renaud, "Human Rights As Radical Anthropology: Protestant Theology and Ecumenism in the Transwar Era," *Historical Journal* (November 24, 2016), 493–518; Heather A. Warren, *Theologians of a New World Order: Reinhold Niebuhr and the Christian Realists, 1920–1948* (New York: Oxford University Press, 1997).

[59] Zubovich, "For Human Rights Abroad," 288.

[60] Carl F. H. Henry, *The Uneasy Conscience of Modern Fundamentalism* (Grand Rapids, MI: William B. Eerdmans Publishing Company, 1947), 20.

speak about missionaries, for example, it was to rebuke them for their cultural imperialism.

As Hocking's career demonstrates, the mid-century human rights project was partly underwritten by ideas rooted in Enlightenment values, including the spread of science and cosmopolitanism, which Hocking called "world culture." The persistence of Enlightenment-inspired liberalism among American Protestants at mid-century made the religious dynamics of the United States quite distinct from the European context. As Udi Greenberg argues, "American ecumenism had a different intellectual agenda and operated in a different political context than its European counterpart."[61] And yet the diversity of American religion has escaped the notice of many scholars of human rights, who pay little regard to the diversity of American Christian thought at mid-century.[62] Contrary to such accounts, Hocking's long engagement with human rights places the emphasis on their roots in the Enlightenment and the long history of Protestant attempts to reconcile their religion with the values of science, human diversity, and individual freedom. Liberal Protestant endorsement of human rights in the 1940s was one marker of a changing public attitude toward imperialism, a new understanding of religious liberty, and increasing comfort among Protestant thinkers with secularism.

[61] Greenberg, "Protestants, Decolonization, and European Integration," 316.
[62] See, for example, Moyn, *Christian Human Rights*.

8   Inside the Cauldron

Rawls and the Stirrings of Personalism at Wartime Princeton

P. MacKenzie Bok

Intellectual influences may follow surprising paths across long distances in any era, but the history of the twentieth century is particularly jumbled in this way. Shortened distances of communication and travel led to constant combination even of ideas first cultivated in very different local hothouses. This intermingling can vex those who wish to label and explicate distinct intellectual milieus in this period, or to trace the history of a concept within a circumscribed sphere. So it is with Christian "personalist" human rights talk in the 1940s. In *Christian Human Rights* (2015), Samuel Moyn attempts to pull specifically on the conservative Catholic European strand of this conversation – and let it stand in for the whole.[1] Aiming to acknowledge the American Protestant strand without exploring it, he mentions briefly "a parallel trajectory" whereby "personalism and the rise of rights as a bulwark against totalitarianism also burgeoned within Protestant networks across the same period." One example of this parallel development, Moyn notes, is the personalist theology of the young John Rawls, who as an Episcopalian undergraduate at Princeton penned a 1942 thesis on Christian ethics as right relations between persons in community.[2] But Rawls's case – and the cauldron of personalist influences in which he was immersed – actually reveals that the Catholic conversation on the topic cannot be helpfully separated from the Protestant, nor the American from the European, nor the conservative from the socialist.

In practice, the Christian discourse that laid the groundwork for the contemporary language of human rights traversed all these boundaries. The rigidity of ideology, and consequently the rigid lens of ideological history, fares poorly when confronted with such

---

[1] My quarrels with Moyn's approach in this book are pursued in greater detail at: P. MacKenzie Bok, "Did the Christians Ruin Rights?" *New Rambler* (February 15, 2016): http://newramblerreview.com/book-reviews/history/did-the-christians-ruin-rights.

[2] Samuel Moyn, *Christian Human Rights* (Philadelphia: University of Pennsylvania Press, 2015), 17–18.

a soup.[3] Yet intellectual historians need not be flummoxed by the challenge here. Instead, we might begin to deconstruct the stew by gazing into a particular cauldron and examining the ingredients. Even far-flung influences are usually specific for a certain thinker, or at a given university. Let the university be wartime Princeton; let the nascent thinker be John Rawls. The example shows not merely the relevance of the liberal American Protestant side of the story but also how many of the paths to "Christian human rights" that have been taken to run in historical parallel can instead be seen to actually meet.[4]

The Study of Religion Emerges at Princeton

When Rawls arrived at Princeton as a freshman in the fall of 1939, the university was shifting onto a wartime footing. Hitler had just invaded Poland two weeks prior; Rawls had been tying up his summer sailboat at the family's vacation home in northern Maine when his father ran out to tell him the news.[5] The year's first issue of the *Daily Princetonian* expressed concern for Thomas Mann, the German novelist who had been given a university lectureship the prior year but was visiting Europe when war broke out and had not yet secured safe passage back to campus.[6] No one knew when the United States would join the fighting, but a large number of Rawls's classmates signed up for the Reserve Officer Training Corps (ROTC) – some with dreams of glory, others with the calculation that it was better than the inevitable draft.[7]

For the university, however, one key academic component of the wartime footing was to literally "get religion." Princeton had a proud Presbyterian institutional history, was home to the Princeton Theological Seminary, and required chapel attendance of its under-classmen. But like other American universities it had reorganized in the

---

[3] Ibid., 67.
[4] The need for more such work "to capture how these coterminous streams of personalist rights talk were related" is noted in Linde Lindkvist, *Religious Freedom and the Universal Declaration of Human Rights* (Cambridge: Cambridge University Press, 2017), 41.
[5] John Rawls, "Autobiographical Notes – John Rawls" [ca. 2002], folder 12, box 42, Papers of John Rawls, HUM 48, Harvard University Archives, 13.
[6] "Vacationing Students Harried by European War," *Daily Princetonian* (September 18, 1939), 1.
[7] Rawls, "Autobiographical Notes – John Rawls," 16. Rawls himself did not sign up for the ROTC and would be drafted into the army as a private in December 1942; he received a month's deferral to February 1943 so he could sit his final exams and graduate a semester early before reporting for duty. He somewhat misremembered this sequence of events in his autobiographical account, but relevant administrative correspondence can be found in John Rawls, box 63, Undergraduate Academic Files, 1921–2010, AC198, Department of Rare Books and Special Collections, Princeton University Library [folder henceforth "Rawls UAF"; archive henceforth "Princeton Archives"].

late nineteenth century according to the German model of specialized disciplines, and therefore offered virtually no coursework in religion to undergraduates.[8] Faced with the rise of totalitarianism in Europe, however, proponents of liberal education such as Princeton philosopher Theodore Meyer Greene increasingly identified the humanities and religion as allies in the common cause of defending democratic values, and urged universities to reintroduce religion into undergraduate curricula.[9] While Greene's philosophical work focused on the likes of Kant and Plato, he had been raised by Episcopal missionary parents in Turkey and was an active member of Holy Trinity Episcopal Church in Princeton.[10] He argued that competency in a variety of separate realms is insufficient; people yearn to "see life steadily and see it whole," so "liberal education, if it is to perform its task, must also help the student find a set of values and a philosophy of life that he can really live by."[11] Questions of God and ultimate concern, Greene asserted, are an important subject of education. Thus in 1934 and 1935 he took an active role on a Princeton faculty committee that recommended the hiring of a professor to teach undergraduate classes in religion.[12] The search would take five years. Only as Rawls took his first freshman exams in January 1940, with war truly launched on the continent, did the university finally appoint George Finger Thomas to establish "a program of instruction in religious thought" for the following academic year, with the goal of launching a religion department soon after.[13]

[8] For more on this broader phenomenon, see Jon H. Roberts and James Turner, *The Sacred and the Secular University* (Princeton, NJ: Princeton University Press, 2000), 91; Darryl G. Hart, *The University Gets Religion: Religious Studies in American Higher Education* (Baltimore, MD: Johns Hopkins University Press, 1999), 12; and Douglas Sloan, *Faith and Knowledge: Mainline Protestantism and American Higher Education* (Louisville, KY: Westminster John Knox Press, 1994), 19.

[9] Theodore M. Greene, Charles C. Fries, Henry M. Wriston, and William Dighton, *Liberal Education Re-examined: Its Role in a Democracy* (New York: Harper & Brothers, 1943), xiii and 66–69. Greene chaired Princeton's Divisional Program in the Humanities.

[10] "Biographical Material about Theodore Meyer Greene," in T. M. Greene file, primary run, Faculty and Professional Staff files, 1764–2009, AC107, Princeton Archives [collection henceforth "Faculty Files"]. See also Rawls's college transcript in Rawls UAF.

[11] Theodore M. Greene, "The Liberal Arts College," in Southern University Conference pamphlet (1941), 108–109, in T. M. Greene file, primary run, Faculty Files.

[12] "Confidential Document: Princeton University Report of the Special Committee of the Faculty on Religious Education" (December 17, 1934), 16; and "Princeton University Report of the Special Committee of the Faculty on Religious Education" (April 11, 1935), 2; both in folder 1, box 50, Collection AC109, Princeton Archives.

[13] Harold W. Dodds, "Introduction," in George F. Thomas, *Religion in an Age of Secularism: The Inaugural Lecture of George F. Thomas, October 24, 1940* (Princeton, NJ: Princeton University Press, 1940), 3–5, in G. F. Thomas file, box 518, Faculty Files.

Greene had been steering a faculty committee of diverse viewpoints toward his own curricular ends, but Thomas's hire marked an outright victory. He and Thomas would become fellow Episcopalian parishioners at Holy Trinity, and the rational liberal Christianity they shared would now guide Princeton's program in religion through its formative early years. Greene likely personally recruited Thomas; the two men already knew each other well from the Theological Discussion Group founded by Henry P. van Dusen of Union Theological Seminary in 1934 to help gather together a group of twenty-five "younger Christian thinkers" for twice-yearly retreat weekends of discussion and debate.[14] The group lasted more than two decades, and is most often invoked as a community of conversation to justify describing prominent members such as Paul Tillich, Reinhold Niebuhr, and H. Richard Niebuhr as all "neoorthodox" theologians, despite their disagreements.[15] What has not received attention, however, is how the theologically liberal Princeton wing of the group carried its own outlook into academia. Greene, Thomas, and Princeton's university chaplain Robert R. Wicks were all Theological Discussion Group members, and not marginal ones either; when the group published a 1945 book of essays entitled *The Christian Answer*, Greene and Thomas wrote two of the six contributions. These Princeton professors became regarded as important advocates for religion's intellectual relevance in the immediate aftermath of the war.[16] Their successful effort to bring religion back into the college classroom at one of America's leading universities is a major unsung legacy of the Theological Discussion Group.

Thomas had studied theology at Oxford as a Rhodes Scholar and earned his PhD in philosophy from Harvard in 1929 under William Ernest Hocking.[17] His field was philosophy of religion, which he had

---

[14] Heather A. Warren, "The Theological Discussion Group and Its Impact on American and Ecumenical Theology, 1920–1945," *Church History* 62, no. 4 (December 1993), 528–542, at 534. Warren has shown that the group's churchmen members deserve attention as well; the likes of Van Dusen, Francis P. Miller, John C. Bennett, and Samuel McCrea Cavert explicitly used the Theological Discussion Group's forums to lay the groundwork for the Oxford Life and Work Conference in July 1937 and for the foundation of the World Council of Churches, both profoundly influential to the direction ecumenical Protestantism took in the 1940s and 1950s.

[15] For further discussion of disputes over the term "neoorthodoxy," consult K. Healan Gaston, "Neo-orthodoxy," in *Encyclopedia of Religion in America, Volume 3*, ed. Charles H. Lippy and Peter W. Williams (Washington, DC: CQ Press, 2010), 1533–1538, at 1537; Douglas John Hall, *Remembered Voices: Reclaiming the Legacy of "Neo-orthodoxy"* (Louisville, KY: Westminster John Knox Press, 1998), 8.

[16] *The Christian Answer*, ed. Henry P. van Dusen (New York: Charles Scribner's Sons, 1945).

[17] For more on Hocking, who deeply influenced Thomas, see Gene Zubovich's contribution to this volume, "William Ernest Hocking and the Liberal Protestant Origins of

previously taught at Swarthmore, Dartmouth, and the University of North Carolina.[18] When he received Princeton's offer, Thomas wrote to Hocking for advice as to whether he should accept; to move into a religion department, he knew, would invite scorn from many fellow philosophers.[19] But Hocking sent Thomas an urgent telegram urging him to take the post; the prejudice of philosophers against religious themes was real, he concurred, but this was too important a pedagogical opportunity to pass up.[20] Thomas took his mentor's advice and accepted, writing back to Hocking:

> I think the young men of America need to have the claims of religion presented to them in rational terms and that our society needs especially a reinterpretation of basic Christian insights. If people who have the training to do this, however poorly, refuse to do it, it won't be done. Thank you again for your encouragement to tackle a hard job.[21]

With this personal decision, Thomas set in motion a series of events with ramifications far beyond his own career. Princeton saw the new program in similarly high-stakes terms. As one pamphlet for alumni declared:

> In America at large the need for men who can lead the nation back to the deeper springs of its democratic way of life and foster knowledge of the history and genius of our religion is being recognized more clearly than at any time during the present century. At this critical hour Princeton has embarked upon a program which will enable her to reclaim her historic role in religion and make a major contribution in education.[22]

Accordingly, when Thomas arrived in fall 1940, the university president arranged for him to deliver an inaugural address on "Religion in an Age of Secularism," which Princeton then printed and distributed not only on campus but also to a multitude of peer institutions.[23] This pamphlet also included a description of the new religion program, which proceeded to roll out according to plan. By 1944, there would be sufficient enrollment

---

Human Rights" (Chapter 7). For another valuable general assessment of Hocking's intellectual legacy, albeit in a more whimsical style, see John Kaag, *American Philosophy: A Love Story* (New York: Farrar, Straus, & Giroux, 2016).

[18] "Biographical Information" (1961), in G. F. Thomas file, box 518, Faculty Files.

[19] George Finger Thomas to William Ernest Hocking, December 30, 1939, letter in bMS Am 2375 (5948), Papers of William Ernest Hocking (*92-M-71), Houghton Library, Harvard University [collection henceforth "Hocking Papers"].

[20] William Ernest Hocking to George Finger Thomas, January 3, 1940, Hocking Papers.

[21] George Finger Thomas to William Ernest Hocking, January 14, 1940, Hocking Papers.

[22] Pamphlet on Princeton's Program of Religious Instruction (Princeton, NJ: Princeton University Press, 1941), 6–7, quoted in Merrimon Cuninggim, *The College Seeks Religion* (New Haven, CT: Yale University Press, 1947), 77–78.

[23] As a result, it can still be found catalogued in many major university libraries on the East Coast.

in Thomas's courses to justify hiring Paul Ramsey as a second professor of religion, and by 1945, Thomas would officially found Princeton's religion department.[24] This department, in turn, served as a model for dozens of other universities as they launched their own programs for the study of religion after the war. Thomas and Greene would crisscross the country serving as consultants in these endeavors.[25] Prior to all this and most immediately, however, the new program launched just in time for the "rationally defended" liberal Protestantism these men promoted – and their particular species of Christian "personalism" – to crucially shape the outlook of the young John Rawls, who would one day become America's most famous liberal philosopher.

Rawls and the Influence of American Episcopalian Liberal Personalism

After initially declaring "Art & Architecture" as his major, Rawls belatedly switched in his junior year to philosophy.[26] This shift in major coincided with a dramatic deepening of Rawls's Episcopal religious faith that year; Thomas's class on "Christian Thought to the Reformation" may have provided some intellectual encouragement on that score.[27] What we know is that as Rawls pondered entering the Episcopal priesthood, he began work on an undergraduate thesis about Christian ethics.[28] And although Rawls would draw upon a host of theologians for that thesis, its framing was heavily influenced by the arguments of George Thomas.[29] Specifically, Rawls appears to have taken his cue from Thomas when he positioned "naturalism" as the foil for his own interpretation of Christian ethics. In Thomas's view, "the real

---

[24] Cuninggim, *The College Seeks Religion*, 191. Ramsey became one of the best-known Christian ethicists in America with the publication of his book *Basic Christian Ethics* in 1951, which John Rawls reviewed that same year.

[25] Cuninggim, *The College Seeks Religion*, 95.

[26] See administrative correspondence about the belated change at David F. Bowers to Robert G. Albion, January 8, 1942, in Rawls UAF.

[27] On Rawls's new religious seriousness in his junior year, see John Rawls, "On My Religion," published in John Rawls, *A Brief Inquiry into the Meaning of Sin and Faith* (Cambridge, MA: Harvard University Press, 2009), 261. His enrollment in Thomas's class in fall 1941 is recorded on Rawls's college transcript in Rawls UAF.

[28] The thesis was first discovered and discussed in print by Eric Gregory. See Eric Gregory, "Before the Original Position: The Neo-orthodox Theology of the Young John Rawls," *Journal of Religious Ethics* 35, no. 2 (2007), 179–206.

[29] For more extensive discussion of the theological sources used in Rawls's thesis, see Robert Merrihew Adams, "The Theological Ethics of the Young Rawls and Its Background," in Rawls, *Sin and Faith*, 24–101. These sources are also explored at greater length in P. MacKenzie Bok, "The Early Rawls and His Path to *A Theory of Justice*" (PhD Diss., Cambridge University, Faculty of History, 2016), 15–48.

enemy of religion in the schools and colleges is the dominant philosophy of naturalism."[30] As he put it in his inaugural public lecture,

Secularism is the theory that men should seek ends which are exclusively human and natural. Its sting is in its assumption that all ends which claim to transcend nature and human life are illusory. In this sense of the term, secularism is a corollary of Naturalism, which accepts as real nothing that is not embraced in nature, the totality of events in space and time.[31]

Materialism was fine for science but dangerous as an overall outlook; Thomas feared that the fading out of the spiritual view threatened the fabric of democracy and misled his contemporaries as to the true nature of reality.

Upon turning to the preface of John Rawls's 1942 thesis, the parallels are obvious. According to the young Rawls, "naturalism is the universe in which all relations are natural and in which spiritual life is reduced to the level of desire and appetition." This attitude toward existence "cannot explain community and personality," and therefore "loses the inner core of the universe," he wrote.[32] The young Rawls believed a mistaken naturalism, influenced by the Greek tradition, had infused much of Christian theology since Augustine and had to be repudiated. In its stead, he proposed a Christian ethics firmly grounded on the distinction between the natural and the personal. While he struggled to define "personality" precisely, Rawls stated as a core assumption "that there is something which we call personality existing in the world, and that persons as such exist."[33] Furthermore, these persons form and exist within the context of "community." And "the realm or the character of the personal and the communal is qualitatively distinct from the realm of nature," Rawls insisted. "By nature we mean what is usually meant by that term, i.e., the expanse of space filled by bodies, all that we see, feel, touch and so forth. As a result of this distinction between the natural and the personal, there are two types of relations, natural and personal."[34] Proper Christian ethical relations with other persons and with God had to be of the latter type. Otherwise one was committing a category error and treating persons as objects. Like Thomas, Rawls thought one had to survey the world from a spiritual point of view, to see the image of God in every person, in order to think rightly about ethics. And thinking rightly

[30] George F. Thomas, Pamphlet on *The Place of Religion in School and College* (Montevallo: Alabama College Press, 1941), 15, quoted in Cuninggim, *The College Seeks Religion*, 251.
[31] Thomas, *Religion in an Age of Secularism*, 9. Compare also George F. Thomas, "The Relation of Philosophy and Religion," *Philosophical Review* 55, no. 5 (September 1946), 564–571, at 566.
[32] Rawls, *Sin and Faith*, 107.   [33] Ibid., 111.   [34] Ibid., 112.

about ethics meant thinking about community, because persons were as securely embedded in community as natural objects were embedded in the physical world.

This claim lay at the heart of personalism: not just to assert the world was spiritually alive, but also to underscore that the character of deep spiritual reality was personal, defined by the personal character of God and the echoing personal nature of humankind. This was the framework that could render "human rights" as a law of nature – because what it meant to respect such rights was to see and treat other humans as the persons that they were. To the young Rawls, this tight connection between spiritual personalist reality and one's moral duties meant that one could not be hived off from the other: "There can be no separation between religion and ethics," he wrote, "since the problems they deal with are in the same nexus of relations, namely those personal relations which involve all persons existing in the universe."[35] Such an assertion might today be more readily expected in a theology thesis than a philosophy one. But since the religion department had not yet taken shape in 1942, philosophy was still for Rawls the logical Princeton department in which to pursue such arguments. Furthermore, Rawls had encountered at Princeton a cohort of professors who worshipped as Episcopalians and thought as philosophers, moving easily between those realms. Aside from Thomas and Greene – the latter would serve as one of Rawls's thesis readers – there was his ethics professor Walter Stace (another thesis reader), who had once planned to enter the Anglican priesthood, and the Wittgensteinian Norman Malcolm, also an Episcopalian, who taught Rawls in a spring 1942 class on "Social Philosophy" that chiefly focused on theology about the problem of evil.[36]

It is Thomas's and Greene's writings, however, that best illuminate the particular fulcrum on which Rawls would come to balance his early Christian ethics. On one hand, they and he were deeply familiar and to a degree sympathetic with the ascendant neoorthodox theology of the day, which emphasized a keen awareness of the sin and fallenness of man. Thomas and Greene went to Theological Discussion Group meetings with Reinhold Niebuhr; young Rawls likely attended Niebuhr's 1942 talk at Princeton and extensively cited the first volume of Niebuhr's *The*

---

[35] Ibid., 114.
[36] On Stace, see Roy Herbert, "Philosopher Stace Is Homey Pipe-Smoker; Calls Moral Relativity Talk 'Disastrous,'" *Daily Princetonian* (January 7, 1949), 2. On Rawls's class with Malcolm, see Thomas Pogge, *John Rawls: His Life and Theory of Justice* (Oxford: Oxford University Press, 2007), 11.

Nature and Destiny of Man.[37] Yet on the other hand, the Reformed tradition from which neoorthodoxy largely emerged remained somewhat alien and alienating to these Episcopalians, whose denominational tradition did not entirely embrace the "salvation by faith alone" rejection of human works. To be sure, Anglicans had since the English Reformation styled themselves as Protestants in contradistinction to "Papists" on matters of church polity, but they had nearly always been just as ready to lambast the perceived determinism of Calvinists. So while they might summon up the moral seriousness of "crisis theology," Thomas and Greene ultimately retained a liberal hopefulness about the possibility of collaborating with God in bringing about God's Kingdom – a vision Rawls also embraced. In fact, even when Rawls leaned heavily upon the writings of neoorthodox theologian Emil Brunner in his thesis, it was to pull out the most liberal thread in Brunner's thought. The upshot of all this was that Thomas and Greene and Rawls would aim to articulate a personalist theology of human nature that could render persons inviolable by virtue of their relationship with God – and yet also kept them free. Interesting, this was the same goal Catholic philosopher Jacques Maritain set himself in establishing a personalist framework to underpin Christian human rights; as we see in what follows, the two endeavors would soon intersect.

According to George Thomas, the ideal of human good was "the fulfillment of personality in a community of free men capable of taking responsibility for their own destiny." This ideal, Thomas opined, was based in a belief in human worth that could be put both in terms of "the Greek and eighteenth century view" of human beings as rational and autonomous, and in terms of "the Hebrew vision of man as a creature made in the image of God and the Christian vision of him as a son of God." The Enlightenment vision of human beings borrowed from classical antiquity – in which the truth-seeking person whose reason triumphed over passion could attain spiritual freedom – was "an indispensable aspect of the democratic theory," Thomas thought. But the latter religious appeal to the image of God imprinted in every person strengthened the case, since it offered "the modern democratic faith" a more durable justification for treating all people as potentially reasonable and responsible and autonomous, even if in practice they were behaving otherwise. Only such a consistent attitude of respect and love toward one's fellows could be the basis for the genuine community that democracy required,

---

[37] On Niebuhr's lecture at Princeton, see "Let Us Clarify Our Ideals," *Daily Princetonian* (November 16, 1942), 6.

Thomas contended.[38] Thomas's dual picture aligns with much of what has been written by American historians about the wartime twinning of "Judeo-Christian" religion and democracy.[39] What it underscores, however, is how neither the Enlightenment in general nor the French Revolution specifically loomed as a bogeyman for most American Protestants. Allying Christianity with talk of democracy, autonomy, and rights did not strike any of Rawls's teachers as an about-face.[40] Indeed, they saw Christianity as the spiritual guarantor of individual agential freedom. Greene, also writing in 1940, described teaching his annual Princeton course on Plato's *Republic*, then asking his undergraduates whether they would like to live under such a regime. "Their answer is a unanimous, emphatic 'No, because we would be deprived of all initiative, free choice, and genuine responsibility!' I submit that this response is motivated by a sound democratic impulse, that is, a sound moral impulse and a sound Christian impulse."[41] Rawls surely heard versions of these arguments; he took Greene's aforementioned Plato class in spring 1941, and then Thomas's "Christian Thought to the Reformation" class the following fall.

In making such arguments about the importance of human spiritual freedom, Greene and Thomas knew themselves to be in disagreement with certain forms of neoorthodox theology. When addressing Christian educators, Greene asserted four tenets of Christianity: "that man is a being of intrinsic worth, that he cannot save himself, that God has taken the initiative, and that man is under moral and religious obligation to meet God halfway."[42] But this last one was a sticking point – for Swiss theologian Karl Barth, for instance, there was to be no talk of man reaching halfway across the unbridgeable ontological divide between the human and the divine; only God could make such a leap.[43] In 1941, in a review of H. Richard Niebuhr's new book, Thomas criticized Niebuhr for adopting similar, Barthian language: "the process is one of 'disclosure' on God's part, not of 'discovery' or 'vision' by man. One wonders whether this Barthian view, as well as the view that it is God rather than Christ or man who revealed, is not an example of that 'totalitarian,' 'either-or'

[38] Thomas, *Religion in an Age of Secularism*, 20–21.
[39] K. Healan Gaston, "Interpreting Judeo-Christianity in America," *Relegere: Studies in Religion and Reception* 2, no. 2 (2012), 291–304.
[40] This is in contrast to how Moyn characterizes the move among European Catholics. See Moyn, *Christian Human Rights*, 9–10.
[41] Theodore M. Greene, "Christian Education and Democracy," *Christian Education* 23, no. 3 (February 1940), 151–158, at 156.
[42] Ibid., 153.
[43] Karl Barth, *The Epistle to the Romans*, trans. Edwyn C. Hoskyns (London: Oxford University Press, 1933), 365.

thinking which Niebuhr seeks so hard to avoid."[44] Thomas and Greene were still theological liberals; they wanted to ensure that "the fashion in certain Neo-Orthodox circles to scoff at the 'perfectionism' of some Christians" not banish the Christian ethical aim of emulating Christ more perfectly.[45] The corrective point that man needed God was useful; the dismissal of man's agency was not. On the other hand, when Julius Seelye Bixler – another member of the Theological Discussion Group – published a 1940 book defending a species of such theological liberalism (*Religion for Free Minds*), Thomas wrote a friendly review but ended by admonishing Bixler:

Its chief weakness is the neglect of certain distinctive insights of Christianity, especially the depth of human sin in the will and the need for divine grace. Only these insights, I think, can save those of us who still call ourselves liberals from falling into the humanism and moralism with which the Barthians reproach us.[46]

So Thomas was willing to take on board the neoorthodox emphasis on sin – but not to let it overwhelm what he considered to be the hope of the Gospel.

Close reading of these academics shows that, despite their association with neoorthodox conversation partners in the Theological Discussion Group, one needs to be attuned to a new *liberal* theology that was also blossoming during the war.[47] When Thomas and Greene wrote about spiritual freedom, they were not picturing the irresolvable paradox of finitude and freedom that was characterized as provoking men to sin in Reinhold Niebuhr's first volume of *The Nature and Destiny of Western Man*.[48] They were imagining a responsible freedom that it was possible to live into. The Christian knew that ultimate hope had to be deposited in eternal life through Christ, not social utopianism or inevitable progress,

[44] George F. Thomas, "The Meaning of Revelation by H. Richard Niebuhr," *Journal of Religion* 21, no. 4 (October 1941), 455–460, at 459.

[45] George F. Thomas, "Central Christian Affirmations," in *The Christian Answer*, 126–127.

[46] George F. Thomas, "Religion for Free Minds by Julius Seelye Bixler," *Journal of Religion* 20, no. 3 (July 1940), 292–293, at 293.

[47] Past scholars referred to a portion of the Theological Discussion Group as "neoliberals," distinct from the "neoorthodox" wing. But they focused on the churchmen (Van Dusen, Bennett, etc.) in this regard, not the academics. See Kenneth Cauthen, *The Impact of American Religious Liberalism* (New York: Harper & Row, 1962); William R. Hutchison, *The Modernist Impulse in American Protestantism* (Cambridge, MA: Harvard University Press, 1976); Gabriel Fackre, "Theology: Ephemeral, Conjunctural, and Perennial," in *Altered Landscapes: Christianity in America, 1935–1985*, ed. David W. Lotz, Donald W. Shriver Jr., John F. Wilson, and Robert T. Handy (Grand Rapids, MI: William B. Eerdmans, 1989). The term "neoliberal" has since become largely unusable in this context, given its other strong contemporary valences.

[48] Reinhold Niebuhr, *The Nature and Destiny of Man, Vol. 1, Human Nature* (New York: Charles Scribner's Sons, 1941), 182–183.

Thomas argued, but God was still the God of history, so "the hope of eternal life does not prevent Christians from seeking to approximate the Kingdom in history as far as their weakness and that of their fellows will permit." Platonic dualism put time and eternity in opposition; in contrast, from a Christian perspective, Christ had entered history and therefore "eternity must fulfill that which time has begun."[49]

Rawls and the Influence of Maritain's French Catholic Personalism

All these themes were extensively echoed in the personalist theology of another Princeton faculty member writing at the same time: French Catholic philosopher Jacques Maritain, the most famous theorist of Christian human rights. Maritain had been teaching an annual course of lectures in Toronto throughout the 1930s and complemented this with various American appointments during the war; he arrived on Princeton's campus as a visiting professor in the spring of 1941, a few months after George Thomas took up his appointment.[50] He returned again to give weekly lectures for the spring of 1942.[51] When the *Nassau Literary Review*, Princeton's literary magazine and oldest student publication, began to prepare for its special centenary issue in the spring of 1942, its editors asked Maritain to contribute a piece.[52] He used the occasion to publish his essay "Natural Law and Human Rights" for the first time in the United States; it was his earliest significant statement on human rights as such, and would later appear as the second half of his short 1943 book, *The Rights of Man and Natural Law.*[53] In that article, Maritain argued that natural law was the unwritten law that claimed obedience from man by virtue of his very nature. But along with universal obligation to that law came universal human rights, Maritain wrote, for:

The notion of right and the notion of moral obligation are correlative, they are both founded on the freedom proper to spiritual agents: if man is morally bound to the things which are necessary to the fulfillment of his destiny, it is that he has

---

[49] Thomas, "Central Christian Affirmations," 133.

[50] "Faculty Personnel Undergoes Changes during Summertime," *Daily Princetonian* (September 24, 1940), 1.

[51] "Maritain to Lecture Tomorrow," *Daily Princetonian* (April 27, 1942), 1.

[52] Jacques Maritain, "Natural Law and Human Rights," *Nassau Literary Review* 100, no. 3 (May 1, 1942), 14–22.

[53] Samuel Moyn notes that this article first appeared as the printed text of an award acceptance speech Maritain delivered in Ontario on January 18, 1942, and then in print in Ireland in the *Dublin Review* of April 1942 (Moyn, *Christian Human Rights*, 203). I have not found any instances of the essay's publication in the United States prior to its May 1, 1942, appearance in the *Nassau Literary Review*.

the right to fulfill his destiny; and if he has the right to fulfill his destiny he has the right to those things which are necessary for this purpose.[54]

Like Thomas and Greene, Maritain linked human beings' spiritual nature to freedom and its necessary accompaniment, moral responsibility. Thomas's mentor William Ernest Hocking made an almost exactly identical argument that same year; as Linde Lindkvist notes, Hocking held that "he who claims a right accepts a responsibility to destiny, and holds his right just so long as he maintains that ultimate bond which rebukes his frivolity and his sensation-yardstick for the worth of living. There are no costless rights."[55] For all these Christian thinkers, claiming one's rights entailed acknowledging one's higher calling and therefore one's responsibilities to God.

Also like these American liberal philosophers, Maritain rejected the Reformed Christian idea that human nature was so thoroughly corrupted that it could do no good; sound Christian theology taught that "grace perfects nature and does not destroy it," Maritain wrote, so with God's help the human agent could genuinely participate in fulfilling his higher destiny. Maritain acknowledged that that destiny lay ultimately outside time; indeed, "the human person transcends the State to the extent that man is ordered to things which are superior to time."[56] But just as Thomas had insisted that the work of eternity began for Christians within time, so did Maritain. For this reason it was essential that fundamental human rights be guaranteed. In enumerating these rights, Maritain offered some persuasive redefinition of the American Declaration of Independence's right to the pursuit of happiness. He described it as the right "to the pursuit of one's human, moral and rational fulfillment, in other words, to the pursuit of happiness, which is above all the pursuit, not of material accommodations, but of moral righteousness, internal strength and completion, with the material and social conditions involved."[57] As this description shows, the *purpose* of human rights was to secure the spiritual, otherworldly aims for which persons existed, but the necessary conditions for achieving these aims involved material, this-worldly realities. Human beings were "ordered to supra-temporal values" for Maritain, but they lived in time.[58] And they were ordered to consciously pursue those supra-temporal values; here too Maritain – like

---

[54] Maritain, "Natural Law and Human Rights," 16–17.

[55] William Ernest Hocking, *What Man Can Make of Man* (New York: Harper & Brothers, 1942), 50; see discussion in Lindkvist, *Religious Freedom and the Universal Declaration of Human Rights*, 54.

[56] Maritain, "Natural Law and Human Rights," 19.   [57] Ibid., 21.   [58] Ibid., 20.

Thomas and Greene – linked the rational to the human spirit without reducing the sacred aspect of human nature to rationality alone.

The similarities between Maritain's theory and that of the liberal Episcopalian philosophers might be attributable to Maritain's own liberal Protestant upbringing in France – he had only converted to Catholicism at twenty-four. It certainly reflected Maritain's wartime immersion in the American rhetoric of rights and freedom; indeed, "Natural Law and Human Rights" featured two prominent references to Franklin Delano Roosevelt's 1941 State of the Union Address, one concerning the positive freedoms of "freedom from want, and freedom from fear" and another concerning religious freedom, the "freedom of every person to worship God in his own way everywhere in the world."[59] More fundamentally, however, Maritain shared with Thomas and Greene the philosophical challenge of articulating a sort of "Via Media" – trying to valorize human subjective action while also pointing to an objective moral order beyond human power to alter. And the Scylla and Charybdis of their mental landscapes were the same: the self-abnegation of neoorthodox theology on one side, various forms of totalitarian human egotism on the other. In light of this shared intermediate position, it is perhaps unsurprising that the French Catholic and the American Episcopalians found their way to personalist conceptions of moral and spiritual life that were deeply similar in structure.

These two strands of personalism became robustly intertwined in the budding moral theory of the young John Rawls. Rawls's senior thesis on Christian ethics mentions Maritain only fleetingly, so one might assume that their paths did not cross at Princeton, or that perhaps Rawls attended one of Maritain's public lectures without taking much from it. A remarkable document, however, shows otherwise. Nestled in the May 1942 centenary edition of the *Nassau Literary Review*, not far from Maritain's "Natural Law and Human Rights" article, is a previously unnoted article on "Christianity and the Modern World" by John Rawls.[60] The piece is a striking call to stem the tide of secularization and make society truly Christian, and it shows Rawls, then a college junior, explicitly adopting Maritain's position on how God's grace transforms and perfects the spiritual freedom inherent in human nature. "Jacques Maritain, in his 'True Humanism,' sums up the whole

---

[59] Ibid., 18, 22. Lindkvist explores quotation of Franklin Delano Roosevelt as a rhetorical strategy adopted by Maritain and a number of Catholics in America in the 1940s at Lindkvist, *Religious Freedom and the Universal Declaration of Human Rights*, 36–38.

[60] John Rawls, "Christianity and the Modern World," *Nassau Literary Review* 100, no. 3 (May 1, 1942), 140–150. I believe I am the first to rediscover this earliest article by the young Rawls, and that the present chapter is the first discussion of it in print.

question," Rawls wrote.[61] Upon examination, Rawls's article turns out to be framed almost entirely in terms borrowed from the 1938 English translation of Maritain's book *True Humanism*, and represents the very first time that the young Rawls would call for the moral reform of social institutions.

"What the word 'Christian' means is indefinite. To some it signifies a religion, to others it implies a moral standard or code, and to certain of us it suggests a pattern for social revolution," Rawls wrote.[62] His aim in his *Nassau Literary Review* piece was to diagnose whether Western civilization could fairly describe itself as Christian any longer – it could not, it was "neutral" at best – and then to call for it to return to faith before it became fully "pagan," as the Nazis, the Fascists, and the Communists already had.[63] Rawls had borrowed the term "pagan" for describing modern post-Christian society from Maritain. To Rawls, it meant either accepting a deterministic view of a fully mechanized world, or else – more commonly – placing a mistaken egotistical faith in the human capacity to triumph in all things.[64] At a minimum, Rawls commented, if one endorsed this latter untrammeled faith in humanity, "the idea of Grace as a factor in human life is allowed to float out the window upon reason and a rational optimism which regards the world as essentially reasonable in all its processes."[65] He identified such optimism with John Dewey, whose views represented "the present day faith in democracy and in man's ability to work out his own problems."[66] But on the darker side, at its worst, such human pride could quickly lead to identifying moral value with "strength and power." This approach, which the young Rawls identified philosophically with Nietzsche, might seem "humanistic" in its glorification of human self-sufficiency, but in fact represented the "annihilation" of humanism by denying all obligations to humble love and service.[67]

This idea that radically secular humanism in fact became antihumanistic was also borrowed straight from Maritain, who had written in *True Humanism*:

Man, forgetting that in the order of being and goodness it is God who has the first initiative and who gives life to our freedom, has sought to exalt his own proper movement as creature to the dignity of the first absolute movement and to attribute to his own created freedom the first initiative towards goodness. Thus his movement of ascension has necessarily been separated from that of grace, and

---

[61] Ibid., 141.   [62] Ibid., 140.   [63] Ibid., 149.

[64] For an example of Maritain's use of "pagan" as a term of art to describe contemporary modern societies, see Jacques Maritain, *True Humanism* (London: Bles, 1938), xvi.

[65] Rawls, "Christianity and the Modern World," 145.   [66] Ibid., 144.

[67] Ibid., 146–147.

this is why the age in question has been an age of dualism, of division, of disintegration, an age of humanism apart from the Incarnation, where the effort of progress must needs follow an inevitable course and itself contribute to the destruction of what is human. In short, we may say that the radical fault of anthropocentric humanism has been its anthropocentric quality, not its humanism.[68]

In other words, personalists like Maritain and now Rawls averred that the humanness of human beings could only be revealed in right relationship to God. "When Nietzsche thought he was negating Christianity, he did not realize that he was negating that whole humanistic stream which made him possible," Rawls wrote. "He stands at the end of 'Pelagian' heresy; he is the final annihilation of grace."[69]

On the other hand, an overemphasis on grace to the exclusion of all human agency in the divine drama – the theological mistake of which Rawls accused Luther and Calvin – would mean that "the central notion of Grace with Freedom is lost, and with it the essence of Christianity." Determinism, whether materialist or theological, "completely destroys the moral life for without freedom there can be no responsibility, and without responsibility the intrinsic worth of doing good is lost."[70] Rawls sounded here a great deal like the undergraduate Plato students Greene had quoted as examples of good Christian Democrats, protesting any picture that resulted in an unacceptable loss of moral agency. He was just as committed as his Episcopalian professors to establishing a theological position that accommodated both divine grace and human freedom. As Rawls summed up his personalist creed:

The central idea of the Christian religion, and the one that underlies all its beliefs is, it seems to me, the mystery of the togetherness between Nature and Grace. It is this conception which underlies the Christian conception of God as a person. . . . Further the Christian notion of the efficacy of moral effort comes from the idea of acting with God together because the very phrase implies that Nature can act positively after the reception of grace – that Nature is not a slave. But note also that this togetherness also means that man must not consider himself able to live alone – such a union implies always two factors, the Nature and the Grace. The intrinsic value of individuals also is derived from this fundamental conception, for it recognizes that each man regardless of wealth and intelligence, possesses value by virtue of his ability to enter into the relation of union between Nature and Grace.[71]

---

[68] Maritain, *True Humanism*, 19.
[69] Rawls, "Christianity and the Modern World," 147. Rawls's antipathy to Nietzsche is a consistent aspect of his intellectual landscape.
[70] Ibid., 143–144.   [71] Ibid., 140–141.

This text is Rawls's earliest attempt to work out the subtle position he would occupy throughout his philosophical life: granting deep value to the activity of human beings, as expressions of human freedom and personality, while also refusing to measure value by success in such activities, all of which had to be regarded as a gift. Maritain offered Rawls in 1942 the best vocabulary he had yet found for describing the apparent paradox that he wished to ardently affirm: "the Mystery of Nature and Grace, and the Mystery of Grace and Freedom."[72] And what Maritain, with his deep Catholic learning, could provide to Rawls that the likes of Thomas and Greene could not was a long theological tradition to claim for this personalist view. To quote the words that Rawls borrowed from Maritain: "When they (referring to the Medieval Schoolmen) affirm at one and the same time the full gratuitousness, the sovereign liberty and efficacy of divine grace, and the reality of the human free-will . . . they were professing purely and simply a conception which is Christian, catholic, and orthodox."[73]

Maritain's insistence on human freedom and moral responsibility, even in light of the necessity of divine grace, was not an incidental point to his arguments for Christian human rights. As we have seen, for him and liberal Protestants alike, this positioning was essential – God's grace was what gave human beings the sacred mission that entitled them to rights, but for there to be reason to respect such rights, they had to be capable of free action in pursuit of that mission. Rights in this framework were always *for* something; one had a divine purpose to live into. And therefore the violation of rights was ultimately an offense against God; this was the special valence with which these Christians sought to endow the language of "human rights" as they codified it in documents such as the Universal Declaration of Human Rights.[74] For this reason, the right to freedom of conscience was especially important to Maritain; there could be no greater frustration of God's purposes for a human being than to block his or her sincere pursuit of right belief.[75] Later, as rights talk became increasingly secularized, such direct appeals to divine purposes would

---

[72] As I argue elsewhere, Rawls's emphasis on freedom in this 1942 *Nassau Literary Review* article undercuts the arguments in Eric Nelson's *The Theology of Liberalism: Political Philosophy and the Justice of God* (Cambridge, MA: Harvard University Press, 2019), which seeks to render Rawls's youthful theology as fundamentally deterministic and to suggest that his later secular moral philosophy is thus reliant on the same determinism.

[73] Ibid., 141, quoting Maritain, *True Humanism*, 4.

[74] For helpful detail on how Charles Malik brought Christian personalist ideas to bear in the drafting of the Universal Declaration of Human Rights, see Lindkvist, *Religious Freedom and the Universal Declaration of Human Rights*, 43–57.

[75] Maritain, "Natural Law and Human Rights," 20–22. Lindkvist explores Maritain's particular interest in the freedom of conscience in Lindkvist, *Religious Freedom and the Universal Declaration of Human Rights*, 36–42.

fade somewhat into the background, but the structure of justifying rights by reference to the free human purposes and "flourishing" that they enabled would persist.

Long before he became an agent of such secularized discourse in his mature work, the young Rawls expressed his impatience with it: "It is not too much of an exaggeration to call modern philosophy a perversion of the Christian truth in one way or another. So great has the perversion become, that the true Faith lies unrecognized behind it."[76] But Karl Barth would have argued that the personalist liberal theology being offered by Maritain, Thomas, and now Rawls was sowing the seeds of inevitable secularization through its own anthropocentric mistake: that of thinking that human beings could have agency in divine purposes that only God could accomplish. Maritain could hear this potential criticism echoing in his head, so in *True Humanism* he took care, as Thomas had, to address the Barthian position directly.

The "archaic" position, we find in a certain school of modern Protestantism, marked by its return to primitive Calvinism. This position is primordially anti-humanist and in a word – despite all the involvements with which a highly intelligent and aware dialectic can decorate a doctrine – one which demands the annihilation of man before God. This, in brief summary, is the standpoint of the great Protestant theologian Karl Barth, who, partly under the influence of Kierkegaard, and partly in a violent renewal of the original Lutheran spirit armed with the sharp-drawn logic of Calvin, has completely reversed the stand-point of Protestantism in Germany. Schleiermacher, Harnack, the old liberalism and rationalism of the nineteenth century, all these are completely gone to dust: the modern objection to Catholicism is that it is too human. It is a return, in short to the pure pessimism of primitive Protestantism. ... Finally, his error is that of Luther and of Calvin: it is to think that grace does not vivify.[77]

On the other side of God's grace, Maritain insisted, stood human beings whose redemption gave them true freedom to act as children of God; their nature was salvageable. The young Rawls had not read Barth, little of whose work had yet been translated into English, but he followed Maritain's critique of Reformation theology. As he commented in the *Nassau Literary Review*,

Luther is no doubt one of our greatest theologians, but despite his great insights he falls into error. He realized along with the great thinkers before him that man alone cannot bridge the gap between himself and God, and that man, if unaided, inevitably falls into sin. But what Luther did not realize fully is the other side of the apparent paradox – mans [*sic*] freedom which belongs to the essence of his nature and which is not taken from him even though grace is necessary to keep him from

---

[76] Rawls, "Christianity and the Modern World," 148.
[77] Maritain, *True Humanism*, 63.

error. By underestimating the degree of man's freedom, Luther is led to accept a deterministic theory of salvation in which grace performs all acts to the exclusion of freedom. Here lies Luther's error – one which becomes even more exaggerated and perverted in Calvin.[78]

That Rawls could so approvingly emulate a Catholic intellectual's criticism of Luther and Calvin reminds us not to use the phrase "American Protestant" as too much of a catchall. Denominational distinctions still mattered theologically in the 1940s, and the Episcopalianism of Rawls and his professors left them feeling particularly free to eschew the more austere arguments of the Reformed tradition. As they sought the "Via Media" and Maritain proved himself willing to write in the liberal language of rights and freedom, these two strands met in that place and time.

Nevertheless, it is likely no accident that John Rawls's senior thesis, completed seven months after his May 1942 essay for the *Nassau Literary Review*, makes little reference to Maritain. Over the summer of 1942, Rawls stayed on campus at Princeton and took a class on "The History of European Thought" with E. Harris Harbison, a proudly Protestant professor of the Protestant Reformation.[79] The gist of Harbison's theory about Europe is conveyed by an argument Rawls cites approvingly in his thesis: European history had been repeatedly marred by the rise to power of "closed groups," beginning with "the Roman Church who called everyone outside the pale heretics" and ending with Nazism.[80] Perhaps Rawls's deepest religious conviction was that theology had to contain redemptive space for all humankind, and Harbison's course seems to have reminded him of the liberal American Protestant commonplace that Catholicism, itself misled by the sin of pride, was prone to imperious exclusions.[81] Such a reminder did not prompt Rawls to repudiate any of what he had taken from Maritain – the theology of the *Nassau Literary Review* essay and the senior thesis are consistent with one another – but he found other proponents of Christian personalism to cite.[82] Chief among them was Emil Brunner – a Swiss neoorthodox

---

[78] Rawls, "Christianity and the Modern World," 142.
[79] For a record of this class, see Rawls's college transcript in Rawls UAF. Harbison clearly thought of history in a Protestant vein; he delivered public lectures such as "The Meaning of History in the Protestant Tradition" and edited a book of "religious perspectives of college teaching in history" for the Hazen Foundation.
[80] Rawls, *Sin and Faith*, 197.
[81] This attitude toward Catholicism would linger for Rawls, who continued to use the Catholic Church as a model of authoritarianism in his writing after the war.
[82] Rawls was not alone in this ambivalence; Lindkvist notes that the 1945 report of the Joint Committee on Religious Liberty, an American mainline Protestant organization led by a Princeton man, "oscillated between viewing religious freedom as a predominantly Protestant idea, and, at the same time, acknowledging the prospect for a broader religious coalition against the forces threatening it," including "a family of thinkers and

theologian often mentioned in the same breath as Karl Barth. Yet to first note the liberal American Episcopalian professors who taught Rawls in 1941, and then to discover how the French Catholic Maritain influenced him in the spring of 1942, is to understand that Rawls's engagement with this third European Protestant strand of personalism was in service to his fundamentally liberal theological outlook, not a neoorthodox one.

Rawls and the Influence of Brunner's Protestant Existentialist Personalism

Brunner was the theologian who served as the first personal ambassador for continental neoorthodox theology in the English-speaking world.[83] After famous German Protestant theologian Adolf von Harnack endorsed the German government's aims in World War I, his student Karl Barth denounced the moral bankruptcy of liberal theology and broke out in a new direction, one that would return to Luther and Calvin and Augustine to dwell in acute awareness of the obstinacy of human sin.[84] Barth subsequently became famous over the course of the 1930s for both his systematic theology and his principled stand against the Nazis, but his colleague Emil Brunner's books were translated into English much sooner than Barth's, so Brunner's writings proved more readily accessible to English readers early on.[85] Brunner himself also traveled in the 1930s to England and America; he even served as a visiting professor at Princeton for 1938–1939, the year before Rawls matriculated there.[86] Perhaps introduced to Brunner's writings by someone who had met him during this Princeton sojourn, Rawls read several of Brunner's books over the latter half of 1942 and wrote in the preface to his senior thesis,

Amongst theologians I think Brunner is the person whom I learned the most from and I think that his work best illustrates what I mean by a theology based on the intimate and personal quality of the universe, together with a clear and unflinching recognition that the universe is a community of Creator and created.[87]

organizations working to ground the principle of religious freedom from a Catholic standpoint," such as Maritain. See Lindkvist, *Religious Freedom and the Universal Declaration of Human Rights*, 72.
[83] Hall, *Remembered Voices*, 75.
[84] Geoffrey W. Bromiley, "Karl Barth," in *Creative Minds in Contemporary Theology*, ed. Philip E. Hughes (Grand Rapids, MI: William B. Eerdmans, 1969), 27–28.
[85] Hall, *Remembered Voices*, 154. Barth authored the 1934 Barmen Declaration, which condemned steps to officially align Protestant German churches with National Socialism, and resigned his German teaching post after refusing to profess his loyalty to Hitler.
[86] Brunner and Rawls's near miss at Princeton was first noted in Gregory, "Before the Original Position," 186.
[87] Rawls, *Sin and Faith*, 108.

The key fact illuminated by this statement is that Rawls's ideas could never have been nourished by Barth's theology, neither were they the result of a general neoorthodox mood. To substantiate his idea of a "nexus" of personal relations between God and all people, Rawls drew on the aspect of Brunner's theology that was most at odds with Barth's uncompromising views about human agency. And he ultimately extended Brunner's ideas in so hopeful a direction that his Christian ethics is most appropriately viewed as a continuation of the liberal theological tradition in a personalist vein.

As Brunner recollected, the Anglophone world initially received him as a representative of both himself and Barth. In his words, "I was regarded more or less as the English mouthpiece of this Barth-Brunner theology, until suddenly the well-known controversy over natural theology made it evident that Barth and Brunner were not identical twins."[88] The controversy was the one made famous by a furious essay Barth wrote entitled simply "Nein!"[89] Brunner had argued that a "point of contact" was possible between God and fallen humanity. In stark contrast, Barth stressed above all else "recollection of the qualitative distinction between God and men."[90] He likened human striving to connect with God to the building of the Tower of Babel, and he rebuked the church for thinking that it could bridge the ontological divide with God.[91] Neither the church nor individual Christians, he argued, can attain grace by "following after" God, because God saves human beings through a miracle they cannot understand or imitate.[92] Instead, Barth insisted, both the church and its members should live bowed down by an awareness of God's well-deserved judgment upon them, a posture that would enable openness to the inexplicable wonder of God's forgiving grace.[93]

With this attitude in mind, Barth expressed his concern that Brunner's resuscitation of natural theology and the idea that human beings could be in community with God was another attempt to domesticate the Gospel, rather than living in awe of its mystery.

I saw Emil Brunner, another member of our group, pursuing a theology that I increasingly came to view only as a return under new banners to the fleshpots of

---

[88] Brunner quoted in Hall, *Remembered Voices*, 154.

[89] Karl Barth, "Nein!" in *Natural Theology*, trans. Peter Fraenkel (London: Centenary Press, 1946), 97. The controversy over natural theology was Brunner and Barth's most famous disagreement. See Hall, *Remembered Voices*, 78.

[90] Barth, *Romans*, 365. The phrase "infinite qualitative distinction" comes from Kierkegaard and is quoted at Barth, *Romans*, 10.

[91] Ibid., 372.   [92] Ibid., 369.

[93] Ibid., 367, 372. Despite his thundering emphasis on God's judgment, Barth held out hope for universal salvation.

the land of Egypt, which I thought that he had left behind once and for all in our common exodus.[94]

Over his time in England, Brunner had been influenced by the evangelical Oxford Group, a Protestant Christian movement of the 1920s and 1930s that focused on the need for self-mastery over sin and mostly targeted the educated and well-to-do in Europe and America.[95] Philip Leon, a thinker Rawls read in Norman Malcolm's class and also cited in his senior thesis, was among the movement's leading figures.[96] In 1936, Barth wrote of the Oxford Group:

One decisive point against it is that while it sets out to be a renewal of Christianity, it fails to respect its mystery, the freedom of grace and the sanctity of the name of God. Instead, all along the line, with all kinds of excuses and changes of terminology, it is turned into humanity and morality. . . . If the church does not resist this movement, in the end it will be completely ruined by it.[97]

In the Oxford Group's exhortations to live a better life, Barth saw the shadow of the optimistic belief in progress and the perfectibility of man that he had rejected for leading Harnack into nationalistic boosterism. For Barth, the only real freedom was the "freedom of grace" that belonged to God, not, as we have seen Maritain contend, a freedom for human beings that could be perfected by grace.

Barth was perhaps unfair to Brunner; his theology remained considerably less enthusiastic than that of the Oxford Group, and Brunner certainly agreed with Barth regarding human beings' utter dependence on God for salvation. On this point, Barth, Brunner, and the young Rawls all followed Augustine, who argued that even the person who genuinely willed to turn away from sin required God's grace to effect repentance.[98] In his thesis as in his *Nassau Literary Review* piece, Rawls repeatedly repudiated Pelagianism, the classical Christian heresy of thinking that humans could right their relationship with God and achieve salvation through their own best efforts.[99] Nevertheless, Rawls went farther than

---

[94] Eberhard Busch, *Karl Barth: His Life from Letters and Autobiographical Texts* (London: SCM Press, 1976), 195.

[95] Its American branch eventually gave birth to the organization Alcoholics Anonymous.

[96] Leon is most famous for his 1939 text *The Philosophy of Courage or the Oxford Group Way*. There is no evidence that Rawls was independently exposed to the Oxford Group through its American operations, although it would be unsurprising if it influenced some of the campus chaplains he encountered.

[97] Busch, *Karl Barth*, 275–276.

[98] Augustine, *Confessions*, trans. Henry Chadwick (Oxford: Oxford University Press, 2008), 131. See also Rawls, *Sin and Faith*, 231.

[99] Rawls, "Christianity and the Modern World," 144. See also Rawls, *Sin and Faith*, 172.

Brunner in the direction Barth decried; crediting some transformative potential to human agency, his thesis culminated with the hope that human beings could contribute to hastening the coming of the Kingdom of God.

Rather than endorsing Barth's conception of an unbridgeable ontological divide, Rawls adhered to Brunner's assessment of the relationship between God and human beings as involving a "point of contact."[100] Citing Brunner's *Man in Revolt*, published in English in 1939, Rawls wrote,

Man was made in God's image, which meant that man was made as a responsible being, as a communal being, and as a being who must answer to his Creator. This capacity to answer was God's gift to man, not a law laid upon him.[101]

This reference to man as "a responsible being" underscores the viewpoint Rawls shared with Thomas, Greene, and Maritain about the importance of human spiritual freedom, even in relations with God. This freedom comes from being made in the image of God. According to Brunner, "the fact that man 'has' intrinsic value – that is, his distinctive being – consists in 'having' the Word, that is, that he knows himself to be in God, and also knows that God knows and recognizes him."[102] Brunner explicitly opposed this view to Barth's contention that "the bond between the *humanum* and the man's relation with God has been severed; the fact that 'man is man and not a cat' is 'quite unimportant.'"[103] In other words, Barth believed that human beings are just as qualitatively removed from God as are all other creatures, though they were once made in God's image. Brunner, in contrast, asserted that human beings, despite being "fallen," retain some intermediate relationship with God that differs from the rest of creation. Humans could communicate with God across the divide between them; God graciously called and people had the freedom and capacity to answer.[104] Brunner's position is essential to Rawls's argument. No "community of Creator and created" could possibly exist across Barth's unbridgeable ontological divide. Barth saw all efforts at human imitation of God as fruitless, whereas Brunner presented God as a divine person on whom humans model their own communication with and love for other human persons.

---

[100] David Reidy has also noted Rawls's agreement with Brunner rather than Barth on this point; see David A. Reidy, "Rawls's Religion and Justice As Fairness," *History of Political Thought* 31, no. 2 (2010), 309–343, at 326.

[101] Rawls, *Sin and Faith*, 204.

[102] Emil Brunner, *Man in Revolt*, trans. Olive Wyon (London: Lutterworth Press, 1939), 96.

[103] Ibid., 95, citing Barth, "Nein!" 25–27.   [104] Brunner, *Man in Revolt*, 97–98.

When drawing upon Maritain seven months earlier, Rawls had described the possibility of human agency in one's communion with God in terms of the "Mystery of Grace and Freedom." If Maritain had marshaled the scholastic traditions of the Church to show that belief in such a mystery was "Christian, catholic, and orthodox," Brunner offered Rawls access to a Christian existentialist tradition that could help him describe the lived reality of that mystery.[105] In his *Nassau Literary Review* essay, Rawls had called for a three-step process: Western society must recommit itself to Christian education, then each person's heart had to be converted, then attitudes on all contemporary social issues had to be reoriented in line with that reconversion. But Rawls was hesitant in describing that second step:

The second step is the reconversion of the will, and this can only come about with the aid of Grace. Naturally there is no mechanical formula here. The final conversion is something that lies beyond ourselves. But we must try to prepare for it, and hope that it will come about.[106]

What Christian existentialism gave him was the idea that one might approach this mystery by thinking of encounters with other human persons as a path by analogy into interpersonal encounter with God (and vice versa). Brunner introduced Rawls to the tradition of describing the capacity for mutual recognition as constitutive of personhood. Brunner's book *Man in Revolt* drew inspiration on this front from Ferdinand Ebner and from Martin Buber, the Austrian Jewish philosopher who had argued in his 1923 book *I and Thou* that the religious experience is one of reciprocal encounter between personal beings, not acquisition of knowledge of a divine object.[107] Brunner's work relied heavily upon this description of religious encounter, and Rawls used precisely Buber's distinction – between the personal relations of "I and thou" and the natural relations of "I and it" – in his thesis, although he had read only Brunner's gloss on it.[108]

In Brunner's view, the genuine recognition of and communication with other persons championed by Buber was only possible in a spirit of love. As he asserted in a passage that Rawls quoted approvingly,

Man is man to the exact extent in which he lives in love. The degree of his alienation from love is the degree of his inhumanity. The distinctively human

---

[105] Rawls, "Christianity and the Modern World, 141.   [106] Ibid., 150.
[107] Martin Buber, *I and Thou*, trans. Ronald Gregor Smith (Edinburgh: T. & T. Clark, 1937). Originally published in German in 1923.
[108] Rawls, *Sin and Faith*, 117. Brunner acknowledged the influence of Buber and his Austrian counterpart Ferdinand Ebner in Emil Brunner, "Intellectual Autobiography," in *The Theology of Emil Brunner*, ed. Charles W. Kegley (New York: Macmillan, 1962), 11. See also Brunner, *Man in Revolt*, 23.

element is not freedom, nor intellectual creative power, nor reason. These are rather the conditions of realization of man's real human existence, which consists in love. They do not contain their own meaning, but their meaning is love, true community.[109]

So the human person lacked not only meaning but even proper existence outside a community of love. And "the source of all unfathomable, generous love" was God; as Brunner wrote, "The love of God, the Primal Word, with which God calls man into existence . . . is the ground from which human existence comes into being."[110] God disclosed this love through self-revelation, both historically, in the person of Jesus Christ, and inside each human being, through the Holy Spirit. This was how Brunner integrated Christian doctrine into his vision: community was possible only because God, in the persons of the Trinity, "bursts in" and speaks to human beings, revealing God's love.[111] Rawls cited Brunner when he described how revelation happens at the moment of conversion, "the Word of God speaking to us."[112]

Brunner, Buber, and Ebner had all been influenced by Søren Kierkegaard's impassioned picture of the relationship between God and man, a picture they boldly extended to apply to relations between human beings. For Kierkegaard, the person was *constituted* by relationship with God, finding the very ground of one's being in that loving connection.[113] Brunner agreed, but went on to suggest that one's personhood was also in this way constituted by all interpersonal relationship – persons were also made by God for community with one another. Brunner's theology on this score is particularly important to the history of human rights talk on the Protestant side; as Terence Renaud has shown, Brunner's *Man in Revolt* provided a key basis for the personalist consensus reached by Protestant ecumenical leaders at their 1937 Oxford Conference on Church, Community, and State. While American neoorthodox thinker Reinhold Niebuhr helped to crystallize a sense of urgency with his rhetoric of paradox and crisis, it was Brunner's relational ethics combined with the political activism of liberal Protestantism that seemed to offer the

---

[109] Brunner, *Man in Revolt*, 74, quoted at Rawls, *Sin and Faith*, 192–193.

[110] Brunner, *Man in Revolt*, 75–76.

[111] Emil Brunner, *Theology of Crisis* (New York: Charles Scribner's Sons, 1935), 32.

[112] Rawls, *Sin and Faith*, 233; Brunner's language is also echoed at Rawls, *Sin and Faith*, 246.

[113] Søren Kierkegaard, *The Sickness unto Death* (Princeton, NJ: Princeton University Press, 1941), 77–78. English editions of Kierkegaard edited by Walter Lowrie had just been published at Princeton when Rawls was writing his thesis, so he read Kierkegaard directly. For more background on Lowrie's popularization of Kierkegaard, see George Cotkin, *Existential America* (Baltimore, MD: Johns Hopkins University Press, 2003), 35–53.

most fruitful way out. The final statement of these 1937 Oxford proceedings paired the intensely personal call to respond to God's saving action
with acknowledgment of the collective social obligations that arose from
doing so.[114] Brunner would later go out of his way to emphasize that these
latter responsibilities were meaningless if transplanted outside a Christian
framework.[115] But his framing shaped the perspective of many internationalist Protestants who helped forge the language of human rights, even
if these obligations to other persons would later be untethered from the
story of obedience to God's call into relationship.

The connection between communion with God and community with
fellow human persons was the "nexus" of "those personal relations which
involve all persons existing in the universe" of which Rawls wrote.[116] The
Protestant intensity of the individual person's relationship with God
could break down the barriers of all "closed groups" and enable universal
human community. Now armed with the language of Christian existentialist passion, Rawls was more willing to directly address the moment of
conversion in his senior thesis than he had been in the *Nassau Literary
Review*: at such a moment, he wrote, God overwhelms all barriers of sin
and pride and renders the person completely exposed and helpless. Aware
of the contrast between the self's wickedness and God's goodness, the self
feels as though it ought to dissolve, yet God's love and mercy sustain it.
This experience shatters the lies of independence and rebellion and makes
the person aware of being utterly dependent upon God, prompting them
to replace claims of merit with an attitude of deep thankfulness.[117] With
egocentrism thus shattered, one is then open to right relationship with
other persons as well. Rawls's youthful writings are striking for the hints
they give of his own likely conversion experience in the prior year. But
they also showcase the development of a line of Protestant thought
according to which a "community" was a networked web of relationships,
rather than a wheel in which each individual related only like a spoke to
God at the hub, or a solid collective into which all personhood was
subsumed. This was a fundamentally subject-oriented picture, too relational to be aptly described as "submission to objective morality," even
though it gave prime position to God.[118] It provides an example of how

---

[114] Terence Renaud, "Human Rights As Radical Anthropology: Protestant Theology and
Ecumenism in the Transwar Era," *Historical Journal* 60, no. 2 (2017), 493–518, at
505–507.
[115] Emil Brunner, "Das Menschenbild und die Menschenrechte I," *Universitas* 2, no. 3
(1947), 269–274; see discussions at Renaud, "Human Rights As Radical
Anthropology," 514, and Lindkvist, *Religious Freedom and the Universal Declaration of
Human Rights*, 41.
[116] Rawls, *Sin and Faith*, 114.   [117] Ibid., 232–243.
[118] Cf. Moyn, *Christian Human Rights*, 87.

Protestant personalists sought to "leave behind the choice between the individual and the collective"; answering God's call was intensely individual, and yet it also placed one most fully in community.[119] Both Rawls and Brunner thought the model of God's love and self-revelation then enabled direct relations of love and mutual revelation between human beings.[120]

There was a difference between them, however, as to what the converted person was empowered to accomplish. Rawls's account of conversion emphasized its dependence upon God's gracious agency, but he still seems to have believed that human beings could hasten the restoration of community by imitating God in their relations with one another.[121] This assertion was his most marked point of divergence from Brunner. While ethical endeavors are necessary as an extension of being in right relationship, Brunner insisted, they do not build the Kingdom of God.[122] Human beings must not lose sight of the gap between this world and the one to come; the eternal community is not an earthly democracy. Offering a classic neoorthodox critique of liberal theology, Brunner stressed that one of the great mistakes of the modern West was to trust in deliverance through human progress when God alone can save.[123] Rawls, by contrast, believed that human beings could be God's saving agents for one another, as the Elect "help bring the totality of the creation before [God]."[124] In this respect, although he relied so heavily upon Brunner for his explanation of the mechanisms by which the mysterious meeting of human freedom and God's grace is accomplished, Rawls's conception of what came next was far closer to Maritain's.

"A Pattern for Social Revolution"

Maritain really did believe in moral progress; he thought that man's knowledge of natural law "increases little by little with the progress of moral conscience" and "will continue to develop and to become finer as long as humanity exists" until "the Gospel has penetrated to the very depth of human substance."[125] He described this as a collective process in which a whole civilization might participate; it should strive to conjure up "a cultural and temporal force of Christian inspiration able to act in history and come to the aid of men." He laid out his vision in *True Humanism*:

---

[119] Ibid., 98.   [120] Brunner, *Man in Revolt*, 176; Rawls, *Sin and Faith*, 153–155.
[121] Rawls, *Sin and Faith*, 244–245.   [122] Brunner, *Theology of Crisis*, 56.
[123] Ibid., 85–86.   [124] Rawls, *Sin and Faith*, 252.
[125] Maritain, "Natural Law and Human Rights," 16.

This new humanism, which has in it nothing in common with bourgeois humanism, and is all the more human since it does not worship man, but has a real and
effective respect for human dignity and for the rights of human personality, I see as
directed towards a socio-temporal realization of that evangelical concern for
humanity which ought not to exist only in the spiritual order, but to become
incarnate; and towards the ideal of a true brotherhood among men. It is not to the
dynamism or the imperialism of a race, or of a class, or of a nation, that it asks men
to sacrifice themselves: it is for the sake of a better life for their fellows and for the
concrete good of the community of human individuals: so that the humble truth of
brotherly love may advance – at the price of constant and difficult effort and of
poverty – to the permeation of the social order and the structures of common life.
In this way such a humanism can make man grow in communion.[126]

Again and again, Maritain emphasized the spirituality of personalism: it
called for an individual transfiguration "whereby man, consenting to be
changed and knowing that he is *changed* by grace, strives to *become* and to
realize the new man who *is* from God."[127] Because "social Christianity is
inseparable from spiritual Christianity," no ordinary temporal political
strategy could bring about a more Christian world. "You can only transform the social order of the modern world by effecting at the same time
and first of all within your own soul a renewal of moral and spiritual life:
by digging down to the moral and spiritual foundations of human existence, and reviving the moral ideas that govern the life of the social body
as such, and by awakening a new impulse in the secret sources of its
being," Maritain told his readers.[128]

Yet at the same time, such inner work would necessarily have material
consequences that transformed social and political life. "This transfiguration should extend really, and not only figuratively, to the social structures
of humanity and so bring about – in the degree to which that is possible
here on earth and in given historical circumstances – a veritable socio-
temporal realization of the Gospels," Maritain wrote.[129] Even transfig-
ured human beings might never become perfect in practice, yet:

Social structures, institutions, laws and customs, political and economic organizations, are not men though they are human: in the very degree to which they are
things, not men, they can be purified of certain particular miseries of human life;
and like many of the works of men, they are made by man and are better than he,
in their order and in certain aspects. They can be measured by justice or brotherly
love, while the acts of men are rarely measured by that measure; they can be more
just than the men who use and apply them.[130]

Thus Christians who grasped the truth of justice and loving communion
could build these principles into their institutions and laws to protect

---

[126] Maritain, *True Humanism*, xvi–ii.   [127] Ibid., 86.   [128] Ibid., 114.   [129] Ibid., 86.
[130] Ibid., 104.

against their own weaker natures. Far from being naïve, this was the definition of realistic utopianism, Maritain thought.[131] As he put it,

> If it is absurd to ask the commonwealth to make all men, taken as individuals, good and fraternal to one another, we can and should demand, which is quite another thing, that it should have in itself social structures, institutions and laws which are good and inspired by the spirit of fraternal love, and that it should orientate as potently as may be the energies of social life towards such an amity which, natural as at bottom it may be, is very hard for the sons of Adam.[132]

Fraternal love could be infused into social institutional life and so into the "secular Christian common task" of achieving the "socio-temporal realization of the Gospel" that would represent "a sanctity and sanctification of *secular* life."[133] To elevate fraternal love to a real governing goal would require demoting economism and politicism – the fatalistic assumption that the raw play of greed and power must inevitably lie at the heart of temporal affairs – and exploring new social forms such as cooperative enterprises and more devolved government.[134] But such a reorientation was fully possible in history, and indeed past due, Maritain believed.

The undergraduate Rawls did not spell out a critique of capitalism or offer any concrete institutional reforms, as Maritain did. But the structure of his argument in "Christianity and the Modern World" was lifted straight from Maritain: society stood at a great crossroads, and had to make "a positive decision." "There are but two alternatives," Rawls wrote. "Either we become Christian or we become pagans. . . . The stress of events will push us into a decision if we do not do so of our own free-will."[135] Despite the sense of crisis that he conveyed, whereby the choice to follow the totalitarians and become fully pagan would mean plunging into another Dark Ages, Rawls's vision of the alternative prospect was like Maritain's deeply hopeful: the possibility of a new Christendom, where adherence to real Christian values would provide the "pattern for a social revolution."[136] He endorsed the idea that, after "re-conversion of the part

---

[131] Maritain elaborates in several places in *True Humanism* on the idea of a realizable utopia, or "concrete historical ideal," as contrasted with an impossible ideal/utopia (Maritain, *True Humanism*, 100, 122). His arguments on this front are strikingly similar to Rawls's much later contention that conceptions of "realistic utopia" could help set long-term goals for political endeavors.

[132] Ibid., 198.   [133] Ibid., 116.   [134] Ibid., 157–158, 207–208.

[135] Rawls, "Christianity and the Modern World," 149. This language of "decision" or "crisis" was very typical of the moment and of the neoorthodox theologians like Brunner and Niebuhr in particular.

[136] Ibid., 150. For an almost identical juxtaposition of either a new Dark Ages or a New Christendom, compare Maritain, *True Humanism*, 250. The "pattern" remark is at Rawls, "Christianity and the Modern World," 140.

of the great majority of our people," then the next step would be "reorientation" in regard to social life: "we must rehabilitate our new knowledge and our new modes of living to the Christian Faith remembering that the latter stands foremost and constitutes our objective."[137] Becoming aware of one's Christian responsibilities was a path toward a far better form of community life.

In Maritain's formulation, this was what human rights necessarily entailed: human duties to pursue a Christian form of politics and social life, achieving "penetration into the temporal and cultural order of a real refraction of the Gospels."[138] Bourgeois humanism, focused on individualist freedoms, had to be dethroned in favor of a true humanism where the same spirit that prompted respect for personal rights also took offense at the oppression of the poor.[139] George Thomas shared the same emphasis on duties alongside rights, and the same criticism of allowing individual liberty to excuse material inequality. As he wrote in his 1940 inaugural lecture:

We have shown ourselves more eager to assert our rights than to acknowledge our duties. Too often we have put our own interests, and those of our group, above the welfare of the community as a whole. Moreover, individualism, with its exclusive emphasis upon liberties and rights, has had much to do with the alarming increase of economic inequality since the Civil War. When one honestly faces the fact that millions of his fellow-citizens live in a state of poverty and insecurity which embitters their relations with more fortunate groups and poisons their faith in themselves and in their country, one sees that the insistence upon unlimited liberty for some means, in effect, the denial of equality of opportunity for others.[140]

What it meant for the individual to appropriately subordinate one's own interests to the common good, Maritain mused, was not to yield to something totalizing (such as the interest "of a race, or of a class, or of a nation"), but rather "each, in subordinating himself to the common task, is subordinate to the accomplishment of the personal life of *others*, of *other persons*."[141] In this Christian picture, the same acknowledgment of humans' spiritual destiny that prompted the recognition of human rights ought also to flower into such mutuality, whereby one affirmed the functional ability of other persons to pursue their purposes as aligned with one's own deepest purpose. Rights alone were not enough.

These arguments alert us to the possibility that, in becoming deracinated from personalist Christian theology over the balance of the

---

[137] Rawls, "Christianity and the Modern World," 150.
[138] Maritain, *True Humanism*, 206.   [139] Ibid., 81, 103.
[140] Thomas, *Religion in an Age of Secularism*, 19.   [141] Maritain, *True Humanism*, 199.

twentieth century, "human rights" would be transplanted out of a context in which they actually *could* have been coherently aligned with arguments in favor of greater material equality. Certainly the writings of Maritain and Thomas on this front belie characterizations of Christian human rights talk – Catholic or Protestant, European or American – as an inherently politically "conservative" endeavor.[142] Instead, personalist Christian theories of human rights seem to have contained the potential for the very breadth of vision about "social revolution" whose loss Moyn has recently mourned.[143]

In fact, perhaps one might say that this road-not-taken was indeed taken: by John Rawls, who found himself in a cauldron of Christian personalist influences as a young man at Princeton, where the ingredients of liberal American Episcopalianism, French Catholicism, and continental dialectical theology all intermingled. Rawls's case is exceptional – an unusual moment at Princeton, a precocious youth whose denominational identity made him particularly open to a variety of such influences – and yet also emblematic of how these currents crossed and whirled together into the stew of Christian personalism. And this case is also significant because of Rawls's subsequent intellectual trajectory: even as he dropped any direct appeal to Christian frameworks, Rawls would ground his philosophical justification of welfare policies on the capacious regard for other persons that he had first learned to trumpet from Thomas, from Maritain, from Brunner.[144] Moyn calls Rawls, in the history of distributive theory, "the last Jacobin"; could he rather be, in this arena, the last Christian personalist?[145]

---

[142] Cf. Moyn, *Christian Human Rights*, 4.

[143] Samuel Moyn, *Not Enough: Human Rights in an Unequal World* (Cambridge, MA: Harvard University Press, 2018), 213. This book addresses more effectively and directly the core concerns about economic and social life that motivated Moyn's arguments in *Christian Human Rights*.

[144] For more on the persistence of Rawls's personalist outlook and his later efforts to transpose it into a moral naturalist key, see P. MacKenzie Bok, "To the Mountaintop Again: The Early Rawls and Post-Protestant Ethics in Postwar America," *Modern Intellectual History* 14, no. 1 (2017), 153–185.

[145] Moyn, *Not Enough*, 40.

9   The Dignity of Paul Robeson

Vincent Lloyd

On December 17, 1951, African American singer and activist Paul Robeson presented a long petition to the United Nations (UN) on behalf of the Civil Rights Congress. Robeson, who was himself a lawyer before he became an entertainer, had spent long hours working with lawyer William L. Patterson to draft the document, *We Charge Genocide: The Crime of Government against the Negro People.*[1] The treatment of black Americans demanded international condemnation, Patterson and Robeson asserted. "Out of the inhuman black ghettos of American cities, out of the cotton plantations of the South, comes this record of mass slayings on the basis of race, of lives deliberately warped and distorted by the willful creation of conditions making for premature death, poverty, and disease," the document begins.[2] In a narrow sense, *We Charge Genocide* made the case that the treatment of black Americans violated the Convention on the Prevention and Punishment of the Crime of Genocide, adopted by the UN General Assembly three years before. But Robeson and Patterson made a broader argument, responsive to the framework of international law emerging in the years immediately following the Second World War. Notably, the petition that Robeson brought to the headquarters of the UN invoked the concept of human dignity to protect the rights of black Americans.

Addressed to the UN General Assembly, the text of *We Charge Genocide* runs more than 200 pages. It is literally a petition: 93 names, including those of Paul Robeson, his wife, Eslanda Goode Robeson, and his son, Paul Robeson Jr., are listed as petitioners. "Many of your petitioners are Negro citizens to whom the charges herein described are not mere words.

---

[1] Martin Duberman, *Paul Robeson: A Biography* (New York: New Press, 2014), 397–398. See also Carol Anderson, *Eyes Off the Prize: The United Nations and the African American Struggle for Human Rights, 1944–1955* (Cambridge: Cambridge University Press, 2003), chap. 4.

[2] *We Charge Genocide: The Historic Petition to the United Nations for Relief from a Crime of the United States Government against the Negro People,* ed. William L. Patterson (New York: International Publishers, 1970), xiv.

They are facts felt on our bodies, crimes inflected on our dignity."[3] The Genocide Convention does not employ the language of dignity, but that was language gaining newfound recognition in international law. The preamble of the UN Charter, adopted in 1945, affirms "faith in fundamental human rights, in the dignity and worth of the human person, in the equal rights of men and women and of nations large and small." The Universal Declaration of Human Rights, adopted by the UN General Assembly in 1948, begins, "Whereas the recognition of the inherent dignity and of the equal and inalienable rights of all members of the human family is the foundation of freedom, justice and peace in the world."

The language Robeson brought to the UN might be seen as an example of ambivalent imitation – somewhere between mimicry and mockery – famously theorized by Homi Bhabha.[4] Oppressed subjects use the language of the oppressor, but with a difference. For Bhabha, such imitation is a site of political struggle, a means by which those who are oppressed can exercise their agency even when their own language has been taken away. But something else is happening in *We Charge Genocide* as well. After asserting that crimes had been "inflicted on our dignity," the petitioners continue, "We struggle for deliverance, not without pride in our valor."[5] This sentence can be read as adding a distinctive dimension to the concept of dignity absent from the discourse of international law. It is not simply that dignity marks the inherent value of every human being – a property of all human beings codified and protected by international law. Dignity here brings with it the connotations of "dignified" and "dignitaries," worthy of particular respect, as the nobles of earlier ages.[6] For Robeson and his fellow petitioners, dignity is attacked by what they name as "white supremacy" in the United States, but it can be regained and in fact perfected by "struggle." Attacking white supremacy is a means to achieve dignity, not just after success but along the way, offering deserved "pride in our valor." In other words, I argue that for Robeson, the dignity enshrined in the nascent human rights regime is important but deficient. It remains a stale abstraction. Genuine dignity is performed. In performance, dignity in the only genuinely meaningful sense of the concept is realized. This can be artistic or activist performance, for each can be directed against white supremacy and other forms of oppression. The

---

[3] Ibid., 7.
[4] Homi Bhabha, "Of Mimicry and Man: The Ambivalence of Colonial Discourse," *October* 28 (Spring 1984), 125–133.
[5] *We Charge Genocide*, 7.
[6] These resonances are explored in Jeremy Waldron, *Dignity, Rank, and Right* (New York: Oxford University Press, 2015).

international human rights regime is not a backstop against human rights abuses; it is an occasion for mobilizing oppressed communities to make real the promises of that regime and, above all, the promise of dignity.

Put another way, a central tenet of the postwar consensus was that human rights flow from human dignity, and the task of theorists and lawyers was to explicate those rights. In contrast, for Robeson – and I suggest this is characteristic of black American accounts of dignity more broadly – what the international community counts as human rights violations attack dignity in the abstract, naïve sense, and such attacks ought to precipitate struggle. Struggle results in those who struggle achieving genuine dignity, not compliance with a set of propositions about human rights. Human rights are not an end point or goal; at most, pointing to their violation serves to stoke indignity and precipitate struggle. I agree with Nick Bromell that attention to indignity is a central feature of the black political tradition: indignity as an experience that may be marked by legal or statistical measures but that always transcends those measures. Indignity is a political affect, and the response is political action – through which dignity is achieved.[7]

Scholars have recently shown the importance of specifically Catholic concerns in the rise of the concept of dignity during the 1940s.[8] This chapter adds another dimension to how we understand the circulation of dignity. I argue that Paul Robeson was not merely imitating the Catholic-influenced idiom of international law. Rather, dignity was a central part of Robeson's vocabulary, not only in the 1940s and 1950s but as early as the 1910s. Dignity was essential to Robeson's self-understanding, and it was a key term others used to describe Robeson as an actor and activist. This concept of dignity was not idiosyncratic to the performer. It was part of a black American tradition of thinking about dignity and acting with dignity, the two inextricably linked. And this tradition of black dignity, as articulated by Robeson in particular but also over its broader history, is deeply tied to Christianity. In other words, I accept the claim Samuel Moyn makes so persuasively that the concept of dignity has deep Christian connections, but I argue that looking from the bottom up, at the language and practices of a marginalized community, we see a linkage between dignity and Christianity that has a quite different character than the linkage found by focusing on European elites.

* * *

---

[7] See Nick Bromell, "Democratic Indignation: Black American Thought and the Politics of Dignity," *Political Theory* 41, no. 2 (2013), 285–311.

[8] Samuel Moyn, *Christian Human Rights* (Philadelphia: University of Pennsylvania Press, 2015).

Paul Robeson was born in 1898 in Princeton, New Jersey, the son of a man formerly enslaved.[9] He had an eventful career. He was a standout high school student; he became the first black student to attend Rutgers University, where he wrote a senior thesis on the Fourteenth Amendment, graduating as the valedictorian, and where he was also a nationally renowned football player. He attended Columbia University's law school, but his fame came as an actor and singer rather than as a lawyer. Spending some of the 1920s and much of the 1930s based in London, Robeson became an international star of the stage and screen. In England he moved toward socialism, aligning himself with working people around the world and celebrating their folk songs. These working people included his own, African Americans, and he gave black spirituals an international audience. As Robeson's left-wing politics solidified, he visited the Soviet Union and associated with organized Socialists and Communists. Back in the United States during and after the Second World War, Robeson's leftist associates brought him under scrutiny by anti-Communist agitators from the FBI and the House Un-American Affairs Committee. In 1949, a riot broke out at one of his concerts in upstate New York, and throughout the 1950s Robeson's career stagnated after he was blacklisted and the US State Department confiscated his passport. During the 1960s, he was finally allowed to travel again, although until his death in 1976 Robeson suffered from poor health, and he never regained his place at the top of the international arts scene that he held during the 1930s. However, Robeson's political activism continued, whether he was in the spotlight or not, and he mentored a generation of black artist-activists who would become icons of the civil rights movement, even as those leaders publicly kept Robeson at arm's length. Particularly notable among Robeson's mentees were Harry Belafonte and Sidney Poitier.[10]

Christianity played a crucial role in Robeson's life. Practically, when he was stuck in the United States and blacklisted by the arts establishment, it was black churches that most often opened their doors to Robeson's performances, and it was in a black church that he created his own recording studio when no corporate studio would work with him. Politically, it was important for Robeson to identify with working-class culture, and the culture of the black working class in the United States was deeply infused with Christianity. Thus, Robeson opens his political

---

[9] The definitive biography is Duberman, *Paul Robeson*.

[10] Richard Iton describes Poitier carrying on Robeson's legacy through "the search for dignified roles for black actors." *In Search of the Black Fantastic: Politics and Popular Culture in the Post-Civil Rights Era* (New York: Oxford University Press, 2008), 59.

memoir by describing his own current life (during the period of black-listing, away from the spotlight) immersed in black Christian culture. "I am a Negro," the book begins.[11] When he walks the streets of Harlem, he can "feel here the embrace of love."[12] He lives around the corner from his brother, the minister of Mother African Methodist Episcopal (AME) Zion Church, and it is there that he communes with his race: "On Sunday mornings I am united with the fellowship of thousands of my people, singing with them their songs, feeling the warmth of their handshakes and smiles."[13] This was not just any black church: founded in 1796, it was the first church of one of the three great black Christian denominations. It was founded by black members of a predominantly white liberal Methodist church that practiced segregation, and Mother AME Zion nourished the spiritual lives of great African American leaders: Sojourner Truth, most famously, with Frederick Douglass and Harriet Tubman members of associated congregations – as Robeson proudly notes.

These reflections Robeson records in *Here I Stand*, his political memoir written in 1958. Blacklisting prevented its wide distribution. Despite Robeson's status as an internationally renowned entertainer, the book was self-published and reviewed only in black American newspapers. (It did find wider distribution internationally, and it was translated into several languages.) The title itself brings together the political and the theological: "Here I stand, I can do no other, so help me God" were the words famously uttered by Martin Luther as he spoke to Emperor Charles V. They mark a commitment to faith in the face of overwhelming worldly power, an experience that certainly must have resonated with Robeson during the Red Scare. Robeson structures his book as part autobiography, part political pamphlet, connecting his own life story and political struggle with the freedom struggles of black Americans more generally and of working-class people around the world. And it starts with Christianity.

Robeson's brother, Reverend Benjamin C. Robeson, opens and closes *Here I Stand*. At the end of the text, as an appendix, is a testimonial from the minister reflecting on his extraordinary sibling. Curiously, Benjamin mentions that Paul is not, in fact, a regular churchgoer, despite what Paul professes on the memoir's first page. Benjamin asserts that despite this questionable public religiosity, Paul in fact embodies a deeper sort of religion, which he attributes to the Quaker sensibilities of their mother. "To understand Paul, one must know this. He moves by his inner

---

[11] Paul Robeson, *Here I Stand* (Boston: Beacon Press, 1971), 1.   [12] Ibid., 2.
[13] Ibid., 1. He describes this brother as "a gentle, gray-haired man of quiet dignity." *Paul Robeson Speaks: Writings, Speeches, Interviews, 1918–1974*, ed. Philip Sheldon Foner (New York: Brunner/Mazel, 1978), 387.

revelations. Experience has taught him to do this. He never fails, is never disappointed or perplexed when he follows his flash."[14] This is not quite so simple as asserting that Paul Robeson has the image of God stamped on him, and through contemplating Robeson, or a certain aspect of him, we can contemplate God. Dignity is not an abstraction ascribed to the entertainer. Rather, Robeson – who, we must remember, represents himself and is being represented as a paradigm of dignity – achieves dignity by allowing "inner revelation" to guide his actions, his performances. He has learned to do this via experience, the experiences chronicled in *Here I Stand*. These are experiences of enduring American racism, struggling against American racism and the global capitalist system of which Robeson believes it to be a part, enduring persecution for that struggle, and persisting in that struggle. Now experienced, Paul Robeson "is never disappointed or perplexed" because he is rightly oriented in struggle and familiar with the machinations of power. In this steadiness, explained by his minister brother in theological terms, Robeson performs dignity. In doing so, in acting or activism, he calls others to join him, to struggle together with him. As Benjamin Robeson puts it, this is Paul's "ministry."[15]

Benjamin points to Paul's performance of the traditional black spiritual "Witness" as exemplifying Paul's religiosity – indeed, as demonstrating that Paul's performance is a Christian "witness." The song begins repeating the line "My soul is my witness for my Lord," then proceeds to name a series of biblical figures who also "witness," and concludes by asking "Who will be a witness for my Lord?" Paul is a witness, drawing others to share his faith – a faith ambiguously Christian or political, perhaps political-theological. But there is something more personal in this "witness" than just the concerns of the day. According to Benjamin, in singing "Witness," Paul becomes "the personification of his father with his own personality added. He is singing then for his Lord and Master."[16] There is a slippage between divine and human paternity here, between God as father and Robeson's own father.[17] The faith Robeson is proclaiming is directed not only politically and religiously but also at the legacy of Robeson's father, and perhaps by extension to his father's father and a certain black tradition that itself, indirectly, is firmly rooted in the political and the religious. This, after all, is how the book started: Robeson anchored his own life in the life of black Americans and black

[14] Robeson, *Here I Stand*, 113.   [15] Ibid.   [16] Ibid.
[17] See Vincent Lloyd, "From the Theopolitical to the Theopaternal: On Barack Obama," in *Common Goods: Economy, Ecology, and Political Theology*, ed. Melanie Johnson-DeBaufre, Catherine Keller, and Elias Ortega-Aponte (New York: Fordham University Press, 2015), 326–343.

Christianity, and out of black religious sociality unfolds the story of his own life and politics.

But there is also a very specific account of Paul and Benjamin's father that matters here that Benjamin is referencing. It is found in the first chapter of his book, after Paul describes his immersion in black faith and life. "The glory of my boyhood years was my father," Robeson begins. "I loved him like no one in all the world. His people, among whom he moved as a patriarch for many years before I was born, loved him, too."[18] How does Robeson describe this beloved father of his? He is a man whose character has "rock-like strength and dignity."[19] How would "his people" who loved him characterize this man? They would speak of "his wisdom, his dignity."[20] In short, *dignity* is the essential trait of the man with whom Paul Robeson so closely identifies, and who Robeson so identifies with blackness, the man who was born a slave and rose to become a patriarch. And Robeson at his best becomes his father: when his performance precisely hits the mark, he embodies dignity.

Robeson's father, like his brother, was a minister. This is why they were in Princeton: Reverend William Drew Robeson was leading Witherspoon Street Presbyterian Church. According to Paul Robeson, it was this Reverend Robeson who "more than anyone else influenced my life."[21] Attending his brother's church was a reminder of a childhood when he attended his father's church. In some ways, Robeson describes his father as having nobility, that older sense of dignity that was "democratized" in modernity. The elder Robeson was quiet and strong, somewhat distanced from others. Even with his children he was not "demonstrative in his love."[22] Because of this high rank expressed in his father, "white folks – even the most lordly of aristocratic Princeton – had to respect him" and "recognized my father's dignity."[23] But Robeson describes his father's dignity as having aspects that went beyond nobility. After all, he was no aristocrat, and he did not belong to some high rank. He was a black man in the era of segregation. How, then, was such dignity achieved? By being embodied and lived. His dignity was reflected in his "physical bearing" and, particularly, his voice – "a deep, sonorous basso, richly melodic and refined."[24] In other words, the way this Rev. Robeson lived in his body, the way he performed every day accorded him dignity in the eyes of his family, the black community, and even white elites.

---

[18] Robeson, *Here I Stand*, 6.   [19] Ibid., 9.   [20] Ibid., 7.   [21] Ibid., 1.   [22] Ibid., 9.
[23] Ibid., 6, 9.
[24] Ibid., 9. Clearly, masculinity is attached to dignity here. But compare Brittney Cooper's attempt to find dignity "beyond respectability" in black feminist intellectuals. Brittney C. Cooper, *Beyond Respectability: The Intellectual Thought of Race Women* (Urbana: University of Illinois Press, 2017).

Paul Robeson describes another aspect of his father's dignity, tied to the others but ultimately, it seems, the most essential. Rev. Robeson's character was formed against a background of forces that would take away his dignity, that would cause him indignity. At a broad level, these were the legal mechanisms of white supremacy at the time – slavery and segregation – and Robeson describes how this manifested on a daily basis. He reflects that his father "quickly resented any attempt to belittle them [the local black community] or to interfere with their rights."[25] Because of the role Rev. Robeson played in the black community, as a minister and de facto community leader, he would often interface with white leaders, including the president of Princeton University. These leaders expected Rev. Robeson to "bow and bend," but in fact there was "no hint of servility in my father's make-up."[26] Rev. Robeson performed dignity consistently, for his own people and for whites. This was not exactly inherent dignity made visible, for example, in preaching. Rather, it was dignity developed in response to systemic injustice and violence, and so felt bodily, performed in the face of and in implicit struggle against white power.

The moral of his father's story, according to Robeson, is "that a so-called lowly station in life was no bar to a man's assertion of his full human dignity."[27] Robeson goes on to demonstrate how asserting one's dignity is more than just a universal human potential. In the case of his father, dignity was most evident in the steadfastness he demonstrated in cases of adversity. The most crushing blow to Rev. Robeson in Paul's childhood did not come directly from white supremacy. It came from within the black community, from the reverend's own congregation. Members of the church split and Rev. Robeson was ousted from his pulpit. To make a living, he started hauling ashes. Despite this diminished social status, Paul explicitly affirms that the dignity of his father was undiminished. Indeed, Robeson would likely go further and say that it is through struggle against such adversity that dignity is forged.

At the same time, we should not forget that Robeson's father was a minister, and the Christian context and Christian idiom were important for Paul Robeson, even as he secularized this idiom. He frames his own struggle to receive a passport from the US State Department as part of the long struggle of black Americans to achieve freedom of movement, so constrained and regulated during slavery and in the Jim Crow South, and

---

[25] Robeson, *Here I Stand*, 6.
[26] Ibid., 11. According to Paul Robeson, his father went to Woodrow Wilson, then president of Princeton, to ask that his children be allowed to attend Princeton. Wilson denied the request.
[27] Ibid.

Robeson frames this struggle itself as continuous with black music, with the spirituals and also the blues. Such music expresses religious and political thought at once, Robeson argues, citing the enslaved singing that they are "bound for glory" and "heading for the Promised Land."[28] These words powerfully equivocate between the other-worldly and this-worldly, freedom in heaven and freedom in the North or Canada. Either way, through song black Americans were able to affirm and theorize the concept of freedom, represented in travel but pointing toward an end to oppression *in toto*.

After surveying the constraints on black freedom using his own story, Robeson turns in *Here I Stand* to a chapter dedicated to "The Power of Negro Action." This would seem to be a purely political, perhaps specifically Marxist framing, but Robeson begins the chapter with Scripture: "How long, O Lord, how long?" (Psalm 94:3). In the second paragraph, Robeson responds in the secular: "The answer is: *As long as we permit it.*"[29] What is needed is action, like the risk-taking of the high school students in Little Rock integrating their school. Even more important than highly visible, essentially one-off action is organizing. Black communities already have organizational infrastructure, Robeson notes, most powerfully in the form of churches, "the strongest base of our power of organization."[30] The question of whether Robeson was a Christian or how often he attended church is much less important than the degree to which his own language and view of the black community was full of Christianity, even when he articulated that Christianity in a way that was oriented by and for political struggle. This is the context in which we should read Robeson's reflections on dignity: neither exclusively Christian nor secular, but responsive to the reality that black American experience and politics cannot be fully articulated outside a Christian idiom. In other words, when Robeson comes to the UN speaking of dignity, he may be responding to the UN's own emerging idiom with its implicit Christian background, but he is responding just as much, if not more, to a black vernacular sense of Christian dignity.

In fact, the language of dignity was at the center of the controversy that proved a turning point in his career, which pivoted him from international superstar of the 1930s and 1940s to national pariah in the 1950s and 1960s. The year was 1949, and the language of dignity was in the air as international human rights norms and practices were congealing. Robeson traveled to Paris to attend the Congress of the World Partisans of Peace, an attempt to cool emerging Cold War tensions. W. E. B. Du Bois was there and so was Pablo Picasso, as well as 2,000 others coming

[28] Ibid., 67.   [29] Ibid., 90.   [30] Ibid., 96.

from four dozen countries.[31] Robeson sang to the gathering and then he spoke about the importance of working-class unity and the horrors of antiblack racism in the United States. He spoke of the need for world peace, and he condemned antagonism toward the Soviet Union. As the Associated Press reported it, Robeson said, "It is unthinkable that American Negroes would go to war on behalf of those who have oppressed us for generations against a country [the Soviet Union] which in one generation has raised our people to the full dignity of mankind."[32] While there is some controversy over Robeson's precise wording, the essence of the claim was certainly true to Robeson's thought, and the idea that the Soviet Union made dignity possible was common in his speeches at the time. Condemnation ensued from all sides, including from mainstream US civil rights organizations. While the focus of the controversy was the patriotism of black Americans, Robeson's use of dignity to motivate his claim certainly captured the American imagination – and prompted disgust. The House Un-American Activities Committee called hearings at which many of Robeson's former friends condemned his remarks, most famous among them Jackie Robinson, whose testimony was carried on the first page of the *New York Times*. Robeson had helped Robinson gain entry into Major League Baseball, but now Robinson distanced himself from the singer, describing himself as "a religious man" firmly opposed to Communism.[33] A few months later, Robeson was nearly lynched at a concert in the town of Peekskill, in New York's Westchester County, as police joined anti-Robeson hooligans attacking pro-Robeson union members who were protecting the singer. As a result of blacklisting and the travel ban on Robeson that followed, his income and public profile plummeted and would never recover.

Careful followers of Robeson's thought should not have been surprised by his remarks in Paris. After he visited the Soviet Union in the mid-1930s, obviously in a quite different geopolitical context, he made similar remarks about the dignity of men and women living there. Indeed, dignity is one of Robeson's favorite words in his speeches and writings, and the frequency with which he employed the term did not dramatically change after it was enshrined in human rights law by the UN. In a collection of Robeson's speeches and writings published shortly after his death, the

---

[31] Duberman, *Paul Robeson*, 341–342.

[32] Ibid., 342. For Communist employment of dignity language, see Ernst Bloch, *Natural Law and Human Dignity* (Cambridge, MA: MIT Press, 1996); O. S. Ioffe, "The New Codification of Civil Law and Protection of the Honor and Dignity of the Citizen," *Soviet Law and Government* 1 (1963), 37–45.

[33] Duberman, *Paul Robeson*, 360.

word "dignity" appears more than seventy-five times.[34] In a 1942 speech in New Orleans, Robeson explained, "I had never put a correct evaluation on the dignity and courage of my people of the deep South until I began to come south myself. ... I see them now courageous and possessors of a profound and instinctive dignity, a race that has come through its trials unbroken."[35] Here again, as in Robeson's memoir, dignity is proven in adversity. Witnessing this puts the lie to intuitions about the kind of dignity that one might begin with, intuitions that treat dignity as an abstraction possessed by all and then diminished in some because of oppression. Contrariwise, dignity is particularly evident in the resilience of those oppressed, and Robeson mixes his own dignity with the dignity he finds in the South. "It is only here that I achieve absolute and utter identity with my people."[36]

While Robeson's remarks in New Orleans might seem to stand between an old era of dignity, attributed to a people, and a new era of dignity, attributed to a human being, Robeson himself uses the term flexibly, not making a firm distinction between the cases. After all, the sort of oppression that matters to him is oppression of a people, and so the sort of dignity that matters most, dignity forged through struggle against oppression, occurs at once collectively and individually. This was the case with respect to African Americans, but also with Africans, and ending colonialism in Africa was a particular focus of Robeson's work in the immediate postwar years. What the European powers are doing in Africa, Robeson writes in the *New York Herald Tribune* in 1946, is a "beastly destruction of human dignity," an "irresponsible degradation of a whole continent of people."[37] At the same time, Robeson describes the struggle against white supremacy as "a fight for human dignity" in 1949, and as early as 1937, writing in London's *Daily Worker,* Robeson uses the phrase "human dignity" to describe what the working class is lacking.[38]

Robeson employs the language of dignity in one of his earliest speeches: his valedictory address at his Rutgers graduation in 1919. In that speech, following on the heels of American victory in the First World War, Robeson lauds a "new American spirit" that is "cultivated and intensified

---

[34] Robeson, *Paul Robeson Speaks.* Robeson is not entirely consistent in his usage of dignity. He is, after all, not a philosopher or a theorist. He is a rhetorician, speaking to particular audiences on particular occasions advancing particular causes. For example, during the Second World War, supporting the Allies, Robeson will write that a goal of the war is to achieve "liberty, opportunity and dignity" for those who have been oppressed (151), seemingly suggesting that dignity is achieved after struggle rather than in the process of struggle. My claim is not that Robeson consistently makes explicit a vernacular theory of dignity but that dignity generally fits in to Robeson's larger political (and theological, if that can be said) vision best when it is identified with struggle against oppression.
[35] Ibid., 143.   [36] Ibid.   [37] Ibid., 166.   [38] Ibid., 218, 120.

by Christianity."[39] This spirit is one of compassion and service: it impels us to lift up those in need and to develop a sense of community. Robeson's politics at this point, in his twenty-first year, had not sharpened, but certain intuitions that would develop later were clearly evident. It is necessary, Robeson intones, for us to "recognize a common lot" and to develop a "fraternal spirit" as we relate not only to family but also to those who share "fellow-citizenship and fellow-humanity."[40] Out of this developing sense of community comes the possibility for people to "receive the respect, honor and dignity due them."[41] Here Robeson equivocates. On one hand, the language of fraternity suggests that respect, honor, and dignity are due to all. On the other hand, Robeson also says earlier in the same sentence that one of the features of this fraternity is that "success and achievement are recognized," suggesting a sense of dignity earned rather than dignity due because of the bare fact of one's humanity. My suggestion is that this apparent tension is later worked out in Robeson's thought by giving political content to "success and achievement." That content is political struggle: it is not that hard work will result in dignity being accorded but that political struggle will result in dignity being achieved, both in the process of struggle and, on an eschatological horizon, when struggle is complete.

As the young Robeson concludes his speech, that sense of struggle is already present. He exhorts his audience "to join with us in continuing to fight for the great principles for which [older generations] contended, until in all sections of this fair land there will be equal opportunities for all, and character shall be the standard of excellence."[42] A fraternity is emerging that will guarantee dignity, and the process through which that fraternity is emerging, indeed the substance of the bonds of that fraternity, is a "fight." In other words, we are beginning to see how the struggle for dignity and the realization of dignity are becoming coterminous. Lest this be interpreted as a purely secular political point, it is also important to note here, in these early days, that Robeson still speaks in a thickly Christian idiom. He concludes his speech by arguing that the fight he commends must persist "until black and white shall clasp friendly hands in the consciousness of the fact that we are brethren and that God is the father of us all."[43] In other words, the fraternity of struggle that Robeson envisions is joined by its shared parentage, by the fatherhood of God.

Robeson wrote about dignity, but he was also widely described in the press and by adoring fans as embodying dignity.[44] Outstanding

---

[39] Ibid., 64.   [40] Ibid.   [41] Ibid.   [42] Ibid., 65–66.   [43] Ibid., 65.
[44] For further discussion of Robeson's image, see Shana Redmond, *Everything Man: The Form and Function of Paul Robeson* (Durham, NC: Duke University Press, 2020).

Trinidadian writer and activist C. L. R. James described Robeson as "the most distinguished and remarkable" man he ever met. Black American actor Ossie Davis described Paul Robeson as "a man and a half," adding, "we have no category, even now, to hold the size of him. Something about him escapes our widest, most comprehensive embrace, and we've never been able to put our finger on exactly what it is." In a sense, these words precisely describe dignity as Robeson understood it. There is something special about Robeson, something difficult to express in words. For the European Christian tradition, dignity has to do with the image of God in the human; for the Kantian, it has to do with the autonomy that makes humans irreducible to price. There is certainly something elusive gestured at by Davis's description of Robeson, but it is not quite an image of God, neither is it autonomy that beckons respect. It is not that Robeson has what every human has – some inherent, incalculable worth. He is human and more than human at once, "a man and a half." These descriptions are set against the background of Robeson's tribulations and his political commitment. The way that such excessive humanity is achieved is through orienting humanity to struggle against oppression.

How did Robeson arrive at this performance of dignity? Robeson does not offer a particularly theological explanation, but he does offer a secularized account of his father's Christian understanding of dignity. According to Robeson, his father did not "make a fetish of perfection," but rather believed that one's goal in life ought to be "the richest and highest development of one's own potential," in line with one's "personal integrity."[45] It is hard to avoid the resonance here with the personalist philosophy and theology that Samuel Moyn associates with the birth of human dignity and human rights in the international legal regime.[46] Moyn sees this as a particularly European Catholic development, but in fact it has many strands. The school of Boston personalists flourished throughout the first half of the twentieth century, with founding father Borden Parker Bowne's book *Personalism* published in 1908. Martin Luther King Jr. went to Boston University for his doctoral studies in order to be at the hub of personalist thought, and he wrote his dissertation on the leading personalist of the day, Edgar Brightman, a disciple of Bowne. According to King, it was through Boston personalism that he found the "metaphysical basis" for affirming human dignity.[47] In light of Robeson's own embrace of this language, perhaps we can go further than King himself. It was certainly not from French Catholics that King

---

[45] Robeson, *Here I Stand*, 18.   [46] Moyn, *Christian Human Rights*.
[47] Martin Luther King Jr., *The Papers of Martin Luther King, Jr. Volume IV: Symbol of the Movement*, ed. Clayborne Carson, Susan Carson, Adrienne Clay, Virginia Shadron, and Kieran Taylor (Berkeley: University of California Press, 2000), 480.

acquired his understanding of dignity, which was so central to civil rights organizing and public discourse in 1950s and 1960s America, though King was not unfamiliar with these currents, particularly the work of Maritain. As Robeson's early embrace of a language resonant with personalism suggests, this may have been part of the African American vernacular, part of a vernacular metaphysics, invisible to the Google N-Grams of which Moyn is so fond when he seeks to expand his analysis beyond the most rarified intellectual spaces. Put another way, is the history of Christianity and human rights told best as a history of ideas, circulating in published texts, or is it told best as a history of social movements challenging domination? In this chapter I am attempting the latter: I agree that commitments to Christianity and commitments to human rights are entangled, but I suggest that these commitments are implicit in practice, and that texts as well as aesthetic performances, memoir, and daily life provide resources for understanding this practice – this vernacular political theology.

Indeed, it is this longer black vernacular tradition of employing the word, concept, and performance of dignity to which I gesture in conclusion. Let us suspend the desire to find intellectual antecedents for Robeson's concept of dignity in European sources, whether liberal or Marxist, or in American personalism. Let us suppose that there might be an intellectual tradition in black America that only leaves traces in the written record. Because this is a vernacular idiom of communities systematically excluded from elite intellectual spaces and resources, the evidentiary trail is thin. However, it is not nonexistent. We find the language of dignity employed repeatedly throughout the career of King, but also later, among King's opponents. Huey P. Newton asserts, "People respect the expression of strength and dignity displayed by men who refuse to bow to the weapons of oppression. Though it may mean death, these men will fight, because death with dignity is preferable to ignominy."[48] But we also find it earlier, in the seminal texts of black political thought: Frederick Douglass's autobiographies. Indeed, at the crucial moment, when Douglass is fighting and defeating the slave-breaker Covey, Douglass gains insight into his humanity. "I was a changed being after that fight. I was *nothing* before; *I was a man* now. It recalled to life my crushed self-respect, and my self-confidence, and inspired me with a renewed determination to be a *free man*. A man without force is without the essential dignity of humanity."[49] In both the words of Newton, from the 1970s,

---

[48] Huey P. Newton, *The Huey P. Newton Reader*, ed. David Hilliard (New York: Seven Stories Press, 2002), 50.
[49] Frederick Douglass, *Life and Times of Frederick Douglass* (New Haven, CT: Yale University Press, 2012), 112.

and of Douglass, from the 1880s, dignity is associated with struggle. It is
not an abstraction applied to each person because of her humanity,
neither is it an elevated status or social rank. Dignity must be performed,
and that performance runs against the powers of the world to oppress.[50]

This black vernacular tradition of dignity, in which Robeson participated, cannot be disentangled from Christianity. Newton may have professed a certain secularity, but he was the son of a Baptist preacher and he
framed his own life story with decidedly Christian tropes. Frederick
Douglass was suspicious of white Christianity, but he also saw potential
for Christianity aligned with black struggle. The connection runs deeper
still. Richard Allen, the founding father of institutional black Christianity
who created the African Methodist Episcopal Church in 1794, preached
about dignity in the early nineteenth century. Addressing those fighting
racial injustice, Allen says, "Your righteous indignation is roused at the
means taken to supply the place of the murdered babe; you see our race
more effectually destroyed than was in Pharaoh's power to effect upon
Israel's sons; you blow the trumpet against the mighty evil; you make the
tyrants tremble; you strive to raise the slave to the dignity of man."[51] Here
the older sense of dignity as high rank or nobility is evoked even as it is
applied to all of "man." Those enslaved are men but they are not treated
with the dignity of men, causing indignation in those who observe such
treatment. This is all expressed in a thickly Christian idiom: the forces of
white supremacy that degrade black Americans are likened to those forces
of domination and oppression represented in the Bible, most famously
Pharaoh. Out of the denial of formal, abstract dignity comes indignation,
and out of indignation comes struggle – blowing the trumpet, making the
tyrants tremble – and then we are back again at dignity, dignity understood anew, as achieved through struggle, in struggle.

When Robeson delivered his demand for dignity to the UN, he was
doing more than mimicking a secularized Catholic legalism. If there is
a stream of subversive mimicry, it joins with the powerful river of vernacular black dignity that ran through the centuries. The language Robeson
brought with him to the Secretary General's office may have appeared
secular, but like the black vernacular idiom, it transcended the sacred-
secular divide. It also transcended the divide between thought and practice: Robeson spoke of dignity, was described as dignified, and performed
the dignity he described, the dignity that circulated around him in black
cultural spaces.

---

[50] I develop this point in Vincent Lloyd, "Black Dignity," *CrossCurrents* 68, no. 1 (March
2018), 73–92.
[51] *Preaching with Sacred Fire: An Anthology of African American Sermons, 1750 to the Present,*
ed. Martha J. Simmons and Frank A. Thomas (New York: W. W. Norton, 2010), 110.

But what of human rights? This is not a phrase native to Robeson's tongue. In the European intellectual tradition, human dignity was first only loosely connected with human rights, becoming the definitive source of human rights with the upsurge of rights activism in the 1970s. Yet for Robeson, the linkage was not even loose, it was nonexistent. Today we would most certainly describe him as a human rights advocate, singing and speaking out on behalf of the working class around the world, but that language is anachronistic and conscripts Robeson into a liberal narrative he spent his life resisting in various forms. Robeson's example opens the question of whether, when we attend to marginalized communities, when we attend to the grassroots, we ought to frame our investigation in terms of Christianity and human dignity, not Christianity and human rights.

Part IV

Beyond Europe and North America

10 On Chinese Rites and Rights

Albert Wu

On Christmas Day 1942, Celso Costantini, the second-in-command at the Sacred Congregation for the Propagation of the Faith (Propaganda Fide), the Vatican's primary institution responsible for missionary-related activities, noted in his diary the reception of two messages. The first was Pope Pius XII's Christmas address, which serves as the opening to Samuel Moyn's *Christian Human Rights*. Moyn points to the pope's address as evidence of a revolution in the Vatican's thinking about human dignity. In 1942, Costantini was electrified by the pope's words. "As always, the Pope, the Universal father, is the avenger of the truth ... he is the avenger of freedom."[1] Days later, he continued to lavish praise on the pope. "A single force is perhaps – as never before – alive and operating in everybody: the spiritual power of the Supreme Pastor. His acts and words inspire a vast resonance in all social classes."[2]

The other Christmas message came from General Chiang Kai-shek, the leader of the Chinese Nationalist government in Chongqing. Chiang's address reflected China's new international position since Japan's attack on Pearl Harbor in December 1941. Once isolated in its battle against Japan, China now belonged to a broader alliance struggling against the Axis powers. "Today," Chiang wrote, "thirty-one nations are united in their struggle against the Axis. The United Nations fight for international justice and for the freedom of humanity." Chiang envisioned the creation of a new postwar world order – one with Christianity as its basis. "I have the firm conviction," Chiang continued,

that at the end of this war, the world will be based on equality and mutual assistance and on the construction of a new world order of peace and happiness. ... This new world order must be created through the love that Christ spoke of. And it is for this that while war rages, I welcome with all my heart the return of Christ as Prince of Peace; and I pray for an early shared

---

[1] Celso Costantini, *The Secrets of a Vatican Cardinal: Celso Costantini's Wartime Diaries 1938–1947*, ed. Bruno Fabio Pighin, trans. Laurence B. Mussio (Montreal: McGill-Queen's University Press, 2014), 150.
[2] Ibid., 153.

victory, so that oppressed people can quickly obtain their liberation and freedom.[3]

The fact that Costantini was able to receive official communication from Chiang represented a sea change in the realm of Sino-Vatican diplomacy. Only two months before, the Nationalist government and the Vatican had normalized relations, even though this created numerous problems for Catholics who still lived in Japanese-occupied areas of China.[4] Costantini himself was a key figure in the diplomatic process; as China's first apostolic delegate, appointed by Pope Pius XI in 1922, Costantini would oversee a transformation in the Vatican's relationship to China within the realm of international diplomacy. He was also instrumental in pushing forward a change in the Vatican's view toward traditional Chinese culture. In particular, he helped revise the Vatican's condemnation of Chinese rites, a position it had held since the eighteenth century. In 1704, Pope Clement XI had issued a decree banning Chinese converts from participating in Chinese rites and Confucian rituals; most importantly, it forbade converts from participating in the cultural practice of honoring the dead. In 1939 – the same year that, as Samuel Moyn has noted, human rights "discourse reached the heights of Christianity" – Pope Pius XII approved the Instruction on Chinese Rites, *Plane Compertum Est*, issued by the Propaganda Fide.[5] Through the document, the Vatican essentially reversed its previous position on Chinese rites, allowing Chinese Catholics to participate in Confucian ceremonies.

Celso Costantini's diary entry on Christmas 1942 thus points us to two revolutions within Chinese Catholicism – in the realm of rites and that of rights – that were shaped by and shaped the Vatican's thinking. Drawing upon Moyn's broader global historical narrative as a backdrop, I argue that these two histories must be understood in relation to each other. For the history of the Chinese rites controversy had, from its inception, been intertwined with broader issues related to the religious rights of Chinese Catholics and Western missionaries. On one level, the Chinese rites controversy centered around whether the Vatican should permit Chinese Catholics to participate in a range of traditional Chinese rites,

---

[3] Ibid.

[4] The definitive history on Sino-Vatican relations has yet to be written in English. In Chinese, see Chen Fangzhong and Jiang Guoxiong, *Zhongfan waijiao guanxi shi* [*The History of Sino-Vatican Relations*] (Taipei: Commercial Press, 2003); Chen Congming, *Zhongfan waijiao shi – Liangan yu jiaoting guanxi* [*The History of Sino-Vatican Diplomacy: Vatican Relations across the Taiwan Strait*] (Taipei: Guangqi chubanshe, 2016). In French, see Olivier Sibre, *Le Saint-Siège et l'Extrême-Orient (Chine, Corée, Japon): De Léon XII à Pie XII (1880–1952)* (Rome: École Française de Rome, 2012).

[5] Samuel Moyn, *Christian Human Rights* (Philadelphia: University of Pennsylvania Press, 2015), 15.

including public ceremonies celebrating Confucius or services honoring the dead.[6] But the struggle over Chinese rites concerned more than questions of doctrine and ritual behavior. Was the Chinese Catholic first and foremost a servant of the Chinese Empire or of the Vatican? Would the Vatican's claims on the loyalty of the Chinese Catholic delegitimize the sovereign claims of the Qing Empire, which itself had only recently established its realm?

The early Qing emperors, following the example set by their Ming predecessors, tolerated the work of the Jesuits, and the court employed the missionaries as astronomers, doctors, geographers, and translators. But Qing Emperor Kangxi interpreted Pope Clement's 1704 decrees forbidding Chinese converts from joining Chinese rites as a hostile act, an attempt to wrest control of the Catholic population away from the Qing state. Beginning in 1706, Kangxi began to adopt an antagonistic stance toward the Vatican, banning missionary groups that did not allow Chinese Christians to participate in Chinese ritual life from entering the empire. In 1724, discerning that the Vatican was not going to relent on the issue of Chinese rites, the Qing emperor went one step further and declared Christianity a heterodox religion, banning Christian missionaries from working in the empire altogether.

These regulations on Christianity belonged to a broader set of economic and cultural policies that restricted Western cultural and economic access to China. Throughout the early nineteenth century, Western missionaries and merchants sought to undermine the Chinese Empire's regulations on both commerce and Christianity. Missionaries snuck into the empire; in one particularly dramatic case, a French bishop was caught and decapitated for his illegal missionary activities in Sichuan in 1816. Similarly, British and American merchants smuggled opium into the country, openly testing the extent of the Qing Empire's ability to maintain sovereign control of its borders.

And just as Western merchants relied on the force of Western colonial powers to open China to foreign trade, missionaries also used the resources of Western imperialism to increase the flow of missionaries

---

[6] The literature on the Chinese rites controversy is vast. For good overviews, see George Minamiki, *The Chinese Rites Controversy: From Its Beginning to Modern Times* (Chicago: Loyola University Press, 1985), and *The Chinese Rites Controversy: Its History and Meaning*, ed. David Mungello (Nettetal: Steyler Verlag, 1985). The Jesuits, the most influential group of European missionaries in China in the seventeenth century, argued in favor of permission: Chinese rites, they believed, were not "religious" ceremonies, but "civic" obligations with little theological significance. Opponents of the Jesuits, primarily the mendicant orders of the Franciscans and the Dominicans, disagreed, taking the view that Chinese rites were "religious." The Vatican sided with the mendicants and decreed that Chinese Catholics should not attend these rituals.

into the country. Starting with the Nanjing Treaty after the Opium War of 1842, Western imperial powers forced the Qing Empire to end its restrictions on Christianity. Missionaries were allowed access to the treaty ports, but not further inland. They continued to smuggle themselves into the Chinese interior, and in 1856, a local Chinese official arrested and killed a French priest who had trespassed into Guangxi. Using the incident as a pretext, the French joined forces with the British to defeat China. The unequal treaties that resulted from the Second Opium War of 1858 and 1860 gave Western missionaries unfettered access to China, granting them the rights to buy land and live in the Chinese interior.

The Second Opium War also established the French Religious Protectorate: the French Empire – not the Vatican – was designated as the main "protector" of all Catholic missionaries in China.[7] To travel and work in China, Catholic missionaries all had to obtain a passport that designated them as French. While the process of applying for passports was often an inconvenience, most missionaries welcomed the imposition, as the French were willing to flex their muscles in the region. In the name of "religious freedom," the French often interfered in local disputes, pressuring local courts to issue judgments in favor of Christians, regardless of the validity of their claims.[8] In the minds of Qing intellectuals, the French Protectorate cemented the connection between imperialism and Catholicism. The extension of religious rights to Chinese Catholics and European missionaries came at the expense of the Qing Empire's sovereign claims over its subjects.

The Vatican Revival and Celso Costantini

The French Protectorate did not just undermine the Qing, it also threatened the authority of the Vatican. In theory, the Vatican was the *spiritual* protector of all Catholics in China. But the Vatican had no military power to back up its claims. The Vatican felt further beleaguered in Europe with the waves of revolution throughout the nineteenth century, and in particular the unification of the Italian states in 1871. In China, the Vatican saw a pathway to regaining the international standing it had lost in the nineteenth century. But the Vatican's attempts to establish ties with China were repeatedly stymied by France. With the founding of the

---

[7] For the best work on the French Religious Protectorate, see Ernest P. Young, *Ecclesiastical Colony: China's Catholic Church and the French Religious Protectorate* (Oxford: Oxford University Press, 2013).

[8] For more on Western encroachment at the local level in China, see Alan Richard Sweeten, *Christianity in Rural China: Conflict and Accommodation in Jiangxi Province, 1860–1900* (Ann Arbor: University of Michigan Press, 2001).

French Third Republic in 1870, the French were motivated simultaneously by anticlerical sentiment and a desire to maintain their undisputed position in China. Until the First World War, the French Protectorate blocked the Vatican's endeavors to establish direct diplomatic ties with China.

After the First World War, the Vatican emerged with an ambitious new diplomatic agenda. As Giuliana Chamedes writes, "the Vatican successfully made use of new legal and diplomatic instruments to regain political and territorial sovereignty, establish formal diplomatic relations with over two dozen countries, and increase its power in international affairs by providing ideological and practical support to political parties in a large number of European nation-states."[9] Pope Benedict XV had already made clear his intentions of expanding diplomatic relations with China during the First World War. Viewing the French as preoccupied with their wartime affairs, the Holy See thought that it could establish direct relations with the new Chinese government. But in 1918, the French lodged an official complaint, once again foiling the Vatican's plans.

Undeterred, the Vatican sought other methods to circumvent the French. One of these avenues was Christian missionary work. For Benedict, missionaries were crucial actors who could extend Catholicism's interests globally in the wake of the catastrophic destruction wrought by the First World War. In 1919, Pope Benedict XV issued his apostolic letter, *Maximum illud*, which, as historian Ernest Young has shown, implicitly addressed the situation of Catholics and Catholic missionaries in China.[10] The apostolic letter argued that missionaries could undercut the French Protectorate by making alliances with the local Chinese. For too long, the letter stated, Christian missions had been a tool of the foreign imperial powers. Missionaries should no longer see Chinese Christians as inferior assistants, but instead treat them as equals. The pope exhorted missionaries to do everything they could to disentangle Catholicism from foreign imperialism.

Benedict XV died in 1922, and his successor, Pius XI, pushed forward the vision laid out in *Maximum illud*. The first task, Pius believed, was to unify the mission field in China, which had long been fragmented not only by geopolitics but also by theology. The Vatican sought to appoint an apostolic delegate, a position without official diplomatic status but nonetheless a representative for the church in China, a person whom it hoped

---

[9] Giuliana Chamedes, "The Vatican and the Reshaping of the European International Order after the First World War," *Historical Journal* 56, no. 4 (2013), 955–976, at 956.
[10] Young, *Ecclesiastical Colony*, 212–214.

would fuse the different church interests in China. The Vatican chose Celso Costantini for the job.

Costantini was, in many ways, a surprising candidate. Born in 1876 in Castions di Zoppola, he had never been to China and had no experience with the language or with diplomacy. Before the First World War, he was a parish priest in Concordia who had made a name for himself through his writing on sacred art. Suddenly he was thrust into one of the Vatican's most complicated, long-standing diplomatic quandaries. In his memoirs, Costantini wrote that he had tried to turn down the offer. Ultimately unable to refuse the pope, Costantini immediately went to the pontifical library in Rome to study up on China and the issues the country faced.[11]

How was Costantini chosen? After the First World War, he had come to the Vatican hierarchy's attention because of his work as bishop of the harbor town Fiume during its occupation by prominent Italian poet Gabriele d'Annunzio. In September 1919, incensed by what he perceived as unfair treatment from the Paris Peace Conference, d'Annunzio led a group of nationalist soldiers and marched on Fiume, which had been given over to the Kingdom of the Serbs, Croats, and Slovenes. D'Annunzio proclaimed the town a regency, with him as the dictator, calling himself Fiume's *Duce*. For fifteen months, Lucy Hughes-Hallett writes, "the place became a political laboratory. Socialists, anarchists, syndicalists, and some of those who had begun earlier that year to call themselves fascists, congregated there."[12]

Costantini had known d'Annunzio before the war; they had met several times through artistic circles in Aquileia. The Vatican, hearing of this connection, sent Costantini to establish the Diocese of Fiume in the regency, with the specific goal of stemming the tide of "materialism" in the city. Costantini walked into a delicate situation. His arrival provoked consternation among the Croatian clergy, who were unhappy that the Vatican had sent an Italian for the job. His first order of business, he noted in his memoirs, was to reopen the cathedral in the city, which had been "shut down by radicals." Costantini recalled that his "hands were shaking from emotion" when he opened the doors of the cathedral.[13]

In the ensuing fifteen-month regency, Costantini would meet with d'Annunzio multiple times. In his memoirs, he wrote admiringly of the

---

[11] See *Zhongfan waijiao guanxi liushi nian. Shiliao huibian* [*Documents on the History of the 60 Years of Sino-Vatican Diplomatic Relations*], ed. Chen Fangzhong and Wu Junde (Taipei: Institute of Catholic History, Fu-Jen Catholic University, 2002), 43 [Hereafter *Documents*].

[12] Lucy Hughes-Hallett, *Gabriele D'Annunzio: Poet, Seducer, and Preacher of War* (New York: Anchor Books, 2014), 4.

[13] Celso Costantini, *Can ye*, Chinese translation of *Foglie Secche: Esperienze e memorie di un vecchio prete*, trans. Stanislaus Louang (Taipei: Archiespicopus Taipeinensis, 1976), 266.

self-proclaimed dictator. He noted their mutual respect, portraying d'Annunzio as a sensitive spiritual being. When the Italian navy began to bombard Fiume in December 1920, hoping to force d'Annunzio to relinquish control of the city, Costantini was a key player in negotiating the accord that allowed d'Annunzio and his troops to leave the city unscathed.[14] Pope Benedict XV and Vatican Secretary of State Gasparri, who had both taken keen interest in the situation developing in Fiume, were impressed by Costantini's handling of the tensions there, and selected him for the position of apostolic delegate to China.

Despite his diplomatic inexperience, Costantini was in many ways the perfect candidate for the job. In China, his relative anonymity became an asset, as he had no prior reputation with the French Protectorate. The Vatican also saw Costantini as a fresh face to implement its vision for Sino-Vatican relations. And Costantini indeed followed the pope's lead: the ideals of *Maximum illud* thoroughly infused Costantini's first official memorandum that he circulated to Catholics in China. He argued that as apostolic delegate, he had purely "religious" goals and explicitly rejected any "political outlook" in China. The Vatican, he reassured, would remain strictly neutral and would not side with the interests of great powers: it had no "imperial ambitions in China . . . the Pope cares about China, and wants China to become strong, so that China can belong to the Chinese."[15] When leaving for China, Secretary of State Cardinal Gasparri made Costantini's mission clear to him. "The Chinese possess a beautiful, ancient culture," Cardinal Gasparri told him. "So how difficult will it be to find several bishops?"[16] Costantini understood that he had one clear goal in China: court and develop an indigenous clergy as a way to undercut the imperial power of the French Protectorate. By recognizing China's sovereignty in foreign affairs, the Vatican hoped to curry favor with the Chinese government and thereby solidify the Vatican's primacy in control over Catholic life in China.

The Vatican and Republican China

Costantini and the Vatican's shift toward the Chinese indigenous church reflected not just the political and diplomatic ambitions of the Vatican but also their increasing concerns about the increasingly unstable political situation for Christians in China. Costantini arrived in late 1922 at the onset of a rising anti-Christian movement. Earlier that year, a broad coalition of Chinese secular intellectuals had organized an anti-

---

[14] For more on the signing of the accord, see Costantini, *Can ye*, 303–308.
[15] Chen and Wu, *Documents*, 46.   [16] Ibid., 45.

Christian federation to protest the Protestant World's Christian Student Federation meeting in Beijing. Like their Italian counterparts, Chinese nationalists were incensed by what they perceived as unfair treatment at the Paris Peace Conferences in 1919, particularly the fact that the victorious Allied powers had not relinquished their extraterritorial powers in China in spite of China having been on the winning side of the war. The persistence of Christian missionaries was perceived as a further insult to Chinese national sovereignty. Anti-Christian sentiment did not abate, and anti-Christian organizations continued to form throughout the country from 1922 to 1928. These organizations launched a series of movements targeting Christians and foreign missionaries. Politically the movement found an outlet during the Northern Expedition from 1926 to 1928, when Communists and Nationalists formed an alliance to unify the country from warlord factions. The advancing troops targeted Christianity by looting Christian property, occupying Christian schools, and threatening the lives of missionaries.

Costantini's commitment to indigenization thus belonged to a broader attempt to carve out a new space for the Catholic Church in an increasingly volatile political landscape. He sought to prove to the Chinese public that Catholicism was compatible with Chinese nationalism. And he aggressively pursued the policy of indigenizing the church by coordinating missionary policy throughout China. In 1924, he convened in Shanghai the first synod for the Chinese Catholic Church. Never before had the Vatican laid a foundation for a coherent and comprehensive policy of indigenization. Most notably, the bishops at the synod agreed to establish a network of new seminaries dedicated to training Chinese clergy. He pushed for the formation of new Chinese Catholic universities, as well as a Chinese missionary order, the Congregation of Discipuli Domini. Costantini would claim quick victories: by 1926, within four years of his having been appointed secretary, the Vatican had ordained its first six Chinese bishops in the modern era.[17]

Drawing on his experience with d'Annunzio, Costantini courted the Chinese Nationalists. In his speeches, he adopted the platforms of Chinese nationalism: he railed against the unequal treaties – and by implication, the French Protectorate – and he asserted that China needed to be accepted as a full member of the international community. From the moment he arrived in China, he kept his distance from the French diplomats, signaling to the Chinese his independence from French

[17] For more on the ordination of the six Chinese bishops, see Paul P. Mariani, "The First Six Chinese Bishops of Modern Times: A Study in Church Indigenization," *Catholic Historical Review* 100, no. 3 (2014), 486–513.

influence. He defied French directives, needling the French officials in China by moving his residence from Hankou to Beijing, where he engaged in meetings with Chinese government officials free from the presence of French diplomats.[18] In 1925, he accused the most important Shanghai French-language newspaper, *L'Echo de Chine*, of being anti-Chinese, which in turn led to the newspaper's suppression. Incensed, the French minister in China called Costantini "an open enemy of the French Religious Protectorate."[19]

While Costantini sought to build bridges with the Chinese Nationalists, he saw no room for compromise with the nascent Chinese Communist Party. The moment he arrived in China, Costantini announced his commitment to resisting the rise of Bolshevism, framing it as a threat to global Catholicism.[20] In an interview with the French consul general in Guangzhou, Costantini attributed the civil unrest in China during the warlord period to the "alliance between bandits and Communists" and "a small group of bandit leaders who had been trained in Soviet Russia who inflamed the ugly side of nationalism and spread the poison of Communism." "Their ideology," Costantini wrote, "is predicated on appropriating other people's private property, killing old bureaucrats and gentlemen, and burning houses and land."[21] Ignoring the contributions of the Communists in the Northern Expedition, he praised the Nationalists for "unifying China in a short period of time, and gaining the trust and support of young people."[22] He praised both Sun Yat-sen, the pioneering leader of the Nationalist revolution, and Chiang Kai-shek, whom he believed could inject "new life" into China.

After the Nationalist purge of the Communists in 1927, it seemed as if Costantini and the Vatican's bets had paid off. In 1928, the pope issued a declaration to the Catholic community in China, celebrating the end of the civil war there. "His Holiness wishes the full recognition of the legitimate aspirations and the rights of a people who are the world's most numerous, a people of ancient culture, who have known periods of grandeur and splendor," the pope stated.[23] Costantini spread the pope's message widely, issuing translations in newspapers throughout the country.

---

[18] See Young, *Ecclesiastical Colony*, 225–226.   [19] Ibid., 236.   [20] Ibid., 225.
[21] Celso Costantini, *Zai Zhongguo Gengyun*, volume 2, Chinese translation of *Con i missionary in Cina (1922–1933). Memorie di Fatti e di Idee*, trans. Matthaeus Kia (Taipei: Archiepiscous Taipeinensis, 1979), 179.
[22] Ibid.   [23] Young, *Ecclesiastical Colony*, 34.

A Revision on Chinese Rites

The Nationalists also saw in the Vatican a potential ally that could help bolster their insecure legitimacy on the international stage. After they gained power in 1927, the Chinese Nationalists dropped their anti-imperial slogans and sought to forge new diplomatic alliances as a way to legitimize their standing within the international community.[24] On June 1, 1929, as part of the Nationalist government's broader outreach, it invited foreign dignitaries to attend a reinterment ceremony of the body of Sun Yat-sen, the leader of the Nationalist revolution. Sun was buried in Beijing, and the Nationalist government wanted to move his body to the seat of the new government in Nanjing, where they had constructed a vast mausoleum. The ceremony was the culmination of the Nationalist agenda to legitimize Sun, who had essentially died a failure, and build a "cult" around him.[25] The location of the tomb was carefully chosen, Henrietta Harrison writes, "signall[ing] his claims to equality with the first Ming Emperor."[26]

The question of what to do with Sun's body had long been a subject of disagreement among Sun's followers. When Sun, a professing Christian, had died in 1925, his family and members of the left wing of the party had clashed. His family insisted on a Christian burial; leftists demanded a nonreligious ceremony. Sun's family won the battle, and leftist party members boycotted the funeral.[27] By 1929, Chinese Nationalists were intent to show that their government was modern and secular. The elaborate preparations for the funeral procession from Beijing to Nanjing, along with the reinterment ceremony itself, reflected the government's attempt to clamp down on "superstition" and create a "secular religion."[28] Henrietta Harrison describes the scene in this way: the "soldiers who lined the route were under orders to prevent either participants or spectators from talking loudly, laughing, eating or smoking. ... Shopkeepers and peddlers were also banned from selling fruit and cold

---

[24] Edmund S. K. Fung, "The Sino-British Rapprochement, 1927–1931," *Modern Asian Studies* 17, no. 1 (1983), 90–91.

[25] For the use of the word "cult" to describe the Nationalist elevation of Sun as a figure, see Marie-Claire Bergère, *Sun Yat-sen*, trans. Janet Lloyd (Stanford, CA: Stanford University Press, 1998), 410–411.

[26] Henrietta Harrison, *The Making of the Republican Citizen: Political Ceremonies and Symbols in China, 1911–1929* (Oxford: Oxford University Press, 2000), 209.

[27] See Frederic Wakeman, "Mao's Remains," in *Death Ritual in Late Imperial and Modern China*, ed. James Watson and Evelyn S. Rawski (Berkeley: University of California Press, 1988), 257–258.

[28] For more on the Nationalist campaign against "superstition," see Rebecca Nedostup, *Superstitious Regimes: Religion and the Politics of Chinese Modernity* (Cambridge, MA: Harvard University Press, 2009).

drinks along the way."[29] The government strictly controlled the proceedings by banning "mass meetings, parades or demonstrations on penalty of immediate arrest," and onlookers had to demonstrate "respectful and disciplined behavior."[30] The Nationalists forbade Communists and left-wing members of the party from attending the funeral procession.

Costantini welcomed the Nationalists' heavy-handed control. In his memoir, he praised the funeral procession for its "solemnity and its decorum. The nationalist government got rid of the superstitious colors of normal Chinese religious rites. The funeral dress was different from traditional clothing ... there were no Llamas or Buddhist monks or any flags with superstitious markings. There were no traditional orchestras, ritual offerings, or burning of paper money."[31] Costantini praised the prevalence of "blue and white" – the colors of the Chinese Nationalist flag – that he saw during the procession ceremony. He did not interpret it as a form of party propaganda, but rather saw it as a rooting out of the "traditional red clothing in popular religion."[32]

Costantini and the Vatican had at first debated whether to accept the invitation to the funeral and procession. Fearing that the burial would be filled with references to Chinese popular religion, Protestantism, or leftist ideas, Costantini wrote in response to the invitation: "Even though we value the similarities between Sun Yat-sen's Three Principles of the People and Catholicism, I must emphasize that we cannot accept any ideologies that influence the purity of our religious faith."[33] In particular, he asked the Nationalists whether the ceremony would include any religious elements, as these would present a conflict for a Vatican representative. The Nanjing government replied that the funeral would be purely "civic" and not religious. Costantini was also informed that the funeral procession would not contain any overt Christian references, even though Sun was Protestant. Reassured that the funeral procession was a purely "secular" affair, Costantini accompanied the Nationalist procession from Beijing to Nanjing.

In Nanjing, a climactic moment arrived when the invited governmental and foreign officials were asked to approach Sun's casket and bow to his body. Without much hesitation, Costantini bowed. "My bowing," he explained later, "corresponded with my respect for the fallen leader." His act broke with centuries of church policy in China: Costantini, the apostolic delegate, publicly participated in Chinese funeral rites. While symbolically important, Costantini's actions did not immediately overturn the Vatican's stance on Chinese rites. The Vatican continued to

---

[29] Harrison, *Making of the Republican Citizen*, 228.   [30] Ibid., 228.
[31] Costantini, *Zai Zhongguo Gengyun*, 116.   [32] Ibid., 114.   [33] Ibid.

forbid Chinese Catholic schoolchildren from bowing in schools to idols and other religious iconography, including portraits of Sun Yat-sen.[34]

But a sea change was afoot in the region. In 1931, the Japanese government, having just invaded Manchuria, made attendance at state Shinto services mandatory. Soon thereafter, a group of Japanese Catholic students at the Jesuit-run Sophia University refused to attend a state ritual dedicated to the war dead at the Yasukuni shrine. The refusal by the Japanese Catholics caused a public row in Japan. In 1933, American Cardinal Edward Mooney, the apostolic delegate in Japan, struck a deal with the Japanese government declaring that Japanese Catholics could attend state Shinto rites. The Vatican intervened by asking the Japanese to make the declaration that state Shinto rituals were rooted not in "religion," but rather in "patriotism" and "loyalty."[35] The Japanese agreed to issue a statement proclaiming the civic nature of the Shinto rituals. In return, the Vatican declared that Catholic attendance at the state rites could be "tolerated."[36] A similar situation played out in the Japanese puppet state of Manchukuo. The Manchukuo government instituted a new Confucian ritual, mandating the population to attend, and local Catholics objected to the rite. The Vatican once again intervened on the side of the state power, declaring that the state ritual did not conflict with the individual faith of the person.

After the Japanese and Manchukuo decisions, the writing was on the wall: it was only a matter of time before the Vatican would decide to reverse its position on the Chinese rites. In December 1939, with Europe now at war, the Propaganda Fide issued *Plane Compertum Est*, declaring that Chinese Catholics could participate in Confucian rites. Celso Costantini, who had since 1935 become the second-in-command at the Propaganda Fide, was the main architect of and cosigned the document. Costantini's writing infused the document's opening statement: "It is abundantly clear that in the regions of the Orient some ceremonies, although they may have been involved with pagan rites in ancient times, have – with the changes in customs and thinking over the course of centuries – retained merely the civil significance of piety towards the ancestors or of love of the fatherland or of courtesy towards one's neighbors."[37] Besides allowing Chinese

---

[34] Chen Tsung-ming, "1930 niandai Luoma jiaoting jieshu 'Liyi zhizheng' zhi yanjiu [Notes on the Holy See's Solution to the Chinese Rites Controversy in the 1930s]," *Bulletin of the Modern History Institute, Academia Sinica* 70 (December 2010), 97–143, at 115.

[35] George H. Minamiki, "The Yasukuni Shrine Incident and the Chinese Rites Controversy," *Catholic Historical Review*, 66, no. 2 (April 1980), 205–229, at 216.

[36] Ibid., 221.

[37] Excerpts of the document can be found in *A History of Christianity in Asia, Africa, and Latin America, 1450–1990: A Documentary Sourcebook*, ed. Klaus Koschorke, Frieder Ludwig, and Mariano Delgado (Grand Rapids, MI: William B. Eerdmans, 2007), 100.

Catholics to participate in Confucian ceremonies, the Vatican acknowledged the Chinese Nationalist regime's sovereign claims over China, opening the pathway for a normalization of diplomatic relations between the two countries.

Conclusion

The end of the Vatican's interdiction on Chinese rites in 1939 has been celebrated within the historiography as a progressive measure. Church historians have seen the end of the Chinese rites controversy as a signal that the church was ready to shed its previous intolerance toward non-Western religions and cultures.[38] In many ways, such an interpretation is true. The decision represented a major revision of how Chinese Christians could relate to other religious traditions in China. It affected, in very real ways, how Chinese Christians could practice their faith.

But the timing of the ending of the Chinese rites controversy renders untenable an unabashedly progressive reading of the event. The Vatican's decision to compromise on Chinese rites came on the heels of pressure from ultranationalists in Japan and the rising tide of global fascism. Japanese nationalists, in pushing Catholics to submit to the rites of the nation-state, had learned from German and Italian fascists.[39] China had also been touched by fascist fever; Chiang Kai-shek modeled the New Life Movement and the wearing of blue shirts specifically after German fascists, and the Nationalist government instituted a series of public rituals that forced Catholics to attend.[40] The Vatican thus signaled to Chinese Catholics that it could not protect the individual consciences of Chinese or Japanese Catholics; it was more advantageous to accept the authority of the states in power. The Vatican's decision on Chinese rites reflected a moral compromise, a willingness to accept the rising tide of fascism in both Europe and East Asia.

At the same time, the Vatican made clear to indigenous Catholics whom it could not compromise with: Communists. Throughout the 1930s, the Vatican emerged as one of the most vocal anti-Communist

---

[38] For an example of this type of interpretation, see Sergio Ticozzi, "The Official End of the Chinese Rites Controversy," *Tripod* 29, no. 155 (2009): www.hsstudyc.org.hk/en/tripo d_en/en_tripod_155_02.html.

[39] For more on Japanese fascism, see *The Culture of Japanese Fascism*, ed. Alan Tansman (Durham, NC: Duke University Press, 2009) and Tansman, *The Aesthetics of Japanese Fascism* (Berkeley: University of California Press, 2009).

[40] For more on the GMD's penchant for fascism, see Frederic Wakeman, "A Revisionist View of the Nanjing Decade: Confucian Fascism," *China Quarterly* 150 (June 1997), 395–432.

voices in China. Costantini was obsessed with the Chinese Communists and constantly sent reports on Communist activity back to the Vatican.[41] In 1931, he wrote, "The most aggressive enemy of the Catholic missions in China at the present moment is Bolshevism."[42] His ideas were mirrored widely throughout the global church. As Samuel Moyn writes, "Christian human rights have been not so much about the inclusion of the other as about policing the borders and boundaries on which threatening enemies loom."[43]

Costantini and the Vatican's antagonism toward the Communists provoked a backlash among grassroots Catholics as the Japanese imperial march into China widened. Missionaries and Chinese Catholics appealed to the Vatican to recognize that the Japanese, not the Communists, posed the bigger geopolitical threat to the Catholic Church's mission in China. As Japanese encroachment into China intensified, Belgian Lazarist missionary Vincent Lebbé used his influential newspaper *Yishibao* to denounce the Japanese. Embedded in the war effort against the Japanese, Lebbé – himself an avowed anti-Communist throughout the 1920s – became a vocal supporter of the United Front between the Chinese Nationalists and Communists, hoping that an undivided China could stem the Japanese march into China. In a letter to Costantini's successor, apostolic delegate Mario Zanin, Lebbé noted of the Communists, "not only do they not oppose us, but they show themselves to be best friends of my mission."[44]

But the Vatican refused to adopt an openly anti-Japanese stance. They conceded to the Japanese by designating a "temporary special delegate" to the areas of Manchuria the Japanese had conquered.[45] Zanin followed Costantini's example, ordering Chinese Catholics to moderate their anti-Japanese positions. He censured priests who overtly criticized the Japanese, requesting them to remain politically neutral.[46] In China, the

---

[41] Chiara d'Auria, "La Propaganda comunista in Cina nella corrispondenza di Mons. Celso Costantini," *Rivista di Studi Politici Internazionali* 80, no. 4 (2013), 593–612, at 603.

[42] Celso Costantini, *Against Hope in Hope* (New York: Society for the Propagation of the Faith, 1931), 7.

[43] Moyn, *Christian Human Rights*, 24.

[44] Cited in Young, *Ecclesiastical Colony*, 245. While it is clear that some Catholics in China like Vincent Lebbé shifted more toward a pro-Communist stance because of the intensification of the Sino-Japanese war, it is unclear to me whether they were reading the global anti-totalitarian literature that James Chappel writes about in his contribution here (Chapter 3) and in his book *Catholic Modern*. More research needs to be done to see whether, in Chappel's terms, the "fraternal" Catholic writers had an audience in China. For an exploration of these ideas, see James Chappel, *Catholic Modern: The Challenge of Totalitarianism and the Remaking of the Church* (Cambridge, MA: Harvard University Press, 2018).

[45] Young, *Ecclesiastical Colony*, 248.   [46] Ibid., 249.

Vatican's silencing of anti-Japanese forces mirrored its global political stance. As Giuliana Chamedes writes, in 1937, the Vatican reaffirmed through three encyclicals that communism, not fascism, "was the greatest existential threat to Catholicism and the world."[47]

The revolution in Chinese rites thus belongs to a broader global moment in which the Vatican sought to redefine and redeploy values and ideas as a way to halt the rise of communism. As Moyn argues, part of the strategy to stem global communism included the appropriation of rights talk, making "what had been secular and liberal into a set of values that were now religious and conservative."[48] The Chinese rites controversy thus serves as something of an inverted mirror to Moyn's findings in the case of human rights. The Vatican changed what had previously been considered religious – the act of civil, ceremonial bowing – into something that appeared secular and "civic." Moyn points out that the Vatican was driven by "a conservative vision of liberalism" to embrace human rights. Similarly, Costantini's embrace of Chinese rites fundamentally advanced a "conservative vision of liberalism." And as Moyn writes, "in different national contexts, rights talk had different fates: the new language of the rights of the human person was not just passively received but creatively interpreted from place to place and moment to moment." In China, rights talk intersected with the centuries-old question of whether Chinese converts could participate in public ceremonies with possible religious underpinnings. The Vatican's new stance on Chinese rites reconfigured the relationship between religious freedom and the Chinese state: the Chinese Catholic was free to practice and participate in state rituals, as long as the state defined these rituals as "civic" or "nonreligious."

That the revolution in Chinese rites was deeply entangled with the Catholic Church's "conservative vision of liberalism" helps explain why Chinese Communists were suspicious toward the Vatican from the moment they gained power after 1949.[49] Chinese Communists did not see the Catholic Church's position on Chinese rites as an uncomplicated directive to decolonize the church.[50] Remembering their exclusion from

---

[47] Giuliana Chamedes, *A Twentieth-Century Crusade: The Vatican's Battle to Remake Christian Europe* (Cambridge, MA: Harvard University Press, 2019), 193.

[48] Moyn, *Christian Human Rights*, 3.

[49] For a detailed study of the conflict between the Catholics and Communists in China from the 1930s onward, see Paul Mariani, *Church Militant: Bishop Kung and Catholic Resistance in Communist Shanghai* (Cambridge, MA: Harvard University Press, 2011).

[50] There is a burgeoning literature on the Catholic Church's relationship to the decolonizing movements of the post–World War II era. See, for instance, Udi Greenberg, "Catholics, Protestants, and the Violent Birth of European Religious Pluralism," *American Historical Review* 124, no. 2 (2019), 511–538; Elizabeth Foster, *African Catholic: Decolonization and the Transformation of the Church* (Cambridge, MA: Harvard University Press, 2019).

Nationalist civic rituals, Chinese Communists suspected that the Vatican's calls to embrace Chinese rites were part of a global political agenda to exclude communists from public life. The Communists saw and continue to see the Catholic appeal to an indigenous clergy as an intervention in the sovereignty of the Chinese government. Seeing the Vatican as intent on retaining its control over the indigenous church hierarchy, the Chinese Communist Party retaliated by appointing its own bishops and forcing Chinese Catholics to declare allegiance to the Communist state. Those who continued to adhere to the Vatican's hierarchy went underground. More broadly, the Chinese Communist Party remained deeply suspicious of Western calls after 1949 to protect the human rights of individuals in China, viewing them as a Western imperial attempt to undermine China's sovereign borders. These mutual suspicions, exacerbated during the Cold War, had their roots in the 1930s, during a moment when both the Vatican and the Chinese state were reconceiving the meanings of Chinese rites and rights.

11 "Expert in Humanity"

An African Vision for the Catholic Church

Elizabeth Foster

In 1967, two years after the conclusion of Vatican II and only a few months following Pope Paul VI's encyclical *Populorum Progressio*, "On the Development of Peoples," prominent African Catholic intellectual Alioune Diop published an article entitled "Note on the Weight of Western-ness in the Christian Experience."[1] In his piece, which appeared in the Dominican missionary theological periodical *Parole et Mission*, Diop criticized the ongoing Eurocentrism of Catholicism in harsh terms, yet also applauded the encyclical and held the church aloft as a beacon of hope for the struggling peoples of the Third World, regardless of whether they were Christian. "Without a doubt," he wrote, "the church is an *expert in humanity*. And most certainly the foremost expert in the world."[2] In Diop's view, the postconciliar church had a weighty role to assume as the leader of a planetary effort to combat widespread poverty, hunger, and ignorance in Europe's former colonies, even as it continued to grapple with its Western heritage, which was inextricably linked to Europe's domination of the very populations who needed its help. As Diop saw it, the church had flaws and had made mistakes, but it was the best institution available to do such work, because it touted a universalist promise that could yet be realized. Indeed, Diop and other devout African Catholic intellectuals, both clergy and laymen, took it upon themselves to hold the church to that promise between the mid-1940s and the 1970s.

Though frequently overlooked by historians, Alioune Diop was not an obscure voice in the wilderness. In fact, he was arguably the most important force behind black internationalism and the negritude movement at mid-century. Though he did not win fame through literary endeavors like his collaborators Léopold Senghor, Léon-Gontran Damas, or Aimé

---

[1] Alioune Diop, "Note sur le poids de l'occidentalité dans l'expérience chrétienne," *Parole et Mission* 39 (1967), 569–578. This piece was reprinted in a special issue of *Présence africaine* on Africa and the papacy in 2005: Alioune Diop, "Note sur le poids de l'occidentalité dans l'expérience chrétienne," *Présence africaine* N.S. 142 (2005), 97–105.

[2] Diop, "Note sur le poids," 569. Emphasis in the original.

Césaire, he created the structures and institutions that gave both franco-phone and anglophone black voices an international platform in the postwar period. Chief among these were the periodical *Présence africaine*, which he founded in 1947, and the publishing house of the same name, established a couple of years later. His bookstore in Paris (also named Présence africaine) became a haven for colonial students in the French metropole and a site of dialogue and cultural exchange between African and European intellectuals. Diop also organized the seminal Congresses of Black Writers and Artists in Paris in 1956 and Rome in 1959. And, while he was one of the few nonwhite members of the prestigious European Society of Culture (SEC) in the 1950s, he founded the parallel African Society of Culture (SAC) to promote the richness and value of African culture to both European and African audiences. In short, Diop did more to organize black intellectuals and to publicize their arguments than anyone in the years that immediately preceded and followed the decolonization of French and British Africa.

Diop's 1967 intervention in *Parole and Mission* reflects that he was also a devout Catholic who was very deeply engaged with the church's rela-tionship to Africa's people both in the continent's colonial past and in its independent future. This is perhaps the least known aspect of his monu-mental yet neglected career. Indeed, he was a leader and sponsor of a cohort of militant and vocal African Catholic intellectuals who proble-matized Africa's relationship with the church and criticized European Catholics and church institutions for failing to practice the universality that Catholicism laid claim to. This Catholic negritude was a fixture in the pages of *Présence africaine* and the activities of the SAC in the 1950s and 1960s.[3] For Diop, the 1967 article in *Parole et Mission* was only the latest intervention in a campaign he had waged to make the church respect all of its believers' "*personnalités*" and cultures since his conversion from Islam in 1944. Diop and his allies resolutely and ceaselessly savaged the church's Eurocentric and condescending stances vis-à-vis the "Third World," its peoples, and their cultures, while simultaneously extolling its promise as a force for good in the developing world.

This chapter highlights the seminal influence of Diop and like-minded African Catholic intellectuals and clergy in the reorientation of the Catholic Church at mid-century. Long ignored by intellectual historians of Catholicism, Africans played a leading role in forcing the European Catholic hierarchy and its missionaries to reimagine the church's relation-ship to the non-Western world in the postwar years. Well prior to the full

---

[3] See Elizabeth A. Foster, *African Catholic: Decolonization and the Transformation of the Church* (Cambridge, MA: Harvard University Press, 2019), chap. 2.

flowering of liberation theology in Latin America, African Catholic intellectuals were grappling with the meaning of the church's deep entanglement in the European colonization of their home continent, and insisting that they had wisdom and perspectives, born of their unique cultures and of their experience of colonization, that European Catholics needed to absorb. For example, they embraced dialogue with leading European Catholic thinkers such as Emmanuel Mounier, but they also critiqued his paternalistic impulses vis-à-vis Africa and its peoples. They adopted the language of Mounier's personalism, but deployed it to amplify their message that Africans deserved respect and recognition of their dignity as people, and that African believers were equal members of the universal church, for the benefit of European and African audiences alike.[4]

When viewed from the present day, this activism casts a long shadow, and not just in the intellectual realm. Diop and his colleagues fervently supported the political decolonization of Africa, as well as a theological and racial "decolonization" of the Catholic Church itself. They exercised a decisive influence on the papacies of John XXIII and Paul VI, helping the church to pivot away from Europe and make itself more hospitable to the constituencies in Africa, Asia, and Latin America that would embody its future. Indeed, when the Vatican instituted the church hierarchy across the vast reaches of French Africa in 1955, replacing missionary territories with dioceses and archdioceses, nearly all the bishops and most of the clergy ministering to the nearly 1.75 million African Catholics in French colonies were still European exports.[5] Yet ten years later, after political independence and the reforms of Vatican II, this picture began to change dramatically. In the ensuing years, adherence to Catholicism exploded on the African continent as it diminished in Europe, and today the flow of clergy has entirely reversed, as African priests come to staff parishes in France. Though Diop did not foresee this outcome, he would doubtless have relished the formidable African presence in the pulpits of the former metropole.

---

[4] Another important European interlocutor was Umberto Campagnolo, founder of the European Society of Culture and a proponent of a conception of a "civilization of the universal" that Diop decried as fundamentally Eurocentric. Drawing on Teilhard de Chardin, both Léopold Senghor and Alioune Diop championed a different vision of a "civilization of the universal" that allowed for all peoples to contribute their wisdom to humanity as a whole – finding a way of conserving local knowledge, experience, and culture while becoming part of a larger whole. On Teilhard and Senghor, see Charlotte Walker-Said, "The Global Reach of Teilhard's Legacy" (September 14, 2013): www.teilhardproject.com/global-reach-teilhards-legacy/.

[5] For detailed numbers, see Délégation apostolique de Dakar, "Statistiques annuelles des missions catholiques en Afrique française," 1954–1955, Archives de la Congrégation du Saint-Esprit (Chevilly-Larue, France) 2F 1.3 a5.

Alioune Diop's Catholicism

Alioune Diop chose to become a Catholic as an adult while living in occupied France during the Second World War, when his birthplace of Senegal was still a French colony. This very particular context shaped his conception of Catholicism and of the role of the church in the world. There were Catholics in his extended family, but he was born in 1910 into a Muslim household in Saint-Louis and began his scholastic career in Koranic school. He moved on to a French elementary school at the age of ten and did very well, becoming one of a handful of black Africans who went on to higher education in the interwar years, first in Algeria and then in metropolitan France. Arriving in France in 1937, he connected with other black artists and thinkers such as Senghor, Césaire, and Damas, as well as notables of the French intellectual scene. Among the most important for his personal development as a Catholic were Father Jean-Augustin Maydieu, a Dominican intellectual who became Diop's spiritual guide and mentor, and Emmanuel Mounier, the devout editor of the nonconformist review *Esprit* and leading philosopher of Catholic personalism.[6]

The war years, when Diop worked in various capacities in French secondary education, proved to be a crucial turning point for him personally and professionally. Living under German occupation and watching Europe implode at close range prompted him to contemplate Europe's faults, weaknesses, and blind spots, as well as the value of his own African culture and experience. In his opening essay for the inaugural issue of *Présence africaine* in 1947, he explained that the idea for founding the review, which he modeled in part on Mounier's *Esprit*, had emerged from this process of reflection in 1942–1943.[7] At the very same time, under Maydieu's influence and instruction, Diop was undergoing a course of catechism and study that culminated in his baptism as a Catholic on Christmas Day 1944. From the very beginning, Diop's engagement with Catholicism involved wrestling with Europe's power in the world, the church's historical identification with the West, and its ambiguous relationship to European colonialism and racism. Some of the arguments he made in the wake of *Populorum Progressio* in 1967 were already implicit in a letter he wrote to his future French godmother in 1943. In it, Diop noted that Europe had the world at its feet and "more riches than it

---

[6] For more biographical detail on Diop, see Foster, *African Catholic*; Frédéric Grah Mel, *Alioune Diop: le bâtisseur inconnu du monde noir* (Abidjan: Presses Universitaires de Côte d'Ivoire, 1995); Philippe Verdin, *Alioune Diop, le Socrate noir* (Paris: Lethielleux, 2010).

[7] Alioune Diop, "Niam n'goura ou les raisons d'être de *Présence africaine*," *Présence africaine* 1 (1947), 7–14, here 8.

needed to live," yet it was self-destructing. In his view, the salvation of Europe lay in the rediscovery of pure and true Christianity (as opposed to how it had often been practiced), and the role of the church was to lead this process by example.[8] In the 1950s, he pushed the church to support the self-determination of colonized peoples, to embrace their cultures and civilizations in the faith, and to initiate dialogue between Europe and the rest of the world. By 1967, after independence, he was again calling for the church to deploy what he saw as its genuine values to lead the palliation of ongoing suffering in Europe's former colonies.

Diop's vision of Catholicism also owed a lot to Mounier's personalism. The two men developed a close relationship and at Diop's urging Mounier took a six-week trip to West Africa in 1947, but Mounier ultimately irritated Diop with his supercilious tone toward the African elite in an essay for the inaugural issue of *Présence africaine*.[9] Mounier's antimaterialist philosophy sought a "third way" between the complete subordination of the individual in communism on one hand, and the unchecked individualism of capitalism on the other. Mounier insisted on the existence and validation of "free and creative persons," defining the person as "precisely that which in each man cannot be treated as an object."[10] Personalism was inherently vague and therefore accommo-dated a wide range of political persuasions: Philippe Pétain invoked it after the defeat of 1940, and Mounier himself initially embraced the Vichy regime before breaking with it in 1941. Personalist language of the dignity of the human person was also common in the speeches and writings of conservative French missionaries who ran the Catholic Church in postwar Africa, such as Monsignor Marcel Lefebvre, the *intégriste* former archbishop of Dakar who was skeptical of African self-determination and who would break with Rome over Vatican II. Yet personalism proved very seductive to African Catholic intellectuals (and French-educated Vietnamese Catholics) with an anti-colonial bent.[11]

---

[8] Alioune Diop to Marguerite Marteau, October 31, 1943, quoted in Verdin, *Alioune Diop*, 100.

[9] Emmanuel Mounier, "Lettre à un ami africain," *Présence africaine* 1 (1947), 37–43. On Diop's reaction, see Iwiye Kala-Lobé, "Lorsque l'enfant paraît," in *Mélanges: Réflexions d'Hommes de Culture* (Paris: Présence africaine, 1969), 71, 74. On Mounier's trip, see Emmanuel Mounier, *L'Eveil de l'Afrique noire* (Paris: Editions du Seuil, 1948).

[10] Emmanuel Mounier, *Le Personnalisme* in *Œuvres*, vol. 3 (Paris: Editions du Seuil, 1962), 429–430.

[11] Much more can be said about personalism and anti-colonialism. It was also important in Québec's Quiet Revolution. On personalism in the Vietnamese context, see Phi Vân Nguyen, "The Vietnamization of Personalism: The Role of Missionaries in the Spread of Personalism in Vietnam, 1930–1961," *French Colonial History* 17 (2017), 103–134, and Edward Miller, "The Diplomacy of Personalism: Civilization, Culture, and the Cold War in the Foreign Policy of Ngo Dinh Diem," in *Connecting Histories:*

Mounier's championing of the "dignity" of the entire spiritual and physical person, embedded in his/her community, struck a chord with Africans who struggled to identify with Eurocentric models of communism or capitalism.[12] Alioune Diop and Léopold Senghor, who celebrated communal solidarity as a particularly African value, and dedicated themselves to the validation, celebration, and championing of African culture, found Catholic personalism deeply compelling. Diop saw the role of the church, if it was being true to its own values, to embrace, encourage, and protect African *personnalité* (personhood) and culture.

Decolonizing the Church

Diop's trajectory is a reminder that the role of African voices and the strategic importance of Africa in the titanic shifts within the Catholic Church at mid-century should not be underestimated. Neither should they be understood merely as part of a Vatican-led offensive against communism in the so-called Third World. The church's grappling with the "modern world" in the 1950s and 1960s involved a reconception of its missionary role in Europe's former colonies. At the urging of African and Asian believers and Europeans sympathetic to their claims, the church gradually moved away from equating conversion to Catholicism with the wholesale adoption of European culture, civilization, and norms.

In some respects, this impulse predated Vatican II – as early as 1919, Benedict XV had warned European missionaries against carrying national chauvinism with them abroad, and in 1926, Pius XI called for the training of indigenous clergy, worrying publicly that missionaries would be expelled if and when indigenous peoples threw off their foreign overlords.[13] Yet there was little urgency until after the Second World War, when political decolonization, both bloody and peaceful, loosened Europe's hold in Asia and Africa. Vatican II, which was announced just when political developments in French and British Africa were rapidly evolving, convened in 1962 in the wake of the Evian Accords ending the Algerian War and a wave of independence across sub-Saharan Africa.

Decolonization and the Cold War in Southeast Asia, 1945–1962, ed. Christopher E. Goscha and Christian F. Ostermann (Washington, DC: Woodrow Wilson Center Press and Stanford, CA: Stanford University Press, 2009), 376–402.

[12] On Mounier's language, see Samuel Moyn, "Personalism, Community, and the Origins of Human Rights," in *Human Rights in the Twentieth Century*, ed. Stefan-Ludwig Hoffmann (Cambridge: Cambridge University Press, 2011), 85–106, here 88.

[13] See Pope Benedict XV, *Maximum illud* (November 30, 1919), in *Selected Papal Encyclicals and Letters*, vol. 1, new and enlarged ed. (London: Catholic Truth Society, 1941), 12–13; Pius XI, *Rerum ecclesiae* (February 28, 1926), in *Selected Papal Encyclicals and Letters*, 17–18.

Though American and European scholars have tended to focus on other aspects of the council, Vatican II was a key step in the church's mid-century pivot from a European institution to a global one. Believers with their roots in the "developing world" – Africans and, notably, Latin Americans in the late 1960s – forced the church hierarchy to reckon with their social, political, and cultural problems and aspirations. The rapid growth of Catholicism in Africa and Latin America, whose Catholic communities now export clergy to faltering parishes in Europe, suggests that the institution ultimately adapted rather successfully to the world realignment after decolonization.

When John XXIII called the council, he certainly did not envision the startling decline of Catholic observance in Europe that would mark the last third of the twentieth century, but he did grasp that Catholicism could have a bright future in Africa, as well as in Asia and Latin America, if it could be disentangled from the European colonial past. He was attuned to the postwar effervescence among black intellectuals and artists in Paris from his time as nuncio to France between 1944 and 1953, and he was also familiar with the challenges facing the poorer regions of the world through his work as the Vatican's first observer to the United Nations Educational, Scientific and Cultural Organization (UNESCO), where he encouraged Catholics to engage in productive dialogue and exchange with those of other faiths.[14] He continued his predecessor Pius XII's pressure on reluctant European missionaries to train local priests in order to hasten the creation of indigenous churches that were not dependent on European personnel. On Easter weekend of 1959, John held an audience with African Catholic intellectuals gathered in Rome for the Second Conference of Black Writers and Artists, organized by Alioune Diop and the SAC, and expressed his sympathy for their project of investigating and valorizing African culture.[15] The following year, he received Diop and nine other black intellectuals, only three of whom were Catholic, in a relaxed and lengthy private session where the conversation ranged over history, the Koran, travel, painting, and the idiosyncrasies of the English language.[16] Between his elevation and the opening of the council in 1962, John issued many messages of congratulation to newly independent African states, and elevated numerous young African clergy to positions in the church hierarchy, including

[14] Thomas Cahill, *Pope John XXIII* (New York: Viking, 2002), 151.
[15] M. Roland de Margerie, Ambassadeur de France près le Saint-Siège to M. Couve de Murville, Ministre des Affaires etrangères, Rome, April 2, 1959, Centre des archives diplomatiques de Nantes, PO1/1389.
[16] Alioune Diop, "Postface," in *Un hommage africain à Jean XXIII*, ed. Société africaine de culture (Paris: Présence africaine, 1965), 113–188, 114.

the first black African cardinal, Laurean Rugambwa of Tanzania in 1960. There is no doubt he had his eye on Africa during his brief pontificate, and African Catholic intellectual leaders greatly appreciated his interest. The SAC gathered his pronouncements regarding Africa in a volume entitled *An African Tribute to John XXIII*, published by Présence africaine in 1965.

John's successor, Paul VI – former archbishop of Milan Giovanni Cardinal Montini – made Africa even more of a priority, before and after his election.[17] In the summer of 1962, just weeks before Vatican II got under way, Montini took a month-long trip to Africa – the first future pope to visit the continent. Leaving behind the intrigues surrounding the organization of the council, he visited missions and African Catholic communities across both francophone and anglophone Africa. According to his auxiliary in Milan, Monsignor Giovanni Colombo, Paul told African audiences, "Fear not, Africa, if the Gospel takes root among your people it will purify and safeguard both your faith and your freedom; and it will also protect and keep intact the heritage of your original culture on which your future surely depends."[18] This message echoed two ideas that were key for Alioune Diop: the power of the church to act as a moral force, and, what might seem paradoxical given its historic entanglement with European civilization, as a guardian of African culture.

When Montini became Paul VI in 1963, in the midst of Vatican II, Diop wasted no time in trying to influence the new pontiff. Together with Cameroonian student Georges Ngango, he went to Rome on behalf of the Society of African Culture and presented Paul with a document outlining African hopes and expectations for Vatican II.[19] Ngango, a devout future professor of economics who later served as Cameroon's minister of information and culture and as the minister of education, shared Diop's insistence on a new relationship between Europe and the rest of the world. "The Christian West must show itself to be consistent henceforth, by ceasing to be a stumbling block and a brake on the awakening of the Third World and becoming instead a true center of influence and comprehension; a force for authentic human advancement in a fraternal manner," he wrote in *Présence africaine* that same year.[20]

---

[17] Peter Hebblethwaite notes that even though Africa was very important to Montini, key biographers have overlooked his engagement with Africa and Africans completely. Peter Hebblethwaite, *Paul VI: The First Modern Pope* (New York: Paulist Press, 1993), 302n3.

[18] Ibid., 301–302.

[19] Jean-Paul Messina, *Evêques africains au Concile Vatican II, 1959–1965: le cas du Cameroun* (Paris: Karthala, 2000), 43. Unfortunately, the exact contents of the document are unknown but are not difficult to guess given Diop's copious pronouncements and writings on what he wanted to see from the church.

[20] Georges Ngango, "L'Occident Chrétien face à l'éveil des non-occidentaux," *Présence africaine* N. S. 45 (1963), 205–211, here 211.

There is little doubt that Diop and Ngango found a willing audience in Paul VI, who largely adopted this stance as he increased the church's public attention to Africa in the first years of his pontificate. In 1964, during the third session of the council, Paul canonized the so-called Uganda martyrs as the first modern black African saints. In the mid-1880s, these twenty-two Catholic converts had been burned alive, along with African Anglicans, by Mwanga II, the ruler of Buganda. They had been beatified by Benedict XV in 1920 but had languished immobile in relative obscurity since then on the road to sainthood, until they became a symbol of African equality within the church. In 1953, Diop had invoked them in a blistering attack on colonialism and Eurocentrism in the church: "but the Ugandan martyrs are not saints. ... Even God, a prisoner of European civilization, seems not to know of us."[21] In 1959, he returned to the theme by publishing a letter of French mystic and Islamophile Louis Massignon, who had made a pilgrimage to the site of their deaths and described them in glowing terms while savaging French policy in Algeria.[22] With Diop's help, the Ugandan martyrs emerged as a totem of African belonging in the Catholic Church – with their canonization, black people could see themselves in the ranks of the saints. It was a concrete step toward redefining Catholicism as not inherently white and European.

The Church, the West, and the Third World

In the late 1960s, Paul VI increasingly devoted his attention and his political capital to the developing world, and to Africa in particular. In March 1967, he released *Populorum Progressio* on the question of development. By addressing it to clergy and faithful of the "Whole Catholic World" and to "All Men of Good Will," he asserted the Vatican's role as a truly global voice that should be taken seriously on the world stage.[23] Seven months later, he issued a lengthy and detailed message to Africa entitled "Africae terrarium," which included a reference to John XXIII's 1958 meeting with Diop's SAC, and a direct plea to the African intellectual elite to "collaborate" with the church for the "revival and development of African cultures, as much for liturgical reform as for the teaching of church doctrine in terms that correspond to African

---

[21] Alioune Diop, "On ne fabrique pas un peuple," *Présence africaine* 14 (1953), 7–14, here 13n5.

[22] Louis Massignon, "Message à M. Alioune Diop," *Présence africaine* N. S. 27/28 (1959), 363–364.

[23] Pope Paul VI, *Populorum Progressio* (March 26, 1967): http://w2.vatican.va/content/paul-vi/en/encyclicals/documents/hf_p-vi_enc_26031967_populorum.html.

mentalities."[24] This went far beyond the mere promotion of African individuals to positions of authority in the church, instead promising the inclusion and valorization of African culture within it – something Diop had been after for years. Finally, in July 1969, Paul VI made the first ever visit to Africa by a sitting pope – a remarkable move that garnered a lot of attention in Africa and across the rest of the world.[25] He spent three days in Uganda and visited the shrine of Namugongo honoring the African martyrs he had canonized in 1964, but he also arranged opportunities to speak to government officials and representatives of Islam and Anglicanism, again claiming a wider audience than merely the Catholic faithful.[26] This reflected the Vatican's determination, in the wake of the council, to engage more fully with the modern world and initiate dialogue with people of different faiths. Diop, as a former Muslim, had advocated for such dialogue. Indeed, he and new African bishops in predominantly Muslim areas, such as Hyacinthe Thiandoum in Senegal and Luc Sangaré in Mali, insisted that a long experience and practice of Muslim-Christian exchange and solidarity was something black Africa could offer the church at large.

Paul's pronouncements on and engagement with Africa and the developing world were influenced not only by Diop and like-minded African Catholic activists but also by French Dominican economist Louis-Joseph Lebret. Lebret, a complex figure who had embraced Pétain's Vichy regime and believed firmly in a European civilizing mission, surfaced in the 1950s and 1960s as the leading theorist of an emerging Catholic school of development thought that rejected both classical economics and the modernization vision of W. W. Rostow and the Charles River School. Lebret, who saw development as a way to counter the spread of communism, did not want to combat it merely with pro-capitalist materialism that tended to benefit the few, or with rigid formulae that failed to take into account the character of the societies in question.[27] He advocated for an approach animated by the true spirit of the Gospels, which would feed the hungry,

---

[24] "Message 'Africae terrarum' de S. S. Paul VI à l'Afrique," *La Documentation Catholique* 1505 (November 19, 1967), 1951–1952.

[25] Paul VI's unprecedented attention to Africa continues to resonate on the continent. See, for example, the proceedings of a 2012 conference in Nairobi on Paul and the church in Africa, which include Peter Cardinal Turkson on "The Responsibility of the Church to Society: Promoting Peace, Justice, and the Development of Nations" and Bishop Barthélemy Adoukonou on "Paul VI et l'inculturation de la foi chrétienne en perspective interculturelle," in *Paul VI and the Church in Africa* (Brescia: Istituto Paolo VI, 2015), 59–74 and 48–58, respectively.

[26] On Paul's various speeches in Uganda, see the Vatican website on the trip: http://w2 .vatican.va/content/paul-vi/en/travels/documents/uganda.html.

[27] Giuliana Chamedes, "The Catholic Origins of Economic Development after World War II," *French Politics, Culture & Society* 33 (2015), 60–62, 65.

cure the sick, combat infant mortality, and help poor countries and former colonies industrialize and improve their agricultural yields in ways that did not merely line the pockets of the richest among them or of Western capitalists. Lebret became remarkably influential, putting his ideas into practice across Latin America and receiving invitations to help from government elites in Lebanon, Vietnam, Dahomey, and Senegal. In 1958, Mamadou Dia, the Muslim prime minister of Senegal, invited Lebret as an official economic advisor and gave him considerable power to shape policy.[28] Lebret served the Senegalese government for the next four years, until the rupture between Dia and President Léopold Senghor.[29] At the same time, Lebret was becoming increasingly influential within the Vatican. As of 1957, he began expressing his wish to see Montini, already an ally, ascend to the throne of Saint Peter, and he became a trusted papal advisor once that took place.[30]

Diop and Lebret knew each other and apparently met often at the Dominican headquarters in Dakar whenever they were both in town in the late 1950s and early 1960s, though little record of their relationship exists in current scholarship, and the extent of their philosophical agreement remains a matter of conjecture.[31] There certainly were crucial points of convergence between them: each man called for a renewed European commitment to what he saw as the genuine values of Catholicism. Both felt this was necessary for the survival of the West, and the rest of the world as well.[32] Both were anticommunist, though they

---

[28] See "Convention générale d'organisation de l'étude dirigée par L. J. Lebret pour permettre l'élaboration du plan de développement du Sénégal," Dakar, January 16, 1959, Archives Nationales du Sénégal (Dakar), Fonds de Vice-Présidence et Présidence du Conseil de Gouvernement du Sénégal, Dossier 00096. On development in Senegal, see Mamadou Diouf, "Senegalese Development: From Mass Mobilization to Technocratic Elitism," in *International Development and the Social Sciences: Essays on the History and Politics of Knowledge*, ed. Frederick Cooper and Randall Packard (Berkeley: University of California Press, 1997), 291–319.

[29] Jean-Claude Lavigne, OP, "Le développement au Sénégal: utopie et réalisme des intuitions du Père Lebret," in *Le Père Lebret, un dominicain économiste au Sénégal (1957–1963)*, ed. Charles Becker, Pierre-Paul Misséhoungbé, and Philippe Verdin (Dakar: Fraternité dominique de Dakar, 2007), 10, 14.

[30] Denis Pelletier, *"Economie et humanisme": de l'utopie communautaire au combat pour le tiers-monde (1941–1966)* (Paris: Editions du Cerf, 1996), 400. See also Lydie Garreau, *Louis-Joseph Lebret, précurseur du Vatican II (1897–1966)* (Paris: L'Harmattan, 2011), 273–277.

[31] Diop attended Lebret's first appearance in Dakar, a lecture inaugurating the Dominicans' new lecture hall across the street from the campus of the University of Dakar on December 17, 1957, entitled "Exigence et condition d'une nouvelle civilization" (Lavigne, "Le Développement," 14). On their meetings in Dakar, and Diop's invitation to Lebret to attend a 1962 SAC conference on African politics, see Verdin, *Alioune Diop*, 340.

[32] Indeed, the title of one of Lebret's most important works was *Suicide ou survie de l'Occident? Dossier pour comprendre les problèmes de ce temps* (Paris: Economie et Humanisme, Editions Ouvrières, 1958).

saw communism through different lenses: Diop saw it not only as soulless materialism but also as fundamentally Eurocentric. Though he died in 1966, Lebret's thought formed much of the basis for *Populorum Progressio*. Paul VI quoted him directly in the encyclical, observing, "We cannot allow economics to be separated from human realities, nor development from the civilization in which it takes place. What counts for us is man – each individual man, each human group, and humanity as a whole."[33] This sentiment aligned with Alioune Diop's personalism, his emphasis on the dignity of African people, and his valorization and championing of African culture and its potential to contribute wisdom to humanity as a whole. Yet Diop's commentary on the encyclical suggests that he thought Lebret and Paul VI could have gone even further in their thinking on the relationship between the West and the Third World.

By the time of *Populorum Progressio*, Diop was preoccupied by the mixed results of political independence for Africa. As he observed in his commentary on the encyclical, "independence did not suffice to cure our miseries and our hungers. Peace is inconceivable within our borders and in the world at large until the war and poverty that the egoism of the great powers keeps alive beyond their frontiers disappears."[34] In these circumstances, Diop saw the encyclical as a wake-up call to the Christians of the West regarding the situation of the peoples of the Third World – conveying the message that while the "West had Christ without the Cross, everyone else had the Cross without Christ."[35] Moreover, Diop suggested that Paul VI had made the case that all peoples are interdependent. It was imperative, in Diop's view, that Europeans understand that "the development of poor countries is linked to the changing of economic structures in the Western World."[36] Diop felt that the pope's words were the first step in what had to be a double revolution: first the West needed to change its approach, so that it could then help the Third World combat poverty, hunger, and illness, and lack of education.[37]

In Diop's view, the Catholic Church was the only existing institution that could instigate and lead these connected transformations. While he praised the "admirable activities" of the United Nations, he noted that it

---

[33] Paul VI, *Populorum Progressio*.
[34] Diop, "Note sur le poids," 576. Diop also acknowledged that a portion of Africa's difficulties could be blamed on its elite, of which he was a prominent member. See Alioune Diop, "Discours d'ouverture," Dossier Table Ronde: "Elite et Peuple dans l'Afrique d'aujourd'hui," *Présence africaine* N. S. bilingue 73 (1970), 45–49, here 45.
[35] Nearly a decade before, Diop had used this same formulation, borrowed from American Monsignor Fulton J. Sheen's comments about Russians, in the preface for a book of his fellow African Catholic activist Albert Tévoédjrè. Alioune Diop, "Préface" to Albert Tévoédjrè, *L'Afrique révoltée* (Paris: Présence africaine, 1958), 9.
[36] Diop, "Note sur le poids," 577.   [37] Ibid.

was largely ignored by the great powers, including those that had founded it. Moreover, in his view, not a single Western political movement or ideology, including communism, had conceived of "an economic revolution within the Occident whose vocation was to liberate the economic possibilities of the Third World." And so far, he claimed, the communist countries of Europe, guided by what he termed "national egoism," had only imagined the redistribution of resources within, and not beyond, the boundaries of the West.[38] In sum, "only Rome" offered a universal vision capacious enough to see and encompass the interconnectedness of the West and the Third World.

Moreover, in Diop's opinion, only the church possessed the moral authority to deploy such a vision. As he had argued in a 1963 lecture to African seminarians that was broadcast on Vatican Radio, Diop saw the church as a guarantor or "security deposit" for "the dignity of man in the Third World."[39] In January 1964, as the pope journeyed to the Middle East, Diop reiterated that the church needed to wield its moral clout far and wide: "At the moment when Paul VI travels to Jerusalem, the reverberations of the first two sessions of the council, of John XXIII's encyclicals, and the immense emotion awakened in the souls of the powerful and the humble together demonstrate just how much the world needs the spiritual and moral authority of the Papacy to strengthen and increase on our earth."[40] He made a similar point in a 1965 article entitled "The 'Third World' and the Church" that appeared in *Le Monde* during the last session of Vatican II. In that piece, Diop developed the theme that the church, as the "oldest global institution," was an unparalleled repository of wisdom, moral authority, and culture. "In this explosive century, where man cannot find a guarantor of justice anywhere," he wrote, "the church, more than any other institution, has a powerful capital of moral discipline, acquired through trials and often [unknown] sacrifices, at its disposal."[41] As a result, Diop argued, Vatican II mattered deeply to the peoples of the Third World, even those who did not believe in Catholicism or were critical of the church, and he urged their political and cultural leaders to pay attention to the council. "These debates concern all of us, and the cultural and social destiny of the peoples of Africa and Asia will partly depend on the decisions that emerge from them," he wrote.[42]

---

[38] Ibid.

[39] "Causerie de M. Alioune Diop à Radio-Vatican (Résumé de sa conférence du 5 mars)," Centre des Archives Diplomatiques de Nantes, 576PO/1 1449.

[40] Alioune Diop, "A propos du 'Vicaire,'" *Le Monde* (January 3, 1964), 2. This title referred to Rolf Hochhuth's 1963 play *Le Vicaire* [*Der Stellvertreter*], which critiqued Pius XII's stance during the Second World War, especially vis-à-vis the Jews.

[41] Alioune Diop, "'Tiers Monde' et Eglise," *Le Monde* (October 3–4, 1965), 13.

[42] Ibid.

As much as Diop applauded the church's new, more overt sensitivity to non-Western peoples and cultures, however, he did not think that *Populorum Progressio* represented the absolute achievement of what he had long championed. As he admitted himself, any amount of rhetoric could not do the hard work required, both in the Third World and in the West, to bring about an end to hunger, ignorance, and illness. Moreover, he was well aware of the lingering gap between European Catholic rhetoric and practice, which likely lay behind his decision to publish his gloss on the encyclical in *Parole et Mission*, a respected journal of missionary theology published by the Dominican order in France. Diop probably thought that the journal's European missionary audience needed more prodding to understand what he deemed to be the real import of the encyclical. He addressed their evangelism in the Third World directly, claiming that it would not succeed without the "comprehension and love" of the Third World's "*civilizations*" and these "living civilizations" could not be protected without "*economic development.*"[43] Only on these two conditions, he argued, could missionary action "deliver itself from a narrow form of charity that distributes surpluses while fearing to meet the human in his diverse finery, and thus remains the parasite of the prosperity of the West." Moreover, he noted frankly, "I know that the Pope's text does not go as far as I suggest it does." Yet, he maintained, it raised consciousness of the problem of development, and, in that respect, made the necessary, interconnected revolutions more feasible.[44] As he had long made a habit of doing, Diop yet again used the church's own rhetoric to validate his conception of its role.

Conclusion

In 1968, church authorities asked Alioune Diop to offer a public comment on *Populorum Progressio* in the Vatican lecture hall on Saint Peter's Square.[45] This invitation revealed how he successfully initiated and maintained a long-term running dialogue with the Catholic hierarchy between the mid-1940s and the late 1960s and, in so doing, helped to persuade its members of his positions. Of the African voices that sought to redefine Catholicism as a truly universalist guardian of indigenous cultures and an advocate for the poor, his was the loudest and the most persistent. At the time, some skeptical readers on the left saw him as an apologist for an institution that had made common cause with European

---

[43] Diop, "Note sur le poids," 577. Emphasis in the original.   [44] Ibid., 577–578.

[45] Fabien Kange-Ewane, "Alioune Diop à travers sa commentaire de l'encyclique 'Progressio populorum' (Rome 1968): le développement solidaire de l'humanité," *Bulletin de théologie africaine* 4, no. 7 (1982), 75–86, here 75.

domination around the world, but he never refrained from criticizing the church's long identification with European civilization and he made clear that he considered that civilization deeply flawed. He felt that the most effective way forward was to pull the church toward his inclusive vision for it by steering it from within and deploying its language and teachings in ways that were difficult for its leaders to refute. As he saw it, the church was not a narrow philosophy or an ideology, but rather a "living experience, complex like the diversity of human experience," and "a vigilant history of the valorization of man."[46] His lifelong goal was to make African experience and wisdom known in the church, to the benefit of all peoples. And despite his condemnation of its past and his ongoing frustration with some of its European thinkers and adherents, Diop never relinquished his conviction that the Catholic Church had a unique role to fulfill as a protector of vulnerable people and their cultures in a violent and troubled world.

[46] Diop, "'Tiers Monde' et Eglise," 13.

12 Neoliberalism, Human Rights, and the Theology of Liberation in Latin America

David M. Lantigua

The emergence of mainstream human rights discourse and neoliberal economic reforms in north transatlantic societies during the 1970s and 1980s is a most curious coincidence. Nongovernmental agencies dedicated to individual civil and political liberties like Human Rights Watch and Amnesty International were born, or experienced unprecedented growth, in both the USA and England. President Jimmy Carter's 1977 inaugural address proclaiming an absolute commitment to the individual at home and abroad ushered in a "crusade for human rights."[1] Concurrently, neoliberalism for the first time attained a status of economic orthodoxy in British and US policy, signaling the ascendency of global finance capitalism under a new transnational corporate class of private owners.[2]

What relationship, if any, is there between these two global economic and political forces? Samuel Moyn has recently visited this question in a characteristically illuminating way.[3] Having narrated the distinct break-through eras of human rights for both emancipatory secularism in the 1970s and 1980s and Christian conservatism earlier in the 1930s and 1940s, Moyn's latest oeuvre explores how human rights came under neoliberal captivity by the 1990s.[4] Moyn argues that human rights politics is a "powerless companion" unable to curtail, much less overcome, the neoliberal transformations of economic life across the globe. Although human rights advocacy has been committed to promoting civil liberties for many and basic social provisions for the needy, the neoliberal age has

---

[1] John Charvet and Elisa Kaczynska-Nay, *The Liberal Project and Human Rights: The Theory and Practice of a New World Order* (Cambridge: Cambridge University Press, 2008), 261.

[2] David Harvey, *A Brief History of Neoliberalism* (New York: Oxford University Press, 2007), chap. 1.

[3] Samuel Moyn, *Not Enough: Human Rights in an Unequal World* (Cambridge, MA: Harvard University Press, 2018) and "A Powerless Companion: Human Rights in the Age of Neoliberalism," *Law and Contemporary Problems* 77, no. 4 (2014), 147–169.

[4] Moyn, *The Last Utopia* (Cambridge, MA: Harvard University Press, 2010) and *Christian Human Rights* (Philadelphia: University of Pennsylvania Press, 2015).

mostly benefited the transnational elite who continue to climb the ever-expansive summit of corporate wealth beyond state regulatory parameters. The "harshest verdict" of all, Moyn writes, "is that the human rights icons and movement were not attentive to the inegalitarian consequences of neoliberalization."[5] Moyn does not merely describe the recent political past of human rights as a missed opportunity. More important, the politics of human rights shared a fatal ideological commitment with neoliberalism: "Human rights, even perfectly realized human rights, are compatible with inequality, even radical inequality."[6]

Human rights advocacy following political detachment from the welfare state has largely become an informational politics unsuited to pursuing egalitarian social reform through just distribution of resources. It therefore remains powerless before the growing disparity between those who can have anything and those who can only ever have what is necessary. Moyn's analysis of neoliberalism points to a more global perspective for the historiography of human rights. Beyond the postwar bipolar militarized politics of East versus West, the neoliberal frame of North and South decenters the standard geopolitical terrain, thereby enabling greater recognition of overlooked regions on the frontiers of economic globalization. These regions on the economic periphery provide another vantage point for analyzing the relationship between human rights and neoliberalism, especially in Latin America where both global forces gained exceptionally strong traction.

Turning to the Southern Cone of the 1970s, investigative journalist Naomi Klein has detected an even more troubling relationship between human rights and neoliberalism than Moyn. After the coup of 1973, the national security regime of General Pinochet in Chile instantly began measures to eradicate remnants of Salvador Allende's democratic socialist state. Klein's analysis focuses on the key advisory role of the "Chicago Boys." These Chilean free market economists recommended to Pinochet's regime the neoliberal trifecta of privatization of public assets, deregulation of the financial sector, and cuts to social spending that they learned from their University of Chicago teacher Milton Friedman.[7] In a visit to Chile, Friedman claimed the country's economy needed "shock treatment," an ominous choice of words for a terror regime set on abolishing workers' organizations and unions by torturing its political prisoners.[8]

---

[5] Moyn, *Not Enough*, 185.   [6] Ibid., 213.
[7] Naomi Klein, *The Shock Doctrine: The Rise of Disaster Capitalism* (New York: Picador, 2007), 94–99.
[8] William T. Cavanaugh, *Torture and Eucharist* (Malden, MA: Blackwell, 1998), 39.

Remarkably, Friedman received the Nobel Prize in 1976 for economics and Amnesty International won the Nobel Peace Prize a year later for its work on documenting torture in Chile. This Chilean nexus of an American neoliberal godfather and a British human rights organization offers an instructive point for Klein. Despite Amnesty's laudatory role in ending some of the regime's worst abuses, Klein argues, it remained blind to the political-economic rationale of Pinochet's policy of terror.[9] The organization's commitment to political neutrality and an impartiality focused on discrete "crimes" compromised the social analysis of underlying structural causes. At the very least, this shortsightedness should be a cautionary tale about the analytic limitations of human rights advocacy in the face of neoliberal economic policies.

Regardless of whether one shares the cutting criticisms of Moyn and Klein, another formulation of human rights was developing among Latin American religious actors in the second half of the twentieth century outside the margins of most human rights histories. As early as the 1960s and 1970s, coinciding with the rise of national security states and the conclusion of the Second Vatican Council, Latin American theologians began promoting an "alternative discourse" (*discurso alternativo*) of human rights specific to their region's historical realities and their lived faith. They spoke of an alternative precisely because they saw a collusion between official human rights speech and adverse economic policies and political actions from the North affecting their region.

Attending to these Latin American voices contributes to the new historiography of human rights in two ways. By tilting the axis to the global South, this chapter first draws attention to the social-critical analysis of Latin American thinkers, mostly theologians, who made the historical link between neoliberalism and human rights associated with the Carter administration. On this score, Moyn's chronological narrative is correct, yet incomplete. Second, this chapter considers the theological articulation of rights in Latin America after Vatican II, which stemmed from a historical faith centered on the preferential option for the poor, rather than universal human dignity. Another genealogy of Christian human rights in Latin America emerges here that is not personalist in orientation, but liberationist. Concluding with a brief treatment of the small country of El Salvador during the 1970s and 1980s, this underappreciated story discloses an important prophetic alternative to the dominant liberal-individualist formulation of human rights. A Christian human rights praxis rooted in the postconciliar Church of Latin America comes into sharper relief. Its formidable resistance to the overreaching powers of

---

[9] Klein, *The Shock Doctrine*, 146–149.

both the nation-state and the global market attests to its ongoing normative value.

The Neoliberal Underside of the Human Rights Breakthrough

Latin American theologians, sociologists, and political analysts were attentive to the liberal economic underside of the human rights breakthrough associated with the Carter administration from the beginning. Before addressing the identifiable link between human rights and neoliberalism observed by these thinkers in the global South, it is important to contextualize the geopolitical background of the national security state in Latin America. For it was the rapid spread of right-wing authoritarian regimes – starting with the military junta of Brazil in 1964 and culminating in the Argentine coup of 1976 – that formed an anticommunist political culture in Latin America open to neoliberal globalization.

The communist revolution of Cuba in 1959 and subsequent support from the Soviet Union made Latin America a strategic hot spot for new revolutions of the Left. With the USA already having executive precedent from the unilateralist Monroe Doctrine and Roosevelt Corollary for policing Latin America against encroaching foreign threats, the hemispheric battleground was not so much a Cold War, but rather a series of "dirty wars" implicating the northern neighbor in the fight against revolutionary politics. The long-standing Good Neighbor policy, which gained new impetus during this postwar era, rested on a "Pan American doctrine of continental self-defense."[10] Presidents Kennedy and Nixon typified the era's self-defense policy of counterinsurgency and national security, suppressing movements deemed leftist in both Southeast Asia and Latin America.

Kennedy, for his part, established the Alliance for Progress with Latin American countries to provide socioeconomic backing and covert operations against communist expansion. He also reoriented the Georgia-based School of the Americas in 1961 to serve as a counterinsurgency training ground for Latin American military personnel, some of whom directly participated in the terror of national security states. The growing national security system of the postwar United States established a federal model of control and secret service through its National Security Council and Central Intelligence Agency (CIA). US involvement through the CIA in Operation Condor – a joint intelligence effort among Southern Cone

[10] Brian Loveman, *No Higher Law: American Foreign Policy and the Western Hemisphere since 1776* (Chapel Hill: University of North Carolina Press, 2010), 243.

authoritarian governments targeting leftist political dissidents – only further entwined the northern neighbor in a bloody web of assassination and state-sponsored terrorism. A new face and ideology for US foreign policy in Latin America was required. Under Carter's administration, human rights and neoliberalism entered this scene together with profound moral and political urgency.

US assistance to national security states with their countless impunities made Latin American thinkers more than skeptical of policy changes from their overbearing neighbor to the north. The national security state had been the American empire's "farthest reaching export," wrote theologian José Comblin in the late 1970s.[11] Yet the Cold War era of realpolitik was giving way to a new political and economic vision of world order articulated by the Carter administration. In 1978, Brazilian theologian Hugo Assmann edited the two volumes of *Carter y la lógica del imperialismo*, a foundational work of critical social analysis for the emergent theology of liberation.[12] The distinctive logic of the new imperialism, according to Assmann and the various contributors, evolved from a well-orchestrated and thoroughly researched argument for an alternative world order, a transnational economic liberalism. Assmann's introduction quoted President Carter, who expressed the new logic of the age in the following way: "It is very probable that, in the near future, the problem of peace and war will have more to do with economic and social conflicts between North and South, than with the problems of militarized security between East and West that has dominated international relations since the Second World War."[13] For Carter, underdevelopment and extreme poverty in a global South cut off from economic liberalization posed grave challenges to the stability of international order.

The sociological underpinning of the new ideology, intensely scrutinized by the contributors to the two-volume work, was the Trilateral Commission cofounded in 1972 by Chase Manhattan Bank executive David Rockefeller. Still in existence, the Commission included key politicians, Democratic and Republican, yet overwhelmingly consisted of business owners, bankers, and executives from many of the largest corporations in the USA, Western Europe, and Japan. As a transnational class of some of the wealthiest elites, the Commission advanced a global vision of cooperation and interdependence in response to international

---

[11] José Comblin, *The Church and the National Security State* (Maryknoll, NY: Orbis Books, 1979), 64.

[12] *Carter y la lógica del imperialismo*, 2 vols., ed. Hugo Assmann (Centroamérica: EDUCA, 1978). Assmann noted at the beginning of the volumes that the essays were published together quickly following an international meeting in October 1977.

[13] Cited in Assmann, "Introducción," in *Carter y la lógica*, 1:15.

economic crises and the socioeconomic polarity between North and South, or rich and poor nations. The structural power inscribed in the mobile, large-scale capital of these transnational economic players could facilitate the exertion of political pressure for policy changes in favor of profit-making and capital accumulation.[14] The new ideological frame of the Trilateral Commission was "the transnational outlook of the multinational corporation."[15]

With the USA spearheading the deliberately hegemonic initiative, the first aim of the Trilateralists was to consolidate the private economic interests of the most powerful corporations from the northern nations comprising the capitalist bloc.[16] In theory, a strategic trilateral front affirming a freer market for corporate expansion and foreign investment would begin the neoliberal process of integrating cooperative underdeveloped countries for the benefit of all nations involved. To achieve that end, Trilateralists sought to neutralize any potential mobilization of the global South through the regionalism and decolonization advocated by the New International Economic Order (1974) and the Charter of Algiers on the Right of Peoples (1976).[17] Proponents of the short-lived New International Economic Order devised at the United Nations (UN) responded to the disparity between rich and poor nations by prizing greater equality between them and protecting the economic self-determination of weaker states.[18] The Trilateral Commission proposed its own alternative ethical solution to the same dilemma of rich and poor nations – what its cofounder and first director Zbigniew Brzezinski called a "planetary humanism."[19] For Brzezinski, solidarity among underdeveloped nations resistant to cooperation stood as a major threat to the international economic system.[20]

According to Trilateralists, the doctrine of human rights was the morality of a neoliberal world order. Carter, a member of the Commission since he was governor of Georgia, became its most visible spokesperson. After his presidential election, he appointed numerous members of the

---

[14] Stephen Gill, *American Hegemony and the Trilateral Commission* (Cambridge: Cambridge University Press, 1990), 112–113.

[15] Richard Falk, "A New Paradigm for International Legal Studies: Proposals and Prospects," *Yale Law Journal* 84, no. 5 (1974), 969–1021, at 1005.

[16] Arturo Sist and Gregorio Iriarte, "De la seguridad nacional al Trilateralismo," in *Carter y la lógica*, 2:219–220.

[17] Pablo Richard, *Death of Christendoms, Birth of the Church: Historical Analysis and Theological Interpretation of the Church in Latin America*, trans. Phillip Berryman (Maryknoll, NY: Orbis Books, 1987), 85–86.

[18] Moyn, *Not Enough*, 113–118.   [19] Assmann, "Introducción," 15.

[20] Holly Sklar, "Trilateralism: Managing Dependence and Democracy," in *Trilateralism: The Trilateral Commission and Elite Planning for World Management*, ed. Holly Sklar (Boston, MA: South End Press, 1980), 1–57, here 27.

Commission to key positions within the administration. Brzezinski became his national security advisor, thus sending a clear message about the trilateral nature of US foreign policy committed to liberal economic globalization and human rights. The Polish-born Brzezinski recognized that after the Second World War the US "empire" had direct political dominance over dependent nations. Yet with the decline of such power by the late 1960s, the imperial vacuum had been "filled by the pervasive but less tangible influence of American economic presence and innovation."[21] The Trilateral Commission worked to make that economic influence more direct and effective through a transnational corporate ideology aimed at subordinating territorial politics to non-territorial economic goals.[22] Even before the official establishment of the Trilateral Commission, Brzezinski already envisioned something like it to foster global cooperation better than the UN.[23] After serving in the Carter administration, Brzezinski would later join the board of directors for Amnesty International.

On the heels of Watergate, the disaster of the Vietnam War, and support for Pinochet's brutal antidemocratic regime, the new morality of human rights adopted by the Carter administration was a strategic effort to restore US credibility before the international community.[24] Although this was not the only expression of human rights at the time, it was highly influential due to its sophisticated theoretical analysis and backing from transnational corporate power and US public policy. It therefore deserves a place in the historiography on the diverse political and sociological origins of human rights. In the spirit of Trilateralism, the Carter administration avoided the egalitarian and national self-determination models of economic world order. Instead, it promoted a human rights policy focused on promoting civil and political liberties, and promising to fulfill basic needs and alleviate extreme poverty.[25] The global vision of interdependence between the rich North and poor South entailed moral support for a "minimum of social justice" by satisfying basic needs and protecting human rights, which was only achievable alongside Trilateral control of economic power through peace maintenance and global trade management.[26]

---

[21] Zbigniew Brzezinski, *Between Two Ages: America's Role in the Technetronic Era* (New York: Viking Press, 1970), 32–33.

[22] Falk, "A New Paradigm," 1006.   [23] Brzezinski, *Between Two Ages*, 297.

[24] James Petras, "La nueva moralidad de Carter y la lógica del imperialismo," in *Carter y la lógica*, 2:210.

[25] Moyn, *Not Enough*, 143–144.

[26] Richard Cooper, Karl Kaiser, and Masataka Kosaka, *Towards a Renovated International System: A Report of the Trilateral Integrators Task Force to the Trilateral Commission* (New York: Trilateral Commission, 1977), 10, 20.

From a Latin American perspective informed by dependency theory and Marxian social analysis, the idea of interdependence associated with Trilateralism and the Carter administration signaled a familiar practice of American hegemony now oriented to the private accumulation of transnational capital.[27] Interdependence and the "magic word" of cooperation were code for the restructuring of an economic world order ethically managed by Trilateralist citizens of the most powerful nations – the ones capable of assisting poorer nations.[28] Ideally, restricted or viable democracies would replace unstable national security states in the global South. These transitional democracies could better conform to the policy dictates of Trilateral nations and international economic organizations like the World Bank, the International Monetary Fund (IMF), and the United States Agency for International Development (USAID) by producing goods on the cheap and opening their natural resources and financial capital to a global market dominated by multinationals.

Notwithstanding its moral idealism, the Trilateral human rights doctrine linked to neoliberal policies promoting interdependence and cooperation appeared entirely suspect to Latin American critics who saw it as more than just a palliative for social unrest. Human rights from the North was the midwife of the new imperialism of global capital.[29] In a memo entitled "From National Security to Trilateralism" written in 1977 by two founding members of Bolivia's Permanent Assembly for Human Rights, the authors, both religious clergy, observed: "Many have come to think that the defense of human rights is the motivating principle of Carter's politics without realizing that it is the consequence of analysis and adopting stances more far-reaching for strengthening and expanding North American power."[30] In other words, the Trilateral Commission's analysis of and response to the economic world crisis was the larger subtext for Carter's human rights foreign policy. Despite the Carter administration opting for civilianism over militarism, and a viable democracy over the security state, the Bolivian clerics alleged that US politics of human rights abroad was not supportive of those democratic popular movements pursuing greater social justice.[31] They concluded that the Carter administration had not invented human rights (*derechos humanos*); neither were human rights reducible to the recent struggle for civil liberty against

---

[27] Arthur F. McGovern, *Liberation Theology and Its Critics* (Eugene, OR: Wipf & Stock, 2009), 120–129, and chap. 8.
[28] Franz J. Hinkelammert, "El credo económico de la Comisión Trilateral," in *Carter y la lógica*, 1:209–210.
[29] Mark Engler, "Toward the 'Rights of the Poor': Human Rights in Liberation Theology," *Journal of Religious Ethics* 28, no. 3 (Fall 2000), 339–365, at 349.
[30] Sist and Iriarte, "De la seguridad nacional al Trilateralismo," 218.
[31] Ibid., 224–226.

military juntas.[32] Assmann and the other ecumenical contributors reminded readers that Christians in Latin America had an "alternative discourse" of human rights, which neither idealized rights as equally accessible for all nor advocated for civil and political rights at the expense of others. Rather, the alternative discourse proclaimed the rights of poor and dispossessed peoples actively struggling to live within a human history oriented toward salvation.[33] This theological vision of human rights in a conflictual mode points to another genealogy of Catholic modernity in Latin America.

An Alternative Catholic Modernity in Latin America

In a momentous decision, the Latin American Catholic Church's council of bishops (Consejo Episcopal Latinoamericano or CELAM) aligned itself pastorally with the poor masses following the Second Vatican Council of the 1960s. This "preferential option" indicated a Church *of* and *for* the poor. It tells another story about the transnational theological and political origins of human rights during the second half of the twentieth century. The 1968 regional breakthrough of Catholic bishops and theologians gathering in Medellín, Colombia, marked a new era in the Latin American Church and paved the way for an alternative Catholic modernity in the twentieth century.[34] When bishops and theologians made the preferential option at Medellín, and later at Puebla, Mexico (1979), they mobilized a transnational institutional response to the dominant structural forces scourging the continent.

The Second Vatican Council (1962–1965) contained the seeds of this institutional paradigm shift in the Latin American Catholic Church. A month before the Council, Pope John XXIII delivered a radio address summoning the Church in the global South to present "itself as it is, and how it wants to be, as the Church for everyone . . . as the Church of the

---

[32] Ibid., 228.

[33] José Míguez Bonino, "Los derechos humanos, ¿de quienes?" in *Carter y la lógica*, 2:337–338; Juan Luis Segundo, "Derechos humanos, evangelización, e ideología," 347; Luis Alberto Gómez de Souza, "La dimensión social del derecho a la vida," 355–365; Assmann, "El tercer mundo comienza a crear un lenguaje alternativo sobre los derechos humanos," 455.

[34] Patrick William Kelly's important study on transnational human rights activism among Christians in Latin America has located the critical turning point in the 1970s when there was an ecumenical Christian response to state repression. See his *Sovereign Emergencies: Latin America and the Making of Global Human Rights Politics* (Cambridge: Cambridge University Press, 2018). In contrast, my argument isolates the definitive contribution of the Latin American council of Catholic bishops (beginning in the 1960s) toward an alternative discourse and praxis of human rights among liberationist clergy and theologians responding to not only state repression but also to global capitalism.

poor."[35] Pope John's message was a catalyst for an international group of cardinals, bishops, and theologians known as the "Church of the poor" at Vatican II. Just days before the closing of the Council in December 1965, the bishops in the "Church of the poor" group made the so-called Pact of the Catacombs. These forty bishops gathered in the ancient Christian catacombs of Domitilla outside Rome. All of them agreed that when they returned to their respective communities, they would live according to the simplicity, service, and voluntary poverty characteristic of the early Christians.[36] They also committed themselves to promoting the cause of justice, especially for the world's population living in substandard conditions.

More than half of the bishops who signed the Pact of the Catacombs were from Latin America. Among them were the Chilean bishop of Talca, Manuel Larraín, and the Brazilian bishop of Recife, Dom Hélder Câmara. These religious leaders, who were close friends and very active in the Church's struggle for social justice, were the original founders of CELAM in the 1950s. The strategic purpose of CELAM was to provide a transnational organization of bishops for all of Latin America similar to what Brazil had for its diocesan bishops.[37] Medellín was their brainchild. Although Larraín did not live long enough to attend the gathering, Câmara did and became one of the most prominent bishops of the poor and proponents of liberation theology for the remainder of the twentieth century.

Inspired by the Church of the poor at Vatican II, the CELAM gathering at Medellín afforded a moment for ecclesiastical leaders to listen to their communities. Pope Paul VI convened the meeting in an unprecedented papal visit. According to the document it produced, the authentic summons of the CELAM gathering was the "muted cry erupting from millions of people begging their pastors for a liberation that never arrives from anywhere."[38] The pastoral attention of the Latin American Church would not be preoccupied with the atheistic challenge of the secular nonbeliever, but rather with the muted cry of the destitute nonperson.[39]

Remarking on the significance of Medellín only a year after the meeting, pioneer of liberation theology Gustavo Gutiérrez highlighted the

[35] Pope John XXIII, Radio Address (September 11, 1962): https://w2.vatican.va/content/john-xxiii/es/messages/pont_messages/1962/documents/hf_j-xxiii_mes_19620911_ecumenical-council.html.

[36] Maria Clara Bingemer, *Latin American Theology: Roots and Branches* (Maryknoll, NY: Orbis Books, 2016), 49–54.

[37] Christian Smith, *The Emergence of Liberation Theology* (Chicago: University of Chicago Press, 1990), 82–83.

[38] Medellín (1968), "Poverty of the Church," in *Las cinco conferencias generales del episcopado Latinoamericano* (Bogotá: CELAM, 2014), no. 2, 189.

[39] Gustavo Gutiérrez, *The Power of the Poor in History*, trans. Robert Barr (Maryknoll, NY: Orbis Books, 1983), 57, 92.

document's focus on the underlying causes of "institutionalized violence" (*violencia institucionalizada*). Notably, the Medellín document included within the scope of moral culpability not only personal and social sins but also *structural sins* that harm vulnerable populations deprived of basic material needs and political agency. Institutionalized violence, a form of the latter sin, signals "a defect of the structures of industrial and agricultural enterprise, of national and international economy, of cultural and political life."[40] A theological advisor at Medellín, Gutiérrez described CELAM's new historical awareness of Latin America's place in the economic world order:

> It is becoming ever more clear that underdevelopment, in a total sense, is primarily due to economic, political, and cultural dependence on power centers that lie outside Latin America. . . . This new awareness of the Latin American situation . . . finds authoritative and clear-cut expression in the Medellín document on peace, which forthrightly speaks of "internal colonialism" and "external neocolonialism." In Latin America, these are the ultimate causes of the violence that is committed against the most basic human rights.[41]

Contrary to a certain misconception from North America, various liberation theologians affirmed human rights and saw their violation as endemic to neocolonialism already in the late 1960s.[42] Deeply influenced by the language of dignity and human rights from twentieth-century social teachings – Pope John XXIII's *Pacem in terris* (1963), the Second Vatican Council's Pastoral Constitution of the Church in the Modern World (*Gaudium et spes*), and Pope Paul VI's *Populorum progressio* (1967) – Medellín charted a liberationist version of modern Catholicism distinct from the continental European variety.

Medellín specifically invoked the language of the "inalienable" rights of the person and "human rights" to scrutinize and oppose institutionalized violence. Yet the evangelical inflection on liberating the poor through ecclesial solidarity was its mainstay in Latin America and the global Church. European Catholicism's "paternal" expression of human rights, concerned with the rights of the family, and its "fraternal" commitment to the rights of the worker could not fully characterize the Latin American situation elaborated at Medellín, even though both of these models were

---

[40] Medellín (1968), "Document on Peace," in *Las cinco conferencias generales del episcopado Latinoamericano*, no. 16, 103–104.

[41] Gutiérrez, *The Power of the Poor in History*, 28. This is an English translation of a 1969 piece that Gutiérrez wrote as a prologue to *Signos de renovación: Recopilación de documentos postconciliares de la Iglesia en América Latina* (Lima: Comisión Episcopal de Acción Social, 1969).

[42] David Hollenbach, *Claims in Conflict: Retrieving and Renewing the Catholic Human Rights Tradition* (New York: Paulist Press, 1979), 179n2. Hollenbach is one of the earliest Anglophone scholars to suggest that "rights language is notably deemphasized in the various forms of liberation theology recently developed within Roman Catholicism." Cf. Moyn, *Not Enough*, 124.

still present in the CELAM documents.[43] In fact, the Church's outspoken defense of workers' rights would occasion its bloodiest confrontation with authoritarian military-oligarchic regimes.

Definitively, Medellín outlined the new pastoral line of praxis for the Latin American Church: "to defend, according to the Gospel mandate, the rights of the poor and oppressed."[44] Gutiérrez has noted how the "new formality" with which Medellín presented the defense of human rights prompted a liberationist language of rights attentive to the conflictive character of Latin American social life, but also critical of a liberal doctrine that believes "society enjoys an equality that in fact does not exist."[45] Unlike the global human rights activism of the later 1970s, which turned on discrete violations of civil and political liberties, Medellín and the Latin American theology of liberation that crystallized and evolved in its wake articulated an alternative discourse and praxis of rights according to an analysis of structural violence from a southern global perspective. Distinct peoples rather than abstract individuals were the agents and recipients of justice.

If the Catholic modern in postwar Europe pivoted between antifascist and anticommunist opposition to totalitarianism on the right and left, the Latino Catholic modern explicitly resisted a new totalizing threat: the international imperialism of money.[46] With Pope Paul VI's first postconciliar social encyclical, *Populorum progressio*, issuing a warning against this new imperialism, another vector of modern Catholic social teaching was forged. Following the lead of his predecessor John XXIII, Paul VI moved the social analysis of the unjust gap between rich and poor from the domestic context within a single nation to an international context between nations. As he noted, the perspectival shift came as a result of visiting Africa and Latin America before becoming pontiff, which brought him "into direct contact with the acute problems" of the global South.[47]

Although the new watchword of papal social teaching after Paul VI would be the *development* of peoples, the Latin American Church focused specifically on the *liberation* of peoples, not least because the term development was fraught with an economic meaning of third-world

---

[43] James Chappel, *Catholic Modern: The Challenge of Totalitarianism and the Remaking of the Church* (Cambridge, MA: Harvard University Press, 2018). Chappel's work deftly analyzes the crucial "modern" moment in 1930s European Catholicism as it shifted "from an *antimodern* institution to an *antitotalitarian* one" (11).

[44] Medellín (1968), "Document on Peace," no. 22, 106.

[45] Gutiérrez, *The Power of the Poor in History*, 87.

[46] Medellín (1968), "Document on Peace," no. 9, 100; Puebla (1979), in *Las cinco conferencias generales*, no. 312, 320. CELAM explicitly referred to Pope Paul VI's *Populorum progressio* (1967), § 26.

[47] Pope Paul VI, *Populorum progressio* (1967), § 4.

dependency on wealthier nations. Beginning with the biblical Exodus and culminating in the Cross and Resurrection, the concept of liberation (from the bondage of sin and death) is native to theological reflection.[48] Going beyond the language of integral development in Catholic social teaching without abandoning it, Medellín introduced the theological category of *integral liberation* to account for God's work in salvation history as an action promoting "human persons in every dimension."[49] The CELAM meeting at Puebla specifically coined the expression "liberating evangelization" (*evangelización liberadora*) to establish the inseparability of the integral liberation of peoples from the Church's missionary activity.[50] According to the postconciliar Church in Latin America, human history and salvation history could not be divorced in the life of God's people.

For an increasing number of Latin American theologians, liberating evangelization was the Church's nonviolent strategy of being robustly political on its own terms without being partisan. In this regard, the Church could avoid the political extremes of communist guerilla tactics (*foquismo*) and the militarized security states.[51] The Latin American bishops roundly condemned the ideologies of Marxist collectivism and national securitization, which represented the modern political vices of communism and fascism. However, this shared ecclesial perspective did not prevent growing tension and even division among the bishops during the volatile political period of the 1970s and 1980s in Latin America. The election of Bishop Alfonso López Trujillo as secretary-general of CELAM in 1972 animated a conservative clerical opposition to liberation theology and its ecclesial social praxis.[52] In the leadership role at CELAM, López Trujillo tried to enervate the liberationist language of Medellín but only exacerbated the ideological conflict between various national delegations. This confrontation came to a head at the Puebla meeting between Colombia, Argentina, and Mexico forming a conservative bloc, and Central America, Peru, Brazil, and others forming a liberationist contingent.[53] Excluded from the meeting were Gutiérrez, along with

---

[48] Gustavo Gutiérrez, *A Theology of Liberation* (Maryknoll, NY: Orbis Books, 1988), chap. 2.

[49] Medellín (1968), "Document on Justice," no. 4, 88.

[50] See the section specifically titled "Discernment of Liberation in Christ," in Puebla (1979), nos. 480–490, 354–356. A chief source for CELAM's theological reflection on liberating evangelization was Pope Paul VI's apostolic exhortation, *Evangelii nuntiandi* (1975).

[51] Comblin, *The Church and the National Security State*, 87–88.

[52] McGovern, *Liberation Theology and Its Critics*, 12, 47–49.

[53] Enrique Dussel, *A History of the Church in Latin America* (Grand Rapids, MI: Eerdmans, 1981), 230–231.

other notable liberation theologians such as José Comblin and Ignacio Ellacuría.

Nevertheless, the attention at Medellín and Puebla to liberal capitalism's neocolonial mode under the international imperialism of money remained CELAM's most prophetic contribution to the social analysis of ideology and structural violence in a global context. As it happened, the new form of domination in Latin America was a complicated nexus of powerful neoliberal actors including multinationals, transnational banking, and the Trilateral Commission, but also the Cold War hangovers of militarism, counterinsurgency, and the national security system. Liberating evangelization and its moral offshoot of rights for historically poor persons directly countered these ideological forces discursively and politically.[54] El Salvador presented an iconic example of ecclesial resistance amidst the social conflict between faith and the forms of domination, old and new, during the 1970s and 1980s.

El Salvador and the Rights of the Poor in History

The powerful nations of today tell us they come to the Third World to make us "rich" and to make us "democratic." But these "generous propositions" contain a distinctive political and economic project. In order to discover and unmask the truth of such a project, one should not look *within the borders* of dominant nations in the West, but instead look precisely *beyond their borders*. There the ultimate effects of the Western project – its chief representative and carrier being the USA – become manifest, showing what it really is and what it pretends to be.[55]

San Salvador, the capital of one of the smallest Central American nations, was a microcosm of the internal colonialism of national security and the external neocolonialism of US interventionism beginning in the 1970s and culminating in the nation's civil war from 1980 to 1992. Two extraordinary prophetic voices of integral liberation for the poor emerged in this violent social context, Monseñor Óscar Romero and Jesuit theologian Ignacio Ellacuría, brothers in Christ who suffered death at the hands of right-wing military actors with US ties during the 1980s. Both Romero and Ellacuría were liberationist critics of their repressive military state, transnational capitalism, and US foreign policy under the banner of human rights. They were also key articulators of the Medellín-inspired

---

[54] Richard, *Death of Christendoms*, 89–90.
[55] Ignacio Ellacuría, "Quinto Centenario de América Latina, ¿descubrimiento o encubrimiento? (1990)," in *La lucha por la Justicia: Selección de textos de Ignacio Ellacuría (1969–1989)*, ed. Juan Antonio Senent (Spain: Universidad de Deusto, 2012), 345–356, here 348. My emphasis.

alternative Latin American discourse and praxis of rights for the poor in their respective capacities as archbishop of San Salvador and rector of the Universidad Centroamericana José Simeón Cañas (UCA).

As early as 1969, the Spanish-born Ellacuría reflected on the truthfulness of human rights discourse – starting with the fundamental right to life (*el derecho a la vida*) – by subjecting it to an historical analysis of social conflict.[56] Importantly, the basic right to life was not reducible to a single individual's personal security and immunity from arbitrary attack or torture. The right to life also included the social and economic rights to pursue work and receive a just wage at the level of individuals, but also at the level of an organized group of laborers. Liberation must first entail "liberation from basic necessities" to overcome the unjust material oppression without which one could not sustain a dignified human life.[57] There can be no genuine liberty without justice for the neediest. This prioritization of the fundamental right to life, as Assmann noted, was a key point of contention between a liberal conception of human rights and the alternative discourse in Latin America.[58]

According to Ellacuría, the historical struggle to survive among destitute peoples indicates that it is precisely the negation of right, or injustice, which provides the basic datum for claiming human rights in the first place. "Structural injustice in its diversely manifested forms," he wrote, "is a fact prior to 'rights.' Rights are formulated because there is an injustice and this injustice is recognized before the expression of any specific right."[59] The truthfulness of rights cannot be grasped apart from a concrete prior injustice experienced by real subjects in history. This injustice consists chiefly in the privation of life's material needs among the poorest of society. The preferential option for oppressed communities marked by real poverty and injustice methodologically allows for a "historization" (*historización*) of human rights that points to an authentic universality while exposing the vacuity of individual rights asserted in the abstract.[60] The historical truth of rights born from the conflictual struggle for liberation by poor and oppressed peoples markedly contrasts with

[56] Ellacuría, "Los derechos humanos fundamentales y su limitación legal y política (1969)," in *La lucha*, 215–216.

[57] Ellacuría, "En torno al concepto y a la idea de liberación (1989)," in *La lucha*, 140.

[58] Assmann, "El tercer mundo comienza a crear un lenguaje alternativo," 455: "All abstract notions of individual freedom, placed before or in contrast to the fundamental rights to life and the means of sustaining life, show the emptiness of the meaning of 'liberal rights,' of which the majority of humanity has been systematically deprived. This necessity of subordinating certain (derivative) rights to others more fundamental is one of the most difficult points to accept, even for relatively open-minded and progressive persons."

[59] Ellacuría, "Respuesta a CETRAL (1980)," in *La lucha*, 295.

[60] Ellacuría, "Historización de los derechos humanos desde los pueblos oprimidos y las mayorías populares (1990)," in *La lucha*, 373.

a universal human rights doctrine ideally applicable to all individuals but only realized by the privileged. "The condition of the oppressed" in history, Ellacuría remarked, "can cast doubt on rights accepted ideologically" and independent of economic and political realities.[61]

From the liberationist view of Catholic social ethics, poverty is an oppressive structural injustice resulting from an inequality of wealth between individuals in society. The extreme gap between rich and poor is evidence of structural injustice. Pius XI's *Quadragesimo anno* (1931) clearly acknowledged the fact "that the vast differences between the few who hold excessive wealth and the many who live in destitution constitute a *grave evil in modern society.*"[62] Echoing Medellín, the Puebla document (1979) provided a social analysis along these lines, stating that poverty was too often "the result of economic, social, political structures."[63] Structural injustice – embedded in social institutions, public laws, and economic policies, and reflected in gross inequalities – is the result of decisions that subordinate labor to capital and persons to profit.

The historical victims of structural injustice in every age are concrete peoples, not abstract individuals. They are the real faces (*rostros*) of children, indigenous peoples, African Americans, *campesinos*, the underemployed, and the elderly who all reveal the sufferings of Christ in the world. In the words of the Puebla document, the *campesinos* (poor rural farmworkers) referred to a particular social group living as "outcasts almost everywhere on the continent, dispossessed of land, caught in a situation of internal and external dependence, and subjected to systems of commercialization that exploit them."[64] Archbishop Romero's powerful presence at the contentious Puebla meeting brought firsthand experience to drafting key teachings regarding concrete injustices in the spirit of Medellín. As a transnational leader in the Church, Romero publicly recognized the injustice of *campesino* suffering and could therefore mobilize a Christian ethic of resisting both state repression and neocolonialism. For this reason, Romero's Jesuit friend and companion to Ellacuría, Jon Sobrino, has rightly stressed the archbishop's political effectiveness at institutionalizing the preferential option for the poor by putting the resources of the institutional Church at the service of protecting and empowering the neediest.[65] Archbishop Romero's homilies and pastoral letters during his episcopacy

---

[61] Ellacuría, "Respuesta a CETRAL," in *La lucha*, 296.

[62] Pope Pius XI, *Quadragesimo anno*, § 58, in *Catholic Social Thought: Encyclicals and Documents from Pope Leo XIII to Pope Francis*, eds. David J. O'Brien and Thomas A. Shannon (Maryknoll, NY: Orbis Books, 2016). My emphasis.

[63] Puebla (1979), no. 30, 268.   [64] Puebla (1979), no. 35, 269

[65] Jon Sobrino, "A Theologian's View of Oscar Romero," in *Voice of the Voiceless: The Four Pastoral Letters and Other Statements*, trans. Michael Walsh (Maryknoll, NY: Orbis Books, 1985), 22–51, 31.

from 1977 to 1980 consistently refracted papal social teaching, especially Paul VI's, through the liberationist historical lens of CELAM in order to speak out for the victims of structural poverty.

At this time, El Salvador was on the brink of civil war due to the political instability of the dominant military-oligarchic rule and its refusal to concede power after losing two elections to the Christian Democrats. The military regime's violent repression of political dissidents only strengthened the cause of the leftist movement, the Frente Farabundo Martí para la Liberación Nacional (FMLN). Central to the nation's political conflict was the social question of agrarian reform going back to the nineteenth-century privatization of land for coffee production and trade.[66] Beginning with the massacre of 1932, El Salvador's poor and mostly indigenous agricultural laborers were the primary targets of military repression whenever economic oligarchs feared peasant organization or uprising. The *campesinos* – victims of material deprivation, kidnapping, torture, assassination, and terrorism by the state – were the principal historical subjects of long-standing dispossession and structural poverty in El Salvador.

Archbishop Romero frequently referred to the Church of and for the poor as "the Body of Christ in history." The Church's preferential option illustrated the faith community's concrete yet divinely inspired struggle for liberation. For Romero, the theme of liberating evangelization encapsulated the transforming power of Christ in history.[67] "Our continent's longing for liberation," he wrote in his second pastoral letter in 1977, "is a clear sign of the presence of God in history."[68] In the case of El Salvador, solidarity with the poor *campesinos* brought the Church into an increasingly persecuted state during the military-oligarchic rule of Generals Arturo Molina and Carlos Romero in the 1970s. The preferential option, according to the archbishop, implicated the Church directly in the poor's painful struggle for justice, just as Christ did by identifying directly with the weakest and most neglected of society.[69]

Through an unflinching episcopal commitment to nonviolent social justice, Archbishop Romero was a paradigmatic embodiment of the liberationist discourse and praxis of Christian human rights in Latin

---

[66] Raymond Bonner, *Weakness and Deceit: U.S. Policy and El Salvador* (New York: Times Books, 1984), chap. 2.

[67] Archbishop Óscar Romero, "Pastoral Message to the National Council of Churches," in *Voice of the Voiceless*, 168–176, here 172.

[68] Archbishop Óscar Romero, Second Pastoral Letter (1977), in *Voice of the Voiceless*, 63–84, here 67.

[69] Ibid., 79–80.

America.[70] In his third pastoral letter, cowritten with Bishop Arturo Rivera y Damas in 1978, Romero defended the agrarian cause of *campesinos* most forcefully. The principal injustice addressed in the letter was the violation of the fundamental right to organize, supported by national, international, transnational, and supranational bodies during the twentieth century. Contrary to El Salvador's constitution, the UN Universal Declaration, Medellín, and the social teaching of the universal Church, military-oligarchic repression directly attacked the right of political parties, trade unions, and rural farmworkers to organize legally in pursuit of their just aims. The authoritative moral weight behind the *campesino* right to organize was not merely a civil and political liberty to participate in the management and self-determination of the country, crucial as that may be, "but the simple basic need to survive."[71]

Along with the problem of political organization in El Salvador, the third pastoral letter analyzed the various forms of violence outlined at Medellín that were rapidly destroying the country. Romero keenly parsed the difference between the repressive violence of the state used against the *campesino* right to organize and the "most acute form" of violence in Latin America: institutionalized violence.[72] Institutionalized violence did not attack civil and political rights, as state repression did. Rather, it was observable through its deleterious economic effect on society – when the majority of people lacked life's necessities. Those responsible for "international structures" and those who "monopolize economic power instead of sharing it" were complicit in this kind of violence, undermining the fundamental right to life even when they remained distant from the victims.

Archbishop Romero's fourth and final pastoral letter, written the following year (1979), returned to the Salvadoran problems regarding the right to organize and institutionalized violence. His analysis of the social conflict became even more refined when he called out the owners of El Salvador's agricultural export trade in coffee, sugar, and cotton for relying on unorganized *campesinos* to sustain their cheap labor force, a practice all too familiar in the country's history since the nineteenth-century liberal reforms. Romero reflected prophetically on the link between the idolatry of power in national security that fed internal colonialism and the idolatry of money in transnational capital that steered

---

[70] For more on Romero as a distinct voice of liberation theology in El Salvador, see Michael E. Lee, *Revolutionary Saint: The Theological Legacy of Óscar Romero* (Maryknoll, NY: Orbis Books, 2018), 188–199.

[71] Archbishop Óscar Romero, Third Pastoral Letter (1978), in *Voice of the Voiceless*, 85–113, here 91.

[72] Ibid., 106–107.

external neocolonialism. Although Romero never shied away from denouncing the secular idolatry of Marxist-inspired political organizations, he vociferously opposed the large-scale violence perpetrated by colonialism, old and new. "Today," he critically observed, "many industrial and transnational corporations base their ability to compete in international markets on what they call 'low labor costs,' which in reality means starvation wages." This new international system of transnational capital relied on the preexisting modern colonial system of oligarchic landownership. He continued: "The ruling class, especially the rural elite, cannot allow unions to be organized among either rural or urban laborers so long as, from a capitalist point of view, they believe their economic interests are at risk. This viewpoint makes repression against popular organizations something necessary in order to maintain and increase profit levels, even though it is at the cost of the growing poverty of the working class."[73]

The absolute commitment to private property, at both the international and national levels, undergirded the irrepressible desire to control political and economic power, without which the rich could not sustain their private interests.[74] In biblical parlance, Romero's social analysis operated with the belief that the love of money was "the root of all evils."[75] Nevertheless, he did not let denunciation and despair have the last word on social life. Conversion was indeed possible for the wealthiest elites. Romero challenged the privileged minority to exercise true charity, which consists "not only in giving others what is their due, but even in giving them something that is one's own."[76] The practice of true charity marked Saint Óscar Romero's life to the very end. He became a martyr by an assassin's bullet while celebrating Mass in a hospital chapel on March 24, 1980.

Archbishop Romero's final homily from the cathedral the day before became his death warrant when he implored soldiers to refuse killing innocent *campesinos* out of obedience to God over national security forces. His prophetic indictment to "stop the repression!" addressed the Salvadoran national guard and, implicitly, President Carter, who was aiding the military junta.[77] Romero would never get a chance to develop his social analysis of El Salvador's neoliberal reforms of the late 1980s and 1990s, which benefited the financial elite more than traditional oligarchs, while extreme levels of poverty among *campesinos* persisted and gang

---

[73] Archbishop Óscar Romero, Fourth Pastoral Letter (1979), in *Voice of the Voiceless*, 114–161, here 121–122.
[74] Ibid., 133–134.   [75] 1 Timothy 6:10.   [76] Romero, Fourth Pastoral Letter, 142.
[77] *A Prophetic Bishop Speaks to His People: The Complete Homilies of Archbishop Oscar Arnulfo Romero*, vol. 6 (Miami, FL: Convivium Press, 2016), 410, 419.

violence emerged. Nevertheless, his ecclesial resistance to the idolatries of wealth and national security can still guide Christian thinking about human rights under Pope Francis in an age when economic inequality widens indefinitely and national security rhetoric dominates executive action. The archbishop's letter to President Carter denouncing US interventionism a month before his death exposed the human rights breakthrough as an unwitting ally of injustice. His letter also revealed the direct confrontation between the Trilateral human rights doctrine and the alternative discourse of Christian human rights in Latin America.

After the October 1979 coup in El Salvador deposed the country's military dictatorship, efforts were undertaken to address national economic disparity through agrarian reform. Assisted by the USA, a 1980 junta involving a reformist faction of the military and the Christian Democrats put forward an economic plan to nationalize banks and export production of coffee. They also supported a political plan to begin democratizing El Salvador through greater respect for human rights. In reality, the agrarian reform mostly benefited the landed elite and thus failed to fulfill the economic redistribution of national wealth, as social-scientific studies at the UCA indicated.[78] The violent military repression waged against *campesinos* increased, which was precisely why Archbishop Romero tried appealing to the conscience of Salvadoran security forces in 1980. Brzezinski, Carter's national security advisor, called Pope John Paul II directly to complain about Romero's lack of support for the junta.[79] In this context, Romero demanded that President Carter, whom he recognized as a Christian proponent of human rights, stop intervening in the economic and political life of El Salvador.

A report indicating that the USA was sending more than $5 million in military assistance prompted Archbishop Romero to inform President Carter that his intervention would make matters predictably worse for the organized agricultural workers, "whose struggle has often been for respect of their most basic human rights."[80] Romero also stated that the new government was a ruse because power had reverted to "the unscrupulous military officers who know only how to repress the people and favor the interests of the Salvadoran oligarchy." His twofold ultimatum to the president addressed both current and future interventionism: forbid

---

[78] Bonner, *Weakness and Deceit*, 188–189.

[79] Matt Eisenbrandt, *Assassination of a Saint: The Plot to Murder Óscar Romero and the Quest to Bring His Killers to Justice* (Berkeley: University of California Press, 2017), 53.

[80] Archbishop Óscar Romero, "Letter to President Carter," in *Voice of the Voiceless*, 188–190, here 189.

military aid to the Salvadoran government and guarantee no more US political, economic, and military intervention either directly or indirectly.

Archbishop Romero's demand represented a remarkable regionalist stand against postwar US hegemony by a Latin American religious leader. He ended his letter by declaring the injustice of foreign powers "to intervene and frustrate the Salvadoran people," who must "decide autonomously the economic and political course" for their future. Notably, Romero appealed to the transnational teaching of Puebla, rather than the UN, to support the legitimate self-determination of Latin American peoples.[81] Romero's regionalist defense denoted a politically rich tradition of human rights in Latin America promoting the sovereignty of weaker nations and nonintervention on the world stage.[82] The official response by the Carter administration came through Trilateralist member Secretary of State Cyrus Vance, who assured Archbishop Romero that US support would professionalize the Salvadoran military for the purpose of maintaining order in the country with minimal use of lethal force.[83]

US assistance only further emboldened the ruthless behavior of an ex-major of the Salvadoran military, Roberto D'Aubuisson, trained in counterinsurgency tactics at the School of the Americas. His role in leading the death squads of the country's security forces put him directly in charge of authorizing the assassination of Romero, which a UN truth commission later confirmed. The tragic fact was that the political rise of D'Aubuisson in El Salvador coincided with his removal of Archbishop Romero.[84] Romero was a direct obstacle to the ongoing impunity of internal colonialism and the imminent rise of neocolonialism. In 1981, D'Aubuisson went on to establish the extreme right-wing nationalist party Alianza Republicana Nacionalista (ARENA), elected on an anticommunist platform to the exclusion of the FMLN. ARENA, which staunchly opposed and peeled back agrarian reform in favor of landed elites, and the Christian Democrats, who supported the implementation of agrarian reform, were the dominant political actors during El Salvador's civil war (1980–1992).

The USA ratcheted up its monetary assistance, now appearing to be a form of civilian aid rather than sheer militarism, to El Salvador during

---

[81] Ibid., 189. Romero specifically cited Puebla (1979), no. 505, 360, which referred to *Gaudium et spes*, § 74.

[82] For more on the twentieth-century contribution of Latin America to international human rights, see Kathryn Sikkink, *Evidence for Hope: Making Human Rights Work in the 21st Century* (Princeton, NJ: Princeton University Press, 2017), chap. 3, and "Latin American Countries As Norm Protagonists of the Idea of International Human Rights," *Global Governance* 20 (2014), 389–404.

[83] Bonner, *Weakness and Deceit*, 171.

[84] Robert Lassalle-Klein, *Blood and Ink: Ignacio Ellacuria, Jon Sobrino, and the Jesuit Martyrs of the University of Central America* (Maryknoll, NY: Orbis Books, 2014), 131.

the Reagan administration. USAID's influence in Salvadoran politics was extensive in this regard.[85] Its development funds initially strengthened the state according to the centrist politics of the Christian Democrats, only to later actively advance the interests of the private sector according to neoliberal policies reducing the state's role. The US agency mainly channeled its political and economic interests in the civilian business sector through the Salvadoran development organization FUSADES, which became a kind of neoliberal think tank. When ARENA came to power in 1989 under a new leader, Alfredo Cristiani, a Georgetown University graduate from a coffee-owning family, it seemed to move away from the earlier militarism associated with founder D'Aubuisson. As a member of FUSADES, Cristiani appointed other members to key positions in his government and restructured the country's programs in a neoliberal direction by reprivatizing banks and export trade. ARENA became the flagship "nationalist" party for the neoliberal economic reforms of the 1990s supported by USAID, but also the World Bank.

Although civilian on the surface, several months into Cristiani's governance, the brutal authoritarian militarist roots of ARENA were exposed. With the strong rebel offensive of FMLN against the right-wing government under way in the heat of civil war, a US-trained counterinsurgency battalion known as Atlacatl carried out D'Aubuisson's original wishes to remove the "communist" Jesuits at the UCA.[86] Ignacio Ellacuría, then rector at the UCA, envisioned that the ultimate objective of the Catholic university was to provide an adequate theoretical response and effective practical solution for addressing basic material needs through the social agency of the poor.[87] The military personnel executed Fr. Ellacuría, along with five other priests of the Society of Jesus, a housekeeper, and her daughter on the university campus on November 16, 1989. Like Archbishop Romero's assassins, the UCA murderers never faced legal justice. In an article written in the last year of his life, Ellacuría incisively noted that the USA may have been effective at operating democratically within its own borders even as it maintained an "anti-democratic position internationally."[88] The case of El Salvador during the 1970s and 1980s bore out this inconvenient truth, showing the

---

[85] Chris van der Borgh, "The Politics of Neoliberalism in Postwar El Salvador," *International Journal of Political Economy* 30, no. 1 (Spring 2000), 36–54.

[86] Lassalle-Klein, *Blood and Ink*, xvii–xxii, 146–147.

[87] Ellacuría, "The University, Human Rights, and the Poor Majority," in *Towards a Society That Serves Its People: The Intellectual Contributions of El Salvador's Martyred Jesuits*, ed. John Hassett and Hugh Lacey (Washington, DC: Georgetown University Press, 1991), 211–212.

[88] Ellacuría, "Quinto Centenario," in *La lucha*, 348.

hypocrisy of the northern neighbor's appeal to the language of human rights.

The spiritual and political itinerary of the Catholic modern in Latin America meant the Church had to endure extensive persecution, even martyrdom, when it opted for the liberation of the poor. From this historical and geopolitical context, an alternative liberationist discourse and praxis of human rights developed in resistance to colonialism from within and from without. With attention to institutionalized violence and structural injustice, its social analysis went much deeper than the 1970s activism characterizing the global human rights regime. It exposed not only the tepidity of a Trilateral human rights doctrine linked to neoliberalism but also the alliance, unwitting or not, between Carter's human rights breakthrough and unjust security states in the joint effort to defeat a common red enemy.

The story of human rights as a powerless companion is a fatalist one of unfulfilled promises and the insurmountable power of money over morality in a global market society. Yet viewing human rights from the underside as the struggle of oppressed peoples in concrete history can engender hope from authentic witnesses who embody unyielding courage. In the case of El Salvador and the heroic examples of Romero and Ellacuría, it becomes clear that the liberationist praxis of rights for the poor is sharply incompatible with gross socioeconomic inequalities. Their nonviolent faith, like that of so many members of the body of Christ from the global South, reveals how the preferential option for the poor can identify and oppose the greatest idol of all – Mammon.

13   Two Sudans, Human Rights, and the Afterlives of St. Josephine Bakhita

Christopher Tounsel

The Republic of the Sudan is an intriguing context through which to examine the interplay between Christianity, Islam, religious freedom, and human rights abuses. National governments have attempted to forge Sudan as an Islamic state for most of its postcolonial history. Southern Sudan, with its long exposure to Christian mission work, rejected this agenda. Southerners waged two civil wars against Khartoum. The government bombed, starved, and enslaved Southerners in its effort to subject them to Islamic rule. During the second war alone, more than 2 million Southerners died and nearly 5 million were displaced.[1]

Josephine Bakhita stood at the epicenter of this maelstrom. Bakhita's face has appeared on hats, key rings, badges, and women's printed clothing in Juba, South Sudan's capital. The city's Catholic bookshop has sold DVDs and books on her life, and a Juba radio station donning her name went on the air in 2007.[2] Who is Bakhita, and why is she so resonant? This chapter investigates the sociopolitical significance of Josephine Bakhita in recent Sudanese (and South Sudanese) history. Born in the nineteenth century, she was a Sudanese woman enslaved in her youth but, once free, became a Canossian sister. During the Second Sudanese Civil War (1983–2005), Bakhita was beatified and canonized as Sudan's first Catholic saint. Pope John Paul II injected her life and legacy into calls for human dignity to be respected in a context rife with abuses that included slavery and religious persecution. Bakhita's name

---

[1] Justin Holcomb, "Southern Sudanese Chaplains: Human Rights and the Embodiment of Peace," *The Other Journal: An Intersection of Theology & Culture* (August 8, 2005): https://theotherjournal.com/2005/08/08/southern-sudanese-chaplains-human-rights-and-the-embodiment-of-peace/. See also Jok Madut Jok, *War and Slavery in Sudan* (Philadelphia: University of Pennsylvania Press, 2001), 40.

[2] Wendy James, "Religious Practice and Belief," in *The Sudan Handbook*, ed. John Ryle, Justin Willis, Suliman Baldo, and Jok Madut Jok (Rochester, NY: James Currey, 2011), 43–53, here 53; "Sudan Catholics Turn to Darfur Saint," Sudan Tribune (September 5, 2008): www.sudantribune.com/spip.php?article28524; Fr. José Vieira questionnaire.

continued to carry resonance after the war through the establishment of Radio Bakhita. In time, however, the station became associated with another human rights concern: attacks on freedom of expression. Radio Bakhita has had multiple run-ins with South Sudanese state security, most recently during the new nation's own internal conflict.[3]

Bakhita's postcolonial afterlife not only exemplifies the ways in which a religious figure can be injected into campaigns against secular social ills; it also shows how a religious icon can become a transmutable symbol linked to different abuses in the same space in different times. A "saint for all seasons," her character has shone a religious light on human rights abuses in one of Africa's most troubled regions.

Civil Wars

Despite Christian missionary assistance, Southern Sudan received minimal investment in development during Sudan's Anglo-Egyptian colonial period. Upon independence in 1956 – when the Southern population constituted roughly 27 percent of the population – national power passed to a small Arab and Muslim elite in Khartoum. Efforts to spread Islam and Arabic usage intensified after a 1958 coup, actions that alienated the small, predominantly Christian Southern educated elite. Armed resistance took the form of civil war by the early 1960s. The 1972 Addis Ababa Agreement ended the war and promised Southern Sudan some political autonomy. However, repeated violations of the Agreement paved the way for a second civil war that began in 1983 and lasted until 2005. The Sudanese Peoples' Liberation Movement and Army (SPLM/A) was the major Southern Sudan-based resistance movement in this conflict. The war ended with the 2005 Comprehensive Peace

---

[3] David H. Farmer, "Bakhita, Josephine," in *The Oxford Dictionary of Saints* (Oxford: Oxford University Press, 2011); Robert S. Kramer, Richard A. Lobban, and Carolyn Fluehr-Lobban, *Historical Dictionary of the Sudan*, 4th ed. (Lanham, MD: Scarecrow Press, 2013), 26, 84; "Address of John Paul II to the Bishops of Sudan on Their Ad Limina Visit," December 15, 2003: https://w2.vatican.va/content/john-paul-ii /en/speeches/2003/december/documents/hf_jp-ii_spe_20031215_ad-limina-sudan.html; Bona Malwal, "Overdue but Welcome UN Action," *Sudan Democratic Gazette* (January 1993), 1. For use of the term "freedom of expression," see "Pastoral Statement of the Sudanese Catholic Bishops Conference on the Signing of the Comprehensive Peace Agreement (CPA) Nairobi, February 26, 2005," *Sudan Tribune*: www .sudantribune.com/spip.php?article8385; "World Report 2018: South Sudan," Human Rights Watch (2018): www.hrw.org/world-report/2018/country-chapters/south-sudan#1b7a9c. For examples of Radio Bakhita's problems, see Ngor Arol Garang, "Sudan SPLM Minister Condemns Closure of FM Radios in Juba," *Sudan Tribune* (March 4, 2010): www.sudantribune.com/spip.php?article34324; "S. Sudan Security Agents Arrest Four Journalists, Shut Down Radio Station," *Sudan Tribune* (August 16, 2014): www.sudantribune.com/spip.php?article52066.

Agreement (CPA), and in a 2011 referendum nearly 99 percent of Southern voters opted for secession.[4]

Religion featured prominently during the civil wars. Missionary schools were nationalized in 1957, and efforts to spread Islam in the South intensified after Ibrahim Abboud's coup the following year. A campaign was made to marginalize foreign missionaries, whose access to the South was increasingly limited. Jafaar Nimeiri, who assumed power in 1969, imposed Islamic law upon Sudan in 1983. Although Nimeiri was over-thrown in 1985, Prime Minister Sadiq al-Mahdi – a Northerner who won election in 1986 – did not act resolutely on the issue of Sharia or Islamization. With the government on the verge of collapse, General 'Umar al-Beshir's Islamist military regime came to power in a June 1989 coup. Beshir allied himself with the National Islamic Front (NIF), which moved to spread its version of Islam. Chief NIF designer Hasan al-Turabi introduced the *shura* system, which he maintained was the only legitimate ruling system for an Islamic state. The government, in its move to Islamize state institutions and economic organizations, refused to negotiate with the SPLM on the issue of removing Sharia as state law.[5]

In addition to the North-South war, Sudan experienced simultaneous South-South and North-North conflicts. In Southern Sudan, fights occurred over cattle, resources, and ethnicity. The SPLA's 1991 split into two warring contingents initiated full-scale conflict between the Nuer

---

[4] Hilde Johnson, *South Sudan: The Untold Story from Independence to Civil War* (London: I. B. Tauris, 2016), 2–3; H. R. J. Davies, "Population Change in the Sudan since Independence," *Geography* 73 (1988), 249 (see Table 1); John Ashworth, Maura Ryan, et al., "One Nation from Every Tribe, Tongue, and People: The Church and Strategic Peacebuilding in South Sudan," *Journal of Catholic Social Thought* 10 (2013), 48–49; William Anderson, Roland Werner, and Andrew C. Wheeler, *Day of Devastation, Day of Contentment: The History of the Sudanese Church across 2000 Years*, first reprint (Nairobi: Paulines Publications Africa, 2001), 386, 388; Kramer, Lobban, and Fleuhr-Lobban, *Dictionary*, 408. Scopas S. Poggo's *The First Sudanese Civil War: Africans, Arabs, and Israelis in the Southern Sudan, 1955–1972* (New York: Palgrave Macmillan, 2009) is an excellent examination of the First Civil War.

[5] Johnson, *Untold*, 3, 5; Øystein H. Rolandsen, "From Colonial Backwater to an Independent State: Reflections on the History of South Sudan," in *One Church from Every Tribe, Tongue and People: Symposium on the Role of the Church in the Independence of South Sudan*, ed. John Ashworth (Nairobi: Paulines Publications Africa, 2012), 20–22; *A Concise History of South Sudan*, ed. Anders Breidlid, et al. (Kampala: Fountain Publishers, 2014), 321; Kramer, Lobban, and Fleuhr-Lobban, *Dictionary*, 23–24, 224, 430; Allen D. Hertzke, *Freeing God's Children: The Unlikely Global Alliance for Global Human Rights* (Lanham, MD: Rowman & Littlefield Publishers, 2004), 241; Gabriel Warburg and Younes Abouyoub, "National Islamic Front," in *The Oxford Encyclopedia of Islam and Politics*, ed. Emad el-Din Shain (Oxford: Oxford University Press, 2014): www.oxfordreference.com/view/10.1093/acref:oiso/9780199739356 .001.0001/acref-9780199739356-e-0356.

and the Dinka, the South's two largest ethnic groups. The North witnessed wars in the Blue Nile, Nuba Mountains, the Eastern Front, and Darfur. In 2003, a rebellion began in Darfur with an alliance of Fur, Masalit, and Zaghawa peoples contending with the Sudanese government and its allies among Northern Darfur Arab groups. The national army launched a counterinsurgency campaign to destroy the rebellion, resulting in 300,000 deaths and 1.8 million displaced. The US government has termed Darfur's humanitarian crisis a genocide.[6]

In 2002, the US Commission on International Religious Freedom deemed Sudan "the world's most violent abuser of the right to freedom of religion and belief."[7] The regime framed its campaign as a holy war. The government dropped bombs that targeted Southern sites of worship, hospitals, civilians, schools, and other locations. Non-Muslims faced persecution, and churches were confiscated and converted to mosques. In December 1992, the UN General Assembly produced a resolution condemning the government's violation of human rights.[8]

Slavery was arguably the war's chief abuse. A feature of Sudanese society since the period of ancient Egypt, slavery during the Second Civil War was typically conducted by Khartoum-armed western pastoralists against non-Muslims in Southern Sudan. The practice was linked with the presence of government militias. The government supported these militias as part of its offensive against the SPLA, and in lieu of pay it encouraged militias to capture whatever they could, including people. The *murahalin* that operated in Kordofan and northern Bahr el-Ghazal were the most devastating militia, attacking several Dinka groups. Enslaved persons, typically women and children, were physically assaulted and regularly forced to convert to Islam. Some estimates of

---

[6] Ashworth and Ryan, "Peacebuilding," 49; Jok Madut Jok and Sharon Elaine Hutchinson, "Sudan's Prolonged Second Civil War and the Militarization of Nuer and Dinka Ethnic Identities," *African Studies Review* 42 (1999), 126; Salah M. Hassan and Carina E. Ray, "Introduction: Critically Reading Darfur and the Crisis of Governance in Sudan," in *Darfur and the Crisis of Governance in Sudan: A Critical Reader*, ed. Salah M. Hassan and Carina E. Ray (Ithaca, NY: Cornell University Press, 2009), 20; Andrew S. Natsios, *Sudan, South Sudan, and Darfur: What Everyone Needs to Know* (Oxford: Oxford University Press, 2012), xxvi–xxvii; Graham Harrison, "Darfur," in *The Concise Oxford Dictionary of Politics and International Relations*, ed. Garret Brown, Iain McLean, and Alistair McMillan (Oxford University Press, 2018) www.oxfordreference.com/view/10.1093/acref/9780199670840.001.0001/acref-9780199670840-e-1518.

[7] *Report of the United States Commission on International Religious Freedom* (2002), 25, as taken from Hertzke, *Children*, 239.

[8] Hertzke, *Children*, 241; Holcomb, "Chaplains"; Kramer, Lobban, and Fleuhr-Lobban, *Dictionary*, 204; Malwal, "Overdue," 1; A. M. Medani, "The UN Resolution and the Tragedy of Human Rights in Sudan," *Sudan Democratic Gazette* (February 1993), 6.

the number enslaved ranged from 20,000 to 200,000. The SPLA was also coercive, pressing abandoned or orphaned children into its forces.[9]

Josephine Bakhita

During the early twenty-first century, former South Sudanese and Nuba victims of slavery wrote memoirs and lectured throughout the United States and Europe. And yet the most famous Sudanese slave during the war was not even alive: Josephine Bakhita. Eve Troutt Powell has written that her 2000 canonization conveyed that her story could no longer be consigned to the history of nineteenth-century Sudan. It mirrored contemporary experience.[10]

Josephine Bakhita was born in Olgossa, Darfur. As a young girl, Bakhita was captured and sold into slavery in el-Obeid. Sold again to a general in the Turkish army, she was tattooed with 140 cuts.[11] During her enslavement she was given the Arabic name Bakhita, or "Fortunate One."[12] In 1882 the general decided to return to Turkey and sold Bakhita to Calisto Legnani, Italy's consul in Khartoum. She sailed with him to Genoa, where she was given to Legnani's friend. Bakhita learned of Christianity through the family's business adviser and became free when slavery was banned in Italy. She was baptized, received the Eucharist, and was confirmed in 1890. Bakhita took the name Josephine after her conversion and took her first vows to become a nun at the Institute of St. Magdalene of Canossa. After the patriarch of Venice – the future Pope Pius X – examined her, Bakhita professed as a Canossian sister and took her final vows in 1893. She toured Italy, showed her scars, and shared her experiences. Bakhita served the poor and became renowned as a holy person. She died in 1947.[13]

The Second Vatican Council convened fifteen years after her death. Bishop Karol Wojtyła was one of the Council's active members. Wojtyła had experienced Nazi and Communist attempts to eliminate the Church as an independent entity and played an important role in formulating *Dignitatis Humanae*, the declaration on religious freedom that linked human dignity and conscience with the right to form churches and

---

[9] Kramer, Lobban, and Fleuhr-Lobban, *Dictionary*, 25–26, 389, 392; *Concise*, 286–287; Holcomb, "Chaplains"; Hertzke, *Children*, 241–242.

[10] Kramer, Lobban, and Fleuhr-Lobban, *Dictionary*, 393; Eve Troutt Powell, *Tell This in My Memory: Stories of Enslavement from Egypt, Sudan and the Ottoman Empire* (Stanford, CA: Stanford University Press, 2012), 5, 202.

[11] Farmer, "Bakhita"; Kramer, Lobban, and Fleuhr-Lobban, *Dictionary*, 84.

[12] Kramer, Lobban, and Fleuhr-Lobban, *Dictionary*, 84.

[13] Farmer, "Bakhita"; Powell, *Memory*, 6; Kramer, Lobban, and Fleuhr-Lobban, *Dictionary*, 84.

practice one's faith without government pressure. Wojtyła was elected Pope John Paul II in 1978. Described by Allen D. Hertzke as a major moment "for the cause of religious freedom around the world," Wojtyła's return to Poland as pope strengthened Polish confidence against the Communist state and helped to generate the Solidarity labor movement that toppled the Soviet-backed regime.[14]

On May 17, 1992, an event occurred that linked this advocate of religious freedom with the former Sudanese slave: the pope beatified Bakhita. In a sermon delivered to more than 1 million people, he praised her virtues and prayed that her grace would lead the Sudanese to reconciliation.[15] "I wish," the pope shared, "to send a heartfelt appeal to those who are responsible for the fate of the Sudan ... that the respect of the fundamental human rights – and first of all the right to religious freedom – may be guaranteed, without ethnic and religious discrimination."[16] The timing and content of his sermon was particularly significant in light of the state's recent reaction to a pastoral letter. Archbishop of Khartoum Gabriel Wako and fellow bishops had addressed the institution of a radical Islamic agenda in the 1991 pastoral letter *The Truth Shall Make You Free*. *Truth* listed government actions in pursuit of its goal and appealed for authentic religious freedom and freedom of conscience. The government seized all copies of *Truth* in early 1992.[17]

This action points to the broader matter of press freedom in the Sudan. Political changes challenged the periodical press during the second half of the century, and particularly during military dictatorships. From 1969 to 1985 the Ministry of Information reserved the right to license all newspapers and censor all news, a policy that was followed by the Nimeiri regime. The 1989 coup imposed strict censorship under the Beshir-NIF military regime. The regime has followed the Ministry of Information's aforementioned policy. During the civil war, all coverage of the conflict needed clearance from the Sudanese military.[18]

Archbishop Wako and other Catholics from Sudan attended the beatification. The delegation had an audience with the pope the following day where Wako acknowledged the realities of their situation.

---

[14] Hertzke, *Children*, 117; Russell Hittinger, "An Issue of the First Importance: Reflections on the 50th Anniversary of *Dignitatis Humanae*," *Journal of Law and Religion* 30 (2015), 465.

[15] Kramer, Lobban, and Fleuhr-Lobban, *Dictionary*, 84; "Slave Girl Puts Sudan Indelibly on the World Christian Map," *Sudan Democratic Gazette* (June 1992), 2.

[16] "Slave Girl," 2.   [17] Anderson, Werner, and Wheeler, *Devastation*, 622.

[18] Heather J. Sharkey, "A Century in Print: Arabic Journalism and Nationalism in Sudan, 1899–1999," *International Journal of Middle East Studies* 31 (1999), 543; Chuck Galli [coauthor], "Media," in Kramer, Lobban, and Fleuhr-Lobban, *Dictionary*, 291–292.

"We will continue . . . to be treated as free slaves without real freedom and forced to beg for our God-given dignity and rights as human beings," he said. However, he continued, Bakhita's beatification "has now brought us a spark of hope which we hope will break out into a burning fire."[19] The beatification was succeeded the following year by the first-ever papal visit to Sudan. John Paul II undertook his tenth African tour in 1993. Benin, Uganda, and Sudan were listed on his itinerary. He stopped in Khartoum on February 10 and conducted an open-air mass. Preaching in Green Square, the pope spoke before statues of Christ and Bakhita. Authorities censored a Church-produced booklet to commemorate the papal visit, an action that included deleting mention of Bakhita. Reference to her being a slave before being purchased by a Christian slave master in Khartoum was apparently offensive.[20]

"Bakhita," the pope preached, "learned from the tragic events in her life to have complete trust in the One who is present everywhere. Using religion as a pretext for injustice and violence is a terrible abuse and must be condemned by all who have genuine belief in God."[21] He criticized the Islamist government for its persecution of the Christian minority and, in comments to Beshir, made what the Vatican described as his most pointed statement on behalf of at-risk Christians since his first papal visit to Poland: "No group should consider itself superior to another. The state has a duty to respect and defend the differences existing among its citizens."[22] Sudan's Catholic bishops issued a pastoral letter to all Christians and Muslims two weeks later. They asked their audience to remember Bakhita: "In the midst of so much hardship, she is your model and heavenly patron. To religious believers everywhere she speaks of the value of reconciliation and love, for in her heart she overcame any feelings of hatred for those who had harmed her."[23]

In his 1996 appeal for a peaceful end to the war, the pope encouraged Christians not to lose hope in God and entrusted his readers "to the intercession of Blessed Josephine Bakhita and Blessed Daniel Comboni,

---

[19] Kramer, Lobban, and Fleuhr-Lobban, *Dictionary*, 84, and "Slave Girl," 4.
[20] Kramer, Lobban, and Fleuhr-Lobban, *Dictionary*, 110; Alan Cowell, "Pope Warns Sudan on Imposing Islamic Law," *New York Times* (February 4, 1993): www.nytimes.com/1993/02/04/world/pope-warns-sudan-on-imposing-islamic-law.html; Powell, *Memory*, 201; Anderson, Werner, and Wheeler, *Devastation*, 623.
[21] Powell, *Memory*, 202, as taken from Roberto Italo Zanini, *Bakhita: A Saint for the Third Millennium* (Rome: Orca Printing and Advertising, 2000), 100–101.
[22] Kramer, Lobban, and Fleuhr-Lobban, *Dictionary*, 110.
[23] "EP1. Believers United for Peace Lent and Ramadan for Peace," as taken from Comboniani Library, Rome, M624/261.8/B/5; Sudan Catholic Bishops' Conference, *Letters to the Church of the Sudan* (Khartoum, 2001), 101, 104–105 (quote taken from 104).

the heavenly patrons of your communities."[24] Three years later, Bishop Macram Max Gassis of el-Obeid crafted a Christmas prayer that included a plea for Bakhita's intercession:

> My people cries out to be saved from *jihad*, the Islamic holy war. . .
> My people cries out to be saved from slavery. . .
> Lord Jesus, we thank you for the gift of the first Sudanese saint, Josephine Bakhita. . .
> May she intercede for her brothers and sisters. . .
> May she obtain for the Church and for Sudan the gift of justice and peace.[25]

Bakhita was canonized in 2000.[26] In December 2003, on the occasion of the Sudanese bishops' Ad Limina visit, the pope invoked Bakhita once again: "Bakhita knew the cruelty and brutality with which man can treat his fellow man. . . . Her life inspires the firm resolve to work effectively to free people from oppression and violence, ensuring that their human dignity is respected in the full exercise of their rights."[27]

Radio Bakhita

In February 2005, the Sudanese Catholic Bishops Conference released a pastoral statement on the signing of the Comprehensive Peace Agreement that ended the Second Civil War. The Conference reviewed their vision for a peaceful Sudan, as outlined in their 1997 pastoral letter. Six freedoms, they had written at the time, would have to be respected and promoted in law and practice: the freedoms of conscience, religion, worship, assembly, movement, and expression. Returning to the present day, the letter referenced Bakhita when expressing hope for peace: "Bakhita's spirit of forgiveness was rooted in her Christ centred compassionate love for all her brothers and sisters and extended to those who had abducted her. . . . Such an example challenges each of us to oppose the culture of hatred and revenge nourished by the civil war."[28]

John Garang, leader of the SPLM/A, was killed in a helicopter crash in July 2005. Salva Kiir was named the new chairman. Although the war was over, violence was common during the CPA period in part because of local clashes and violent disarmament campaigns. In March 2008

---

[24] "Pope's Message to the Christians in South Sudan," *NSCC Magazine* (December 1996), 6–7 (7 for the quote). Comboni was an Italian Catholic missionary with long experience in the Sudan. See Scopas S. Poggo, "General Ibrahim Abboud's Military Administration in the Sudan, 1958–1964: Implementation of the Programs of Islamization and Arabization in the Southern Sudan," *Northeast African Studies*, New Series, 9 (2002), 70.
[25] As taken from Zanini, *Bakhita*, 206–207.   [26] Powell, *Memory*, 188.
[27] "Address of John Paul II."   [28] "Pastoral Statement."

tensions rose over conflict between the SPLM and an Arab militia in the oil-rich Abyei region. Tensions persisted on the transparency of oil production data and the transfer of oil revenue, and by 2009 critical national security legislation remained undecided. While the Sudanese church was once credited with mediating thirty local peace agreements during the war and laying the basis for the CPA, churches and religious organizations had a limited ability to assist in solving conflicts in the post-CPA years.[29]

While none could have known it at the time, the Bishops Conference's vision of a peaceful nation that respected freedom of expression would be sorely tested, and the conflict would in fact center upon a radio station adorned with Bakhita's name. Run by the Catholic Archdiocese of Juba, Radio Bakhita 91 FM went on the air on February 8, 2007. It was the Catholic Radio Network's (CRN) first and central station.[30] Fr. José Vieira, a Comboni missionary who worked for three years as a Radio Bakhita news editor, explained that it broke ground in several ways. It "brought new dynamics to the airwaves with its phone-in live programs and the mix of news, formation and entertainment. Bakhita . . . had many programs with a religious content and programs targeting specific listeners: children, youth, women. It had programs on health, politics, local and gospel music." Sr. Cecilia Sierra Salcido, the station's first directress, was responsible for naming it after Bakhita. With support from Archbishop of Juba Paolino Loro, she chose her name because Bakhita was the first and only Sudanese Catholic saint and her "life story was a tremendous inspiration for the people of South Sudan."[31]

Bakhita Radio began broadcasting programs in several languages, including English, a local Arabic variant, Madi, Acholi, and Dinka. In addition to this diversity of languages, Radio Bakhita's demographic of staff and trainees at one point included Madi, Bari, Acholi, Zande, Kakwe, and Didinga workers. *Catholic Sentinel* noted that its offering of different languages afforded a versatility that helped it reach those who had not felt included in the South's political development.[32] In addition to noting that people could use Bakhita Radio to express their perspectives as citizens and Christians in their own tongues, Sr. Cecilia provided

[29] Johnson, *Untold*, 10, 12; Rolandsen, "Backwater," 26; "South Sudan Profile – Timeline," BBC (August 6, 2018): www.bbc.com/news/world-africa-14019202; Ashworth and Ryan, "Peacebuilding," 48n1.
[30] James, "Belief," 53; Vieira questionnaire; Martin Agwella questionnaire.
[31] Vieira questionnaire.
[32] James, "Belief," 53; C. Salcido, "Bakhita Radio USA Article," email attachment sent to author, June 7, 2018; "Catholic Radio Gives Citizens Voice on Democracy in Southern Sudan," *Catholic Sentinel* (December 16, 2010): www.catholicsentinel.org/Content/Ne ws/Nation-and-World/Article/Catholic-radio-gives-citizens-voice-on-democracy-in-So uthern-Sudan/2/34/13612.

the following description of the station's offerings: "With clear and sound broadcasting programs, Bakhita became a forum for thinkers and intellectuals to dialogue with audiences. In partnership with other organizations, our Radio station engaged on civic education, gender, health, and religious programs, prayer vigils, meetings, and training workshops."[33] *Bits and Pieces*, its most prominent evening program, launched on April 18, 2007. The first live phone-in program, it offered commentaries on news and current events. Writing in 2008, Sr. Cecilia noted that the station was then broadcasting from 7:00 AM to 1:00 PM and 4:00 PM to 10:30 PM daily. The signal covered a radius of more than thirty kilometers and had a potential audience of more than a half million listeners.[34]

Fr. Martin Agwella was the Juba archdiocese's secretary-general from 2006 to 2012. His office oversaw Radio Bakhita. Noting "the significant contribution the Radio project was meant to make to the service of peacebuilding and reconciliation," Agwella acknowledged challenges. Apart from issues like finances, poor infrastructure, and capacity limitations, he noted that security was the chief problem: "We had recurrent tensions with security operatives regarding some programmes they didn't want to be aired."[35] In 2008, Sr. Cecilia was called before the minister of internal affairs. Asked who had given the station a mandate to discuss politics, she responded and asked Archbishop Loro to publicly elucidate Bakhita Radio's mandate. According to her, Loro stated that the Church had given the mandate and that "nobody has any right to tell the church it should or should not be doing this." The following year, some protestors in Juba objected to unpaid teacher salaries. Fleeing police, they took refuge inside Bakhita Radio's compound. Several police officers entered and started beating one of Bakhita Radio's female employees (they allegedly assumed she was a protestor). They left after Sr. Cecilia stated that she was calling the archbishop.[36] In March 2010 the *Sudan Tribune* posted an article detailing another thorny encounter at the station. According to Sr. Cecilia, an officer came to her office and asked that the station be closed immediately. The officer took her to Major General Johnson Losuk, head of national intelligence and security service in Central Equatoria. According to Sr. Cecilia, Losuk asked for a tape of an interview held with a political candidate and stated – among other things – that the next time the station aired such a program, its equipment would be seized and the station closed.[37]

---

[33] Taken from Sr. Sierra questionnaire.   [34] Salcido, "Bakhita Radio USA Article."
[35] Agwella questionnaire.   [36] "Catholic Radio Gives Citizens Voice."
[37] Garang, "SPLM."

Catholic Sentinel ran a story on Radio Bakhita weeks before the referendum. If Southern voters opted for independence, Sr. Cecilia was quoted there as saying, "the issues to talk about won't be those far away in the North. Instead, we'll be talking about the issues close to home, like tribalism ... our elbows will be bumping together ... it will be good to have rules for the media and government ... so that they don't get in my area nor I get in theirs."[38] Southerners went to the polls in early 2011 and voted for independence. On July 9, 2011, SPLM Chairman Kiir announced that freedom had come to the new South Sudanese nation.[39]

Radio Difficulties and Renewed War

Though independent, South Sudan did not begin from a *tabula rasa*. Issues over the border and oil resources remained unresolved, and though Beshir and Kiir reached an agreement on several issues in September 2012, conflict continued in South Kordofan and Blue Nile. By 2013 seeds of ethnic violence appeared in Jonglei state (along with rebel action against the ruling SPLM). Kiir dismissed his cabinet in July 2013 and chose not to reappoint his deputy, Riek Machar. Tensions between troops loyal to Kiir and Machar grew, and in December violence exploded between presidential guard soldiers. This conflict developed an ethnic tenor between the Dinka (Kiir's ethnic group) and the Nuer (Machar's ethnic group). During this war at least 4 million people fled their homes, and according to one estimate, at least 50,000 were killed. Human Rights Watch (HRW) reported that each side committed war crimes that included indiscriminate attacks on civilians, arbitrary arrests and detention, rape, and extrajudicial executions. In September 2018 Kiir and Machar signed a peace deal formally ending the conflict.[40]

Radio Bakhita's problems continued through independence. In December 2011 two politically focused shows went off the air after threats were made against the hosts and their families. Two months later, security guards guarding the National Assembly beat Mading Ngor, host of a Bakhita show. Ngor explained that he entered the assembly, took his

[38] "Catholic Radio Gives Citizens Voice."   [39] Johnson, *Untold*, 1, 15.
[40] Christopher Riches and Jan Palmowski, "South Sudan," in *A Dictionary of Contemporary World History*, 4th ed. (Oxford: Oxford University Press, 2016): www .oxfordreference.com/view/10.1093/acref/9780191802997.001.0001/acref-978019180 2997-e-3614; "World Report 2018"; "Civil War in South Sudan," Council on Foreign Relations, last updated June 25, 2018: www.cfr.org/interactives/global-conflict-tracker# !/conflict/civil-war-in-south-sudan; "South Sudan President Signs Peace Deal with Rebel Leader," *Aljazeera* (September 12, 2018): www.aljazeera.com/news/2018/09/south-sudan-president-signs-peace-deal-rebel-leader-180912185452831.html.

recorder out, and began recording the proceedings before someone approached him and asked why he was seated there. Ngor's explanation proved insufficient, and the man ordered security to throw him out. Found guilty of violating the Assembly's code of conduct, Ngor was banned from covering its proceedings. In August 2014 security agents stormed Radio Bakhita. Four of its journalists, including director Albino Tokwaro and news editor David Ocen, were arrested and the station shut down. These actions were taken after the station aired news of renewed fighting between rebels and pro-government forces in Unity and Jonglei states, clashes confirmed by the UN Mission in South Sudan (UNMISS). Bakhita's management apologized to the security officials days later and demanded that Ocen be released. Security officials did not return the station's keys until a month after their seizure.[41]

What, then, did freedom of expression mean in South Sudan? As of late January 2013 the country had not enacted a media law. Human Rights Watch stated that in the absence of laws establishing a legal apparatus to ensure media freedom and allow the media to defend its reporting, editors and reporters claimed that they were vulnerable to security forces (including arbitrary arrest and censorship).[42] The *Sudan Tribune* reported in August 2014 that UNMISS had noted "increasing efforts to curtail operations of media houses and the work of journalists covering the conflict in South Sudan, including the forced closure of Radio Bakhita and other impositions of restrictions on freedom of expression and freedom of the media."[43] The following month, in what many described as the start of a new era between government and the press, Salva Kiir signed the nation's media bills into law.[44] However, HRW reported that in 2017 the government continued to suppress critics, restrict media, and unlawfully detain people for perceived opposition.[45] Warring parties signed a cessation of hostilities agreement in December 2017 that called for

---

[41] "South Sudan 2012 Human Rights Report," *Sudan Tribune* (April 20, 2013): www.sudantribune.com/spip.php?article46289 [reprinted US State Department Bureau of Democracy, Human Rights and Labor Country Reports on Human Rights Practices for 2012 South Sudan]; "Journalist Assaulted, Humiliated at S. Sudan Parliament," *Sudan Tribune* (February 6, 2012): www.sudantribune.com/spip.php?article41524; "S. Sudan Parliament Bans Journalist," *Sudan Tribune* (February 12, 2012): www.sudantribune.com/spip.php?article41589; "S. Sudanese Journalist in Hiding over Arrest Fears: CPJ," *Sudan Tribune* (August 7, 2014): www.sudantribune.com/spip.php?article51954; "S. Sudan Security Agents"; "Bakhita Radio Submits Apology, Pleads for Journalist's Release," *Sudan Tribune* (August 18, 2014): www.sudantribune.com/spip.php?article52092; "S. Sudan Security Returns Catholic Radio Keys," *Sudan Tribune* (September 13, 2014): www.sudantribune.com/spip.php?article52383.
[42] "South Sudan: Threats to Free Speech," Human Rights Watch (January 31, 2013): www.hrw.org/news/2013/01/31/south-sudan-threats-free-speech.
[43] "Apology."   [44] "Catholic Radio Keys."   [45] "World Report 2018."

media protection and prohibited parties from participating in "any forms of hostile propaganda or hate speech, or us[ing] any media, including social media to foment ethnic or sectarian hatred."[46]

Pope Francis postponed a planned 2017 trip to South Sudan with Archbishop of Canterbury Justin Welby. According to Welby, this postponement was done in order to ensure that the visit would have the greatest impact in helping to establish peace. Warring parties asked the South Sudan Council of Churches – which had led the churches' combined efforts to successfully influence the 2005 peace deal – to help them overcome their differences during negotiations in Addis Ababa. A week after the June 2018 Ethiopia talks, both sides signed a peace agreement in Khartoum.[47]

Bakhita and the Fight against Human Trafficking

While Pope Francis's trip to South Sudan may have been postponed, the pontiff has nevertheless found occasion to follow John Paul II's precedent of marshaling Saint Bakhita's figure in the cause of human rights. Following President Donald Trump's executive order banning travel to the US from seven predominantly Muslim countries, Pope Francis reiterated previous comments about building bridges of understanding rather than walls during the International Day of Prayer and Awareness against Human Trafficking. The occasion happened to coincide with Bakhita's feast day, and he inserted the saint into his remarks. Urging government leaders to help fight human trafficking, the pope mentioned that the "enslaved, exploited and humiliated girl in Africa never lost hope" and "persevered in her faith and ended up as a migrant in Europe." He called for prayer to Bakhita "for all migrants and refugees who are exploited and suffer so much."[48] While the decision to reference Bakhita may have been purely circumstantial – it was her feast day, human trafficking was in the spotlight, and she is the patron saint of trafficking victims – the backdrop of President Trump's immigration

---

[46] Information and quote taken from "Report on the Right to Freedom of Opinion and Expression in South Sudan since the July 2016 Crisis," UNMISS-Human Rights Office of the High Commissioner, February 2018, 7n30: ohchr.org/Documents/Countries/SS/ UNMISS-OHCHR_Freedom_of_Expression.pdf. The report cites the Agreement on Cessation of Hostilities, Protection of Civilians and Humanitarian Access, signed in Addis Ababa on December 21, 2017, Article 4 (1).

[47] James Jeffrey, "Church and Conflict in South Sudan," Inter Press Service (July 3, 2018): www.ipsnews.net/2018/07/church-conflict-south-sudan/.

[48] Lindsey Bever, "Pope Francis – Not Naming Names – Makes Appeal "not to Create Walls, but to Build Bridges," *Washington Post* (February 8, 2017): www .washingtonpost.com/news/acts-of-faith/wp/2017/02/08/after-trumps-immigration-ban-pope-francis-prays-for-migrants-and-refugees/.

ban added a politically pointed layer to the pope's invocation of the saint. Two years later (and after the same Day of Prayer), the pontiff similarly called for an end to human trafficking and encouraged Catholics to pray for Bakhita's intercession.[49]

Papal mentions of Bakhita aside, others separated by great geographical distances from Sudan have deployed her legacy in the fight against human trafficking. In 2017 Bishop Terry Brady – chairman of Australia's Bishops Commission for Pastoral Life – noted that Bakhita's feast day was "an opportunity to raise awareness about human trafficking involving children."[50] The Bakhita center for female trafficking victims opened in Lagos, Nigeria, in March 2019 and, three months later, the Caritas Bakhita House opened in London. A ministry of the archdiocese of Westminster and Caritas Westminster, Bakhita House provides women who have fled from their captors with safety and support. Staff focus on helping trafficked or exploited women adjust to normal life.[51]

Conclusion

Sudan and South Sudan have spent most of their postcolonial histories embroiled in conflict. Amid government attempts to forge the nation as an Islamic state and violent Southern resistance, human rights abuses have further marred the years of war. Against this disconsolate backdrop, Catholic saint Josephine Bakhita stands as a luminous figure. During the Second Sudanese Civil War, Pope John Paul II and others invoked her in calls for peace and reconciliation. Though Juba's Catholic radio station was named Radio Bakhita after the war, it soon faced pressure during the post-CPA interim and this continued after South Sudanese independence. Now Bakhita's name, through the eponymous station, has a central role in the narrative concerning freedom of expression within South Sudan. Outside of the country, her name – by virtue of being the patron saint of trafficking victims – has been marshaled by Pope Francis and others in the fight against human trafficking.

---

[49] Courtney Mares, "Pope Francis: Pray with St. Bakhita for the End of Human Trafficking," *Catholic News Agency* (February 10, 2019): www.catholicnewsagency.com/news/pope-francis-pray-with-st-bakhita-for-the-end-of-human-trafficking-75927.

[50] Caroline Smith, "Feast Day of St Josephine Bakhita the Focal Point for Efforts against Human Trafficking," *The Record* (February 9, 2017): www.therecord.com.au/news/local/feast-day-of-st-josephine-bakhita-the-focal-point-for-efforts-against-human-trafficking/.

[51] ANSA, "Order of Malta Warns Criminal Gangs Involved in Trafficking," Info Migrants (July 29, 2019): www.infomigrants.net/en/post/18448/order-of-malta-warns-criminal-gangs-involved-in-trafficking; Dale Gavlak, "Women Who Were Trafficked Find Relief at London's Bakhita House," *Angelus* (June 21, 2019): https://angelusnews.com/news/life-family/women-who-were-trafficked-find-relief-at-londons-bakhita-house/.

Asked what Bakhita represents within the current context of ethnic conflict, Fr. Vieira argued that she "is like a lighthouse shining in the darkened skies of South Sudan. She teaches pardon and reconciliation, two basic ingredients for healing and peace at a time South Sudan is at war with itself."[52] Agwella offered that "her example could be of inspiration to the bitterly divided and polarized ethnic communities of South Sudan to focus not on the . . . pain of the war but on the oneness of humanity as the basis of human relationship." He opined that Radio Bakhita and CRN should "design context specific programmes tailored to promoting community dialogue that may lead to healing, trust-building and reconciliation . . . as the Church is the voice of the voiceless, the radio should cautiously continue to disseminate the messages of the Church."[53]

Modern appropriations of her life and legacy are evident in multiple ways. On one hand, they confirm the contemporary relevance of religious history and historical figures. As Sudan's first Catholic saint, Bakhita was a prominent symbol for a religious minority living under the jurisdiction of an Islamizing state. As an enslaved woman, Powell has noted, the narratives of her life provide a vocabulary about slavery and its history for many Sudanese (a sensitive topic still).[54] Invocations of Bakhita also reflect the capacity for religious history and figures to provide a lexicon to fuel contemporary campaigns against human rights abuses. For John Paul II, Bakhita was a benevolent weapon who could be repeatedly fired in the defense of human rights in the Sudan. Maria Kofes has written that Bakhita's biographical narratives have also been used to present, re-present, and cast her as a model for Afro-diasporic and Afro-Brazilians to follow in the fight for equality and as a connection between Africa, Europe, and Latin America. Finally, the recent conflict presents another opportunity for the saint to become a symbol of hope in the face of more abuses. In February 2018 Reuters reported that rebels had snatched a girl named Bakhita as one of thousands of children forcefully recruited by armed groups in the war.[55] Given Saint Bakhita's own abduction more than a century earlier and her status as the patron saint of trafficking victims, this episode represents a dark irony.

To borrow from Agwella, it appears that the need for Bakhita's example to inspire focus on "the oneness of humanity as the basis for human relationship" is as urgent as ever.

---

[52] Vieira questionnaire.   [53] Agwella questionnaire.   [54] Powell, *Memory*, 202.

[55] Maria Suely Kofes, "Roots and Routes: The Biographical Meshwork of Saint Josephine Bakhita," *a/b: Auto/Biography Studies* 30 (2015), 54; Denis Dumo, "Children Recount Trauma of Abduction after Mass Release by South Sudan Rebels," Reuters (February 7, 2018): www.reuters.com/article/us-southsudan-child-soldiers/children-recount-trauma -of-abduction-after-mass-release-by-south-sudan-rebels-idUSKBN1FR2Z9.

Index

For EU product safety concerns, contact us at Calle de José Abascal, 56–1°,
28003 Madrid, Spain or eugpsr@cambridge.org.

www.ingramcontent.com/pod-product-compliance
Ingram Content Group UK Ltd.
Pitfield, Milton Keynes, MK11 3LW, UK
UKHW020431240426
470322UK00017B/453